KENNEDY ON NEGOTIATION

For Beatrice

KENNEDY ON NEGOTIATION

Gavin Kennedy

Gower

Published by
Gower Publishing Limited
Gower House
Croft Road
Aldershot
Hampshire GU11 3HR
England

Gower
Old Post Road
Brookfield
Vermont 05036
USA

British Library Cataloguing in Publication Data
Kennedy, Gavin
    Kennedy on negotiation
    1. Negotiation in business
    I. Title   II. On negotiation
    658.4'052

ISBN 0 566 07302 1

Library of Congress Cataloging-in-Publication Data
Kennedy, Gavin.
        Kennedy on negotiation / Gavin Kennedy.
            p.   cm.
        Includes index.
        ISBN 0-566-07302-1 (cloth)
        1. Negotiation in business.   I. Title.
        HD58.6.K464   1997   97-10301
        658.4'052–dc21   CIP

Typeset in Century Schoolbook by Raven Typesetter and printed in Great Britain by Biddles Ltd, Guildford and King's Lynn

CONTENTS

LIST OF FIGURES

PREFACE

There has been a limited amount of original material on negotiation published lately. Occasionally someone has something new to say, or brings some specific and noteworthy experiences or original research to our attention. Mostly, however, monotonous repetition jades one's sense of wonder and excitement. Nobody to my knowledge has discussed the best original material from several sources in one volume.

Kennedy on Negotiation germinated from refereeing the manuscript of a particularly poor work on negotiation for an American publisher. The text was wholly derivative from the unacknowledged works of others and, worse, its author misinterpreted the ideas he passed off as his own. My referee's report supplied the bibliographical sources for the purloined works and recommended rejection. The commissioning editor wrote enthusiastically of my referee's report and also asked me to accept the 'usual reader's fee of $50' and a copy of the book when (!) it was published. I took the fee and declined the book.

Negotiation texts are in danger of sliding into a dead-end. The so-called popular market in books on negotiation is going nowhere, except in the endless re-cycling of most of what we already know about negotiation and of the most effective ways to train negotiators. The problem is that 'what we already know' is dispersed in numerous books and a few video packages, with little cross-referencing to or even recognition of the others. Surprisingly, there are few on-going public controversies between the competing schools of negotiation practice. Their authors keep their work very much to themselves and eschew mention of each other.

Fundamentally different approaches to negotiation remain in isolation as if their authors were too polite to contradict others in the field. Surely studies of negotiation practice are now mature enough for a more vigorous debate?

The three main approaches are:

1.   negotiation as a phased behavioural process;
2.   negotiation as a streetwise manipulative game;
3.   negotiation as a principled search for a rational solution.

Each approach, of course, has several important tributaries feeding into and off it, and there is some very limited but usually hidden cross-feeding from each to the others as well.

If these approaches were merely different insights into the same phenomenon they would be of interest only to specialist trainers and a few academics. The audience for *Kennedy on Negotiation*, however, is much wider. All practitioners, trainers and students of negotiation can benefit from a robust – even slightly polemical – review of the main differences in current negotiating practice. Why? Because ineffective practices usually have their roots in theories asserted by people who have little practical experience and who have misunderstood the title they have practised.

There are other approaches too, such as academic works on game theory, economics, social anthropology, social psychology and history that have contributed to our understanding of negotiation. Some of them also contributed to the misleading advice that is available to practitioners and, where appropriate, I shall comment on their mis-interpretations.

Let me be clear, however. This is not an exhaustive survey of the literature on negotiation. I remain a practitioner and a tutor, not a bibliophile. My only concern is with the works that improve the practice of negotiation. If I delve deep on occasion, it is only to root out the source of the errors that lead the innocent practitioner into costly negotiating mistakes.

Eliminating poor negotiation practice contributes as much to personal development as does the adoption of effective practice. Effective negotiating, however, can always be contaminated by poor practice creeping back in. So knowing what to avoid, but not being sure of what to do instead, means that you suffer the fate of the rabbit caught in your headlights.

The present lack of debate on the competing approaches and a lack of rigorous testing of the advice they offer, produces a suffocatingly bland genre that gives negotiation texts and training courses a bad name. Some texts state the blindingly obvious while others are positively dangerous. Practical negotiators asking for bread receive a stone.

The lack of controversy, and, as important, awareness that there are controversies, means that the acquisition of effective negotiation skills is a matter of the chance choice of approach occasioned by which book or training course you happen to come across first.

For this reason a book examining various works has a readership among practical negotiators. Hence, *Kennedy on Negotiation* studies the claims and assertions of important authors and their negotiation work (as in opus) and is also an assertive statement that practical negotiation when guided by sound ideas and practice does indeed work (as in achievement). *Kennedy on Negotiation* shows why on certain occasions negotiation works, and why alas, on other occasions, when guided by silly ideas, it doesn't.

Having read the text, you are invited to test what you have learned – and retained – in a short Practice Examination (Appendix 3), based on the type of examination set at Edinburgh Business School (Heriot-Watt University) for the MBA elective in Negotiation. This consists of a short case study with some pertinent questions, and some longer essays (choose four out of ten) on some of the themes of the book.

Of course, you *can* cheat but you won't learn or prove much that way! Alternatively, you can set aside two to three hours and attempt the questions just like in a normal examination. Please use your own words and not just copious extracts from my text (I will recognize my work if you do!).

Should you like me to assess what you have written – and you do not have to agree with my versions of the issues to pass, because well argued dissent is always welcomed – please follow the instructions when you send your answers to me. I will reply to every set of examination answers I receive with a set of model answers plus my comments on your work (and, no, you will not receive invitations to buy time shares and double glazing or to invest in 'get-rich-quick' scams!). Good luck!

Ex bona fide negotiari

Gavin Kennedy

 ## NOTE ON SEX ROLES

Happily we live in a less male-dominated world of business but when quoting from works of the 1970s and 1980s I have not, of course, interfered with contemporary biases in their language.

In *Kennedy on Negotiation* I alternate, roughly, between 'he' and 'she' when referring to negotiators, rather than choosing 'he' alone, or relying on that monstrosity 'him or her' every time I refer to a negotiator, while 's/he' did not bear thinking about.

ACKNOWLEDGEMENTS

This book owes its appearance to the enormous patience of my publisher, Mr Gower. I started it five years ago and, like the fable, I kept halving the distance between where it was in manuscript and its completion date. This caused deadlines to slip. In my defence I blame the commercial activities of Negotiate Limited for continually raising the opportunity cost of writing. Success, however, in 1996 finally enabled me to take time out to finish the book.

The usual suspects I have mentioned on other occasions in my other books also contributed to *Kennedy on Negotiation*. My first debt is to the management of the Shell-Haven refinery on the Thames estuary, where I observed and analysed the productivity bargaining negotiations with the craft-based trades unions during 1969–71. Shell began my abiding interest in the negotiation of prices and terms of trade in the real world (in Shell's case, the price of labour and the working practices of their craftsmen), as opposed to how I taught price theory at the time as an academic economist.

Recently (1994–95), I revisited labour negotiations as a negotiation consultant to the National Health Service (NHS). It was a time-warp back to the 1970s, as if nothing had happened during Margaret Thatcher's governments. Nevertheless, the Management Executive of the NHS in Scotland enabled me to re-test many of the 'certainties' I had taken on board from observing similar processes at Shell-Haven twenty-five years earlier.

However, my main work as a consultant negotiator remains in the commercial world. The men and women (increasingly, more of the latter) who are moving up the management grades of private companies and numerous boards of directors have been a constant source of inspiration. New purchasing policies are attempting to replace the adversarial negotiations of the past. Sales negotiation has moved a long way since the 'benefits not features', 'overcome objections' and 'keep closing' exhortations of the 1960s. Cross-cultural negotiations are coming to the fore too. Virtually hundreds of negotiators engaged in these areas have influenced my thinking and practice and I thank them for all the (often unintentional) help they provided.

As ever, a family plays a significant role in the writing of any book and mine, yet again, have been their normal patient selves. I wrote the earlier versions of the text and undertook almost all the re-editing of the final manuscript at Doulezon in France, occasionally disrupting family holidays. For accepting such collateral disruption with their usual equanimity, I can only express my eternal gratitude to those concerned.

I have dedicated *Kennedy on Negotiation* to my daughter, Beatrice. If I could write as well as she plays the piano, your journey through the following pages would be dreamlike. Unfortunately, I can't.

GK

PROLOGUE

PROLOGUE

NEGOTIATION

Two people meet to reconcile their different solutions to the same problem. They interact, behave in variously different ways, attempt to change each other's perceptions using various forms of language, recover from crises of mutually exclusive expectations, settle on a common solution by which one of them gets some of what they want through trading with the other person, who acquires some of what they want in exchange, and they both agree on how to implement what they agreed. Then they separate to go about their other business. An everyday occurrence? We call it a negotiation.

Because I have views about the competing explanations of what happens when you negotiate and different prescriptions about how to improve your performance, you will read here differing views on negotiation.

One authority writes, for example, that 'Negotiation is a basic means of getting what you want from others'[1] and this is fine as far as it goes, but their definition could apply equally well to stealing, begging, panhandling, conning, or coercing. Hence, I suggest a definition of negotiation that isolates the unique feature that makes it different from other methods of getting what you want and other forms of decision making.

DECISION MAKING

Decision *making* is about choosing what is to be done, and by whom. Decision *taking* concerns accepting somebody else's decision about what is to be done, when you are bound by circumstance, position, or

3

habit so to do. Competing forms of decision making exist. In some forms you can influence the outcome, in others you cannot.

In *arbitration*, for example, your influence on the outcome ends when you make the final submission of your case to the arbiter – she is free to choose a compromise solution, taking into consideration the merits of the rival cases. Sometimes, she also considers the politics of a party's disappointment if she rules too far to one side at the expense of the other.

True, you can so design your final submission as to be more likely to attract the arbiter's support for your case. This happens in *pendulum arbitration*, where she must choose solely between the final submissions of the rival parties: it is your submission or theirs with no compromises between them permitted. You seek the arbiter's favour by making your submission more reasonable. If both of you modify your original stances with doses of reasonableness, you could move so close towards each other from the original unreasonable stances that you no longer need arbitration. That is why pendulum arbitration codes should be included in negotiation procedure agreements and commercial contracts.

Other decision-making methods competing with negotiation include:

- ○ *Persuasion*   You use language, and sometimes pure rhetoric, to elicit responses that address your wants (often used in selling, propaganda, and politics).
- ○ *Gambling*   Coin tossing (heads or tails?) or 'putting your money where your mouth is', and so on.
- ○ *Command decision*   The person in authority makes the decision (a platoon commander, for example). It is advocated when any command decision in a desperately dangerous situation is better than no decision at all.
- ○ *Instruction*   Presumes that the decision is reasonably clear cut, perhaps routine, and the person in charge instructs the persons paid (or pledged) to accept the legitimacy of the instruction and carry it out.
- ○ *Litigation*   You sue the other in a third party legal process that decides, from precedent perhaps or from reference to a legal statute or from the 'Solomon'-like qualities of the judiciary.
- ○ *Coercion*   The more powerful party makes the decision, which could be the state with the legal means to implement it (prisons, armies and police). Extra-legal coercion comes from the gang boss, the street gang, the rampaging mob, the terrorist, or the biggest guy on the block.

All decision-making methods are appropriate in some circumstances but not in others. Their use depends on the people, the circumstances and the options. No method is uniquely superior to the others and, therefore, there are no implications of moral rectitude, or a failure thereof, in preferring one method to another. Using only one method on all and every occasion, for all and every circumstance, however, is not wise. In sum, you should be situationally flexible when making decisions.

 ## WHAT IS NEGOTIATION?

You need to distinguish negotiating from other methods of decision making by focusing on what is unique to negotiation and is not shared by its competitors. Hence, my definition:

> Negotiation is a process by which we search for terms to obtain
> what we want from somebody who wants something from us.

Negotiation is an explicit exchange or trade between parties who want something from each other. It is also a voluntary exchange, in the sense that the parties can exercise their veto not to agree to the offered terms, whereas in a purely coercive process there are unpleasant consequences if you say 'no'. In a negotiated exchange the parties are much more free to say 'yes' when the terms are 'right' enough for them to do so, and 'no' when otherwise. The threatened menace implied in the Godfather's 'offer you can't refuse' is not within the ambit of negotiation because negotiation requires that you are free to refuse any offer.

My definition comes from long observation. That negotiation is an interactive process between people who want something from each other is observable in the conduct and the content of what happens when people negotiate. The intriguing paradox that all negotiations are unique yet also conform to a common process, is something I shall resolve later. Suffice to note here that unless negotiation processes had common elements, it would not be comprehensible as a process and, for that reason alone, your negotiating performance would be immune to behavioural improvements.

Negotiation is a searching process. Neither party knows whether agreement can be reached. You may search in good faith and not find what you are looking for. We talk about the 'failure of the negotiations' to find an acceptable solution as if failure to agree was always a defeat. Some failures are inevitable and it is appropriate that they do fail when gaps between the parties' aspirations remain. Some negotiations that fail today may succeed tomorrow when circumstances change, or are changed by war, terrorism, sanctions, strikes and the manipulation of public opinion.

Searching for terms describes what negotiators do. You make tentative suggestions, you probe each other, you test for better offers, you signal and you explore each other's reactions and responses. When you stop searching you usually have agreed or you are stuck in a deadlock.

You search to find the terms to obtain what you want. By terms, I mean the terms of trade – what you get for what you give – which is the main mechanism leading to a solution, if there is one. The essence of negotiation is that there is more than one set of terms that could produce an agreement. This is both a help and a hindrance. Because it is easier to find one of several possible needles in a haystack, rather than the proverbial one alone, the existence of several possible settlements is a help. But because there is more than one possible settlement you do not necessarily accept the first one that you find and this could become a hindrance.

If there are other solutions available, some perhaps better than the first one you find, you should continue the search for what may be better solutions awaiting discovery. This pressure to improve on what is on offer, becomes a hindrance when, by continuing the search, you risk losing the first solution you found. In short, you push too hard and wait too long in the futile hope that you can improve on what you already have.

Explicit in my definition is your dependence on somebody else wanting something from you. If they do not want anything at all from you a negotiated solution is not possible.

True, I may not realize that I want something from you and it is up to you to convince me that I do. No matter how persuasive you are, it is possible that I remain unconvinced. Negotiation in these circumstances is inappropriate. You must do without whatever it is that you want from me, or find somebody else who wants something from you, or find another method of obtaining what you want, provided you have alternatives to hand. Steal perhaps? Use violence? Sue me for it? Whatever you do it will not be within the ambit of negotiation.

Trading by its nature requires a voluntary exchange, tangible or intangible. Without explicit trading there is no negotiated decision.

 ## HAGGLING AND HORSE TRADING

When some authors acknowledge the role of trading they call it 'haggling' and 'horse trading,'[2] as if trading was disreputable and succeeds only by sleight of hand.

The disreputable aura ascribed by many people to 'haggling' has a long tradition in 'polite' society. It was certainly beneath the mores of the Victorians – only the poor had a need to quibble with tradesmen! To be dismissed from polite society with sneers that you were 'in trade' as a retailer is one of the ironies of Victorian Britain, then the greatest trading nation on earth.

Remnants of this mind-set occur today among people who, when shopping, never deign to 'haggle', barter or trade over the price on the tag. They regard questioning a price as bad manners, beneath them and an embarrassment similar to creating a 'scene' in a public place. Many people confess to being unable to haggle, yet when they try it they enjoy it, as callers have testified on radio phone-ins I have been on.

The line: 'If you ask how much it costs, you cannot afford it' is an example of price snobbishness. Challenging a price, however, is neither shady nor shabby. It is only sensible as long as the potential pay-off from the price challenge is worth the time and effort of making one. Negotiation is about gaining some control over your life. The alternative is to accept whatever somebody else chooses for you.

Challenging other people's plans for you, whether at home, work or play, is a good habit. Readers who live in societies where you can exercise your negotiating skills at will in any field of endeavour you choose have a personal advantage over those readers who live in societies where it is not safe to challenge anything.

In negotiating you may not always be successful, the deals you get may not always be the best ones and you may sometimes regret having spent too much time and effort on agreeing to some of them, even the better ones. Thankfully, for those with the option of negotiating it is as common to us as obeying orders and accepting our lot was as common to our recent forebears.

 ## PROMISES

Traditional negotiation, based on trade or exchange, has a long history. The practice of trading survives in 'archaic' societies in the African bush, the Amazon rain forest and the uplands of Papua New Guinea, and trading long pre-dates the emergence of capitalism. It has taken many forms, not all of them using money. Some cultures show curious deviations from explicit trading through what amounts to implicit gift-exchange.[3]

The mere existence of contracts and compacts, such as marriage or military alliances is conditional on your ability to make promises about the future,[4] *and to keep them*.[5] Once out of your partner's sight, you might abandon your promises at your convenience unless the fear of the consequences of doing so forces you into compliance.

Over time, enforcing compliance entailed various levels of brutality until the enforcement of contracts became subject to the rule of law and not the rule of violence. People in the past who cheated and who broke their promises suffered severe punishments until they learned by dreadful example to behave differently. If you could not keep your promises you suffered the consequences if you were found out. The beginnings of buying and selling were 'soaked in blood thoroughly and for a long time' as people took their gory revenge on those who broke their promises.[6] Now legal sanctions force compliance, but the principle is still the same even though, thankfully, the means of enforcement are different.

No evidence is, nor can be, offered for these assertions, though an aged Arab trader in the Gulf recently told me that when his great grandfather made an agreement for a joint venture with the Emir, he sent his ten-year-old eldest son to live in the Emir's household as a visible pledge of his family's commitment to carry out his promises. By this gesture I understood that the viability of the boy's throat was at risk if his family had failed to keep its side of the bargain. Thankfully they kept their promises because the young hostage survived to become my Arab informant's grandfather.

Not everybody feels comfortable defining negotiation uniquely as a process of exchanging promises. Some feminist academics reject negotiation as an exchange process altogether because they believe that this roots it in the experiences of the male sex, which influence apparently 'obscures relations of domination and power' (I would have thought it highlighted them). Instead, they prefer to analyse how negotiation affects people who closely identify themselves with each other, such as 'friends, dating couples', etc. They want to shift attention from the anonymity of markets to minority perspectives of personal relationships.[7]

I think we should be more concerned with negotiation as a trading process – for that is what the large majority of people, male and female, experience when they negotiate – than what it might mean for a few introspective dating couples on American campuses. Therefore, I think it is more productive to see negotiation as an *explicit* exchange between people whatever their relationships.

NOBODY EVER SAW TWO DOGS NEGOTIATE OVER A BONE

There is a propensity for people to negotiate.[8] This propensity is not found in animals because they know nothing of contracts or promises. Nobody, for example, has ever seen two dogs negotiate over a bone and nobody ever saw an animal signify to another that it was willing to give 'this for that'.[9] Animals distribute the bounties of nature, primarily food, mates and territory, among themselves by violence and the threat of violence.

Barbarian societies behave similarly to animals when consuming the bounties of nature and the fruits of human labour. Exponents of the 'Genghis Khan school of wealth accumulation' take what they want and leave their victims to fend for themselves. But while it is certainly possible to violently redistribute the bounties of nature and the fruits of human labour, it is not possible by violence to sustain the *creation* of human wealth nor to protect nature from becoming a desert.

The behaviour of two dogs, therefore, is significant. If humans can arrange their affairs differently from dogs, by practising traditional negotiation, they can create and distribute untold quantities of the fruits of labour and the bounties of nature, beyond the wildest dreams of only a few centuries ago.

INTERESTS AND CHARITY

People are (or rather, can be) different from animals in their behaviour. Civilized people need the co-operation and assistance of millions of others. Yet a whole lifetime is scarcely sufficient to gain the friendship of but a few persons and while friendship has many rewards and joys it is not a sufficient way to acquire most of what we want.

'A friend in need is a friend indeed' has more than a grain of truth in it. I do not suggest that friends are unimportant (on occasion they can be life-saving) but you do not have enough friends to provide over prolonged periods your daily necessities of life. Hundreds of thousands, perhaps millions, of people in our global village are necessary to produce the multitude of things you want. If you know only a few people and, of them, even fewer who are close to being your friends, how can you rely solely on them and they upon you to produce but a fraction of what you all want?

Millions of negotiations occur every hour of every day and involve people you never meet nor know. These negotiations occur whatever your loves or dislikes of other people. Of one thing you can be certain: unless you reciprocate with the necessary efforts required for you to access the products of their labour, you will do without them. Such is the power of the global market, that, whoever you are, you rely on the anonymous co-operation of others for the most basic of your necessities and the most trivial of your luxuries. And they depend on you playing your part too.

This leads to the absolute necessity of negotiating to meet the *interests* of the other party. If you disregard their interests you must rely on their charity to get what you want, but you will be more likely to prevail in this quest if it is to their own advantage to do for you what you require of them.[10]

Whoever offers you a bargain of any kind says in one form or another: 'Give me that which I want, and you shall have this which you want'. It is in this manner that you obtain the far greater part of those things of which you stand in need. It is not from the benevolence of others that you should expect your dinner but from their regard to their own interest. That is why it is better to address yourself 'not to their humanity, but to their self-love; and never talk to them of [y]our necessities, but of their advantages'.[11]

These statements contain controversial ideas. Some people object to them on ethical grounds. They feel that people *ought* to do everybody else favours because it is good for them to do so, and not because it is in their self-interest. Frankly, such criticism is naive. An ought can never be an is, and to rely on what people ought to do is to risk (life-threatening?) disappointment.

If everybody relied on everybody else acting like those few friends on whom you can depend *on occasion*, we would as a species rapidly reduce our living standards to levels not seen since the Ice Ages. If you were to rely on unknowable strangers, abiding by 'rules' (agreed and ensured by whom?) that they should supply you with everything you want, under no more than their sense of their charity, you might wait a long time for anything.

In the meantime, I suggest that you make traditional arrangements for your dinner.

 ## NASH AND THE BARGAINING PROBLEM

The bargaining problem is not so much related to the definition of negotiation as it is to the questions of why and how people negotiate. These questions are not just academic (though many academics offer their views on them) but neither is the problem as easy to solve as it first looks. So this and the following chapter may become very slightly technical, prompting me to assure you that I have made every effort to keep it simple. As practitioners, neither you nor I have time for exposure to purely academic debates, so let me assure you that this topic is vitally important to all practising negotiators and that the trespassing of academics into this field is not a proof of its irrelevance.

Your answer to why you negotiate is that you do so because presumably it makes you in some sense better off. Given that you volunteer to accept or not accept the offered deal, it follows that if you accept the deal you are in some way better off than if you don't. What is true for you must be true for other negotiators, so it is fair to conclude that both of you negotiate because you both gain something.

Briefly put, the bargaining problem is about how you arrive at a solution when, for whatever reason, there is a gap between your conflicting aspirations on some important issues. You may or may not also have common interests on other issues.

Unfortunately, in practice there is not one but two problems. The lay person's riposte that obviously there are joint benefits for both parties in negotiating, otherwise they wouldn't negotiate, is partly right but might be less convincing to observers of bargaining behaviour. And the first attempts to solve the bargaining problem were as far away from what observation and experience of bargaining behaviour showed as you could get.

Economists for more than a century fully understood how markets set prices but for many years it remained an irritatingly grey area before economists understood how bargainers set prices. John Nash took up the challenge in 1950 and initiated a whole avalanche of research contributions to the mathematics of bargaining theory. Nash showed how his solution was mathematically determinate, given his idealizing assumptions.

Nash asserted that the situations of monopoly versus monopsony, of trading between two nations, and of negotiation between employer and labour union were bargaining problems. His was a theoretical discussion of the bargaining problem, which he conceived of as establishing a definite 'solution' to the amount of satisfaction each individual should expect to get from bargaining, or, rather, a determination of how much it should be worth to each of these individuals to have an opportunity to bargain.[12]

The mathematics of utility theory are very limiting and for those not previously exposed to economics the Nash assumptions seem almost naive in comparison to the circumstances commonly found in real world bargaining problems.

Nash, for instance, assumes:

○ highly rational 'bargainers who can accurately compare' each other's 'desires for various things';
○ bargainers who have 'equal bargaining skills';
○ bargainers who 'have full knowledge of the tastes and preferences of the other';
○ bargainers who desire 'to maximize' their gains in bargaining.

Fortunately, we do not need to develop the mathematical argument here because Nash also provides a simple arithmetical example to demonstrate his solution, using two individuals, Bill and Jack, who are considering exchanging some goods they own and which they want to barter.

His model of the bargaining problem uses von Neuman and Morgentstern's[13] numerical utility theory. Utility is an economist's way of 'measuring' the satisfaction, however defined, that an individual receives from possessing units of a good. In Figure P.1, the players' utilities appear as 'numbers'.

For example, the book for Bill has a utility of '2' and for Jack a utility of '4'. Crudely, take that number '4' to mean that the book for Jack would have a greater amount of satisfaction for him (however Jack defines his satisfaction) than say, the ball (1), and that for Bill (however Bill defines his satisfaction) take the '2' to mean that the book has much less satisfaction for him than, say, the pen (10).

Now, given the original distribution of the goods between them and the utilities of the goods for each of them, what exchange of the goods, asked Nash, would maximize their satisfaction?

Nash postulated that the solution to the bargaining problem in this and every other case would be where the 'product of the utility gains is

Bill's goods	Utility to Bill	Utility to Jack
book	2	4
whip	2	2
ball	2	1
bat	2	2
box	4	1
Jack's goods		
pen	10	1
toy	4	1
knife	6	2
hat	2	2

Figure P.1 Utilities of the goods to Bill and Jack[14]

maximized'. The bargainers would agree to exchange the goods in whatever way that maximized their joint gains in utility.

For Bill and Jack, Nash asserted that they would trade as follows:

Bill gives Jack: book, whip, ball and bat

Jack gives Bill: pen, toy and knife.

Now what is interesting about the Nash solution is that the utilities of the goods are final offers only and are not subject to any bargaining. In other words, the unique exchange that maximizes the differences between the utilities the players receive from the goods they offer against the utilities they give up in exchange, are first and final offers from both of them. As, by assumption, both negotiators know the utility that each of them ascribes to each of the goods, it would, of course, be pointless to think in terms of other than final offers.

Nash (safely) assumes that the players will trade those goods that they value less for those that they value more. And as Bill and Jack have perfect information about each other's preferences, neither can bluff the other into 'paying' more for a good because they know the utilities each of them places on all the goods. Given this, we can set out the Nash equilibrium trade for Bill and Jack as in Figure P.2.

	Bill				**Jack**	
Total utility before they bargain	12				6	
Goods received in trade				Goods received in trade		
	Gains	Losses			Gains	Losses
knife	6	2	book		4	2
pen	10	2	whip		2	1
toy	4	2	ball		1	1
		2	bat		2	
Totals	20	−8			9	−4
Net gains	12				5	
Total utility after they bargain	24				11	

Figure P.2 Net utility positions for Bill and Jack after trading

Compared to their original utility positions (12 for Bill and 6 for Jack) and given the utility endowments of the items they traded, they have both increased their utilities (to 24 for Bill and 11 for Jack). The product of their net gains is $12 \times 5 = 60$. Nash affirmed that no other combination of traded items could produce a gain in utility that was greater than 60. The product of their net gains in utility was 'how much it should be worth to each of these individuals to have this opportunity of bargaining.'[15]

Nash's solution followed inescapably from his idealistic and restrictive assumptions. We could ask whether it was a bargaining solution at all, in that the strategies of both players must produce the defined solution and their bargaining skills *per se* are eliminated by assumption. For an optimum bargain to be concluded it would have to be one that made both players better off than they were before they traded. If you made either one of them better off than the optimal bargain, you could only do so by worsening the other's position. The Nash solution conforms to this condition.

Nash's derivation of the players' utilities assumes away the conditions of the real world. Nash players have fixed relative values for each item. They have perfect information about each other's preferences and utilities. The outcome of their 'bargaining' necessarily is to maximize their joint gains.

As a solution to the bargaining problem, Nash's model is plausibly compelling. It predicts that the bargainers will reach the optimal solution. That they don't reach the Nash solution in practice is not a definitive refutation of Nash. Because bargainers in practice operate in different conditions from the assumptions of the model, this explains their variations from the optimal solution. Mathematically, however, the Nash solution is robust.

The Nash solution is also fruitful if we consider a loose version of it to explain a transaction that you and I might undertake. Remember that Bill's gain in utility is the net difference between his valuation of the items he receives and his valuation of whatever he must give up to Jack in exchange. Applying this idea to our trade, say I value the utilities in the package I obtain from you at '100' and I trade items worth to me '65', my net gain in utility is '35'. In the same transaction, if you value the items you obtain at '75' and you value the items you trade at '25', then your net gain in utility is '50'.

As neither you nor I reveal (nor can we do so in a meaningful way) our subjective valuations of the transaction ('35' for me, '50' for you), there is no way by which we could compare our relative performances, nor can we calculate what the deal is worth to the other. That we agreed to the deal, is the only evidence that there was some additional utility present for both of us. What that utility is, or what it consists of, is unknowable. Therefore, whether we have maximized it is also unknowable. But it does have some value as an explanation of our agreeing to the deal. If you think of the Nash solution as being vaguely precise (!) you have probably taken it as far as you need to go as a practitioner. The problem with the Nash solution is somewhat more worrying. Theorists should occasionally look out of their study windows, so to speak. For Nash assumes behaviour from his bargainers that does not correspond to the common experience of most negotiators. And the most devastating evidence for this came shortly after the Nash solution appeared in 1950.

A small group of researchers, working out of the Rand Research Centre, in Santa Monica, California, invented a modestly simple game that they played repeatedly. It is now fairly common in negotiation skills and team-building workshops. It produces remarkably consistent results.[16] It is called the 'dilemma' game, and it is a game without content though it has strict rules. The players aim to 'maximize their positive scores'. They do this by playing for points, which are not worth anything other than being a convenient way to keep a score. The status of the points is roughly analogous to notions of utility, with the objective being to 'maximizing one's utility'.

There are two ways of playing the game as the players discover for themselves. Nobody tells them which, or any, way to play nor even that two ways exist. People coming to the game for the first time are thus uninfluenced by prejudices or notions of 'correct' behaviour other than their own. They are the perfect material for an experiment in pure behavioural choice!

The two ways of playing the dilemma game correspond closely to the dichotomy of negotiation behaviour. If the individual interprets the object of the game as being how they can maximize their personal gains at the expense of the other player, they will demonstrate *zero-sum* or *non-co-operative* behaviour.

The partner, whatever her first interpretations of the way to play the game, will be forced to retaliate using zero-sum behaviour too. Their scores at the end of the game will not maximize their joint gains and, worse, could minimize their joint gains leaving them both with negative or very low positive individual scores.

If, on the other hand, an individual interprets the object of the game as being how their joint scores can be maximized, *and this coincides with the predilections of the other player*, they will demonstrate *non-zero-sum* or *co-operative* behaviour.

Their eventual positive scores, in this case only, are maximized (at 48 points each) and they are as close to a Nash solution as is possible ($48 \times 48 = 2304$). You can test this by multiplying any combination of scores that sum to 96 ($48 + 48 = 96$) and you will see that no combination exceeds 2304. For example, $40 \times 56 = 2008$; $30 \times 66 = 1980$; and $20 \times 76 = 1520$, and so on.

What surprises researchers are the very few cases where the players individually choose to interpret the game as a co-operative game and behave accordingly. On the contrary, few players choose or persist with a strategy of play that would lead to a Nash solution!

After 12 years' experience of observing managers playing the dilemma game, I can report that the majority of those who play the game for the first time adopt non-co-operative strategies and many of the others who try initially to play a co-operative strategy switch to non-co-operative behaviour in retaliation. Nash joint maximizing behaviour is remarkable by its almost total absence.

Note that the rules prohibit the players from discussing the game or the appropriate behaviours they should use before they begin playing. They are both bereft of defence but able to attack before they open the play. That, incidentally, is the dilemma! In my experience, only about 8 per cent of pairs of players simultaneously hit on a co-operative Nash solution to the dilemma game and go on to gain 48 points each. Other researchers[17] report as many as 12 per cent in Britain and 25 per cent in the USA playing a co-operative strategy but I have no information on exactly what briefing they offer to players before they start the game, which might explain this difference. It still leaves between 75 and 92 per cent of players faltering with less than optimal Nash scores of 48 each, though some recover from initial non-co-operative play to gain scores in the thirties.

Just under half of the players individually choose behaviour in the first round that suggests that they see dilemma (assuming they obey the 'rules' and make a conscious choice) as a co-operative game, but, after a few rounds most of them find they cannot alter the non-Nash behaviours of a partner who behaves non-co-operatively. Some, of course, find it impossible to alter their partner's behaviour over ten rounds and they both end up with low scores.

Maximizing joint gains as a bargaining objective is a minority choice of the thousands of negotiators I and my colleagues have observed. Depressingly, for the Nash solution, most bargainers behave as if they reject joint gain as their objective. The overwhelming majority of bargainers have sub-optimal, non-Nash, outcomes.

Some players, by defecting on their promises (there are two short sessions after rounds 4 and 8 where they may negotiate with each other) manage to gain high positive scores (greater than 48) purely at the expense of their hapless partners who believed what they were promised. The arithmetic of these high positive scores still does not beat the Nash solution because what they gain over 48 points, their partner loses and the higher their own score the more it reduces their partner's score. The product of a negative and a positive number is always a negative number and one well short of a Nash solution.

 ## THE REAL PROBLEM WITH BARGAINING

The real bargaining problem lies in the dichotomy of zero sum and non-zero sum, or non-co-operative and co-operative behaviours in the negotiation process. Maximizing the distribution of the benefits depends upon the behaviours of the bargainers. Experience suggests that in most cases they behave in ways that fail to maximize their potential gains. This conclusion did not pass unnoticed by observers and practitioners, when the first detailed studies of working negotiators got under way in the United States in the early 1960s.

If, using the language of Walton and McKersie,[18] you choose to be, or you meet with, a *distributive* bargainer you can only benefit at the other negotiator's expense. Only if you choose to be, *and meet with*, an *integrative* bargainer can you both make joint gains at neither party's expense. Lax and Sebenius[19] neatly called this a choice between being a 'claiming' or a 'creating' bargainer, though, strictly, this is only a *quasi*-choice because the gains you seek from your individual choice are not independent of my choice – and behaviour. This is the real bargaining problem – it's not just what you choose that counts, it's what we both choose separately.

Exchange can produce jointly created benefits, both tangible and intangible. A joint benefit does not mean that it is, necessarily, a shared benefit. What benefits me may not have any corresponding benefits for you. Benefits express themselves differently, use different currencies and are invisible except to the party that receives them.

Hence, there are two distinct methods of negotiation producing different solutions to the bargaining problem depending on the congruence or otherwise of the behaviours independently adopted by each of the negotiators. Not understanding this fact of life leads to many of the real problems you experience when negotiating. Idealizing negotiation into a joint gaining game and acting as if your idealization is always true, leads only to disappointment.

The purpose of your tithe on my granary could be to distribute some of my grain to the starving, with which objective I would have some sympathy. You could, instead, live off it and all the other tithes you collect in the area, in the style of the Sheriff of Nottingham. In so far as I can negotiate at all with your tithe collectors (be they the Little Sisters of the Poor, or thugs with psychopathic tendencies), the issue for negotiation is going to be the single one of 'how much of my grain qualifies for your tithe?'

How your emissaries set about their task is decisive, as is what I think of them. The Little Sisters may be well meaning but if I believe that the so-called starving poor are an undeserving lot of layabouts, shiftless in the extreme and successful preyers on guileless nuns, I am going to haggle harder with the nuns than with the mouth-foaming, blank-staring gorillas you sent instead and with whom I choose to be prudent. Before I create the wrong impression, this merely illustrates a case and is not smuggled in as gratuitous social comment. (While I have long been sceptical of the 'Robin Hoods' of this world I have never had any doubts about the intentions of the 'Sheriffs of Nottingham'!)

Claimers see negotiation as the distribution of a fixed amount between them and you. The bigger their share the smaller is yours. It is a zero-sum transaction; what they gain, you lose. Where claiming predominates, manipulative ploys, tricks and power perceptions are the tactical imperatives of the negotiators, reaching their 'highest' level of competence in 'street-wise' negotiating.

Creators are different. Lax and Sebenius[20] identify three ways to create a joint gain. First, an agreement that you both voluntarily enter into is likely to be better than no agreement at all, on the safe presumption that, as both of you have the right to veto any deal with which you are uncomfortable, it is the value created by the deals you agree to that makes you say 'yes' rather than 'no'. In saying 'no' to any deal, you prefer to forgo what you would 'gain' from saying 'yes'.

Second, by accepting another deal, replacing one that is unacceptable to one or both of you, it must create additional value to you both in some way. If it does not, because, for instance, it made one of you worse off than no deal, the loser would veto it.

Third, negotiators moving towards an agreeable deal, making both of you better off or no worse off, who discover a previously unthought of solution, 'whether a new trade, a different option, or a changed schedule of payments', create additional value.[21]

Lax and Sebenius introduce the ideas of *private* and *public* value in this context. Private value is something exclusive to the person, who can only get more of it at the expense of less of it for others; public value is akin to the economists' idea of a public as opposed to a private good, in that the consumption of any amount of the public good does not detract one iota from anybody else's consumption of the same good. For example, a defence budget spent on deterrence equally defends all the citizenry. No part of the territory receives more defence than another when the defence budget deters invasion of all of it (it might be different if deterrence fails and war breaks out). Another example could be, if the environmental budget, in conjunction with laws, produces cleaner air, no amount of extra breathing of the cleaner air by one person will reduce the amount left for others to breathe.

In negotiation we have a third and important source of value creation, not identified by Lax and Sebenius, which does not come within 'the measuring rod of money'.[22] I refer to the idea of *subjective* value. This has the characteristics of a private good, in the sense that it is something I feel I gain from the transaction and which I do not have to share with anybody else, and it also has the characteristics of a public good, in the sense that my subjective consumption of my private gains in no way reduces the subjective gains you receive from your side of the transaction. In the Nash example (Figure P.2), Bill's net gain of 12 in utility is not at the expense of Jack's utility net gain of 5. Both enjoy their satisfactions to the full without diminishing the other's.

In my view, subjective value is a significant motive for negotiating the joint creation of value. It explains much negotiating behaviour and the outcomes that certain behaviours produce. Its only drawback as a practical activity at present is that much of the analytical ingenuity in coping with the role of subjective value in negotiation is highly technical and beyond the mathematics of most negotiating practitioners. While it is, of course, a challenge to authors on negotiation to 'popularize' useful ideas into operationally valuable techniques for both practitioners and trainers, we shall have to leave you with the idea of subjective value and move on.

That joint gains are possible from creating value rather than merely distributing it, is unchallengeable. The real bargaining problem is that it is not easy in practice to do so:

> many parties do not automatically know what opportunities for co-operative action there are to exploit. The parties must explore – imperfectly – the arrangements they may jointly be able to create. In practice many gains go unrealised. Inferior agreements are made. Impasse results and conflict escalates when co-operative action might have been better for all. Understanding where private and common value really come from should make jointly creating it more likely.[23]

This constitutes the essence of the real bargaining problem: if joint gains are preferable, how do bargainers achieve them, and why, we must ask, do so few negotiators seek them?

First, you should note that the failure of Nash to provide a general solution to the real bargaining problem merely makes your practitioner's quest more realistic. Recognizing the tendency of players to behave as if a zero-sum gain is their objective alerts you to the need to develop behaviours that can successfully produce joint gains. The idealization of negotiating behaviour specified by Nash is a boundary on the range of possible behaviours exhibited by negotiators in the real world. What you need to do now, with your back to the Nash boundary, so to speak, is to take in some of the behavioural terrain we intend to march across in what follows.

It is not entirely a case for despair. The constant struggle between claiming and creating behaviours is the single most important feature of the terrain with which you will have to come to terms. There are no other routes open to practical negotiators. Acting as if the Nash boundary dominates the behavioural terrain is naive; substituting other idealized boundaries is pointless. Negotiators have a choice in the way they behave and understanding the severe limitation of that choice – we are dependent, too, on the other negotiator's choices – is the first step to proactively expanding on those limitations.

The best way to establish these points is to show that negotiations to change current arrangements can be better for both parties and that behaving to make things better for both parties has more going for it as a bargaining choice than seeking only to better one's own position.

 ## THE BENEFITS OF BARGAINING

We begin by recognizing that negotiators have a common interest because the consequence of non-agreement means that they are both stuck with the status quo they have before they negotiate to change it. As the benefits (however defined) of the status quo are available to them both without their expenditure of the time and effort needed to agree to change it, and neither of them takes that option, it must be because they both recognize that they could be better off individually if they negotiated to change the status quo. It follows that if they succeed in changing the status quo by negotiating, then they are both better off collectively too.

A simple diagram might add visual clarity to my verbal exposition. Using utilities to represent degrees of satisfaction experienced by the negotiators, Figure P.3 graphically represents the benefits of bargaining. Careful attention to this diagram pays high dividends in understanding to those who make the effort.

Before they negotiate (Figure P.3) the negotiators are at A. This is the status quo. If they fail to agree they remain at A and enjoy only the utilities available to them both at A. At A, negotiator P (Patricia) enjoys a utility of p' and negotiator Q (Quentin) enjoys a utility of q'. Any increase in utility that benefits Patricia but not Quentin, means Patricia moves vertically from A to R and increases her utility to p''; likewise any increase in utility that benefits Quentin but not Patricia

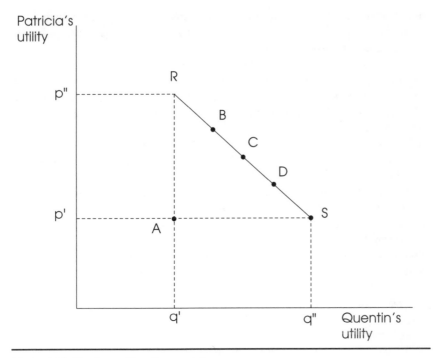

Figure P.3 The benefits of bargaining

moves Quentin horizontally from *A* to *S* and increases his utility to *q"*. A proposal from Patricia to benefit herself without a corresponding benefit to Quentin (and vice versa) illustrates pure claiming behaviour. Quentin receiving such a one-way proposal from Patricia is likely (and is advised) to reject it. As Patricia cannot move herself to *R* without Quentin's consent because he has the negotiator's veto, Patricia will remain with Quentin at *A*.

Alternatively, a creating strategy could benefit both negotiators. Visually this moves them both from *A* (the status quo) in a north-easterly direction to points such as *B*, *C*, or *D*. In each case, such moves benefit both negotiators because they now have more utility without taking anything from the other.

Of course, the negotiators are not indifferent to which of the points, *B*, *C*, or *D*, they move to. Patricia prefers *B* to *D*, and Quentin prefers *D* to *B*. Can you see why? Moving to *B* gives proportionally more utility to Patricia and moving to *D* gives proportionally more utility to Quentin, with correspondingly smaller increases in utility to the other. Patricia and Quentin might propose to move to these points respectively because they improve on the distribution of utilities they each get from the status quo at *A*. In the negotiation dance that follows, the negotiators might gradually move to a position, such as C because it unambiguously equally benefits both of them. They might agree to C on these grounds alone.

You can think of the boundary line as being scribed between the extremes of Patricia getting all the available extra utility (p''), including what they both enjoy at A, or Quentin getting all the available extra utility (q''), with the other player at these extremes getting none. The RS boundary scribes through all the possible combinations of extra utility distributed between Patricia and Quentin. Neither can move to a position outside the boundary because combinations of utility are not available beyond that boundary. The negotiators can only distribute utility between themselves by being on or inside the boundary.

Now to reach any point north-east of A, the negotiators have to at least *co-operate* enough to prevent either of them using their veto. If either of them uses their veto, they will both remain at the utility distribution represented by A and forgo the potential benefits of additional utility to each of them from jointly agreeing to move north-easterly towards the boundary line. Negotiating is an act of tentative co-operation no matter how hostile they feel towards each other as rivals or deadly enemies. This constitutes one of the common interests of negotiators.

Apart from co-operating in the act of negotiating, parties have common interests in a negotiated outcome. If they freely negotiate an outcome, then the benefits of their agreement will address some of the interests of each party. In so far as these interests originate differently for each party, then they have a common interest in reaching and in implementing that agreement.

Moving from a visual exposition involving Patricia and Quentin, we can look at an example to demonstrate the analysis of Figure P.3.

Two siblings inherit a farm and meet to decide how to divide it. They could agree to sell it and divide the proceeds. Now suppose Morag is a farmer and wants to keep the family home as a working farm. Suppose Andy does not. He prefers his share of the money from selling the farm. It could be a stalemate, unless Morag can agree with her brother that, say, she keeps the farm and pays Andy a rental for his half share. He agrees on condition that he gets their mother's Jaguar car and Morag accepts responsibility for looking after Grandma.

Andy needs Morag's consent to pay him regular income, to forgo the Jaguar, and to take responsibility for Grandma; Morag, perhaps, wants the farm more than she wants the Jaguar. Selling the farm at this time could mean a low price, with, perhaps, most of the money they raised going to fund Grandma's retirement in a home, rather than her continuing to live in the farmhouse. In these circumstances, Andy and Morag (and Grandma) are better off if they can make a deal.

Down the road from my Edinburgh office there is a junk shop. It is full of delightful surprises for browsers. One such object caught my eye. It was an old wooden chair. While I was in the shop, I noticed other people looking the chair over. What intrigued me was the range of ages, clothing styles and income levels, represented by those who talked to the owner about the chair. It covered a wide spectrum of social status (though all that glitters is not gold and everybody who is scruffy is not poor).

If I was to speculate, I could surmise that their interest in the old chair stemmed from a variety of reasons:

○   The guy in the buff coat could see it as a comfortable seat.
○   The woman in the tweeds saw it as an antique.
○   The young woman in jeans and off-white T-shirt could see it as a prop for the play she was producing in the nearby university.
○   To the rather snooty thirty-something woman it could be a trendy form of decoration for her hallway.
○   For the young 'poser' it was a possible investment (he was already on his mobile phone to his bank).
○   For the man in the antique trade it could have made up the three identical chairs he had recovered in a house clearing into a more valuable set of four.
○   The aged scrounger could have noted its potential as firewood.
○   The young couple who surveyed it might have seen it as a repainted chair for their kitchen, or a temporary 'clothes rack' for their spare bedroom.
○   To the pensive smoker it was a hole in her bank balance.
○   For the middle-aged well-dressed woman it was a possible present for her son's new home.
○   For me it was necessary for my daughter's chairless flat.

People perceive the same item, the same contract, and the same service in a multitude of different ways, according to their attitudes and beliefs, and their momentary moods.

In different circumstances you want something different and not what is on the set menu or in the pre-printed contract. Your wants are entirely subjective and mostly private. The people examining the chair do not articulate their motives or thoughts. If they express them at all they would not do them justice. Subjective feelings, moods, notions and such like, though keenly felt are seldom defined or definable. You do not reveal your subjective values, though they play a large part in your decisions on the objective costs of changing the status quo to obtain the items you negotiate over. Hence, you must consider the influence of subjective values in negotiating because they play an important role for everybody involved.

Like other social skills, you negotiate with varying degrees of success and your behaviour can also degenerate when you turn from voluntary trading to coercive relationships, or seek to manipulate perceptions by various forms of posturing.

These defects are neither inevitable nor endemic to traditional negotiation. Idealization would suggest that two parties freely enter into a search for the terms upon which they can exchange what they value less for what they value more. If they find such terms, they agree; if they do not, the negotiation aborts, freeing both parties to attempt to contract with others. It also leaves them without the gains they could have made if they had found acceptable terms. They stick at *A* in Figure P.3 and cannot get closer to *C* because each insists on distributions such as *B* or *D*, neither of which is acceptable to the other.

Negotiation, therefore, is worthy of study and practice because it:

○   is a democratic and ethical mode of decision making;
○   requires voluntary consent;
○   ensures that neither party can be coerced;
○   enables the parties to form a bonding relationship when they implement what they agreed.

Negotiation, in my view, is a force for personal and collective liberation in all aspects of human endeavour and excludes nobody from its benefits if they practise the precepts that work.

The *Dialogue* that follows covers the best of advice on how to raise your ratio of success and self-fulfilment by negotiating your way for a bigger say in what happens to you. It also contains criticism of some of the nonsense said about negotiation from time to time. Learning about errors and the sources of errors is a necessary part of learning how to negotiate properly. Of course, not everything I criticize is so bad as to be always pernicious, nor is everything I praise, for that matter, so good as to be always positively beneficent. Life is much more complicated than that.

DIALOGUE

NEGOTIATION AS A PHASED PROCESS

MODELS OF NEGOTIATION

Of the various models of negotiation practice I shall focus on one I have been associated with for over twenty years. One author calls it a *processual*[24] approach but I have always had difficulty saying this without stumbling. I prefer to call it a phased process. Take your pick.

My own work on negotiation began in 1969 while observing labour productivity negotiations at a Shell refinery near London. Before I had completed my research[25] my attention switched from what the negotiators were doing to *how* to negotiate effectively. There were no books and precious few articles in the UK on how to negotiate and these did not begin to appear until after 1972. By the mid-1980s there was a veritable flood (I had written four of them myself by 1985). Bibliographies on negotiation now encompass thousands of individual items, far too many to mention but a fraction of them here. Where once there was a desert, today there is a lush and fruitful Eden. On a personal level, it thrills me to be part of it and, even more, to have been in at the beginning.

My eight-steps training model developed independently of what I later discovered to be earlier work by Ann Douglas[26] in the United States. It pre-dated the fascinating study by Philip H. Gulliver of the comparative negotiating practices of the Arusha people of Tanzania and labour negotiators in America.[27]

If intelligent people observe and analyse the practice of negotiation they will likely come to similar conclusions. Douglas, Gulliver and I based our insights on detailed observation of live negotiations and it is not surprising that we independently identified similar processes at work. In Douglas's case, she used a verbatim record of an industrial dispute, plus her considerable experience from other labour negotiations, to arrive at her phases' model. Gulliver too, developed his phases' model from detailed observation of negotiators at work in two distinct cultures and in doing so he uncovered and confirmed the phased patterns all three of us saw.

Herbert Simon,[28] by way of contrast, produced a deductive phased model of *rational* choice, which preceded the inductive models of Douglas, Gulliver and myself, and is echoed today by the Harvard school of 'principled' negotiation (Fisher and Ury, among others).[29] Assumptions of rationality are often misleading as guides to action by professional mediators and their academic advisors.

These rational models came from deductive (theoretical) research, with occasional anecdotal forays into live observations. In stark contrast, the phased negotiation modellers display an inductive bias from observing what negotiators did, with occasional forays into deductive theory.

Though Simon preceded the inductive studies that produced the phases' models of negotiation, I shall defer commenting on his model until Chapter 5. Meanwhile, I shall examine the original phased models, highlighting their practical foundations and how they can improve your performance. They observe what real negotiators do, and, by implication, what you are doing when you negotiate, whether you are aware of the models or not.

 ## DOUGLAS'S THREE-PHASE MODEL

Ann Douglas produced a three-phase model of the labour negotiations she observed. Her phases were:

○   *Phase 1:* establishing the negotiation range.
○   *Phase 2:* reconnoitring the range.
○   *Phase 3:* precipitating the decision-reaching crisis.

Phase 1 is a 'thorough and exhaustive determination' of the range within which the parties will do business.[30] In this phase the negotiators make long speeches and strive 'for a convincing demonstration that they are impossibly at loggerheads' and that there is substantive disagreement between them. Those familiar with labour negotiations and international disputes, will recognize the behaviour she observed.

Douglas asserted that the deeper the negotiators dig into their opening positions 'the more they enhance their chances for a good and stable settlement at the end'. She also noted that 'antagonism between the parties is the lifeblood of this first phase but that personal antagonism between individuals would be highly detrimental to the psychological activity that is foremost in the second phase'.

She specifically recommended that the negotiators should *not* attack each other personally but that they should concentrate on their differences over the issues. Her advice reappeared thirty years later in Fisher and Ury's prescription to 'separate the people from the problem'.[31]

In *phase 2*, the 'negotiators search earnestly for signs of tacit agreement, long before in their public exchange they can afford to profess anything but continued strong disagreement'.[32] Observing the rhetoric of this second phase in labour negotiations, we see this happening in statements and re-statements of their initial positions and references to 'wide gaps' and 'no signs of movement' (by the other side!) until, suddenly, we enter the third phase.

In *phase 3*, the negotiators precipitate a 'decision crisis' by consulting their respective constituencies and trying to conclude an agreement from what they have learnt of the other party's willingness to settle, and the prospects, if any, for improving on what is now on offer on the table.[33]

 ## GULLIVER'S EIGHT PHASES

Gulliver identified an eight-phased process. He labelled them:

1. search for an arena;
2. composition of the agenda and the definition of issues;
3. establishing maximal limits to issues in dispute;
4. narrowing the differences;
5. preliminaries to final bargaining;
6. final bargaining;
7. ritual affirmation;
8. execution of the agreement.

Gulliver's eight-phase model is a mixture of task and behaviour. He acknowledges immediately that his linear numbering does not mean that the process is necessarily linear or congruent with chronological time.[34] With this I completely concur. Negotiation is seldom a highly structured experience because there are numerous opportunities for diversions, distractions, back-tracking, and cyclical variations, that can be a cause of confusion, even distress, to the uninitiated.

In Gulliver's phase 1 – the *search for an arena* – the parties recognize that they have a problem and that they need to agree to meet somewhere to negotiate an outcome. This could be difficult if one of you refuses to meet or to acknowledge that there is a problem and forgoes the prospects of a negotiated settlement because he is happy with the status quo.

Trivially, if you want to negotiate you must at least make a joint decision on exactly where the meeting is to take place. I do not think, however, that this is a large issue for the overwhelming majority of private negotiations in economies like the UK, though it is not uncommon for lawyers tactically to delay meetings. Internationally, we see occasional disputes over the meeting place and even the shape and layout of its furniture (e.g. the Vietnam peace negotiations in Paris, or the negotiations to formally end the Iran–Iraq war in Geneva). As negotiators regularly ask whether it is better to meet in their own or in somebody else's premises, these issues must be important in some circumstances.

In phase 2 – *composition of the agenda and the definition of issues* – you have to establish what it is that you are disputing. This is never as clear in practice as it seems rational to suppose in theory. What triggers a negotiation may be only a small part of what eventually lands on the table. Some disputes explode from a vague discontent into a whole list of other issues, especially in labour disputes of the spontaneous 'walk-out' variety. These rapidly spread like wildfire and, as new entrants join the walk-out, this often increases the list of issues in dispute and the players' militancy. When these disputes catch the management and the official union leaders by surprise, it is extremely difficult to agree on what the dispute is about.

Other negotiators tussle over the agenda and introduce preconditions to force their own views on what is negotiable. A serious dispute over preconditions stultifies progress. Britain, for example, will not negotiate – or even discuss – the sovereignty of the Falkland Islands; Argentina, meanwhile, takes every opportunity in every diplomatic forum to discuss the sovereignty of the Malvinas. In so far as disputes before negotiating on substantive issues are common enough, Gulliver is probably right to make them a separate phase.

Substantive issues dominate the third phase – *establishing maximal limits to issues in dispute* (echoes of phase 1 in the Douglas model) – which, for most practitioners, constitutes the real opening of the face-to-face negotiations. It is also the phase most notably misunderstood by novices, where a great deal of high-blown rhetoric dominates the proceedings.

If you took to heart what is said in this early phase, or become influenced too much by the tone of the alternating monologues, you might wonder if negotiations were going to take place at all. Following the line that the best method of defence is attack, you launch into spirited attacks on the other party's expected positions and make extreme cases for why you cannot move on issues that they claim are fundamental to their principles.

This is the phase that caught in the craw of Fisher and Ury and their strictures against the behaviour of positional bargainers have most validity in these opening rounds. Tension is undoubtedly high and often personal. It is an uncomfortable time for the faint hearted and those least used to adversarial behaviour.

At the beginning of a negotiation over something important to you, anxiety and uncertainty about the outcome is at its highest. There is a long way to go, of course, before you resolve the issues, but the normal anxiety you feel enforces upon you an expected hostility against the other negotiators who stand in the way of you getting what you want. Imputing insincere motives to others produces tension, and, if reciprocated in tone and manner, the noise of conflict might get worse before it gets better.

Experienced negotiators (not those Lord Nelson before the Battle of Copenhagen described as the 'children of war') hear enough verbal abuse not to let it rattle their sense of purpose. They have heard the long speeches and listened to the other side's claims to the moral high ground on all and every issue, not to fall into the argument traps lying in wait for ill-informed beginners.

The opening rounds of many negotiations are not a place for kindly professors used to more genteel lifestyles and to modes of controversy commonly found in post-graduate seminars, though, come to think of it, I have heard more than one 'kindly' professor launch into an extreme diatribe against something or someone, and usually both at the same time, who proposed to change something dear to their sense of worth (for example, any mention of removing parking privileges for senior faculty!).

The rhetoric and tone of this phase is part of the 'theatre' of negotiating and something you get used to. One thing the uninitiated must not do is take it all too seriously and consequently make unnecessary – or any – concessions in a fatuous attempt to calm tempers. Concessions won by rhetoric alone only encourage irascible players irascibly to demand more. If you jump when they go 'woof, woof', don't be surprised if they see just how high you will jump if they keep 'woofing'!

Sometimes, eventually 'woofing' gives way to calmer interchanges. This is Gulliver's fourth phase – *narrowing the differences* – when you move from rhetoric towards detailed consideration of the issues. In so doing, you exhibit more co-operative tones as you sift through the issues and ponder tentative suggestions on how you both might deal with them. The calmness and the lowering of tension, however, is only relative compared to the third phase. Exploration is a more fitting word for this phase than exhortation. Conditions exist for what I call signalling.

Gulliver identifies five sub-strategies to narrow the differences. They are not necessarily mutually exclusive. They provide useful insights into some of the problems that in my experience negotiators raise regularly at workshops.

First, the tempers of the third phase are cooled with a strategy of considering issues one at a time, in what Gulliver calls a 'simple agenda approach'.[35] Working your way through a list of items has the benefit of being orderly, but it risks manipulation to secure advantage through eliminating some issues from further consideration, on pain of a row breaking out again, to isolate and highlight issues important to one side. My advice is always to be careful of separating issues, particularly in agenda lists and in multiple-clause contracts.

Second, you can nominate the two or three most important issues for you and see if agreement is possible on these, in the expectation that the remaining, less important, issues will go through quickly. I caution against this approach too, because what appears to be important at the start of the negotiation could have less significance towards the end. When the remaining issues come up for consideration, you might want to revise your stance on the earlier issues to facilitate your stance on these later ones.

The interaction often reveals new information about the relative value of the issues to each of you and, by using up your negotiating capital on the early 'more important' issues, there may not be enough flexibility left to make it matter in the later issues. When you realize the implications of the proposals on the later issues or become aware of how their proposals weaken what you thought you had gained on earlier issues, you might be less happy with a strategy of nominating the important issues for negotiation first. Remember an issue is not a proposal, it is only an agenda item.

Third, you can reduce the issues to a single objective such as their contribution to profit or their impact on personal prestige or, *pace* Fisher and Ury, to some form of objective criteria.[36] You can eliminate from the negotiation those issues that do not make a contribution to the identified main objective thus simplifying the remaining agenda. However, it still requires mutual acceptance of the main objective and in the case of objective criteria, agreement on which criteria to use to derive a settlement. For completeness, Gulliver's inclusion of this strategy is interesting but I am not sure of its practicality.

Fourth, you could agree to deal with the issues in reverse order of their importance or their expected levels of disagreement. This is a regular question in seminars: 'Should we seek agreement on the easy-to-settle issues before we tackle the difficult ones, or vice versa?' I usually answer that it depends on the context. By this I mean on the totality of the issues on the table. Is there one issue that is far too controversial for agreement without a great deal of difficulty – if at all – and which if pursued now could jeopardize the physical continuation of the negotiation? If so, it might be advisable to 'park' this issue to one side and move on to issues of lesser difficulty. This is not quite what Gulliver alludes to, but this is the proper context in which to look at the efficacy of tackling the 'easier' issues first.

Remember this device does not remove the conflict over the most difficult issue, assuming they agree that this is *the* most difficult issue and you feel it is right to park it to one side. In some contexts, postponing the main issue helps, in others it hinders.

Gulliver reports that the Arusha and Ndendeuli negotiators likened this sub-strategy to creating a new field in bushland, using as a metaphor 'the clearing away of bushes and undergrowth to reveal the larger trees that must be cut down in order to complete the task'.[37] Some even larger trees 'may be too large to fell, and must therefore be left untouched' (i.e. in our terminology, parked).

Gulliver's *fifth* sub-strategy is to engage in trading among the issues: 'we give way on this issue if you will concede on that one; we agree to compromise on one if you will agree to do the same on the other'. He saw this as a way of clearing away problems by 'horse trading'.

I am cautious about Gulliver's unassertive negotiating language here, as well as the implications of his statement that 'The recognition of such reciprocity may be explicit and subject to some hard bargaining, though it is often tacit as one party offers a conciliatory concession in the endeavour to draw a comparable response from the opponent'. In my experience, relying on tacit rather than explicit trading is too risky a business for a negotiator (it has its uses for an influencer) and is worthy of severe criticism. What happens when the other negotiator does not reciprocate is ignored by Gulliver.

He adds that this fifth sub-strategy requires an ability to evaluate and compare which issue is more or less important to each negotiator and, dangerously, on which there is a 'willingness to make concessions'. In my view, while it is essential to be able to 'evaluate and compare certain issues', i.e. prioritize them, it is more essential that you know the difference between being willing to *trade* and being willing to *make* concessions.

Over the years, I have excused Gulliver this slip because he honestly reported on what he observed the negotiators, both effective and ineffective, were doing and was not prescribing what they *should* do. But I would not want to leave you not knowing the difference between trading and conceding.

He reveals a version of this sub-strategy in the form of packaging, and adds that 'this may be no more than the explicit, reciprocal linking of two issues' and 'that it can be more complex than that, involving a number of issues that are, or can be agreed to be, interconnected'.[38] This is a restrictive view of packaging because there is no reason why packaged issues have to be 'interconnected' at all.

A negotiated package, just like one you receive through the mail, can consist of a multiplicity of unconnected items. I also consider the role of trading and packaging of far greater importance to a negotiated outcome than it being merely one of five possible sub-strategies for the narrowing of differences.

Phase 5 in Gulliver's approach – *preliminaries to final bargaining* – consists of one or more preliminary activities. The negotiators:

O   continue the search for a viable bargaining range;
O   refine persisting differences;
O   test the trading possibilities;
O   try to construct a bargaining formula.[39]

The first activity concerns trying to identify the settlement range: are the current offers and demands within the exit points of the parties? If they are (for an explanation, see p. 59) it promotes movement to the final bargaining phase.

The second activity is about simplifying the remaining differences ('what exactly are we in dispute about?'). Instead of driving into the sand on details, you might aim at an overall generality, such as, for example, proposing *ad valorem* percentage increases rather than a detailed grading revision.

By 'testing trading possibilities', Gulliver means encouraging one side to drop a complex issue in exchange for the other side dropping something complex somewhere else and then focusing on trades that might be possible.

The last, the bargaining formula, is imported by Gulliver from Zartman, who developed the idea into his 'Formula-Detail' approach.[40] Observing international diplomatic negotiations, Zartman noted that they tended to follow a pattern of the parties first exploring for a formula and then negotiating the details according to the guidelines of the agreed formula.

With phase 6 – *final bargaining* – we reach the nub of the process. Gulliver, somewhat tentatively to be sure, considers the dominant behaviour in the final bargaining phase to be 'some form of convergent concession-making'. He admits being influenced as much by the prevalent concession-convergence models of the bargaining problem from economic theory, as by his observation of negotiations in Africa. These observations convinced him that 'such incremental convergence is the most common mode for both quantitative and qualitative issues'.[41] I shall withhold comment on this conclusion, until I discuss economic concession-convergence models in greater detail in Chapter 4.

Gulliver does not find a central role for the principle of explicit conditional bargaining. Perhaps, because he observed what the negotiators did through the framework of plausible concession-convergence modelling, he did not consider prescribing the behaviour that the negotiators should follow. You only see what you look for.

Gulliver's last two phases – *ritual affirmation* and *execution of the agreement* – complete the process as he observed it. While culture prescribes the form of ritual affirmation, it is common in the West to sanctify a deal by a handshake symbolizing the promise to keep to the terms of the deal. Negotiators often celebrate too with a drink or a meal together. Phase eight requires some form of execution of the agreement, usually the sooner the better. After all, we negotiate to make a decision and the next most important step is to implement it.

 ## KENNEDY'S EIGHT-STEP MODEL

The most direct way to discuss my own phases' model is to give some short extracts from the first edition of *Managing Negotiations*:

> We believe that negotiations can be seen as a loosely ordered sequence of distinct steps which can be presented to managers in a credible and simple form (the Eight-Step Approach). Because these steps can be seen to be common to all negotiations and appropriate to all combinations of personality it is not necessary for people to first 'change the world' before they can use them. The eight steps provide a framework for coping with negotiating as a process and permit the development and practice of skills specifically related to each step.
>
> Our approach to negotiating is not evangelical. We are not attempting conversion to a new way of negotiating. Our approach is based on what negotiators do, not what they ought to do. Nor does our method depend for success on negotiators only meeting other negotiators who use the same method. It is not like the truck drivers club of some years ago where the XYZ Company [Bedford] offered drivers of its trucks insurance for a token premium. They were covered for £1,000 in the event of their death arising from an accident while driving the XYZ Company truck. This seemed a good deal until you read the small print; to qualify for the death benefit they had to be killed in collision with another truck made by the XYZ Company ...
>
> What then is the Eight-Step Approach? Briefly, the negotiating sequence is broken down into the eight main steps through which negotiations will go, if agreement is to be reached, though not

necessarily in a rigid order, nor with equal attention or time to each step. We make the central assumption that negotiation can be analysed within the eight-step framework whether the negotiators are aware of the eight steps or not. They will take minutes to learn, not days. They can be used straightaway and, more importantly, long after you are first made aware of them ...

It is our experience, that people are able to absorb the necessary elements in each step with little effort and can use them to evaluate critically their current performance as a negotiator. They can also use them to evaluate what their opponents are attempting to do. Readers ... will be able to grasp a framework for understanding their negotiations in one go and apply that framework immediately: they will know what is going on at any moment in the negotiation, where they want to go next and what they have to do to get there.[42]

I wrote that extract six years after I began disseminating my newly discovered training approach. Its somewhat bullish tone reflects just how exciting it was to have developed a training method that worked. Today, the phased approach is an important training method in many countries. In this respect, as its creator I would rather be plagiarized than ignored, but as a businessman I would, of course, rather be paid than plagiarized.

The phased models of Douglas, Gulliver and my own came from close observation of the phenomena of negotiation. We applied analytical methods in a search for patterns within the process and we drew conclusions about what we thought was going on. I took the 'what the negotiators should do' aspects further than Douglas and Gulliver, by asking prescriptive questions about *how* to improve a negotiator's performance.

Gulliver's model supplied detailed comment on and interpretation of what he observed negotiators doing in each of eight phases. My approach became prescriptively biased. I shall examine these prescriptions in summary and, in later chapters, I shall explore the practical applications of the skills of each of the phases.

The original eight steps (1974) were:

1.   Prepare
2.   Argue
3.   Signal
4.   Propose
5.   Package
6.   Bargain
7.   Close
8.   Agree

The eight phases in the observation mode are about what negotiators do, implicitly or explicitly, well or otherwise. Of course, the extent to which individual negotiators are skilled in the tasks of each phase will determine the quality of the deals they achieve.

The need for *preparation* is almost a cliché in management activity, often done badly and usually under pressure, but always recognized by managers (though almost as often, seldom carried out) as an essential prelude to anything that is important to their roles (and job security). Prioritizing objectives featured strongly in the original eight steps. We distinguished between the negotiator's 'most favoured position' (MFP) and his 'limit' or break point, corresponding to points on Walton and McKersie's negotiation and settlement ranges.[43]

To prioritize the negotiator's objectives, we used 'M-I-L' as a mnemonic for the objectives you *Must* achieve, those you *Intend* to achieve or those it is *Important* for you to achieve, and those you would *Like* to achieve. We replaced our 'M-I-L-it' mnemonic[44] by 'L-I-M-it', following advice from a retired trainer employed to assist us by International Computers in England, who suggested we reversed 'M-I-L-it' to 'L-I-M-it', a word more commonly understood by negotiators.[45]

In preparation, you must also consider the information you intend to reveal to the other negotiator and the information you will seek, if only to confirm the assumptions you have made. And you must assign to the team the three roles of leader, summarizer and recorder.

The name for the second step has always been somewhat troublesome. I chose 'argument' because that is what I observed negotiators doing, though I may have been over-influenced in the early days by the opening phases, tones and manners of industrial relations negotiations.

I have already remarked on just how rowdy and sometimes personally unpleasant the behaviour experienced in this phase can be to the uninitiated and to those used to politer people in pleasanter circumstances. In *Managing Negotiations* I put it thus:

> People with different interests are likely to argue. This is natural. Most people are accomplished arguers and even saints can become emotional when interests close to their heart are threatened (witness Christ scourging the money changers from the Temple) which is one reason to be wary of those who forswear arguing – clearly they have short memories or nothing they value is threatened.[46]

Some people claim they do not argue but they admit to debate or discussion. The beauty of the word argue is that it can mean two distinct things, one reasonable and constructive (two philosophers engaged in discourse, two advocates pleading legal arguments, a mathematician establishing the arguments of her functions), and the other unreasonable and destructive (two adversarial politicians, a tired and emotional bore, an outraged fanatic). Over the years, by dint of the influence of training film producers and sensitive training managers, I have tended to avoid the word 'argue' and replace it with 'discuss,'[47] 'debate',[48] and even 'explore'. [49]

The importance of the second phase exceeds the heat generated by what we call it. Over 80 per cent of the time that negotiators spend face-to-face involves the behaviours associated with 'argue', 'discuss', 'debate', 'exploration', or whatever else you call it! *Debate* phases domi-nate negotiation. Negotiators open in the debate phase and sometimes stay in it until they deadlock. They can slip in and out of debate until they make a relatively short dash through proposing and bargaining to an agreement. If things go wrong they are likely to go wrong during the high proportion of time negotiators spend debating. Therefore, much training time is devoted to correcting unhelpful behaviours.

Indeed, behaviourist trainers[50] have made significant contributions to the improvement of negotiating behaviour in the debate phase. Debate behaviour is dividable into destructive or constructive forms. Our early efforts concentrated on getting negotiators to eliminate destructive behaviour from their repertoire, the need for which, unfor-tunately, is often easier to acknowledge than to practise afterwards, especially by those most in need of it.

'Negative argument', we wrote, 'reinforces the inhibitions of your opponent. These inhibitions prevent an open negotiating stance and sometimes prevent agreement on an issue even when agreement is mutually advantageous'.[51] (Note our own use of the word 'opponent' to describe the other negotiator, which dates the tone even in a book dedi-cated to rising above the negative behaviours and perceptions normally accepted at the time.)

On the constructive side, behaviours that involve listening rather than talking, positive questions rather than sarcastic statements, sum-marizing truthfully rather than using a summary to launch another attack, and clarifying the other negotiator's positions rather than merely reciting a destructive response to them, are more likely to move the negotiations forward:

> If you have identified your opponent's inhibitions, commitments and intentions you will have formed a judgement about the possi-bility of negotiation on the issue of dispute. If that possibility exists then you can proceed to negotiation.[52]

This brings us to the strategic problem for all negotiators: how to move without giving in? For every issue in dispute there are two initial solutions, yours and the other person's. You know that to get agree-ment you have to discover a third solution, which is normally different from either of the two solutions with which you started. But how to get there? If you move in the hope that they will move too, observation and experience suggest you will be disappointed.

It is more than a case of a need for courage, or even faith. The essence of negotiation is the management of movement because without movement no negotiation can succeed. Bearing in mind that you are operating in the opening phases of debate (remember Gulliver's description of his third phase with its emphasis on differences?), when prospects of movement appear to be slim because both of you are presenting your strongest cases for your opening positions, it is likely that ill thought-out movement here will cost you dear later. A negotiator who 'magnanimously moves to his resistance point at an early stage' may fail to agree because he has nothing left to trade.[53] The message received, if you move unilaterally – though not the one, perhaps, that you intended to send – will be that by them refusing to reciprocate they might move you again and again. They believe you are on the slippery slope to surrender. Not moving at all does not help, because you signal total commitment to an unviable position and risk 'losing what goodwill remains in the relationship'.[54]

There are three conditions necessary for movement, two implicit and one explicit. Each negotiator implicitly must 'have sufficient power to persuade the other to move, but insufficient power to force a total surrender'; each party must be 'willing to move from their stated positions ... because each party sees greater benefit in reaching settlement', and, explicitly, 'there must be an indication of willingness to negotiate in spite of the difficulties'.[55] Yes, but how can you indicate 'willingness' without them misinterpreting your message?

People, I noticed, were often not listening and were sometimes 'behind' in the unfolding exchanges and, in consequence, continued to contest earlier positions, some time after the other negotiators had intimated that they might move to new, more flexible, ones. So they carried on arguing as if nothing had changed. What they had missed were *signals*:

> A signal is a means by which parties indicate their *willingness* to negotiate on something. It is also more than that: it implies a willingness only if it is reciprocated by the other side.[56]

Signals use a different language from that of of the early argument phase. This is why I made signals one of the original eight steps. The problem for signals is that they can pass unnoticed if you are queuing up to blow the other negotiator out of the water with yet another devastating broadside.

If noticed, the signal may not be understood and if understood, it may not be acted upon. Like anything fragile, signals can have a short and unproductive life. The other negotiator reacts to your non-reaction to her signal, and withdraws back to her ramparts. And you lose an opportunity to break out of the argument phase with her. Another opportunity might arise, then again it might not.

You do not learn about signals for the first time on a negotiation course because you are already familiar with them from the game of life. What is courtship but a convoluted, and sometimes embarrassing, exchange of signals? Signals are ubiquitous, if you listen for them. They place qualifications on absolutist language:

'There is no way we could agree to your demands'

is a firm rejection, unless they add, perhaps *sotto voce*,

'in their present form.'

At once, potentially, the situation is different. As so often in negotiating, while what you do is important, what is done next is decisive. If you fail to hear the signal and carry on challenging the previously fixed position, nothing can save their willingness to move from fading away. Hours later, you could go home absolutely convinced that they totally and implacably rejected your 'modest' demands.

You could respond positively to her signal, however, and by doing so change the pace of the game. The signal, 'in their present form', is a cue for an exploratory question:

'When you say that our demands are unacceptable in their current form, what do you mean by that?'

is one possibility, and so is:

'What would make our demands more acceptable to you?'

Depending on what you ask, and what they answer, mutual movement is now in prospect.

They are not saying that they will move, and neither are you, but both of you are indicating that discussion on the exact form of your demands is possible. This might be achieved, perhaps, by expressing them differently or by shaping them in some way. Nobody is at risk of a collapse of their position; you are only at risk of finding out whether more acceptable terms are possible.

Signalling weakly hints at possibilities for movement and sets out the ground for possible proposals. I refer to signals as the 'bridge' from argument to proposals. Signals are tentative and require a different response from that of the positional posturings of the argument phase.

Negotiators can be trained to recognize, respond and capitalize on signal behaviour.

We put less emphasis in the early days on the necessity for conditional language when making *proposals* (Step 4). We focused more on the delivery styles and responses to proposals, but always using the IF–THEN format. The main need was to ensure that the negotiators highlighted their proposals – tentative solutions – with clarity and organization. 'Shambolic rambles' were derided because they mixed-up explanation, justification and rebuttals in muddled proposals.[57]

Argumentative behaviour that carried over into the proposal step usually reduced to some abrupt way of saying 'no', or something yet more irascible, often before the negotiator had time to really understand the proposal put to him.

A 'no questions asked nor answers wanted' approach is fairly common and we tried to replace this with more positive responses. Asking questions took the negotiations back to the argument phase but did so under conditions that would not re-start argumentative warfare. The more they responded to questions about their proposals, the more they revealed about their thinking, their motives and their areas of flexibility. These created possibilities for the fifth step – *packaging*.

In responding to questions you reveal both your interests and your inhibitions. The former motivate you to say 'yes', the latter motivate you to say 'no'. If by re-packaging a proposal to take on board some of the legitimate points they have made and if you can also address their interests positively and reduce their inhibitory concerns openly, the prospects for an agreement begin to look promising.

It was in the sixth, *bargaining*, step that we opened up explicitly on conditional bargaining – using the expression 'the Big IF' to highlight the importance of the IF–THEN format:

> The most important single rule for the bargaining step is to make all propositions and concessions, indeed practically any statement at all, *conditional*. Nothing, absolutely nothing, is given away free. Everything, absolutely everything, is conceded in exchange for something else.[58]

Certainly the theme of the first edition left no doubt of the role of conditional bargaining:

> Placing an 'IF' in front of a statement protects it from being misappropriated by your opponent. Without an 'IF' he can simply say 'Thank you very much' and pocket your concession without reciprocating. And most times that he is precisely what he is invited to do by inexperienced negotiators who for some reason assume that if they are generous to their opponents they will eventually persuade them to be generous in return. What is more, many negotiators,

despite the evidence of experience, continue to try the generosity gambit and fail to see the connection between their failures as negotiators and their behaviour as the bestowers of gifts.[59]

We also addressed the choices of *linking* or *separating* – coming down firmly on the side of linking issues – and of always endeavouring to place your conditions before your offers so that the listeners address your condition.

The final two steps, *closing* and *agreeing*, completed the eight-step approach, though there were still some obvious pitfalls for the unwary. Knowing how to close is easier than knowing when to close. Close too early and you risk deadlock by slipping into ridiculous 'my final offer' gambits. Close too late and they wear you away into concessions way beyond what you intended. Several 'closes' were identified and offered for consideration. Our *traded concession, summary, adjournment, or else*, and *either/or* closes have since become part of the general literature on negotiation.

Advice about agreements came solidly from bitter experience. Letting people leave the table without a written agreement is dangerous. No subsequent misunderstanding ever really recovers from the feeling that someone tried to 'slip one over you' and a reputation for 'misunderstandings', with actual agreements unsupported by written evidence, can ruin a relationship – and a reputation – for years.

The eight-step approach, as originally conceived, addressed a client's (Scottish & Newcastle Beer Co.) requirements to train several hundred of its negotiators. It was heavily prescriptive in content, as would be expected since it was meant to train people to become better at negotiating than they were before they attended the course.

The eight steps themselves are the steps that negotiators go through, not the steps that they ought to go through. The prescriptive skills content for each of the eight steps, however, was about what they ought to do in each step. Most of the prescriptive advice came from wrestling with the negative behaviours of negotiators and finding the means by which they could avoid repeating the same old mistakes. Effective negotiators, we observed, used different behaviours (or skills) from the ineffective ones, and we incorporated these effective skills (or behaviours) into the prescriptive advice of what to do and what to avoid in each of the eight steps.

 ## TWO MODIFICATIONS

The switch from eight steps to the current presentations as four phases was not deliberate. The accident of preparing the script for *The Art of*

Negotiation, a training film based on *Managing Negotiations*, in 1981,[60] initiated the changes.

The scriptwriter insisted that he could not include eight distinct steps into a 25-minute film without everything appearing to be too 'jerky' and overly 'abrupt', so 'could we cut it to four instead?' John McMillan, co-contributor to *Managing Negotiations*, assigned by the authors to work on the film project, settled for the four main phases: *prepare, discuss, propose* and *bargain*, and Rank's scriptwriter tucked signalling, packaging, closing and agreeing into the script relatively unobtrusively.

We acknowledged the four main phases in the second edition of *Managing Negotiations* (1984) without altering the book's eight-step chapter structure. Since then, I have used McMillan's four-phases selection instead of my original eight steps as the basis of our training programmes, and he has cut the main phases in 1995 to three (prepare, argue and propose).

The more important modification was to adapt Colin Rose's wants approach[61] in 1985, which fitted in well with the four phases. He had independently developed a six phases' model for negotiation (i.e. prepare, wants, propose, bargain, agree, and follow-up), which is how we got together.

He asserts that people negotiate to get what they want. From this it was an obvious step to present the four main phases of negotiation as identifying yours and the other party's wants and then searching for the terms to exchange them. Such simple ideas appeal to practical negotiators. It cuts right through much of the obfuscation about negotiating behaviour and gets right to the main point of the process.

Rose's 'wants' approach prescriptively tasked the four phases. This transformed the names for the four phases from mere labels into precise and focused tasks (Figure 1.1). It also formed the basis for my 1992 training film, *Do We Have a Deal?*[62]

Phase	Task
Prepare	What do *we* want?
Debate	What do *they* want?
Propose	What wants *might* we trade?
Bargain	What wants *will* we trade?

Figure 1.1 Four phases prescriptively interpreted as tasks

Negotiation is about the ratio of the tasks in the preparation phase ('What do *we* want?') to the tasks in the debate phase ('What do *they* want?'):

$$\text{Negotiation is the ratio of} \quad \frac{\text{what we want}}{\text{what they want}}$$

In the proposal phase this ratio is a possible deal: what might we trade? and in the bargaining phase it is an explicit deal: what will we trade?

Preparation, for example, is finding out what you want and why you want it. If you are not working on these tasks in preparation, you are squandering scarce preparation time in non-preparation activity. Thus, negotiators who complain that they have too little time for preparation – the majority? – might also simultaneously use up what little time they claim to have on activities that do not contribute to their preparation. They are, therefore, in a double bind.

Debate is about finding out what the other negotiators want, mainly by effective behaviours like asking questions and listening to the answers. It confirms your assumptions about their intentions and expectations and uncovers their priorities. Because what is true for them is true for you, debate is also about revealing your wants, without disclosing, of course, how far you are willing to go to get a deal. If you are merely arguing, or generally behaving badly, you simply extend the amount of time spent in debate at best and jeopardize the prospects for a deal at worst.

The third and fourth phases are about searching for trades by iterating from tentative suggestions for exchanges (i.e., what wants *might* we trade?) to firm conditional offers (what wants *will* we trade?).

Negotiation as a phased process has a 35-year pedigree. It is the longest lasting of the approaches to the analysis and practice of negotiation. Its origins lie in observing what negotiators do across the whole process and these descriptive origins have caused a normative bias.

Negotiators trained or not, and in the overwhelming majority of cases it will be the latter, pass through a common process. It follows that if you can identify those behaviours that work more effectively than others, then training to improve your effectiveness is possible. Behaviour changes, and when it changes for the better, training becomes cost effective.

The normative conclusions, and positive insights, of many authors in negotiation is easily integrated into the process models. This has been the predominant experience of training in the eight-step/four phases approach. Other developments in negotiation scholarship, research, practice and some controversies, where appropriate, can aid training in, and understanding of, the complexity of the phenomenon.

The processual approach is not under threat from rival approaches because it can accommodate new insights to help negotiators to become more skilled, without collapsing into contradictions. In this respect, it is much like the English language which is, according to some linguists, on its way to becoming a global language, because English absorbs vocabulary and phrases from non-English languages like a sponge.

The hypothesis of the phased approaches is that negotiations have a common phased structure, no matter what they are about, who they are between, what the stakes are, which culture they occur in, which currencies they exchange, or the levels of technology of the societies their participants live in.

Gulliver's work demonstrated the commonality of the negotiation phases in north America and east Africa. Likewise, in presenting the four phases all over the world, I have not (yet) come across a country or a culture that has resisted in any way its applicability to their negotiating practice. I have not yet read a single line of criticism of the phases approach by anybody. (Please note, that is not a challenge. On second thoughts, it is!)

The four phases are not necessarily, nor even primarily, congruent in chronological time. They run in any order you like, for there is no requirement for them to be linear. The one certainty is that negotiators are in one or other of the identified phases at any one moment.

Identifying which phase you are in, and using behaviours that are appropriate for effective and successful processing of that phase, enables you to do better than, perhaps, you would otherwise. Some negotiators, unaware of the phases of negotiation, obviously on occasion can do just as well, even better, than negotiators who are aware, but they are unlikely to do so regularly.

The rest of this book examines how awareness of the main phases of negotiation improves skills and how learning to practise the most effective skills enhances performance in each of the phases.

CHAPTER

PHASE ONE – PREPARING TO NEGOTIATE

TIME TO PREPARE

I have never met a negotiator yet who claims that she has enough time to prepare properly. However, many negotiators, like students with essay deadlines, start preparing with only a few hours (moments even!) to spare, no matter how long they have known of the deadline. Inevitably, other people interrupt and distract them in the time they do set aside to prepare. Many believe that preparation is a chore, necessary but disagreeable, like washing dishes, or ironing, or visiting the dentist.

Yet preparation is the key to most of the important negotiations you undertake. It underlies everything you do as a negotiator. It is often the difference between a good deal and an average deal, and, as often, no deal at all. If you want to you can always 'out prepare' the other party on most occasions and if you use your limited discretionary time to good effect. And it is a perfectly fair way to compete too, because time taken by you to prepare takes nothing from the other party. How well they prepare is their decision alone and one for which they enjoy or suffer the consequences. The remedy is in their hands.

Preparation takes time but it is time well spent because inadequate preparation prolongs the negotiation. Instead of initiating movement and responding speedily to what develops in the debate or proposal phases, you must go cautiously because you have not prepared as you should have before you started listening to them.

Without preparation you choose your opening positions without adequate consideration and, if pushed to explain or justify your positions, you are unsure of why you want what you claim you want in the forms that you demand or expect. Hence, you ask, and are asked, for things neither of you wants to give on terms you cannot accept and to deadlines you resist meeting. And when you hear demands that disturb you,

47

your response is usually to attack the other negotiator, who as invariably replies with a counter-blast. Before long, you head for confrontation and all that this implies in wasted time and, perhaps, unnecessary disappointment. If, however, you start by thinking about possible solutions to the problems you face you enhance your effectiveness.

For much of the time you are just too busy to prepare properly and, if you have discretionary time, you often do not know where to start and how to allocate what time you have. Therefore, you need a system of preparation that is flexible and compressible enough to cope with relatively simple negotiations, and expandable if the negotiations are more complex. In all cases, it must enable you to use time efficiently, irrespective of the amount of time available.

 ## WHAT IS THIS NEGOTIATION ABOUT?

An obvious question not always asked by negotiators. 'Negotiation is negotiation' is a self-deluding but comforting mantra for the unprepared who turn up ready to 'negotiate' without a thought about what you want, nor why you want it. You 'wing it', hear what we have to say and 'play it by ear' and hope for the best.

Thankfully for the unprepared, business negotiations are often repetitive and seldom 'one-offs'. The past is the unprepared's only guide to the present. While we are talking you can always 'work something out'. But even routine negotiations of the kind you do daily need to be thought about to some degree if you are to do better than good enough.

For a start, you could ask:

O   What is the nature of the problem for which we seek a negotiated solution?
O   What is the relevant data we need if we are to form views about the problem? (In God we trust, all others must use data!)
O   What is the relationship at present between ourselves and the other party to the problem?
O   What happens if we don't resolve the problem?

Is it simply a case of moderating the employees' wage claims to the lowest sum you can get away with, or is it time to develop a reward strategy that delivers the people you need to do the jobs you require them to do to meet your overall business plan?

Is it simply a case of battering your suppliers to get the lowest unit price possible, or should you develop a buying strategy to lower the cost

of supply, which might mean paying more per unit for your requirements?

Is it simply a case of dumping as much product as you can onto your
customers at the highest price you can get, or should you develop a
partnership strategy with your customers to create long-term relationships and barriers to entry by competitors?[63]

Naturally, you may not be able to answer in detail all of these questions every time you negotiate, nor should you need to do so, but part of
your professional preparation for your negotiating activities should
develop a strategic guide to the myriad of negotiations you undertake
in your particular function. Once you settle on your strategic imperatives, you can ask what this negotiation is about and let the answers
direct you to your previously prepared strategic policy guidelines for
the individual negotiations you are about to undertake.

 ## WHAT ARE YOUR INTERESTS?

Negotiators who start their preparation with the identification of the
issues are jumping the gun. It is a natural error, committed by 'know
alls' in a hurry. Sometimes the issues are obvious – wage negotiations
are about an amount of money, likewise an acquisition, likewise a sale
of a business, and so on. But then the next question is about 'how much
money?', and before long you firmly fixate on a fixed position.

A necessary step is missing. Before deciding what the issues are, and
how to quantify or qualify them, you should ask: what are my interests,
that is, why am I seeking this or that negotiated decision? You uncover
your interests by asking 'why' questions:

○   Why do I want this problem solved?
○   Why do I want the problem solved in this or that particular way?
○   Why is it necessary to adopt this or that position?

Unfortunately, by going straight to the issues you focus too soon on
what you want and only sometimes ask why you want it?

In Figure 2.1, behind the negotiable issues' box – *what you want* – is
another box, offset to the side, labelled interests, because behind your
wants are your interests. Your interests have a big influence on your
wants, though not as a perfect correlation.

Forgetting, or not knowing, of this simple relationship between
interests and issues causes confusions and errors. Interest-based bargaining can be the major means to a breakthrough in an otherwise
deadlocked negotiation.

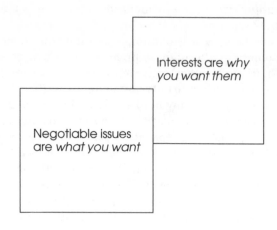

Figure 2.1 Wants and interests

Interests are the reasons why you want something. They are your concerns, fears, hopes, sense of duty, your Maslow-type psychological needs, core desires and their negatives, core hates and the things you feel you must avoid. They are the truth behind your endeavours. They matter to you and because they do, they matter in your negotiations. Seldom will you knowingly work against your interests, or consciously agree to anything that works against them. Regrettably in practice, it is possible for you to work unconsciously against your interests without realizing it at the time. Sometimes your interests are obvious and you can refer directly to them in the negotiation: 'we cannot accept your current proposal because it will damage our long-term profitability'. Where long-term profitability is an interest, it is appropriate to protect it.

On the contrary, sometimes you won't want to identify your interests because, while your interests drive your wants, it might be embarrassing for you to openly acknowledge them or use them to promote what you want. Unions, for example, seldom demand more pay for health sector or educational employees without wrapping their claims in the rhetorical virtues of a healthy or educated society, as if more pay to their members guarantees these outcomes. More pay for these employees without other changes in working practices could just as easily lead to a more expensive health and education provision, with no improvements in performance.

I recall a students' campaign for higher grants, conducted under the slogan that 'if you think education is expensive, you should try ignorance'. Why higher free grants for students (the taxpayer already pays their university fees) would necessarily avert ignorance was neither explained nor explainable. The increase in their student grants is their want and the amount of an increase they aspired to is their position, which, if they obtained the increase, raises their living standards (their interests) at the expense of non-students, most of whom never have opportunities to go to university. Educating a minority is not necessarily the same as reducing the ignorance of the vast majority.

The overall ends served by this or that action summarizes the meaning of interests. A person's wants derive from, and serve, their interests, and, of great significance, more than one set of different wants can, in principle, deliver the same interests.

This is another reason for considering your interests before you negotiate: because the particular set of wants you decide to pursue, in ignorance of your interests, may not deliver your interests to the same extent as some other set of wants you could have chosen to pursue instead.

Examples of interests include:

O   Raising living standards is an interest because you acquire more options if you have higher living standards.
O   Becoming more profitable is an interest because you decrease the risk of unemployment (among other things) if you are more profitable.
O   Reducing crime is an interest because you feel safer if there is less crime.
O   Satisfying your customers is an interest because satisfied customers decrease your risk of unemployment.

To uncover your interests just keep asking 'why' questions about your wants. Why do I want a bigger budget? Why do I want more volume? Why do I want to hold what I have? And question your answers by asking 'why?' Negotiators who ask 'why' often discover that they have several levels of interests and several different interests, some competing with the interests of the other negotiator and some compatible with them.

A union negotiator, for example, could have three levels of interests in a pay claim. Overall, he wants to improve his members' living standards, possibly by a pay rise; he wants his members' living standards maintained, possibly by moderating their pay claims; and he wants to prevent their living standards from falling, possibly by resisting a pay cut. If the choice was a pay cut or a fall in employment, he might agonize as to which interest should predominate (living standards by changes in pay levels or living standards by maintaining employment levels?). Either way, the different interests he serves will produce different sets of negotiable issues and stances on the resultant positions. A compatible interest shared by his members with the employer could be the survival of the enterprise because this maintains and, perhaps, enhances his members' employment.

Interest-based preparation does not preclude the necessity of incorporating detail into the negotiated solutions; quite the contrary. It only precedes it. Interests properly precede detailed consideration of the issues. Too early a total focus on the detail obscures your consideration and reconsideration of your interests served by that detail.

By recognizing the need for detail, you move seamlessly from vague and general terms as is normal when considering interests, like 'security', 'time', 'territory', 'risk', 'living standards' and so on, to the specific issues and positions necessary to decide between workable alternative agreements that serve your interests. You must also constantly check the detail against your interests to ensure you see where particular trees fit into your forest.

To put an interest-based solution, such as 'land for peace' for example, into practical effect we still must reconcile the details of each side's positions. For example:

○   How many crossing points on the Golan can the Syrian army use to effect their re-occupation without creating security fears in Israel if the Syrians advanced *en masse* all along the Heights?
○   How far in miles, or how long in hours (minutes), must be maintained between the withdrawing Israelis and the advancing Syrians?
○   How should this be monitored and supervised and by whom?

Similarly, with a nuclear test ban treaty we must focus on detailed questions like:

○   How many inspections meet the criteria agreed for verifying a Test Ban Treaty?
○   What constitutes an inspection?
○   How many inspectors per inspection team?

Practical negotiators know that 'the devil is in the detail'. Some solutions look good at the general level of your interests but break down when you examine the practical detail agreed to satisfy your interests. This signals a need to seek a different or amended detailed solution to deliver your interests.

When negotiations on detail are successful, it is often because the negotiators spend a great deal of time pouring over alternative wording, alternative numbers and alternative timetables, and so on. Negotiators require patience to negotiate detail, which is why negotiators who are competent and patient with details always have the edge over those who are better at plausible generalities than they are at the practical details serving those generalities.

Without a grasp of detail you are vulnerable to those who grasp them better. Without an ability – preferably pre-planned – to manage the movement along the ranges of your positions on all the issues, the outcome is vulnerable to whichever party can force the biggest shift in the position of the other.

 ## WHAT ARE THE NEGOTIABLE ISSUES?

A negotiable issue is *anything* that the negotiators must *jointly* decide before implementing a decision. You cannot impose your decision on her. If you could impose it, you would not be negotiating with her. Indeed, why negotiate when you can get your own way unilaterally?

Negotiation is, therefore, a joint decision. Negotiable issues include what you want, how much of it is available, when it should happen, and who is to get how much of it. They are about who gets how much of what, where, and when. They can include the quantums and varying qualifications of wording (such as 'use best endeavours' through to 'will ensure'). They can also include a 'yes' or 'no' joint decision.

Negotiable issues should help to deliver our interests. For example:

○ You want a pay rise (negotiable issue) to raise your living standards (interest). The amount of the pay rise is negotiable.

○ You want to avoid discounts on your prices (negotiable issue) to become more profitable (interest). Whether you agree to a discount and the size of the discount is negotiable.

○ You want to increase the police department's budget (negotiable issue) to reduce crime (interest). The amount of the increase in the budget, and what the police spend it on is negotiable.

○ You want to extend their product warranties (negotiable issue) to increase your satisfaction as a customer (interest). The extent and specifications of the warranties are negotiable.

However, emotions, principles, opinions, values, beliefs, who is to blame, who started the argument, who is ethical, who dishonest, and such like, are simply not negotiable, though observation suggests that this in no way prevents people from acting as if they are! What happens when you concentrate on these topics is a destructive and testy argument and not a negotiation.

WHAT ARE YOUR PRIORITIES?

You do not prepare well if you assume that you are in conflict because both of you value every issue equally. There are different valuations of each issue, even for the same negotiator, as well as different valuations between two or more of them.[64] Part of preparation assesses the value to you and, where practicable from experience, intelligence or deduction, the value to the other negotiator, of each issue and sub-issue. This can only be provisional because you cannot see inside the head of the other negotiator, but it is almost inevitable that you ponder it. When you are in contact with them, you will spend some part of the time confirming or otherwise your estimates of the ranking of how important the issues are to them.

The negotiable issues do not have the same degree of importance. Some issues are more important to you than others. For example, it could be more important for you to be paid sooner than to wait longer for a larger amount. The colour of the used van may be less important than its mileage, or vice versa. Getting them to agree to sign a ceasefire may be more important than having the signing ceremony filmed for television news.

This requires you to rank the negotiable issues by their relative importance or value to yourself. Simply ranking the issues in their order of importance, from high through medium to low, forces you to think of negotiation as an exchange of things you want less for the things you want more. The other person presently controls the things you want.

You would surely prefer that what you get back in exchange is worth more to you than the value of the things you give up to get them, otherwise you would be foolish to exchange them voluntarily. This, of course, does not preclude in certain unhappy circumstances that you would be forced to give up something of great value to you to get something worth much less if only circumstances were different.

A 'fire sale' deal could see you exchanging an item of great sentimental or intrinsic value because of the exigencies of circumstance, such as your sweetheart's locket for water in a desert or medicines for a loved one. This does not contradict the basic principle of preference for higher value exchanges because at the moment of transaction the value of satisfying your pressing needs usurps your longer-term valuations of what you give up.

Some issues are 'must get' (*high priority*) if an agreement is to be reached, others are 'like to get' (*low priority*) and the rest are 'important to get' (*medium priority*) (Figure 2.2).

My interests are:

Negotiable issues	Priority ranking
	High
	Medium
	Low

Figure 2.2 Interests and priorities organizer

High priorities are so important to you that you would probably 'fail to agree' if you were unable to obtain them. Medium priority issues are important but are less likely to be deal breakers, though you tend to judge, and are judged on, your performance by the extent to which you obtain them. This leaves low priorities as relatively unimportant to you but it pleases you to obtain them nevertheless, though you would be unlikely to 'fail to agree' to the deal if you were unsuccessful.

Because you value or prioritize the issues differently, it is possible – and practical observation supports this proposition – for you to trade mutual movement on your lower priority issue(s) for favourable movement on your higher priority issue(s). This is sometimes a paradox: they are not cheap 'give-aways' just because your low priority items have little comparative value for you. If they have much higher priorities and therefore are of greater value to the other party they give you high comparative negotiating power. Similarly with your medium priorities.

It is your high priorities that are your weak spots because you depend on trading other issues to obtain them. Too many high priorities among the negotiable issues constrain your flexibility to agree to trade on low issues. Conversely, your low priorities, if the other negotiator values them more than you do, could be your strengths.

Morrison,[65] fatally for his credibility in his otherwise constructive exposition of preparation methodology, describes issues of low priority as 'give-points'. But it is wrong to imply that low priority issues are 'give aways' and, if his book influences beginners, it undermines their effectiveness if they practise what he preaches.

Ideas of 'give-aways', 'easy concessions' and 'throw-ins', when applied to negotiating behaviour are disastrous. The give-away approach, reflected in the language often heard from negotiators, lies deep in the psyche of even quite experienced negotiators, proving that 'experience' is often just the long-term and constant repetition of the same errors.

The three Figures, 2.3, 2.4 and 2.5, illustrate these important points. Assume for the sake of the exposition that you can see into the priority preferences of two negotiators.

In Figure 2.3, the negotiators have identical priorities for all the negotiable issues. What one considers of high priority so does the other, and similarly with their medium and low priorities. Agreed that this would be unusual but if it occurred it could be difficult to agree as things stand. I will explore later how you can negotiate to agreement in practice. Generally, when negotiators have identical preferences it is difficult to achieve a negotiated solution. Usually, unable to agree, you must do without what you both covet, or resort to violence.

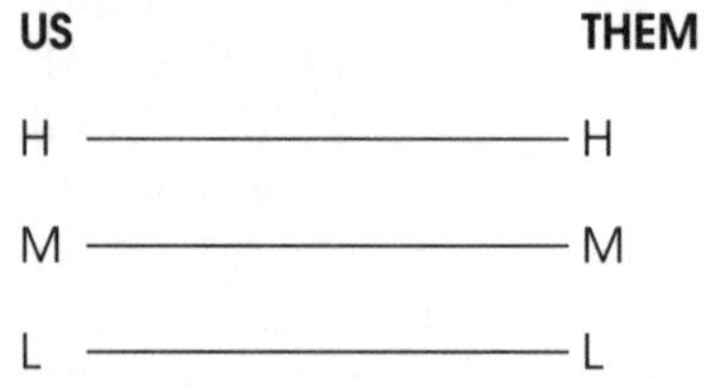

Figure 2.3 Identical priorities

In Figure 2.4, the parties have identical high priorities but differing medium and low priorities. This makes a negotiated outcome more probable because they may trade their low priorities for medium priorities and, in doing so, compensate each other for some trade off on their high priority.

Where the negotiators rank every negotiable issue differently (Figure 2.5), it makes agreement fairly straightforward if they discover the extent of their differing valuations. Each can exchange movement on those issues they value less for favourable movement on those issues they value more.

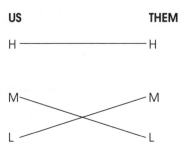

Figure 2.4 Common and differing priorities

It is the differences in the priorities or valuations that enable you to find solutions to problems because each of you wants something from the other and, by negotiating, you can find mutually acceptable terms for the transaction.

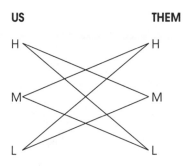

Figure 2.5 Differing priorities

As an example of the principle that in trading you exchange things that you value less (low priorities) for things that you value more (high priorities) we return the arithmetical example used by John Nash to illustrate his solution to the bargaining problem. Putting his arithmetical example into a Negotek® PREP format, we see directly how the two negotiators accomplish their transactions (see Figure 2.6).

Prioritizing is a crude though analogous indicator of the relative utilities of the issues. We simply stretch the meaning of prioritizing to indicate, in some way, the relative utilities of the goods to the negotiators, Bill and Jack. Placing the utility rankings of 1 to 10 on the vertical axes they align roughly with the three levels of priority – high: utilities of 7–10, medium: utilities of 3–6, and low: utilities of 1–2, as shown in Figure 2.6.

	Bill's utilities	Jack's utilities	Priority
pen	10	10	High
	9		
	8		
	7		
knife	6	6	Medium
	5		
box, toy	4	4 book	
	3		
book, whip			Low
ball, bat, hat	2	2 knife, whip, ball, bat, hat	
		1 pen, box, toy	

Figure 2.6 The Nash solution in a Negotek® PREP format

The slopes of the lines link the valuations of the goods as they would appear if we contrasted their priorities. Items of low valuation (1) to Jack, for example, the pen, has a higher utility (10) for Bill. If both trade items of different priority for them this confirms the particular exchange of items identified in the Nash bargain:

Bill gives Jack: book, whip, ball and bat

Jack gives Bill: pen, toy and knife.

Thus, Jack exchanges the knife and the toy for Bill's book because the knife and the toy together are worth 3 to Jack and Bill's book is worth 4, while for Bill the book is worth 2, but Jack's knife and the toy together are worth 10. Similarly, Bill exchanges the whip, ball and bat for Jack's pen because the pen is worth 10 to Bill and the whip, ball and bat are worth 6; for Jack his pen is worth only 1, while Bill's whip and bat are worth 2 each and the ball is worth 1.

They do not swap the hat for the box because Jack would have to give up a hat worth 2 to him to acquire a box worth 1 and Bill would have to give up a box worth 4 to him to receive a hat worth 2.

 WHAT ARE YOUR NEGOTIATING RANGES?

You increase your competence by thinking in ranges of positions from where (a number, a wording, a timing) you plan to open (your *entry* position) to where you intend, as things stand, to close (your *exit* position), rather than by thinking solely in fixed positions.

Walton and McKersie[66] describe how practical wage negotiators addressed the issue of a new wage rate by selecting a varying range of positions during preparation. These authors were responsible for the well-known diagrams of the single-issue negotiation that amost everybody uses in their own expositions.

What Walton and McKersie established beyond doubt is that it is the norm for negotiators to determine a range of positions rather than a single position. Some critics of 'positional bargaining' have failed to grasp the difference between the allegedly fixed immutable position of a positional posturer and the more normal range of positions adopted, often explicitly, by the majority of negotiators.[67] The very use by negotiators in their daily discourse of such words as 'fallback positions' underlines just how common it is to find them thinking in terms of ranges. Positional posturers are much scarcer on the ground.

To underline the assertion that positional negotiations are seldom one-shot decision-making situations, Walton and McKersie stressed over thirty years ago that negotiations involve a series of decisions interspersed with performance activities,[68] and they provided some albeit anecdotal support for their claim that negotiators identify 'more than one intermediate position':

> Consider the following statements: 'I hope to get 7 cents, and must have at least 5 cents'; 'I'd be happy with an 11-cent package, but we couldn't go below the pattern of 8 cents under any circumstances.' The words or phrases such as 'hope', 'happy with', on the one hand,

and 'must have at least' and 'couldn't go below,' on the other hand, certainly refer to different points of prominence on the bargaining spectrum as conceived by the negotiator.[69]

These behaviours contrast sharply with the claim that negotiators decide upon a single position, fortify it and fight like a hell cat to stick to it. On the contrary, even a negotiator's pre-planned range changes under the pressure of events and the unexpected opportunities that arise during negotiation. A fixed immovable position, therefore, is a poor negotiating strategy and owes more to the literary licence of certain authors than it does to experience of the real world.

In practice, negotiators the world over do not think of single positions because the price they want is seldom the price with which they open. If you think only in fixed immovable positions, then your 'negotiating' strategy requires the other person to accept the first and only position you offer them. This is tantamount to expecting them to surrender, give in, pay the price on the tag, and abandon any aspirations of their own. Experience suggests that this is not the normal behaviour of negotiators, and certainly not for hagglers. A 'take-or-leave it' strategy works only if the other person absolutely must take it because they cannot bear the consequences of leaving it.

The norm in negotiation is for both parties to open where they do *not* expect to settle. They usually end up somewhere else. If there is a difference between where they open (their *entry* position) and where they settle, inescapably they have a *range* of possible settlements in mind and not a fixed position.

For most negotiable issues, numerous positions are possible; money positions are limited only by the smallest division of the currency. Pounds, francs and dollars are divisible by 100. Money also comes in 10s, 100s, and 1000s, and so on to unimaginable ceilings (Italian lire, for example). Something less obviously divisible – a permission to do something, for instance – divides into small units of time measurement. Does permission begin in one hour, two or more hours, 30 days or more, next year or the year after? It is also divisible by degrees of precision – what is permissible, for how long is it permissible, who can change it, what degree of discretion does the permit imply, for whom and to what ends? The divisibility and variation of the issues leads to the practice of thinking of ranges.

An example will clarify the implications of these assertions. Take a student, Bob, who is in the market as a buyer looking for a used car, and his professor, Sarah, who is in the market as a seller intending to sell her used car. Circumstances lead them both to consider completing a transaction between them. Bob has a limited budget and intends to open the negotiations with an entry price for the car below what Sarah has advertised as her entry price in the small ads in *Campus News*.

What is true for Bob is true for his professor, Sarah, whose entry price is higher than others that would delight her. Neither Bob nor Sarah knows, however, what price, if push came to shove, the other would willingly settle at. And even if Sarah had not advertised her car with an entry price on it, they both know there would be a gap between Bob and Sarah's entry prices. How do I know that? Because experimental research (and personal observation) shows that no matter what somebody is selling — even junk items — they pick a higher price for it than the entry prices offered by buyers. Hence, negotiations invariably begin with a price gap. Sometimes that gap is large and sometimes it is small, though largeness and smallness are relative. Gottchalk[70] visualizes negotiation as identifying the Gap, narrowing the Gap and closing the Gap, which is a neat way of expressing it.

Your negotiating task is to find ways of exploring to close the gap. This might involve only one of you moving towards the other or, more commonly, both of you moving towards each other. The former is much more difficult to achieve, and consequently rarer in practice, because it implies that you move without the encouragement of corresponding movement from the other person. Incidentally, if you normally make unreciprocated movements, you can safely stop doing that from now on and this alone will improve your negotiated outcomes!

It is more common for both negotiators to move towards each other, not necessarily in equal steps nor at the same pace. Joe Gormley, a former boss of the mineworkers' union in the UK, eloquently summed up his negotiating experience by revealing that he saw wage negotiations with the employers as each side moving towards each other, with the employers moving in bigger steps and at a faster pace than Joe's union.

But look closer at the implication of recognizing the gap between the parties. If people have a range of potential prices that they will settle at, they must have some notion of a limit to their own range of potential settlements, that is, they also have a notional *exit* price. In preparation at least, they intend not to go beyond their exit price.

So Bob has a maximum (his exit price) he will pay and Sarah has a minimum (her exit price) she will accept. But where are their exit points? That is the rub.

Bob knows his own entry and exit prices and, if he has any sense at all, he will find out Sarah's entry price once the face-to-face negotiations get underway. If Sarah had not revealed her entry price in *Campus News*, he must ask her for it ('How much do you want for the car?'). What Bob does not know is Sarah's exit price — the least she will accept — and she is most unlikely to tell him what it is. Sarah, of course, is in a mirror-image position. She knows Bob's entry price, or will soon find out ('How much will you offer for the car?'), but she does not know Bob's exit price – the maximum he will pay. She, too, knows her entry and exit prices but she only knows Bob's entry price.

The negotiating range has great tactical importance and it is essential that you consider your entry and exit prices for each negotiable issue during your preparation. There is no formula to determine the exact quantums of your negotiating ranges. What entry prices you choose depend on a myriad of factors – some of which you get right and some you get wrong. The essential advice for considering any entry position – be it a price or a choice of wording – is that your entry positions must be credible when presented to the other negotiator.

It is not much use your responding to a question on why you want liquidated damages set at 4 per cent with the answer that as your daughter is four years old you thought this was an appropriate number! Your listener may feel you are less than credible. Part of your presentation in the debate phases will justify your entry positions and all and any positions thereafter up to your exit position. Defensible and credible positions between your entry and exit points have a better chance of surviving scrutiny than the other kind.

Figure 2.7 adds your negotiating ranges to your interests and priorities (Figure 2.2) to form the Negotek® PREP planner. The recommended layout in the Negotek® PREP planner sets out your tasks in a neat and easily remembered way. A glance at the planner shows you what you have to do to cover the basics of preparation. The extent to which you cover each task in detail is a matter of choice and circumstance. The more important the negotiated outcome, the more detail

Our interests are:

Negotiable issues	Priority ranking	Negotiation ranges Entry	Exit
	High		
	Medium		
	Low		

Figure 2.7 The Negotek® PREP planner

you will have to go into and the more judgemental you will have to be when considering individual aspects of preparation.

Some tips, based on observation of many people using the planner, might be helpful. The organizer is a template not a mandatory imperative.

You will find it useful as a guideline if you stick to answering the five questions for the basic steps or preparation:

1. What is the negotiation about?
2. What are your interests?
3. What are the negotiable issues?
4. What are your priorities?
5. What are your negotiating ranges (entry and exit points)?

The best advice, when short of preparation time, is to *keep it moving*. Do not spend disproportionate time on any one question, such as trying to formulate a perfect statement of your interests or agonizing over whether a negotiable issue is marginally a high or medium or a medium or low priority, or whether you should set this or that exit point. It is best to move on if undecided and come back to those questions you are not sure of just yet. There will inevitably be some iteration in your choices anyway as later thoughts and insights suggest that you should re-cast earlier decisions.

Having noted that keeping moving is usually better than analysis paralysis, it is still worth taking more time over setting your entry position than setting your exit position, because you justify your entry positions before your exit positions and you would expect to be well into the negotiations before you consider your exit positions.

Some people suggest that while exit positions are of significance for medium and high priority negotiable issues they surely are of little or no significance for your low priorities? By definition, your low priority issues are 'like to gets' and are most unlikely to become deal breakers, and exit positions on low priority issues may have less significance than medium or high priority issues. However, because your low priority issues could be more highly valued by the other negotiator than by you, they can have a high trading priority for you — what can you get back in exchange for them? For this circumstance, some notional idea of your exit positions for low priority issues is prudent.

Generally, where your time is at a premium, and the value of the negotiated outcome is not high enough to justify using scarce discretionary time on preparation, my advice is to keep moving. Where the outcome is of significant importance to you the same advice to keep moving applies, though the time assigned to each task will be greater.

THE NEGOTIATORS' SURPLUS

The selection of entry and exit positions in preparation has great significance for when face-to-face contact begins. To appreciate the significance of this preparatory work, you must take a short diversion into territory overlapping with the behaviour of the debate phase.

Our discussion focuses on the practice of not revealing true exit prices to each other. Sure, you often claim that you are at your exit positions, even implying that your entry position is the best you can do on the issue. However, few people believe totally what you tell them about your 'best' price, etc., and most are wary of what they hear, particularly when they too are gilding the lily a little. This creates a tactical problem. It is impossible to verify your claims that you are at your exit position on an issue because there is no foolproof mechanism that enables negotiators to know each other's true exit prices. If asked to reveal your true exit position, you have every incentive to be economical with the truth.

Raiffa[71] valiantly attempted a method for simultaneously revealing true exit positions, but he also admitted that 'no one has yet discovered how to apply it to real-world situations', adding that 'it would be wonderful if someone could'. But they can't, and I am not so sure that it would be so wonderful anyway.

The best way to understand the negotiator's tactical problem on exit positions is to explore the idea of the *negotiators' surplus*, which assumes an omnipotent theorist not involved in the negotiation. Of course, the omnipotent theorist does not exist, except in our imaginations but, if using our imagination helps elucidate a negotiation problem that certainly does exist, it is worth playing a harmless mind game to achieve so important a result. I readily accept that we do not draw explicit diagrams to negotiate, though as readily I assert that the contents of these diagrams are implicit in real world negotiations.

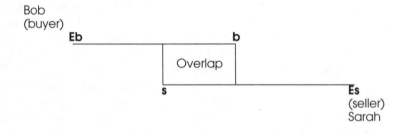

Figure 2.8 Distributive bargaining[72]

In Figure 2.8, I have adapted Walton and McKersie's standard distributive bargaining model. Bob, the buyer, is on the left and Sarah, the seller, is on the right. Their entry prices are Eb and Es, respectively. Their exit prices are b and s.

In Figure 2.8, the omnipotent observer sees that s is smaller than b (i.e. $s < b$), signifying that the lowest price Sarah will accept for her vehicle is less than the highest price that Bob would pay for it. In this case the exit prices for each negotiator *overlap* to create a positive *settlement range* of prices, any of which, including s or b, could be an agreed price for the vehicle. A settlement range exists, therefore, whenever the negotiators' exit prices overlap.

The tactical problem for negotiators is that they do not know each other's exit prices, which means that they do not know if there is a settlement range at all. Where s and b do not overlap (because $s > b$), there would be no settlement range – the least that Sarah would accept would be higher than the most that Bob would pay.

Walton and McKersie's presentation illustrates the tactical situation in the negotiation of a single issue, such as a wage rate, or the price for a used car. The parties are in the dark about the existence or otherwise of a possible overlap of their exit points. The lack of such fundamental information explains much of the behaviour of the parties in the single-issue negotiation.

As long as s and b are stable, the overlap of s and b, i.e. the settlement range, is the *negotiators' surplus*, which is a fixed sum (because the range is of finite duration). Negotiation is about how to divide the negotiators' surplus between the parties. The existence, let alone the extent, of a negotiators' surplus is unknown and unknowable to the real world negotiators.

Suppose the omnipotent observer notes that Bob is right up at his exit price b when agreeing a deal with Sarah. This means that she would acquire all the surplus because, unbeknown to Bob, she could accept a price as low as s but got the price of b instead. Conversely, if Sarah is right down at her exit price s, then Bob acquires all the surplus, because, unbeknown to Sarah, he could pay as much as b.

In between the extremes of one or other of them acquiring all the negotiators' surplus, there are innumerable settlement prices, p^*, between s and b, that divide the available surplus between Bob and Sarah. The only constraint, obviously, is that the sum of the negotiators' surplus divided between Bob and Sarah is always equal to the total of the available negotiators' surplus. But, remember, neither of them knows nor can they know, the exact amount of the negotiators' surplus that is available for them to divide. Implicitly, they know it is there, as evidenced in the negotiators' remark that they 'don't like to leave money on the table', which is another way of expressing the concern that there was more negotiators' surplus available than they managed to extract in the deal they did.

Only when there is a known fixed amount, such as the amount of profit from a partnership deal, will the negotiators know the total negotiators' surplus. Both partners know the amount of profit available for distribution before they start to negotiate. Apart from this circumstance, and perhaps excluding secretly acquired intelligence too (though you can never be sure that they deliberately leaked the secrets to fool you by disinformation), it is essential to know the unknowable – each other's exit points – to calculate the available negotiators' surplus.

Is the idea of negotiators' surplus then a blind alley? Not really. It explains the roots of the behaviours of negotiators in a single-issue negotiation. Bob and Sarah, for instance, have a symmetrical interest in misleading the other as to their willingness, even ability, to contribute to the closing of the gap between their entry prices. How low should Bob offer, how high should Sarah demand? Once their entry prices are on the table, who should move first, how far should he or she move, and when should he or she dig in? These are dilemmas for every pair of negotiators, and like all dilemmas the solution is not obvious – if it was it would not be a dilemma!

Experiments, not surprisingly, have been tried to discover the answers. Raiffa[73] reports on one of them, credited to John Hammond, concerning the sale of a used car, using a simulation exercise with confidential data handed out to players designated as sellers and buyers. Hammond, of course, knew the negotiation range because he wrote the simulation! Here the researcher is the omnipotent observer and he is able to study the results obtained from the players and relate these to the data in the simulation.

Interestingly, Hammond found settlements right across the settlement range from s to b. Of the settlements, 1 per cent agreed to prices outside the settlement range (perhaps they misunderstood the instructions like a buyer in one of my workshops who ended up paying more for the car than the seller opened at!).

Raiffa in his simulations found that 3 per cent did not settle at all. In the car sale simulation,[74] which opens the Negotiate Workshop, about 5 per cent (1 in 20) do not settle in the time allowed, even with the generous settlement range (£17,950 to £15,372) that is programmed into their confidential briefings.

Raiffa's other findings were that if the mid-point of the negotiators' declared entry prices fell inside the settlement range (between s and b), then this was a good predictor of the final settlement price, p^*. He also noted that if the mid-point of the participants' entry prices fell outside the settlement range, it was hard to predict where p^* would settle.

Fine, but what is the significance of this? Well, for a start, when you contemplate an issue in preparation you choose an entry position from whence to start. Choosing entry positions is a universal requirement for a negotiation and, having chosen an entry point, there is a compelling necessity to choose or imply an exit position.

In Bob and Sarah's single-issue negotiation, there is only the price of the car to settle, and this is important to both of them, irrespective of how much Bob tries to convey his cool interest in buying Sarah's particular car and how much Sarah tries to impress Bob with her indifference to selling it to him.

Single-issue negotiations are difficult. What Bob gains – a price closer to Sarah's exit price than his own – Sarah loses. Which suggests why, although a settlement range may exist, it is no guarantee of a settlement. Much depends on how the negotiators behave while positionally posturing. If it becomes too heated and emotional, the parties could tire of trying to do business; if Sarah feels she has moved much more than her 'fair' share – wherever her notions of fairness come from or how realistic they are – she may well break off even while Bob's last offer on price is well within her range, Es to s; and if Bob feels he is being personally humiliated by being forced to concede too much, he might break off negotiations too.

Go back to the notion of the negotiators' surplus for a moment. Note, that because you do not know the other negotiator's exit point it does not preclude the existence of a negotiators' surplus. It merely means that neither of you can measure it precisely. But negotiating a settlement that is different from the initial offers and demands – represented by you and your negotiating partner's entry prices – indicates that a settlement range, or negotiators' surplus, existed, although its limits were invisible to both of you.

You have no way of knowing whether the agreed p^* was her actual exit price or somewhere well short of it. If the agreed p^* was close to her exit price and far from yours, you gained most of the available negotiators' surplus, or if it was well short of her exit price and closer to yours, she gained most of the available surplus.

Does this matter? It does, judging by the behaviour of negotiators who keep challenging each other's current positions. Interviews suggest that negotiators do not like to feel that they did less well than they think they could have done. The fear of 'leaving money on the table' may be a triumph of imagination over reality, but these fears are real enough to those influenced by them. The saying that 'what the eye doesn't see, the heart doesn't grieve about' is probably true (ask any *sous-chef* in a restaurant) but the most stressful grief, however, comes not from what you see, but from what your inner eye imagines, as any lover's outbreak of suspicious jealousy amply demonstrates.

Often, negotiators delay making known their entry position on an issue until they are sure that it will not be short of what they could achieve. The psychic pain from opening higher than the seller's entry price causes a buyer to hold back and the psychic pain from opening below a buyer's entry price causes a seller to hold back. If both of them hold back, it can lead to a long dance before they reveal their opening positions: 'How much do you want for it?', asks Bob. 'How much will you offer?', responds Sarah.

Negotiators behave as if there is a negotiators' surplus on each issue, which is good news, because this can resolve deadlocks in multi-issue negotiation. If you feel that you can gain negotiator's surplus by being closer to your entry positions from some issues sufficient to compensate you for being closer to your exit points on others, you can close gaps across the issues instead of being stuck in a gap on a single issue.

This is not to say that you calculate, even roughly, the distribution of the multiple sources of negotiators' surplus. Negotiators' surplus is implicit more than explicit, though it is real enough for all that. Listen, for instance, to a negotiator explaining the outcome of a multi-issue negotiation to her boss. She will almost certainly talk about the compromises she felt forced to make on the issues 'over here', and she will minimize these 'losses' by talking-up (perhaps genuinely believing) the 'gains' she made on the issues 'over there', emphasizing how she is, and why her boss should be too, more than pleased with the net outcome.

Any senior sales or purchasing manager knows of innumerable cases in which she listens to her staff deliver an 'on-the-one-hand and on-the-other-hand' rationalization of net gains that masquerade as an objective report of a recent negotiation. If you ever report to anybody about a deal you negotiate you too will recognize the phenomenon. This shows that negotiators act *as if* they were 'counting' implicitly their share of the negotiators' surplus gained from the totality of the issues they negotiate.

I worry less about self-delusion, which must be present on some reporting occasions, than I do about ensuring that you recognize the implicit role of the negotiators' surplus created by the gaps in your own and your counterpart's exit positions.

Negotiators with whom I have worked have found the notion of a negotiation surplus helpful in boosting their confidence when they conduct the face-to-face phases.

It is possible that you could use the Negotek® PREP planner to roughly quantify your aspirations in the difference between your entry and exit positions. Where these ranges are quantifiable – a cash difference, for instance – you can compare them with the settlements you achieve and can express these results as a percentage of the total range between your entry and exit positions. Thus, if your range comprises an entry position of 100 and an exit position of no less than, say, 60, your aspiration range would be 40. If the eventual settlement position was, say, 80, your achievement position would be 50 per cent of the aspiration range (100 − 80 = 20 and 20 is 50 per cent of 100 − 60 = 40). Similarly, a settlement position of 70 would be 75 per cent of the aspiration range, 60 would be 100 per cent and 90 would be 25 per cent.

Crudely, you have a measure of your negotiating success, all other things being equal (or *ceteris paribus*, as classical economists used to say). Your task is to minimize the percentage of your aspiration range that you must move to get a settlement. This is merely another way of saying that, ideally, you had to move relatively little to get a deal. If you must go beyond your exit position to get a deal, you will move more than 100 per cent of your aspiration range; if you do not have to move at all – the other negotiator accepts your first offer – you move only zero per cent of your aspiration range.

Where there is more than one issue to negotiate, and assuming your ranges are quantifiable, the measure of your success would be the percentages of your aspiration ranges by which you moved to get a deal. Caveats apply, however, in that it is not realistic to net the percentage movements across the issues to produce a 'global' quantum to measure your success or otherwise in the deal. Issues may not be cross-comparable nor equally weighted. A 50 per cent movement on an issue worth £10 million is not comparable to a 50 per cent movement on a sub-issue worth £2000. Nor might it be meaningful to compare percentage movements for issues of different relative value to the negotiator. Minor movements on high priority issues are more significant than major movements on low priority issues. And everything may be of different significance if major movements occur on non-quantifiable issues, such as contract wording, and minor movements occur on the quantums of other issues. How does one compare a failure to achieve an extended warranty with an acceptance of open ended liability?

That these comparisons occur in practice is not challengeable – sit in on any contract review meeting and you will hear them. What is debatable is that they are captured by an issue by issue quantification, and can then be reduced to a single success indicator. This is a topic worth further research and experimentation. If it worked, it might prove helpful when trying to assess your staff's negotiating prowess across large numbers of routine or repetitive negotiations.

 **TRADABLES**

Negotiators do better if they explore as many issues as they can to form a negotiated package. Numerous issues, and sub-issues, are the practitioners' currency in the search for packaged solutions. Creating new *tradables*, i.e. anything that can be traded, which in many cases is a quite extensive list, creates opportunities for package bargaining (see Figure 2.9).

Searching for tradables is not exactly a revolutionary idea because effective negotiators (many of whom cannot spell 'Bob' backwards) already do it every day. Any business eager to improve its performance can do so by asking its negotiators to list all the tradables they can think of, or can invent, that could assist them in getting a deal in the typical negotiations they undertake in their product or service lines.

Anything tangible or intangible over which the negotiators have discretion and upon which at least one of the parties places some value, can become a tradable. Tradables widen the focus of the negotiation from one or a few issues to several or many issues, including some of the sub-issues upon which you become stuck.

Price	Discounts	Returns policies
Quantity	Liquidated damages	Leasing
Quality	Consequential loss	Assignment
Delivery	Retention money	On consignment
Payment terms	Performance bonds	Letters of credit
Warranties	Spares	Exchange risk
Support	Response times	Licensing
Intellectual property	Exclusivity	Maintenance
Agency terms	Copyrights	Insurance costs
Trade marks	Training	Service levels
Maintenance	Third party use	
Insurance	Inspection	

Figure 2.9 Commercial examples of tradables[75]

Tradables unlock deadlocks, such as if we stick on the tradable of price you might achieve movement if you agree to the tradable that you pay me later. Tradables have different values for each negotiator, which is their most potent power in a blocked negotiation. You might value the invoice total less than that you can pay me six months later.

A useful exercise for you is to list all the tradable variations that are possible in your line of work (Figure 2.10). Think of the usual main list headings of the negotiable issues and then subdivide them to as varied a degree as possible, including all of the potential legal tradables that assist in securing agreement.

When I invited partners at Jones, Lang Wooton, one of the world's largest firms of chartered surveyors, to do this exercise they uncovered tradables, and different ways of concluding business, that many of them knew of but had forgotten through long periods of disuse. They also discovered new tradables that their colleagues had developed from recent practice.

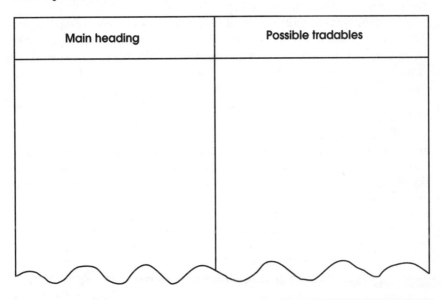

Main heading	Possible tradables

Figure 2.10 What are the negotiable tradables in my line of business?

The minimum duration of a lease was for five years but it was not in widespread use as a tradable prior to1980. Now it is so commonly used as a tradable that it hardly warrants a mention. Some partners were beginning to sell minimum durations of two years and a few brave, and younger, partners were signing them for even shorter terms. They introduced this practice to address a growing market for shorter term leases.

Companies planning and conducting takeover strategies, for example, where security of their intentions and their plans for implementation are important, preferred to lease premises on a short-term basis so as to separate the bidding team from the rest of the management at head office. Corridor gossip can too easily leak to the target firm and to rivals. Even announcing a need for secrecy lets the world know that you have secrets! In other cases, empty property stays empty if the five-year lease duration is too risky for potential tenants, while signing shorter leases not only creates rents for clients, more importantly, perhaps, they also create fees for Jones, Lang Wooton.

Incidentally, one partner at the workshop objected to the drift towards shorter leases on the 'practical' grounds that all the leases he used were pre-printed for durations of not less than five years, hence he could not accept the practice of shortening the minimum duration because his leases would need reprinting!

The necessity to examine, critically, all those non-negotiable preconditions entrenched long after the circumstances that made them necessary are no longer relevant, and probably have long since been forgotten is included in the search for tradables in your line of work. Hence also ask: 'what in my line of work is non-negotiable and why?' Companies that address changing circumstances do better than those that stick with solutions to problems that no longer exist.

Drawing up lists of tradables and sharing them around the management team for consideration is also a productive activity. For example, using this approach Digital (UK) listed 34 tradables for its computer sales negotiators; The Royal Bank of Scotland listed tens of tradables for negotiating overdraft facilities and business term loans; KPMG produced long lists of tradables for negotiating audit fees.

Lists of tradables also help to induct new managers into an organization's negotiating practice. For a start, the new entrants can avoid reinventing the proverbial wheel if they have such lists to hand and, through experience, they can contribute overtime to the continuous process of adding to the lists of tradables from their fresh ways of looking at routine practice.

 THE EXTENDED NEGOTEK® PREP PLANNER

The five basics of preparation set out in pp. 48–63 are necessary but not sufficient for every level of negotiation planning. There are six additional steps we must consider, to extend the template of the Negotek® PREP planner for all levels of preparation. I shall illustrate the extended planner through a banking assignment I conducted in 1992–94.

The bank's shares, at the time, traded well below competing banks because the market judged that the bank's capital base should produce greater returns to its shareholders. This put the bank in a difficult position: either it improved its results or succumbed to a hostile takeover by somebody better able to increase shareholder value. Rumours of a possible bid were, perhaps, the only reason the shares were performing at all. They might have plunged further in the absence of bid rumours. (Ironically, four years later the share price was four times the bid crisis price, and the bank became subject to bid speculation again – now it was ripe for takeover as a successful bank!)

Negotiate's contribution to the turnaround strategy was to train several hundred managers who negotiated to supply bank products with corporate, i.e. non-personal, accounts, ranging from small corner shops with less than £50,000 turnovers right through to £50 million enterprises. About 20 per cent of the bank's corporate accounts at the time were unprofitable and a fair slice of them made losses – the bank could save money if these customers re-banked elsewhere.

The bank divided the target corporate accounts into three categories:

O   loss-making or non-profitable accounts;
O   profitable accounts but open to the sale of additional bank products (the average product sale to all bank customers was only 1.3 per customer, yet the bank had over 200 products to sell);
O   selected customers of rival banks.

To prepare the bank's corporate negotiators for a systematic campaign of targeting accounts in the above three categories we produced a preparation template combining the basic Negotek® PREP planner, with six additional elements added to focus on practical actions the relationship managers should take.

Posing these tasks as a series of questions provided the data for the extended Negotek® PREP planner.

WHAT IS MY STRATEGIC OBJECTIVE?

A strategic objective is what you want to achieve in the scheduled period. In this case the bank's strategic objectives were to be selected from (depending on the type of account they were servicing):

O   to eliminate all loss-making accounts;
O   to make all remaining accounts more profitable;
O   to win profitable new business.

Normally a business plan determines the strategic objectives in the time horizon of three to five years. The bank, however, had months, not years, to achieve the first of its strategic objectives.

WHAT ARE THE BANK'S TACTICAL IMPERATIVES?

Tactical imperatives, if achieved, deliver the strategic objective. These were, in the case of delivering the strategic objective of eliminating loss-making and unprofitable accounts:

○   to raise bank service charges and to charge full costs for any additional servicing of these accounts;

○   to raise interest rates on the renewal of overdraft facilities (usually annually) and to impose penal charges for unauthorized overdrawn positions;

○   to raise interest rates on new business term loans (current rates were fixed for the term of current loans);

○   to introduce fees for all special services, such as:

  −   arrangement fees for the work involved in arranging an over-draft or loan (including the costs of credit checking and risk-reward analysis by senior credit teams)
  −   renewal fees for processing renewal applications (as above)
  −   non-utilization fees for facilities like overdrafts which were not drawn down
  −   legal fees for processing all legal work required by the bank.

Achieving these tactical imperatives would deliver the bank's strategic objective for these accounts. Of course, similar tactical imperatives were relevant when they negotiated with their already profitable accounts, some of which, for one reason or another, currently under-charged for some or all the bank's services they consumed.

The managers selected the tactical imperatives appropriate for each of their clients. Some clients were marginally, others horrifically, unprofitable and they targeted them with different mixes of the tactical objectives to achieve uplifts in bank income and profits.

Selection required the manager to study the history and relevant data from the customers' accounts and to integrate this with the rele-vant bank profit targets for their business sectors. Property develop-ment companies, builders, hotels and over-geared restaurants, were experiencing hard times and the risk premium for these sectors was higher than it was for some cash generating businesses. Farming and fishing were two other higher risk premium sectors and were the sources of many of the 'horror' lending cases in certain parts of the UK.

Interestingly, some of the additional income generated by this activ-ity came from simply mailing standard letters to customers, most of whom accepted the re-pricing of their bank products and paid up with-out a murmur. Those that 'murmured', of course, took up a dispropor-tionate amount of the managers' discretionary time, though the authority from the bank to their relationship managers to invite dissi-dent customers to re-bank if they did not wish to pay appropriate fees and charges for services and support, gave the managers new options normally forbidden in the bank's existing culture of 'not losing a connection'. This culture, while understandable, was also one of the main causes of widespread unprofitability in the target accounts.

WHAT IS THE STANCE?

A stance is a mantra repeated regularly by the negotiator, privately in the main, but sometimes directly to the customer – summarizing the purpose of the negotiation agenda. Under the pressure of difficult negotiations – of which, attempts to introduce or raise fees are among the most difficult – it is often easier to buckle to the pressure and back off. The mantra adds a bit of 'backbone' to a negotiator under that sort of pressure – bearing in mind that many of the bank's personnel in these new and unfamiliar roles were untrained in selling or in negotiating, and many of them privately expressed severe reservations about their new roles (many resigned or took early retirement). It is remarkable, however, what a simple mantra-type stance can do for your resolve when the other person is looking you in the eye and is confident that they have got your measure.

A suggested stance for these purposes, for instance, could be: 'Only profitable banks can support their customers'. If this kind of stance is in front of the negotiator's mind, it gives solid purpose to what she is about when the going gets that bit tougher.

WHAT ARE MY JUSTIFICATIONS?

This is one of three interconnected topics. Even somebody who can't spell Bob backwards asks how you justify your entry positions on the negotiable issues! Not having thought through a position in sufficient detail to answer the (inevitable) questions: 'How did you calculate that number?'; 'What is your rationale for that proposal?'; 'What is in it for me?', etc., risks your reputation for seriousness. Not asking the other negotiator to justify her positions compounds your error.

You should thus use some preparation time to consider your strongest justification for each issue and the position that you are advocating. As always, it is best to confine your justifications to one, maybe two, strong reasons and not to dilute them with progressively weaker ones. The other negotiator, if he is so minded, is likely to concentrate his return fire on the weakest justification you use and ignore the strong ones.

A number of justifications for the bank's proposals suitable for a particular category of customers came from the managers themselves, largely from their experience.

In the case of arrangement fees for overdrafts – an innovation for the bank and many customers – this proved to be a necessary exercise, as for some reason the bank had not briefed its managers on how they persuade their customers to pay for something that had been free in the past. Perhaps, from the sheer urgency to raise income immediately, the bank had no time to prepare its managers for what followed. Some managers could not accept that arrangement fees were necessary, or fair, to their customers, and showed great reluctance to carry out this part of the bank's new policy. Resignations and early retirements, in consequence, continued throughout the programme.

Among the one-liner justifications from the workshops were:

○   Unprofitable banks cannot survive.
○   Interest rates do not cover the bank's overheads in servicing your account.
○   Customers must pay the appropriate bank's fees.
○   Free banking is not an option.
○   To be supportive the bank must cover its costs and make a profit.

These one-liners are from justifications consisting of much longer sentences and paragraphs, but a one-liner is easier to remember and to read off the Negotek® template. Trying to talk while reading detailed notes, or a script, is not advisable during a negotiation.

WHAT ARE THE LIKELY COUNTERS?

The mangers expected that the bank's customers would make counter-statements and, predictably, they found it relatively easy to identify and to rehearse the more common ones. It was surprising just how many of these counters were familiar to the managers from their experiences and how often customers raised them across the country. Among the most common ones were:

○   You are punishing me because of the losses the bank made in Third World debt.
○   Why are you picking on me?
○   Look, this is no time to increase my charges given the financial state of my business.
○   Look, I've only just come through a difficult time and these charges will make me unprofitable again.
○   It's a rip off. All you banks are at it.
○   I'll be glad to pay more when the bank improves its services.

Managers in many business sectors are also familiar with their customer's counters. You should spend time and resources identifying your sector's common counters and preparing your people to deal with them effectively.

In selling skills programmes, effort goes into 'handling objections' because sales suffer if they are not handled properly. Up to this point, the bank had largely ignored the vast amount of experience their managers had collectively accumulated about the reactions of customers to the bank's policies. This experience circulates informally among managers who compared notes on social occasions, for instance. It should be harnessed in training programmes.

WHAT ARE MY RESPONSES?

Dealing with counters on an *ad hoc* basis can be dangerous. The ill-considered response is a hostage to fortune. Some thought beforehand helps the credibility of your response when it is necessary to reply to your customer's counters. Exchanging 'war' stories in the workshops also helps dissemination of quality responses to the group as a whole, in much the same manner as lists of tradables can be disseminated within a company.

Some suggested responses for the above counters included (in summary form):

O   The crisis in Third World debt did affect a lot of banks, but our bank was hardly involved in Third World lending and I can assure you that Third World debt has played no role in my discussions with you about what needs to be done about your account.

O   There is no question of the bank singling you out. All accounts in the bank – 60,000 of them – are being reviewed and you are being treated no differently from the others.

O   It is precisely because of the financial state of your business that we must review the support we have been providing to you. At present you are a much more risky account than you were two years ago and the bank must take steps to cover its increased risks.

O   I know how much effort it has taken for you to get through the difficulties of the recent past, and we supported you then when you needed it most but now that you are moving into profit the bank has to feature in your future costs in order that we can continue to support you and the many others that need help. I am here to discuss with you the amount of your contributions to the costs of our support and I have no fixed contribution level in mind. Perhaps we should discuss it?

○   While I cannot speak for other banks, we do not 'rip off' our customers. I am sure that when we discuss yours and the bank's
problems we will be able to work something out that is mutually
satisfactory. What the bank cannot do is ignore the problem in the
hope that it will go away. For this exercise to be successful the
bank needs your co-operation if it is going to continue to be supportive.

I am not claiming that any of these responses would always work or
that they are appropriate for every customer who raises them. I am
only reporting on some of the initial responses that the managers
themselves came up with in their syndicates.

Discussion with their colleagues refined the responses and many
suggested response 'scripts' were rejected and only a few survived
intact. This process alone illustrated to them, and I hope to you, that
your initial responses to counters, verbalized straight off the top of your
head, are likely to be unsatisfactory, even downright provocative, and
that some consideration by you before you use them is prudent
preparatory behaviour. Also, attempting to explicitly verbalize them
during preparation (Figure 2.11) suggests necessary changes in the
justifications of your initial positions and averts provoking some 'difficult' counters.

Within 18 months the bank's share price had more than doubled –
and then it doubled again. We contributed in some small part to that
happy consequence by training corporate managers in systematic
preparation techniques and then setting them to work with their customers to apply what they had prepared.

 INTRODUCING POWER INTO PREPARATION

Power, like the wind, is felt rather than seen.[76] Ever present in negotiation, surprisingly, it is seldom discussed. Most seminars I have sat
through skip through power, if they mention it at all. A few books for
theorists discuss power but still fewer books for practitioners mention
power in any detail, usually mouthing blatantly obvious but non-
practical maxims.

'Who has *the* power?', for example, is the wrong question to ask
before you negotiate, particularly if you are looking for an 'obvious'
answer, as if, by looking at the question the answer suggests itself.
Power is a much more subtle force, with far greater implications for the
negotiators, than identifying the alleged power holders. For a start,
power is a relatively unsettled topic in social science and not very well

Our Interests are:

_____

What is the strategic objective?

_____

What are the tactical imperatives?

_____

What is my stance?

_____

Negotiable issues	Priority ranking	Negotiation ranges	
		Entry	Exit
	High		
	Medium		
	Low		

What are my justifications?	What are the likely counters?	What are my responses?

Figure 2.11 The extended template of the Negotek® PREP planner

Note: Negotek is a registered trade mark of Negotiate Limited

understood by practitioners. We are often in the state of mind where we cannot define power, though we know it is present when we feel it.

I shall discuss in later sections the influence of power, particularly why and how considerations of power can influence your preparation activities and how your perceptions of power can influence your behaviour, once you are face-to-face with the other party, and when it is often too late to adjust your play to the emerging realization of the power dimensions of your negotiation. I shall also examine in greater detail different approaches to power and highlight those approaches that are of practical use, ignoring for the most part those theories that, while interesting, are of little practical value.

Like most other practical negotiating tools, the uses to which you can put ideas of power depend greatly on the available time and detail but, when the stakes are high and the outcomes are important enough, time spent on assessing the power balance before the negotiation opens, and re-assessing it during the face-to-face phases, is well spent.

Though power is ever-present, any given balance of power is open to the counter-influence of changes in the tactical objectives that shift the existing balance of power between the parties. We need to understand power, its uses and limitations, and not become paralysed like a rabbit caught in your main beam.

 WHAT IS POWER?

Power is the ability to make someone do something that they otherwise would not do,[77] and, we might add, the ability to stop them doing what they otherwise would. As a working definition this covers most situations that negotiators experience. It does not, however, amount to a practical guide. Left to the definition alone, you are high and dry in a choice between using power, if you have it, to get what you want, or, if you haven't got any, giving in and taking what you can get. That's not much of a choice. It's all or nothing.

We can modify our definition slightly to include your ability to resist the power of another, and re-assess power as the amount of resistance (however quantified) that you must use to overcome the exercise of somebody else's power.[78] This at least introduces the prospect that power can be overcome when push comes to shove. You need not be a victim of somebody else's apparent power over you, which must be good news.

There is also a wider context in which power influences not only how you might overtly behave but also how it might influence your attitudes as a prelude to changing your intended or usual behaviours. This is why power is felt rather than seen. You intend, for example, to resist a proposal by your employer to cut your pay but following further consideration of the ability and intentions of the company to end your employment if you resist their proposal, you change your attitude from one of defiance to one of (albeit sullen) compliance, hence you submit without overt resistance. As nothing in your thinking process is visible to others, no overt use of power has been, nor needed to be, exercised by the company. But its power to change your intentions has an effect every bit as real as if it had been.

There are varying sources of power that help us to flesh out the above definition a little. Power as an ability to do something can come from different sources that motivate (positively or negatively) the person who feels it. Without exhausting the sources of power, we can look to the ability to reward you for doing what you otherwise would not do. This leads to the idea of power arising from the control of those resources, such as money, that can be used to motivate you, but just as important in certain circumstances, we can cite rewarding compliance with the power of promotion, or the power of access to people whom you wish to meet or mix with (think of the power of those legendary Hollywood producers, or present day pop stars' roadies, even football club employees),or the power that engenders hero worship, or sexual attraction, or personal loyalties, or simple love and affection (which is why parents negotiating with their children are so hopeless), or the power that goes with title or rank (a long gone power, alas, once associated with the title of professor!), or the power of the legitimate authorities of the state, such as courts, parliaments, and prisons to enforce compliance with their dictats, democratic or otherwise.

French and Raven[79] famously systematized the (most quoted) sources of power into five types: reward power; coercive power; legitimate power; referent power and expert power. Embedded in the sources of power is a relationship between the parties through which power impacts one way or the other. Changes in the sources of power will change the relationship (woe betide a Roman Senate that failed to provide bread and circuses) and changes in relationships alter the distribution of power (leading to advice to treat sensitively those you meet on your 'way up' because you might meet them again on your 'way down'). Power cannot function without a relationship to convey it from its apparent holder to its object.

This moves us closer to a practical meaning of negotiating power. We could suggest, for example, that negotiating power enables you to secure terms of agreement favourable to yourself, though this still does not tell us if you have power or not, particularly power that manifests itself as an outcome and not as something you can assess before or during negotiation. By the time you know whether you have power, it is usually already too late to exploit your knowledge. The game is over, the stumps pulled, and the negotiators have gone home. This is an illuminating though tautological concept of power and it is not practical.

What you require is something enabling you to assess the role of power in the forthcoming negotiation so that you can prepare tactically to deliver your overall strategy. Given that bargaining power infects all of your actions in the negotiation – some of which you control, some of which the other negotiator controls – you need to have practical means of analysing what you can do and what you must avoid. This is a big step forward to operationalizing ideas of power. Negotiating is a process and the tactical moves to enhance or reduce power can play an important part in that process. Negotiating power is subjective, it's in your head, and, because there are at least two parties to a negotiation, it is in two or more heads.

The items to be exchanged may be tangible or intangible, such as goods for money or honour and integrity, but the power dimensions that condition and effect your exchanges are wholly subjective and judgemental.

I do not go so far as to deny *any* objective measure of power. A half-mile long queue of customers outside my plant is objectively a more encouraging sign of my market power than an absence of customers altogether. Your perceptions of which of you has power, whether right or wrong, in my view, play a greater role in your negotiating behaviour than any objective measure of power. And, as power only becomes available to you through your perceptions, your judgement about its relevance in your negotiations is purely subjective. With subjective judgement comes uncertainty and risk, both of which mitigate the practical relevance of an objective measurement of power.

 ## DEPENDENCY AND COMMITMENT

Samuel Bacharach and Edward Lawler[80] published their work on bargaining power over fifteen years ago and nobody has captured its essence more clearly than they did. True they developed their work on power from the works of others, notably by Blau[81] and Emerson,[82] but then who doesn't? Isaac Newton, a genius, spoke modestly about himself standing on the shoulders of giants to create his own awe inspiring contributions to mathematics and physics. Only the ungracious immodestly think they stand on the shoulders of pygmies. Bacharach and Lawler applied a blend of their own and existing ideas about power to the negotiation process and produced excellent results.

The essence of their approach lies in two concepts, dependence and commitment. Broadly, dependence is the degree to which the negotiating parties 'have a stake in the bargaining relationship'.[83] A dependency relationship is 'variable across and within settings and can be manipulated objectively and subjectively in the course of bargaining'. A dependency relationship 'is inherently ambiguous, and the nature of that relationship is often an implicit or even manifest issue at the bargaining table. In other words, bargainers negotiate not only the specific issues to hand but also the nature of their dependence on each other'.[84]

Union-management bargaining provides evidence of the role of dependency. Both sides clearly have a high degree of dependence on each other, for, failing the repetition of rarely occurring events, like the Wapping strike at News International in 1980, it is unusual for a management to replace an entire workforce in pursuit of bargaining objectives, as it is unusual for a workforce to resign *en masse* to take up employment elsewhere. Commercial suppliers and purchasers are also dependent to some degree, and if their dependency is not so strong as that in labour relations, it is certainly a very real one nevertheless.

Significant suppliers are seldom dropped overnight. The heavy transaction costs of switching from a major supplier, such as a bank, an auditor, or a supplier of inputs that form a significant contribution to a company's added value, act as relatively strong barriers to entry to their rivals. It is not, however, impossible to switch and, when severely provoked, this can happen despite the transaction costs.

One example of a sudden switch in suppliers was when the Scottish & Newcastle Beer Company (S&N) sacked its bankers, the Royal Bank of Scotland (RBS). S&N felt that they were severely provoked to do this when RBS put up some of the bid funds for a hostile takeover of S&N by Foster's lager. S&N, not surprisingly, regarded this act by RBS (albeit as a very minor player in the bid funds) as totally incompatible with its status as S&N's banker. By way of an apologetic explanation, an RBS spokesperson expressed the, perhaps insensitive, view that it was a purely commercial decision. S&N, in retaliation, stated that it was also 'a purely commercial decision' with whom it banked. As the bid failed, RBS lost a major customer and did not profit from its involvement.

Bacharach and Lawler point out that your bargaining power comes from the other negotiator's dependence on you. The general statement of a dependency relationship is summarized in the proposition that an increase in your dependence on Melisa, increases Melisa's bargaining power. This creates a two-way dependency relationship and, as a consequence, a two-way distribution of bargaining power. As we shall see, this has important implications when assessing bargaining power in your preparation for a negotiation, and when attempting to influence the power balance in the subsequent face-to-face contact.

There are two dimensions to a dependency relationship.

○   First, there is the dimension of 'the degree to which parties have *alternative* outcome sources'.

○   Second, there is the dimension of 'the degree of *commitment* to the outcomes at issue'.

The availability of alternative outcomes clearly must influence your dependence: if I am the only game in town, your dependence on me is greater than if there is no house in town where there is not a game. This notion is similar to advice from Fisher and Ury that you should consider your best alternative to a negotiated agreement, or BATNA, if you want to increase your bargaining power.[85] By identifying the alternatives to the deal likely to be offered and by comparing it with your best alternative, you are likely to negotiate more assertively – *in extremis*, you can always reject their offered deal and switch to your BATNA.

By commitment, they mean the degree of importance of the outcome to you. If you need a particular outcome badly, your commitment is greater than if you are relaxed about it. If you need a plumber because right now you *need* a plumber, it is unlikely, while up to your waist in water, that you will bargain hard over the call-out charge, irrespective of how many plumbers there are in the *Yellow Pages*.

Changes in dependency and commitment occur for various reasons, some of them outside your control and others subject to your influence. Recognizing these circumstances enables you to turn Bacharach and Lawler's theory of bargaining power into a practical tool. Merely identifying the dependencies of the other negotiator, even if they are beyond your control, provides clues to their behaviour in the forthcoming negotiation. If you can also influence their commitment, or simply recognize its format, you could also affect their perceptions of the power balance and through this produce different behaviours from those that might otherwise be prevalent. Ignorance, or disregard, of dependency and commitment, puts you at the mercy of how awake they are to their opportunities to influence your perceptions of their power.

We can summarize the influence on bargaining power of changes in these dimensions:[86]

1.   A decrease in a supplier's alternative customers, increases its current client's bargaining power.

2.   A decrease in its client's alternative suppliers, increases a supplier's bargaining power.

3.   An increase in a supplier's commitment to the outcome (e.g., a desperate need for the supplier to get a toe-hold in the market for a new product line), increases its client's bargaining power.

4.   An increase in a client's commitment to the outcome (e.g., a

desperate need to acquire scarce inputs for its new product line),
increases the supplier's bargaining power.

It should immediately spring to mind that it is essential, if you want to
take advantage of a shift in bargaining power, or to avoid becoming a
victim of such a shift, that your preparation must include research into
the business circumstances of the firms that you depend upon for your
supplies and for customers. You must become aware of the increase or
decrease in the other negotiator's alternatives and commitment. If you
remain ignorant of these changes you could miss bargaining opportunities, or become one for somebody else.

For example, Reed Packaging, a management buy-out from Reed
Plc, was able to attract a premium price above its tangible asset value
because it was the last independent major packaging business in the
UK. Fortunately, the directors recognized this as the crucial factor in
determining their bargaining power. City financial analysts, on the
other hand, estimated Reedpack's book value at £800 million. It sold a
little while later for just over £1 billion to a Swedish company, whose
strategic goal, and therefore commitment, was to gain access to markets in the European Union (Sweden at the time was not in the EU).
The difference over book value that the Swedes had to pay was the
premium for their commitment to enter EU markets. Their commitment alternatives (other major packaging companies) were non-
existent. If the Reedpack sellers had not realized this they would have
sold their company for less.

If you carelessly reveal a detrimental change in your alternatives
('We're losing market share'), or your levels of commitment ('I desperately need these supplies today') you should expect a less favourable
outcome. Careless reporting of sensitive information in the commercial
press is a rich source of knowledge (as long as you remember not to
believe everything that you read in the newspapers). That caveat aside,
there is no doubt that information about circumstances that are likely
to affect your bargaining power has tactical implications in the conduct
of a negotiation. Events influence them, as does how you report them
and how your negotiating partners interpret them.

An example of the consequences of misreading, or being ignorant of,
commitment shows up in the preparatory analysis of the strategic
interests of unions and management in their recognition negotiations.

The one context where a union's commitment to the outcome is
usually at its highest is when they negotiate for recognition for collective bargaining purposes. Unions cannot function without recognition
agreements that are signed by the employers with whom they wish to
negotiate. The union's *raison d'etre* depends on securing recognition
agreements that define their legitimacy as representative negotiating

bodies for collective bargaining on behalf of their members. This, then normally should be a moment of high opportunity for employers, enabling them to enforce stiff conditions – or, at least, to resist union biased demands – in exchange for recognition.

The alternative conduct for an employer, who is not aware of the union's relative vulnerability, is to accept the union's stiff demands. Union inspired draft recognition agreements naturally reflect the union's version of their collective bargaining rights and usually include restrictions on management's ability to manage, while awarding over-generous facilities for union members to conduct union business in company time and at the company's expense.

Recently, Negotiate provided consultancy support to 18 different employers in the higher education and health service sectors in the UK. Our support included the drafting of collective bargaining recognition agreements and our detailed amendment of union drafted versions. Despite our strenuous efforts to persuade some of these employers to use their bargaining power in these unique circumstances, they disregarded the significance of what they signed up to (against our advice). If they do not use their bargaining power when they have it, what will they do when they don't? It is no accident, therefore, that these employers are destined to be burdened unnecessarily with expensive and extensive restrictive labour practices. They also have some of the lowest paid employees in the UK.

It should be obvious that unions have no alternative sources for different outcomes in a recognition dispute. On recognition issues they have no BATNAs. They can only sign a recognition agreement for their members with the employer who employs them. This gives bargaining power, for once, to their employer, even in organizations long dominated by public sector unions that impose restrictive employment and working policies.

So, six of the 18 health and education employers were so uncommitted to an appropriate, and winnable, outcome, i.e., a recognition agreement that permitted the employer to manage the organization and the union to exercise its more modest functions (and not the other way round) that they handed bargaining power, in spades, back to the same unions by signing, without amendment, union inspired recognition agreements! Schiller got it about right: *Mit der Dummheit kampfen Gotter selbst vergebens* ('against stupidity even the gods themselves struggle in vain').

ATKINSON ON POWER

We now consider the work of Gerald Atkinson on power assessment in the preparation phase. My first reaction on reading Atkinson on the practical application of his concepts of power,[87] was one of extreme scepticism. My earlier views of Atkinson's application of power (regrettably) appeared in *Managing Negotiations* (1980):

> an over-complex probability approach leaves a great deal to be desired. The parties are expected to make estimates of the probabilities of various outcomes and then calculate the various rewards associated with these outcomes weighted by the probability of them occurring. This provides a spurious accuracy to the preparation of a negotiating position. In its most extreme form ('Game Theory') it is both illuminating and operationally limited. The negotiator is thrown back on subjective judgement – a guess. But the illusion of accuracy is maintained. The effort required to calculate the outcome is fairly demanding, especially under time pressure. It creates the possibility of the participant rationalising practically any negotiating position or preference by adjusting either of the expected rewards to an outcome or the likely probability of its occurrence. If both parties are in error on these counts – both choosing mutually conflicting outcomes – we are back in the uncertain world of negotiation as represented in this book. In our view one might as well start there, without the arithmetical hassle.[88]

I quote this embarrassing assessment to show how easy it is to err. My only (feeble) excuse is that at the time I was concentrating on practical negotiating tools and Atkinson's presentation of power assessments were a trifle far-fetched for the level of managers I was training. They were largely engaged in single meeting, single decision, small stakes negotiations. They were not negotiating for larger ticket items of the kind that took several months and many meetings to conclude. Primarily it was a matter of scale and my inexperience.

In 1990, Atkinson published a second book on negotiation.[89] It is one of the best books on preparation for negotiation I have read. It includes a chapter – 'assessing power and using it'[90] – which is the best 30 pages worth you could study on the subject. I have since used versions of Atkinson's model of power assessment for the bigger ticket negotiators, and, though a few reactions have been negative, the majority of the participants successfully applied his method to their cases.

Atkinson pointed out that while the sources of power (from French and Raven)[91] and the personal skill and ability of the negotiators are important, these factors are 'seen by the other party in the context of the third factor: *your proposal*.' The key question in preparation is: will he prefer to accept or reject your solution to the problem? And, since you are going to be facing him with your potential proposal, he will take whichever course of action he judges will hurt him least.[92] The point here is 'the course of action that will *hurt* him least'. In this idea there are echoes of Stevens,[93] who adapted a psychological choice model – 'avoidance-avoidance' – in analysing wage negotiations.

Atkinson properly acknowledges his indebtedness to Neil Chamberlain[94] and H. V. Levinson.[95] Chamberlain wrote: 'We may define the bargaining power of A as being the cost to B of disagreement on A's terms relative to the cost of agreement on A's terms'.[96] This is a fascinating insight into bargaining power. It is obviously a real time decision.

The responder to the negotiator's proposal contemplates the relative disadvantages of rejecting or accepting the current proposal according to which course of action (to accept or reject it) leaves him least worse off.

Levinson[97] expressed the power problem as a ratio written, with my minor verbal adjustments, as:

$$\text{Her negotiating power} = \frac{\text{The costs or disadvantages to him of rejecting her proposal}}{\text{The costs or disadvantages to him of accepting her proposal}}$$

You should treat the (=) sign as meaning negotiating power is 'a function' of the ratio and not as an arithmetical 'equals' sign. Also, note the incision of the word 'disadvantage' alongside costs. This is to remind you that costs extend beyond money and other measurable quantities. The disadvantages, cover what *hurts* him and extends to other consequences, like loss of face, reduced flexibilities, reduced alternatives, changes in importance of the outcome, even the psychic costs of despair, demoralization, loss of heart, loss of coalition support, and such like.

Immediately obvious, I hope, is the opportunity for you to attempt to influence the power ratio, once you identify its elements. This operationalizes the use of power assessment by making it a practical tool for strategic and tactical decisions before the face-to-face phases of negotiation.

Atkinson's method is very simple and only uses arithmetic to derive some feeling for the weight of the ratio. This is where a few practitioners quit. They know that power is an elusive notion because, presumably, they do no more than subjectively assess it when they negotiate. If you ask 'which of you has the most bargaining power?', they are able to give some sort of an answer in specific cases. If you ask why they believe whatever they believe, they usually shrug their shoulders. However they respond, they will almost certainly be unwilling, or genuinely unable, to offer much detail on why they came to their decision, or why they chose this rather than that set of factors to make their assessment.

One negotiator, for instance, told me: 'it's all too complicated to explain to you; I just know this is what it is and that's that'. Admirable, of course, but hardly helpful to others who do not have his insights and talents (assuming he was not just making it up as he went along). Such subjective and unexplainable assessments could be inclusive, because they consider all the pros and cons, or exclusive, because they only consider some prominent ones that attract their attention but which may not be decisive. Using this undefinable method, they either assign significant bargaining power to themselves, or conclude that they have none. Both conclusions are as likely to be wrong.

Atkinson's method of assessment (Figure 2.12) requires that the negotiator score on a 0–10 scale the factors considered to be important disadvantages to the other negotiator and weight them by the probability (0–1) that they will occur. By multiplying the two weightings for each of the 'hurting' factors, the ratio becomes two numbers, one above the line and the other below it. When divided through, these two numbers collapse to a single value for the ratio, from which you assess the power balance.

The procedure involves some simple arithmetic. If the weighted number below the line (the disadvantages of accepting your proposal) is bigger than the weighted number above the line (the disadvantages of rejecting it) then the ratio is less than 1 (because a number divided by a bigger number is always less than 1). It is likely that he would reject your proposal, because to accept it would hurt him more than rejecting it.

Similarly, if the weighted number above the line (the disadvantages of rejecting your proposal) is bigger than the weighted number below the line (the disadvantages of accepting your proposal) then the ratio is greater than 1 (because a number divided by a smaller number is always greater than 1). His inclination is to accept your proposal because it would hurt him more to reject it.

In the former case, where the ratio is less than 1, you do not have power over him because it is in his interests to avoid the greater hurt to him of saying 'yes'. In the latter case, where the ratio is greater than 1, you have power over him because it is in his interests to avoid the greater hurt to him of saying 'no'.

A worked example of a typical weighting procedure, using Atkinson's method, for the (unspecified) terms of a substantial bank overdraft is shown in Figure 2.12. The bank has power over the customer if the

Disadvantages of them saying 'no'	Weighting		Probability		
	(1–10)		(0–1)		
Withdrawal of overdraft	7	×	1.0	=	7.0
Hassles of transfer to new bank	8	×	0.8	=	6.4
Disruption in relationship services	8	×	0.4	=	3.2
Closing meetings/letters/forms etc.	6	×	0.2	=	1.2
Credit 'scares' on news of change	8	×	0.5	=	4.0
			Total	=	21.8

Disadvantages of them saying 'yes'					
Increased bank charges	4	×	1.0	=	4.0
Loss of 'face'	5	×	0.5	=	2.5
Precedents for future	2	×	0.3	=	0.6
			Total	=	7.1

Figure 2.12 Power dimensioning using Atkinson's method

ratio is greater than 3:1; the bank does not have power over the customer if the ratio is less than 3:1. The ratio in Figure 2.12 is 21.8 / 7.1, which is greater than 3:1. The bank, in this example, has power over the customer. Anything nearer parity (1:1) is clearly negotiable. Anything much above 3:1 and you should be asking: 'Am I asking for enough?'.[98]

The appropriate tactical ploys that follow from this assessment are to try to enhance the costs and disadvantages to them of rejecting your proposal (by addressing the elements above the line to worsen the hurt felt by the other negotiator by saying 'no') and to reduce the costs and disadvantages to them of accepting your proposal (by addressing the elements below the line to reduce the hurt felt by the other negotiator from saying 'yes').

It is important to understand that among your efforts to adjust the results of the analysis you must not (ever!) adjust the numbers and their consequent weightings. This would be spurious in the extreme. Your efforts must, instead, concentrate on preparing to influence the various factors themselves that cause the disadvantages of accepting or of rejecting your proposals. This is an altogether different activity though not obvious. It is similar to the rules of statistical analysis – once the null hypothesis is tested against the hypothesis, massage of the data is prohibited. This is sometimes difficult for research students to accept and, regrettably, in my experience of supervising masters and doctorate theses, it is sometimes difficult to persuade them to follow.

The list of disadvantages includes both quantifiable and intangible elements and some part of your tactical effort aims to change the other negotiator's perceptions of the weightings. This normally costs you less than simply conceding. His perceptions of the intangibles, using persuasion and other similar techniques, such as casting 'fear, uncertainty and doubt' (the so-called 'FUD' factor) over the intangibles you wish to increase in significance below the line, and those you wish to reduce in significance above the line, is a legitimate task in the face-to-face phases. Identifying in preparation the factors that you will attempt to influence is part of the strategic planning in the preparation phase.

I haven't yet directly answered my original objections to Atkinson's method, namely that the subjective evaluation involved could lead to 'the possibility of the participant rationalizing practically any negotiating position or preference by adjusting either of the expected rewards to an outcome or the likely probability of its occurrence'.[99] Of course it could, and if negotiators want to 'rationalize' in this way to justify any course of action, nothing will stop them.

Errors in subjective judgement from treating the assessment of power as an unknowable 'black box' are more likely to occur than are errors arising from attempts to make explicit statements about what is in the black box, which, in principle, are checkable by colleagues. Even a mere listing of factors, assumed by those negotiators who reject the 'precision' implied in Atkinson's method, and checking them for inclusions and exclusions, is a step forward in assessing power. Naturally, listing promotes discussion about the identified factors in the power assessment and it would not be stretching credulity at all to suggest that this discussion would likely include an implicit weighting of each factor, such as making remarks like: 'this one is more important than that one'.

Some sceptics, who resist going even this far, make it appropriate to apply to them (and not to Atkinson!) my 1980 strictures against their vague assessment of the components of power which can rationalize practically any negotiating position or preference they choose to make. The vague subjectivists have more to answer for in their unspecified judgements than those who apply Atkinson's method.

 PREPARING THE MANAGEMENT AGENDA

There are two ways to prepare for a wage negotiation: one is for it to be budget driven; the other is for it be strategically driven. Unfortunately, many managements believe they amount to the same thing.

Budget driven preparation is almost entirely tactical. The executive directors agree the maximum amount available for wage increases, given their assessment of 'the going rate', under coercion from the trade unions or from labour market recruitment pressure, and they set this as the upper boundary of the range, within which the personnel function has to secure a settlement.

The personnel function tasks itself to achieve a result within this, usually low, budget. This normally means spreading the 'jam' thinly across all employees, including management, which usually 'freezes' the current distribution of earnings. It is easier to justify equalizing misery than it is to risk provoking envy between 'winners' and 'losers'. When the pressure is too high to keep the employees' aspirations below the upper boundary of the budget, the remedy usually involves job cutting, variously known as 'downsizing', 'right-balancing', 'right-sizing', or 'cost cutting'. They all amount to the same thing – the company attacks its most precious asset, its human capital.

In these tactically driven distributive negotiations, the unions demand more than the available budget and the management offer less. The result is the conventional 'set to' between management and labour, with its attendant rhetorical 'noise', perhaps some disruptive action by the employees, including strikes, and prolonged negotiating sessions until they agree. Then 'peace' reigns until the next annual round.

These disputes also usually feature the management responding to the union's claims and seldom initiating its own. The management uses its tactical energy to mitigate the union's claims in a classic zero-sum outcome: what the managers 'save' below their budget the union 'loses'; what the union's 'gain' above the budget, the management 'loses'. Those personnel managers who are good at this game prosper; those who are not so 'talented' don't.

The alternative strategy follows the steps in the Negotek® template:

O   It aims to link the strategic objectives in the company's business plan to a *management agenda* for the negotiations.
O   It is not tactically driven, though tactical imperatives are present.
O   It does not react to the demands of employees or external unions; it initiates a proactive management agenda.
O   It is not zero-sum negotiating; it is non-zero sum package bargaining. Wage increases, and other changes in the reward and benefits package, are conditional on necessary changes in the way managers and employees work together to achieve the objectives of the organization.
O   It is not necessarily confined to annual pay rounds on general wage increases, nor is it confined to unionized environments such as are still common in the public sector, though less so elsewhere.

The organization's *Business Plan* states the organization's strategic objectives for the next two to three years. True, there are business plans and there are business plans. Their quality varies from expressions of pious intent – as found in some so called 'mission statements' – to clearly stated and measurable goals to which the organization commits its resources. The managers know whether they have achieved their strategic objective as they approach the time horizon of their business plan.

If the business plan is a vague declaration of intent, managers will not know how well they are doing nor what they have to do to correct for shortfalls, nor what resources to mobilize to push for success. For instance, I read one company's 'business plan' that contained a non-discriminatory employment policy as its primary feature! This is not a strategic objective; it is a policy (and a legal requirement). Another plan consisted of a long list of action points for each department to undertake over the next two years, suggesting the departments merely listed what they were going to do in their functional areas and not what the organization as a whole had to achieve. On enquiry, the personnel director told me that her colleague, charged with putting together the business plan, told her she 'should write no more than a single page on her human resource strategy' and that 'no, she could not read the overall plan first as none of the other departments was ready'!

Without strategic direction, everything is tactical. The business twists and turns on a daily basis, comforted by the cliché that 'the whole is greater than the sum of its parts', which it rarely is in this managerial environment. Departments 'freeze' where they are, and act to protect what they have, resulting in functional managers at 'war' with each other. The whole becomes less than the sum of its parts.

Developing a reward strategy to deliver the organization's strategic objective is not primarily a tactical or a budgetary activity. The process requires managers to establish a seamless connection between the strategic objectives of the business plan and the management agenda for the negotiations. They accomplish this by detailed analysis and planning that consumes management time and other resources. It is better not to leave this work to the personnel function to do alone. The managers negotiate not simply to mitigate the total wage award. They could do this without costly preparatory effort to achieve strategic insight to create and deliver the management agenda. In this light it is easier to avoid the effort by relapsing into budgetary driven pay policies.

I shall illustrate the method by reference to an NHS hospital group. Necessarily, as with the banking example, I shall remain discreet about confidential matters and I shall restrict the example to one element of the assignment only. The strategic approach, it should be noted, is applicable in commercial and public sector organizations.

The first stage was to ensure that the hospital's business plan was a proper plan and not just an extended mission statement. It was also necessary to ensure that the senior managers, who were to participate in the determination of the management agenda for the forthcoming pay negotiations, were sufficiently familiar with their business plan that they could derive necessary strategic objectives from it. Unsurprisingly, it is not uncommon to find that even senior managers in many organizations confess to not having read their business plan, at least to a level where they could engage in discourse about it. Unsurprisingly, these organizations tend to be tactically and not strategically driven.

The first step is to require the managers to derive from the strategic objectives of their organization about five *commercial imperatives* that the organization must achieve if it is to deliver its strategic objectives in the business plan.

In the case of the NHS, we switched some terminology from 'commercial' to *service imperatives*, to accommodate the largely non-commercial culture and (self-asserted) 'humanist' values said to prevail in the health sector. One non-executive director, for instance, objected to using the term 'business plan', hence we suggested 'service plan' instead '(a rose by any other name', etc.) because we had enough to do without challenging an individual's beliefs.

Managers who had never done this sort of exercise before, demonstrated no lack of insight into what were their commercial imperatives. This initial step in the exercise usually takes about 45 minutes only and produces up to eight imperatives, a few of which drop out after discussion.

Taking a typical one of them as our example, we shall follow it through to its conclusion into a management agenda. From an acute hospital, we consider the service imperative to 'increase the provision of day surgery'. This imperative arises from changes in medical technology and new thinking about delivering certain surgical health care procedures to patients. Older styles of provision in 'Florence Nightingale' wards required overnight stays, even for minor surgery, which were caused more by a hospital's administrative convenience and not by the patients' medical requirements.

Once, however, you contemplate a new method of delivery of your services, you immediately create another set of imperatives that are necessary to implement the changes that benefit patients. Trying to deliver things differently without changing the existing configuration of resources (human, financial and consumables), is a recipe for inefficiency and a potential waste of scarce resources. *Ad hoc* adjustments to long-term changes are inefficient.

Permanent changes in the delivery of services cause changes in the use and mix of resources. In health care the people employed are the main resource and therefore we are keen to identify the *people imperatives* to deliver the identified commercial or service imperatives that will deliver the organization's strategic objective.

To meet the commercial imperative 'to increase day surgery facilities' requires people imperatives that usually include but are not limited to:

○ Consultants willing to concentrate their work on more routine surgical procedures (veins, bumps, cysts, vasectomies, etc.) and to supervise discharge assessments and procedures.
○ Nurses able to undertake more generalized work and able to become enskilled to cover some of the procedures currently undertaken by medical practitioners, including supervised roles in anaesthetics, minor surgery, and prescriptions.
○ Nurses and assistants able to work flexibly in intensive pre-op and post-op functions.
○ Paramedical support services to be undertaken at a time to suit patient progress and not laboratory opening hours.
○ Support staff able to facilitate patient progress through the unit to medically supervised discharge.

Managers were able to dentify as many as eight people imperatives per commercial imperative, irrespective, interestingly, of their own functional roles in the hospital. The consequence of change in specific departmental functions appeared to be 'obvious', to a surprising degree, even to those not directly employed in the function. Indeed, little or no 'professional' resentments were evident with people protecting their patch, in contrast to the normal protective reaction against outsiders discussing changes in their roles, a feature traditionally most evident the more 'professional' the hospital personnel affected.

For example, it is common for senior medical staff (consultants and registrars) to resist managerial scrutiny of their roles under the camouflage of 'clinical judgement'. The senior consultants who took part in these exercises soon appreciated what it was doing for them, in that it revealed information about the effect of necessary, and inevitable, changes of role for them and their colleagues. They soon recognized that they needed to know about the consequences of service and people changes if they were to develop the professional, as opposed on occasion to the personal, interests of themselves and their patients.

From the people imperatives, the managers uncovered the *personnel policies* needed to deliver the appropriate people into their changing roles to meet those people imperatives that would be required to deliver the commercial imperatives and, in turn, deliver the business plan.

When concluded, this process forges seamless links from business plan to the hospital's reward strategies.

Personnel policies cover a multitude of issues and what you select for analysis depends on the organization's circumstances, technology and business sector. We selected five areas of policy:

1. employee relations;
2. training and development;
3. recruitment (including decruitment);
4. organizational change;
5. manpower planning.

Management syndicates were each given one employee group from the people imperatives and asked to examine the personnel policies that would affect that employee group over the planning horizon of the business plan.

Briefly, Figure 2.13 shows a typical output from a syndicate that analysed the nurses' employee group for the service and people imperatives of increasing day surgery provision. This is just for one employee group delivering one of the five commercial imperatives. There are about six employee groups in a hospital: medical and dental; professions associated with medicine, or PAMs; qualified nurses; unqualified nurses; auxiliary staff; support staff.

You must conduct the same exercise for each employee group and for each of the five commercial imperatives.

The method requires your attention to detail and it creates much

Employee relations	Training and development	Recruitment	Organizational change	Manpower planning
Union-led resistance	Nurse practitioners	Higher quality and qualifications	Team working	Turnover and retention rates
Morale problems and uncertainty	Enskilling Flexibility Responsibility	Tests for suitability	Flatter org. structures	Current age profiles and retirements
Loss of shift allowances	Team and leadership training	No night shifts Pressure working		Surplus staff in older style wards?
Better prospects for some not others		Redundancies?		

Figure 2.13 Personnel policies to deliver the people imperatives (nurses' employees group) in an acute NHS hospital

data. For instance, with five commercial imperatives developing up to eight people imperatives each, there are 40 candidate people imperatives to consider. Taking up to five personnel policies per employee group per 40 people imperatives across up to six employee groups, you can generate 1200 personnel policies. This would almost be unmanageable except that the most common entry in the people imperatives and the personnel policy lists is 'ditto above', i.e., many of the imperatives and policies are common to the employee groups and to the personnel policies. For example, team working is a common requirement of changes in the delivery of hospital services, so is enskilling and de-skilling, and so on. This makes the exercise more manageable, to the evident relief of those undertaking it!

Once you complete the initial investment in the task it does not need to be repeated from scratch again every time you review your business plan. Each review to account for the passing of time and the inevitable changes in strategic priorities, or the impact of changing medical technologies and procedures in the health service, changes the original data by amendments and adjustment only.

The exercise also has the benefit of fully informing the management of their organization's roles to a level of detail other processes can't match. Their place in the main picture and the imperatives of change needed to deliver their organization's goals indelibly etches into their consciousness. Moreover, in considering the details of the obstacles to achieving their strategic objectives they become fully informed of, and committed to, the *management agenda* needed to drive the organization's policies in the negotiations with their employee groups.

The purpose of detailed preparation is not just to educate and energize management into how they plan to deliver the organization's services in the next three years (though that is a worthwhile exercise in its own right), it also provides the data on what they require from their employees if they are to deliver these services in their changing formats. Management is no longer reacting to employees' money wage demands and their habitual resistance to all necessary change, because it is analysing to ensure that it leads rather than follows, that it asserts rather than hopes, and that its reward strategies are solidly founded in what the organization requires, rather than what a tactical budgetary approach allows it to 'afford'.

Data collected from the personnel policies part of the exercise indicates the substantial agenda for change that lurks unnoticed in many organizations. Failure to undertake the necessary policies causes failures in the delivery of the business plan. True, there is a need to be selective and to prioritize among these policies. Management implements some of them by normal managerial discretion, some through consultation and some through negotiation.

The size of the agenda is not an excuse for managerial paralysis. Claims that 'it's too big', 'we can't cope', 'we'll never manage it', etc., are common reactions. On the contrary, its sheer size is a managerial asset! If the size of the change agenda was a debilitating problem, there is something clearly wrong with the business plan from which the change agenda is derived. No management need run out of things to negotiate about with an agenda this big. Particularly as it does not need to, nor can it, do it all at once.

The management agenda determines the appropriate reward strategy to deliver the personnel policies that will, in turn, deliver the people imperatives that will then deliver the commercial imperatives that will deliver the business plan. As change is incremental – you are not doing it all it once – so are the pay and benefits proposals you choose for negotiation. To determine the reward strategy, you start from where the organization is now and design the reward strategy to suit where it is headed.

In the NHS, the established method for the distribution of rewards – the 'Whitley' system through national pay bodies – is of extremely limited relevance in helping to supply what the hospitals require to deliver their changing services. Every management group, irrespective of their previously expressed preferences for or against the national Whitley system, that answered the question: 'Does your current pay and benefits system help or hinder the delivery of the policy imperatives you have identified?', overwhelmingly (i.e., just a few people short of unanimity) concluded that the Whitly system hindered them.

The appropriate pay system to deliver the policy imperatives required:

○ flexibility not narrow grading bands;
○ consolidated pay not myriads of allowances (accounting for up to a third of the total pay bill);
○ money to be recycled into growing services from declining ones;
○ some element of defensible differentials and not those based on tradition, sex or professional restrictions.

A management agenda in preparation for pay negotiations should derive from a strategic approach and not from the habits of residual budgeting. Of course, affordability is a budgetary constraint in any management decision but this does not contradict the need to allocate changes in rewards to support necessary changes in the configuration of a hospital's resources.

It is not a case that the budget is unimportant. Of course it is, when, using the data from the management agenda, the budgetary limit forces the recycling of cash resources by relative generosity to those needed for the change (and who make the changes) and relative stingi-ness to those not needed (or who won't make the changes). While the budgetary approach determines the amount, it must not determine the distribution.

In commercial organizations the same conclusion is even more evi-dent. Using exactly the same analytical approach, management should derive its negotiating mandates not from holding the lid on all changes in pay and by the freezing of historic distributions, but from recycling its budgets to deliver its changing strategic objectives through its changing commercial and people imperatives.

3

PHASE TWO – DEBATING
FACE TO FACE

 DEBATE

According to observations, negotiators spend approximately 80 per cent of face-to-face sessions in debate. While you are in the other phases you return repeatedly to debate. You question a proposal or bargain and this brings you both back to debate. The other negotiator's reply keeps you there. Where, and when, you go next is optional. You could return to preparation to examine more closely the implications of the proposal or to get fresh policy instructions, or you could move on to a proposal phase or stick with debate.

If things go wrong in a negotiation there is a high chance that they went wrong in debate, if only from its duration and dominance during face-to-face contact. There are so many verbal traps, opportunities to over-react, options to threaten, and tensions and frustrations to suffer, that it is not difficult to foul up the interaction by slipping into negative behaviours.

Failure in debate can also be less dramatic. One of you loses heart in 'selling' whatever you are pushing; the other changes her mind about whatever she thought of 'buying'. The deal dies of its own accord. You make your excuses and leave: 'I'll think about it'; 'I'll check with my sister'; 'Don't call us, we'll call you'.

It's as if in debate 'everything you say will be taken down and may be used in evidence'. Debate:

○ *Shapes the tone of the negotiation*   Open with threat and you set a coercive tone; open with an assurance and you set a conciliatory tone.

○ *Removes or creates obstacles to agreement*   Clarification can remove obstacles, qualifications can create them.

○ *Conditions expectations*   Expectations of the outcome influence the debate, hence manipulative ploys use deliberate forms of mis-leading words.

○ *Confirms prejudices or eliminates them* People with stereo-typical prejudices search for confirmation of their prejudices in your debate behaviour.

○ *Opens up options and possibilities or shuts them down* Closed debating behaviour such as blocking closes options while more open behaviour, such as suggesting and exploring, opens options.

○ *Reveals or hides what the negotiators want* The main task of debate is to find out what people want.

Debate involves communication, usually verbal, so what you say or do sends a message to the other negotiator, which – always remember – may not be the message they receive. They interpret what you commu-nicate according to their perceptions of what you mean and once their personal filters decode the message into their terms, it might take much effort to change their minds. Hence, you should be careful rather than casual when communicating because once the dogs of bitter argu-ment get loose it is difficult to rein them in again.

This is why debate promotes, slows down, hinders or deadlocks a deal. For this reason, we discuss next the manipulative ploy behaviour with which you must be able to cope in face-to-face negotiation.

BEHAVING BADLY

Negotiation has always had associations with behaviours that, to be blunt, are devious and manipulative. Ploys vary from the secretively sly through to bare-faced rip offs. Meeting with manipulators without adequate protection is risky. This creates a training niche to meet the demand for protection from manipulation in its varied forms. Though such protective training adds little to the quest for efficient, effective and wise agreements, it cuts your costs in time and effort when negoti-ating with manipulators and ploy merchants. Delivering such training, even as short spots in a negotiation workshop, or inserting some chap-ters on manipulative ploys into a book, could stir up suspicions of ethical confusion.

For example, at the end of a short negotiation workshop I delivered *pro bono publica* in Newcastle to staff employed by charities, com-munity and special interest groups, I asked if there was anything I had not covered fully. A voice from the back shouted out: 'Give us some dirty tricks, Gavin', at which point I realized I had wasted, at least on her, a whole day on the positive pay-offs to negotiators who deal openly, but always conditionally, with the people with whom they do business. Nothing wrong, of course, with her asking the question; it was just that she was asking it at the wrong seminar.

Afterwards she cornered me to explain that it was not that she wanted to use these tricks herself (perish the thought!), but she hated losing out to 'ruthless' politicians and public servants who used dirty tricks to take funds away from her charity to prevent her from getting help to those who needed it. She wanted a 'level playing field' on behalf of her 'disadvantaged clients', and so on.

The marketing pitch for an overtly manipulative approach is different — 'you should wise up to what the sharks out there can do to you; forearmed is forewarned; you don't get what you deserve, you get what you manipulate; and so on'. 'Wising-up' about how negotiators really play is an investment to avoid the fate of all suckers, who never get an even break (*pace* W. C. Fields).

The promoters of the genre argue that learning about the dirty tricks that *others* might try on you is an urgent necessity if your income depends upon negotiating for a living. Hard pressed sales and purchasing people, who are out to do better, or do just well enough to keep their jobs, learn how to deal with all those *other* people who are tricksters. And, they believe, they can learn without feeling guilty. They are not at a 'dirty tricks' seminar to learn how to do it themselves — of course not! — they are there to find out how *other* people manipulate them and what they can do to avoid suffering the sucker's fate.

In the view of the serial manipulative player, you are the enemy and it is surely prudent of them to be suspicious of you because you will use any means to get what you want and do them down in the process. If they can't see the particular ploy you are using at this moment, that is only because you are so devious that they haven't spotted it — yet.

Paranoia is not healthy. It is the ante-chamber of counter-manipulation. It drives you into a state of 'ploy alert', and, while you are at it, you 'get your retaliation in first' by using counter-ploys to protect yourself from what they are (probably) about to do to you. A small step later, and you are using the very same ploys you learned to recognize in 'streetwise' seminars, which is probably what you wanted to do all along.

We are in a bind: we must study ploys because, like sexually transmitted diseases, they are a fact of life. Ploys are common enough in negotiations for you to need to be aware of their consequences for you if they are 'successful'. Idealists are virgin cynics, and exposure to manipulative negotiation soon hardens the nicest of people. The danger is that in your disappointment about certain kinds of conduct, which leaves you feeling cheated, you, in turn, cheat others.

Those negotiators whom I interview because they express some predilection for manipulative negotiation, or whom I observe behaving in this manner, usually claim that they manipulate because others manipulate them. They deny any intention to exploit others and claim they manipulate only to protect themselves.

My advice is that all manipulative players attempt to exploit you and you should heavily discount any excuse you hear about their desire only to protect themselves. What is more, their excuses are irrelevant. What they do – how they behave – is more important than uncheckable claims about their intentions. Bad ploy behaviour looks good only to somebody who avoids looking in mirrors.

 ## MANIPULATIVE PLOYS

All ploys have a purpose. They aim to influence your expectations of the negotiated outcome. The connection between ploys, gambits, tricks and so-called 'tactics', and your expectations is obvious once you think about it. There would be no point in engaging in ploys if your manipulation did not pay off in some way. It would be perverse to manipulate just for the hell of it – though I do not entirely exclude the possibility in the case of some people with whom I have dealt. Negotiators, who use ploys regularly, do so because they intend to 'win' that pay-off. There is a larger group of occasionally manipulative players, who resort to ploys because they just cannot help it when they see an opportunity to 'win'.

Your expectations of an outcome are derived from your perceptions of the other party's power over you. Briefly, if you believe that your power over me is high, you are likely to be bullish about the outcome. You expect to do better than in the opposite case, where you perceive your power over me to be low. The more powerful that you feel I am, the less well you expect to do.

Figure 3.1 illustrates the relationship. Power perceptions run left to right from low to high and your expectations of the outcome run right to left from low to high. It is in practice an inverse relationship: the less power you believe I have, the higher your expectation of the outcome in your favour.

Your perceptions of my power are subject to all kinds of influences, some of which are mere whims and fancies and others with some degree of substance. Observation suggests that people make assessments of relative power on the flimsiest of data. The ploy merchant takes advantage of your neglect of real evidence. They manipulate the context and the environment to portray their power over you as greater than it is.

Few people properly prepare Atkinson's relative power assessment

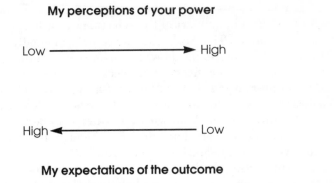

Figure 3.1 *Relationship between my perceptions of your power and my expectations of the outcome*

and even fewer consciously monitor the sources of their shifting expectations during their face-to-face negotiations. That psychological balance, experienced by negotiators and by players of sport, that inexplicably seems to change in the other person's favour, causes the 'head to drop', the body to slump, and you to lose what glad confidence you had only moments previously. This is a possible sign that they have manipulated you into giving up unnecessarily. Yet what was the substance of the change? Why have you revised your expectations? What did they do to strike such a body blow at your self-confidence? Often it is only a vacuous shift in your perceptions.

For years, I have asked my 'Camel Question' in my seminars all over the world, including in countries where camels are a common bargaining currency. You may try it now by marking the answer you think is closest to your immediate assessment:

An Arab with six camels approaches an oasis in search of water, where another Arab stands beside a sign: 'Water, all you can drink, price one camel'.[100]

Who has the power:

  a)   the Arab with the camels?

  b)   the Arab with the water?

  c)   impossible to say?

Most respondents mark either a) or b). A few respond with c). The arguments used in support of the selections a) or b) are numerous and often imaginative. The Arab with the camels, allegedly, for example, is thirsty and, therefore, needs water to satisfy his immediate and relatively unpostponable need, and, because there are vast distances between water springs in the desert, he may not be able to wait until he reaches the next oasis, and, anyway, the price for water may be higher there. Meanwhile, the Arab with the water is under less pressure and he is in the more powerful position. Fair enough, if true.

However, and alternatively, the Arab with the camels, I have been told, is conducting an hydrographic survey and is not searching for water on his own behalf but on behalf of the Water Ministry(!). The man with the water is without a camel and needs one to make an emergency visit to his dying father in an oasis too far away to walk! This means the Arab with the camels has the power. Also fair enough, if true.

In the question I ask, however, neither a) nor b) is true. The additional information that imaginative participants invent and rely upon to make their decision, is totally absent from my question. This makes my point. Without more data you cannot sensibly make an assessment of the relative power of the two Arabs. Yet the majority of respondents who choose answers a) or b) do just that! And from observation, and not a little introspection, I think that we all fall into the error, from time to time, of judging, on severely limited data, who has the most power in our negotiations.

As a result, we often accord greater relative power to other negotiators than the context warrants and we lower our expectations accordingly, and as often without thinking about what we are doing. In short, we negotiate with ourselves. We accept less than we might because we expect less than we could realize if only we approached the power balance in the negotiation in a different frame of mind.

No wonder manipulative behaviour successfully exploits this very human weakness. It would require a mass adherence to a self-denying ordinance not to exploit opportunities to influence other peoples' expectations. Though such self-denial is within the known range of human behaviour, not everybody signs up to it. If an opportunity exists to gain from behaving in a certain way, somebody will behave that way. Acknowledging this is not the same as endorsing what some people do in the privacy of their interactive behaviour. It is merely a realistic acknowledgement of human nature as it is and not as it ought to be. An *ought*, we must always remember, is never an *is*.

Whenever people interact, the possibilities for defection from what people ought to do are real, and, in many cases, defection will occur. Two disciples of Jesus, surely men who were most committed to His teachings, defected in the last two days of his life: Judas 'betrayed' Him and Peter 'denied' Him. And even He 'defected' from His teachings in His last moments on the cross by asking why God had 'forsaken Him'. This is what made all three of them so human, hence, your chances of negotiating on occasion with manipulative defectors are real and, probably, vastly large.

Power is the ability to make someone do what they otherwise would not do and manipulative tricks and ploys are about making you do more than you otherwise would. In short, manipulation coerces you to concede more.

All ploys belong to one of three main categories: dominance, shaping and closing. First, those ploys that seek to increase their *dominance* over you, while not confined to the early sessions of a negotiation, are more common in the opening bout of 'oratorical fireworks'. Achieving dominance from an early stage enables them to set the tone and the tempo (not to say temper) of the following sessions. It coincides with the most conflict-ridden phase of negotiation because the struggle for dominance involves conflict enhancing behaviours. Characteristically, dominance behaviour is concerned with:

○   defending extreme positions;
○   appearing to be intransigent;
○   revealing narrow grounds for manoeuvre – if any;
○   bullying you into early concessions.

Second, in the middle phases of negotiation, with the concentration of the parties on debating the parameters of a possible settlement (signalling, proposing, packaging and bargaining), numerous opportunities appear to manipulate the *shape* of the deal. This is where ploys flourish and the literature abounds with often curiously named 'tricks' (some of which names I invented myself!). Shaping ploys do just that – they shape perceptions of what is possible and shape expectations of what is likely. Some are outrightly 'dishonest' and do not have any ethical justification. They are concerned with cheating in its crudest form and if you use them you are using disreputable methods – true 'dirty' tricks.

Third, certain ploys flourish in the end game or the *close* of the negotiation and are about *pressurizing* you to settle on their current offer. Some of them are well-known and obvious but they still work in the right circumstances when used against those who do not notice what they are up to. Thus, you can usefully divide most manipulative ploys into these three main groups, roughly but not uniquely, corresponding to the opening, middle and closing phases of a negotiation. They range in sophistication from the subtle to the obtuse. Most ploys are well known.[101] But what is more important, they all have counters, which you can use to defeat the ploy's purpose of lowering your expectations of the outcome, i.e. by tricking you into giving away far more than you intended.

To combat the use of ploys you need to neutralize their effects. That begins with your understanding of their purpose and of the intentions of people who rely upon them. *A ploy neutralized is a ploy defeated.*

To neutralize a ploy you must first identify it. Your options from then on are to expose the ploy or to counter it. Exposing a ploy risks embarrassing the perpetrator, which may concern you if you wish to maintain the relationship with them and because the outcome is more important to you than 'winning' an interpersonal contest. Standing on 'moral high ground' can be more good for the ego than it is for business. It can also lend a touch of the sanctimonious to your stance.

There is another risk worthy of consideration. Exposing or countering what you believe is a ploy could be disastrous if it is *not* a ploy. Instead, it could be that the other party's 'ploy' move was genuinely unintentional and fair, as seen by them. Accusing people of 'crimes' they have not committed, or crimes that they can deny plausibly, could be short routes to interpersonal disasters.

Identifying, but not exposing a ploy, seems by far the better response, with some slight risk that they might interpret your countering moves, if any, as your ploy. Fortunately, to neutralize a ploy normally only requires that you identify it, which you can keep, of course, to yourself, and you can refrain from counters.

Most of the books and seminars on ploys originated in the United States, though it may be inevitable that, within such an individualistic and competitive culture, there would be numerous books and seminars designed to appeal to minorities of practitioners. I have often reflected on how the American passion for high stakes, fast scoring games of sport and chance (such as baseball, football, hockey, poker, blackjack and craps) produces negotiation language borrowed from competitive gaming, such as 'big pot', 'up the ante', 'game plan', 'call their bluff', 'raise the stakes', 'nice guys come last', 'come out of left field', 'block them', 'keep the score', 'hard ball', 'low ball', 'don't get mad, get even' and 'tactics', and so on.

Such a culture legitimizes competitive tactics and ploys. 'Winning' is not a dirty word (apparently, it is an essential word on covers of American books about negotiation). Even a book titled *Winning through Intimidation*[102] was a best seller. 'Winning' is no place for patsies either. If you 'can't take the heat, get out of the kitchen'. Truly, 'when a man with money meets a man with experience, the man with the experience ends up with the money, and the man with the money ends up with the experience'.

All of this, and more, adds up, in the practice of some American negotiators, to a dynamic fast moving, high scoring, get-up-and-go negotiation environment, and any means that helps them do even better, apparently, is 'OK'.

 ## STREETWISE?

Levin's interesting little book[103] is a typical example of the joys of ploys:

> The best tacticians are the people who grew up street smart. They know how to defend themselves. They can outmanoeuvre anybody who tries to stab them in the back. They know all the tricks of making people who disagree with them come round to their way of thinking – and love it. They never let anyone box them into a corner. Watch their techniques. Add them to your repertoire.

Levin's book contains all sorts of advice on how to do better in making deals than you thought you could. He has a chapter on 'Fighting Dirty',[104] which is, of course, about fighting those *other* people who play dirty, for which task he advises that 'you had better be able to spot them'.

Now there may be a line between 'getting the best of any deal'[105] and the 12 hard-luck 'dirty tricks' Levin identifies,[106] but judging from the rest of his book, I am not so sure that some negotiators think there is a line, thin or thick, at all. Chapter 5 is entitled: 'Preparation for Battle', and Chapter 6 has sub-headings that include: 'believable threats'; 'brinkmanship'; 'chipping away'; 'don't mention it and it will go away'; 'feigned ire and insanity'; and 'deadline devices'. These sub-headings are not in the chapter about the dirty tricks.

Levin is not the 'worst' example of the vicarious ploys genre by a long way but he typifies the hyper-competitive approach that so easily licenses the reader to start ploy playing on her own account. Much closer to the bone is Sperber's *Fail Safe Business Negotiating*,[107] which contains advice for people who, I can only suppose, are ethically confused if they implement it.

Another author in this genre is William Koch (1988), whose *Negotiator's Factomatic*™ contains almost every negotiating situation, including the nightmares, that you could encounter. His contents pages alone use the word 'opponent' 41 times and, in the text, 'opponent' appears enough times to be at battalion, nay, divisional, strength.

The short-term horizons of ploy makers are their greatest handicap because they require an incessant supply of victims. Through time they run out of negotiating partners because their reputation precedes them. In certain business sectors – used cars, real estate, double glazing and time shares – the streetwise are found out for what they are and this makes them as good as street-dumb.

 ## POWER PLOYS

A survey of well-known ploys would be exhausting to tabulate and probably would not be exhaustive enough to cover all their possible variations. Karass[108] comes close with an 'A to Z' listing of about 200 ploys, while others, Schoenfield,[109] Fuller[110] and Gottchalk[111] make impressive use of their shorter tabulations. My limited selection is confined to the more prominent ploys and their counters. I shall also keep to my three main categorizations of ploy purposes – dominance, shaping and closing – and distribute some well-known ploys between them.

I consider here only those ploys that are predominantly played in the debate phase, and leave until later (see pp. 208, 261) other prominent ploys that are more commonly applied in the proposing and bargaining phases. I think this is a more useful approach than merely listing ploys alphabetically, because it emphasizes how ploys aim at changing your expectations about the outcome, and that they are more dangerous when played against you in the appropriate phase.

Those of a bullish disposition feel the need to achieve *dominance* in the early (debate) phases of negotiation. They dominate to control the situation. Their inexperience of handling tough (for them) decisions, in which there is a real prospect of your saying 'no' rather than 'yes', fires their drive to limit the prospect of any other decision than the one they want, just in case you are awkward enough to say 'no'.

Dominance ploys can begin before the negotiations get under way. In an earlier book[112] I referred to the 'props' of negotiation. These include all those symbols, signs and stage settings that create an image of the power balance between you and them, and are aimed at softening you up to ensure that you make the most movement.

Sales negotiators should be familiar with those buyers' props that are deployed to intimidate you into a bout of the wasting disease of negotiating with yourself. Government departments can exude something similar. For example, in the Foreign and Commonwealth Office, in London, and in the more important embassies, they do it well. These granite solid buildings, steeped in history, their gold-framed portraits of heroes and gallant servants of yesteryear, the antique furniture that was bought when new, the priceless carpets, draperies, decoration (see that hand-painted original cornice!), the silver decanters and their fine crystal glassware, and everything but everything about them, tells you that this is an *important* department of state (perhaps Lord Palmerston sat in the very chair you are kept waiting in?).

In big business they do it on a grand scale too, though the furniture is more likely to be reproduction, not genuine, like the 'Picasso' prints on the wall and the mini-fountain in the corner. Dominance is intimidation and, while the props are passive and less obvious than verbal versions, nevertheless, they have as powerful an effect on your perceptions and they can be even more powerful for being so subtle.

The remedy? A good place to start is by understanding why the props are there. They are not rewards for the faithful servants you have come to see. They are there to make a statement about them and their business to you. You are the visitor and they have all this splendour around them. What do you have, by contrast? If the comparison is unfavourable, and you notice this enough to covet their surroundings, it's a 'gotcha'. You have taken the first step to lowering your sights.

Better to remind yourself that splendid foyers, complete with fountains, atria and super-silent lifts, are the early signs of insolvency (followed closely by company jets and helicopters, yachts and a penchant for the fast life). A short walk down the 'back stairs' at the Foreign Office, with its tatty decorative disorder that suggests it has not been painted since Lord Palmerston was in charge, or at least since the 1950s, works wonders on the otherwise awestruck. Overcome your envy of big business executives and their mini-palaces with a sober sense of pity for them and determine that their splendid props are an incentive for you to up your prices and to insist on cash up front.

Just before you are face-to-face with the other negotiator, as if on cue, the verbal dominance ploys begin. The *preconditions* ploy sets the scene between you. Either you comply with their preconditions or there is no purpose in meeting. Their preconditions include insistence on 'vendor's contracts only', 'assignment of intellectual property rights', 'prohibitions on working for competitors', and such like. These are tricky ones to contest.

Preconditions are often tried in extremely difficult negotiations where the parties have a history, often a bloody one, and each side demonstrates its reluctance to negotiate their differences by attempting to impose preconditions.

To be sure, some preconditions enable the parties to accept negotiation as the solution to their problems. Distinguishing between blatant ploys and trust-building measures is a matter of circumstance and context. 'No negotiations under duress', or 'No negotiations with terrorists', can be ploys to stop negotiations beginning by creating insurmountable barriers between the parties, thus adding another problem to the one that causes them to be under duress. This precondition ploy demands the (unlikely) surrender of the strikers or the terrorists, which is acceptable only if you can break the strike or defeat the terrorists.

As confidence-building measures, some preconditions and the willingness of the parties to accept them create the right conditions for a negotiation to begin. Those preconditions that are part of a propaganda war between the parties are not about confidence building. They are simply part of the wider conflict between them. Negotiating the release of some hostages – the sick, the young, the aged – is a useful precondition to build confidence between the terrorists and the authorities for the more difficult negotiations that must follow. In business, similar preconditions can be a useful test of intentions.

A colleague recently negotiated funding from a venture capitalist, whose advisers questioned the probity of allowing him to cash cheques from the company account. 'You are at great risk', they warned the venture capitalist, if he allowed this. 'You should insist on a joint account, requiring both signatures before he can withdraw any of your money.'

I was asked how he should respond. His inclination, naturally, was to agree to the precondition, but I felt that there was a confidence issue lurking behind the provocative tone of the advisers' statements. I suggested that he not merely agreed to the precondition but that he also tackled head-on the trust implications half-hidden behind it.

If all cheques required two signatures, because the venture capitalist's advisers did not trust my colleague, he should insist that only the fundholder could sign cheques. This would show that he had no reservations about the fundholder who should have none about him.

Closely aligned to the precondition ploy is the assertion that some issues are *non-negotiable*. This widely used ploy prohibits re-negotiation of the fixed terms and conditions insisted on by powerful vendors and buyers. Vendors include in their non-negotiable issues their 'standard terms of sale', often printed in closely set type (I have seen them printed in grey ink making them almost invisible) and they use legal language to intimidate anybody with a notion to challenge them. Whether you accept that they are non-negotiable depends a great deal on how you perceive the relative power balance.

Before mainframe computers became a commodity item, the big vendors, such as IBM, Digital, SUN, and so on, imposed vendor's contracts on their customers. As substitution into smaller forms of computing power became prevalent, the major customers of these suppliers, often large public utilities and government departments, insisted on contracts that included *emptor* clauses, and they successfully insisted on buyer's contracts only. Now the big computer buyers play the non-negotiable ploy on the sellers.

Many will argue that non-negotiable terms and conditions are

merely prudent business and are not negotiating ploys. I have no wish
to challenge that belief here. Every contract is the written expression of
the distrust one party has of the other, and much of this distrust arises,
not from a specific concern with a specific person but from unfortunate
experiences somebody has had with somebody else in the past. Given
the billions of transactions across the globe, it is no wonder that solicitors add more and more clauses to what should be fairly simple contracts to cover this or that unlikely possibility that might occur some
day somewhere.

One of my clients produces contracts to buy training services that
have grown from a single letter of contract five years ago, to a 14-page,
tightly worded formal contract, written with the usual legal jargon.
Indeed, the most recently added clause is one that prohibits suppliers,
like me, from even mentioning to anybody, in or out of the firm, that I
have a contractual duty to confidentiality in all matters relating to the
client! I have no idea what atrocity somebody committed to make it
prudent for inclusion, nor am I sure what it means exactly (and, anyway, I have just broken it!).

Demands that issues are non-negotiable are a well-known dominance ploy. They aim to weaken your negotiating stance by taking
away the possibility of you weakening theirs. Sometimes they are
emotional, sometimes tactical. Such is the emotion that clouds judgement that they will not discuss other issues unless you agree to certain
issues not being discussed. You can accept this in total or you can bend
tactically by suggesting that, for the moment, you will set aside the forbidden issues and see what progress you can make on the others, while
reserving, or at least intimating, that the whole deal depends on all the
issues being aired.

If the demand for items to be non-negotiable covers items of great
importance to you, it could be a deal blocker until you overcome the
obstacle. Context will determine the best way to move on.

The authorities can (and should) make the release of convicted persons non-negotiable when dealing with terrorist incidents. This does
not prevent negotiations continuing on the early release of the
hostages, the supply of food, etc., and communication links to the outside world, or even agreements to publish their (usually unreadable)
manifestos.

The brute fact remains that if they have enough power to enforce the
non-negotiability of anything, they will probably get their way. It
depends how much you value a negotiated outcome, what cards you
have left to play, how much you fear what they threaten if they do not
get their way, and how much time you have to reverse their demands.

Similarly, they could attempt to rig the agenda, either by rigging
the content or by rigging the order of business. Generally, unilateral

determination of either the agenda or the order of business is not compatible with normal negotiating practice. Both parties have a veto on what they negotiate about – if they won't attend your meeting you cannot negotiate for them – and the order in which you go through an agenda.

Not all deals proceed in the same order at the same pace. The other guy can start with:

○ *The krunch*[113] 'Your competitor's offer is much better.' (Why, then, is he still talking to you?)
○ *A phoney deadline* 'We must decide by 3 pm, otherwise it's a no deal.' (Who set this deadline and why?)
○ *The Mother Hubbard*[114] 'I would love to do business with you but my budget is $10,000 less than your best price.' (Is the cupboard really as bare as they imply?)

The early (too early?) shaping ploy warns you of their intentions. The most fatuous one of all is the 'final offer' ploy in the opening exchange, before much has been said by either party. 'That's my final offer' is so crude it is a wonder anybody takes it seriously. How can your opening position be a final offer, unless you have the absolute power to enforce it? And if you have that kind of power, why are you bothering to negotiate? If you haven't the power, why should they take you seriously, except perhaps out of embarrassment for your position in the hole you have dug for yourself?

Publishers (excepting Mr Gower!) often try the intimidating *fait accompli* ploy of sending a signed contract to an author, with an implication that it is in their best interests to sign and return it without resorting to the 'messy' business of challenging any of its clauses, because delays and troublesome queries might induce the publishers to quit the deal and withdraw their 'generous' offer to publish your work. Many an author has meekly signed a publisher's contract so as not to 'antagonize' him with querulous detail. I recently negotiated a fiction author's contract and I must say her sheer nervousness at the possible consequences of my stances worried me, to the point that I spent more time bolstering her morale than I did in facing down her publisher's first offer (they published her novel six months later).

The most prolific scope for manipulative ploys occurs in the shaping phases of negotiation. Manipulators begin shaping the deal throughout the debate and they even try to close (*fait accompli*) in their opening sentences.

Shaping ploys shape deals in their favour. Every deal can be cut several ways and the manipulator aims to pick up concessions here and there, often without offering much, if anything, in return.

Probably the most famous shaping (and any other) ploy is that of *tough guy/soft guy*. Almost everybody sound in body and mind knows of it, so I wonder why it still works? I know of no book on negotiation 'tactics' that does not mention it. Somebody asked me, for example, only the other week, if I thought it was a good 'tactic'. Naturally, I replied 'that it all depends'.

The 'B-movie' story line for tough cop/soft cop is a cliché. An easily irascible cop interrogates the patsy. The cop shouts a lot, physically intimidates, perhaps slaps the patsy around a little, threatens dastardly outcomes, and leaves him physically cowering and whimpering.

In comes a nicer cop. He oozes humanitarian sociability. Off go the lights in the eyes, he releases the cuffs, and produces cup of coffee and some cigarettes. The patsy's gratitude to be re-united with the human race is such that he co-operates with him, as long as he can avoid dealing with his partner. In a really convincing performance, he helps the patsy fill in an official complaint form, while offering his private view that it might just prejudice the judge against him. If his hints are ignored, he shreds it when he ends his shift.

In negotiation, you meet the players of this ploy in many guises. They can appear as two people, ostensibly independent of each other but in reality working as a team. This helps you to identify the game they are playing.

Alternatively, they can be a single person, using the device that while they are amenable to your position they have a distant committee or an unsympathetic boss to answer to and unless you help them by making concessions, they will be unable to help you. If you are convinced by this plausible line, you go out of your way, even beyond your budget mandate, to 'fix' the deal with them, and you wish them luck when they negotiate for you with the, probably fictional, superiors they created to play the tough/soft guy role against you.

An obvious counter is to create your own tough/soft guy scenario with you playing the role of the softer guy. 'I understand your position', you could exclaim, 'and if it was up to me, I would endorse it immediately but I still have to convince my boss who is, I admit, living in the past and still thinks the world owes our company a living. To effect the decision in your favour — and believe me, I want your project to succeed, if only to show some of the out-of-touch people on my board that they are dinosaurs living in the past — I will need your help to cut off dissent on one or two clauses. If you can help, just a little bit, I believe I can outwit these people. Now what can you do for me so I can do my best for you?' A blocked-off ploy is a dead ploy. Now you both have 'tough guys' on your sides.

I tackle the tough/soft guy ploy with humour and perhaps you will also find this successful. I tell them: 'That is the best example of the tough guy/soft guy ploy I have seen in twenty years. Now let me write it down for illustrative use in my next seminar.' This gets the message across and it seldom provokes more than an embarrassed half-smile.

As with all ploys in negotiation, what you think is a ploy isn't on occasion. Admittedly this is a rare occurence, but it is just possible that she does have a tough guy in the wings and he is giving her a hard time over the deal with you. There is no sure way of finding out whether it is a very good play of the ploy or whether it's just the plain truth. The least you should do is block it with your own tough guy pitch, but be careful of overdoing the humorous counter if you suspect she is being truthful. Nothing in this situation, however, implies that you must make a unilateral move to soften her tough colleague with concessions. If you offer only to move conditionally – as you always must – you protect yourself from falling for the phoney tough guy/soft guy ploy and from the, albeit rarer, genuine plays of its truthful cousin.

 VERBAL PLOYS

Not all ploys are manoeuvres in the sense discussed so far. People also manipulate you by the way they argue their case. If you buy what they say, you will buy what they sell. But what they sell could be as phoney as the argument they use to sell it.

You must be careful before accepting – or rejecting – arguments used to support a case. Some coverage of the common verbal ploys used in argument is part of any serious negotiation workshop. Some simple tips to spot phoney lines of argument in others might also stop you using fallacious arguments yourself and thus force you to prepare more carefully for the debate.

Michael Gilbert's little 1980 classic, *How to Win an Argument*, [115] lit up the arid field of academic logic and created a popular sub-genre in its own right. Without doing justice to Gilbert's work, I shall cover similar ground here.

How someone argues depends upon the purposes they expect the argument to serve. Gilbert categorizes arguments into two forms: creative and attached.[116] Gilbert describes *creative argument* as:

> when the arguers are willing to explore a position in order to determine its value, when you and your partner are willing to alter or reconsider a position if strong arguments are brought against it.

Attached argument is the opposite:

> You or your partner have a strong commitment to a position, and

an emotional or psychological stake in seeing one conclusion triumph.[117]

While accepting Gilbert's definitions, I prefer to call his two categories *open* and *closed*, because training has most impact on behaviour if it uses foghorn messages. Open argument suggests it is open to contradiction, amendment, other views and perspectives, and nuances of meaning. Closed argument is shut. There is no room for any other view or interpretation than what the closed arguer has brought to the debate. Closed minds are congenial with closed arguments. You should note that while open arguments are rarer than closed arguments, most people's arguments, open or closed, are simply false.

If two negotiators strongly commit to their mutually exclusive outcomes, their closed debate is fraught, to put it mildly. They are 'unwilling or unable to change their minds, they tend to become stubborn and unco-operative. They have no genuine desire to understand and deal with the opposing arguments. All that matters to them is holding on to their beliefs.'[118] If you cannot stand having your case or beliefs challenged, even gently, you are over-committed to your (closed) positions.

Faced with a negotiator over-committed to their views, you limit your choice if you insist on challenging their beliefs head-on. The more successfully (in your eyes) you expose the contradictions in their beliefs – and all belief systems have contradictions, some fatal – the less likely they are to agree with you, or even beg to differ. You can save yourself much heartache and grief by avoiding, where possible, disputes with over-committed people who rely on closed arguments.

Before joining one of those informal debates on controversial subjects that sometimes surface at social occasions, like dinner parties, I ask the initiator if she will change her mind if I put forward a strong enough case? I tell them – and mean it – that I will certainly change my mind if their case is strong enough against mine. If they say 'no', I drop out of the debate, leaving those who join in to suffer the inevitable wrath of a clash with the committed. This does not stop me identifying, for practice, the various fallacious arguments that are deployed by the participants. If, however, they say 'yes', I join in, though somebody saying 'yes' is so rare that I have noticeably reduced my post-social stress levels!

Negotiators dealing with fractious issues, such as a strike, a terrorist incident, highly charged and emotional conflicts (Northern Ireland, Palestine, South Africa, or Bosnia), have a difficult task in trying to shift the parties from a closed to an open debate. It usually takes a cataclysmic event, perhaps brokered by a third party, to bring the combatants to their senses – an atrocity too far, or a sudden shift in the balance of power. Otherwise, the weary and, often, bloody stand-off continues.

Negotiators do not have too many opportunities to benefit from the services of third parties who might conveniently spring to their assistance. There are far too many arguments going on for the world's supply of mediators to have time enough to intervene. Hence, most of us must rely on our own devices when arguing in a negotiation. What we need, therefore, are simple guidelines to follow, when caught up in an argument, to test the merits or falsity of what they are telling us.

The general principle, applicable in most cases, is that it is important to understand the nature of the other person's argument. This puts a premium on listening and on understanding what is said. Open arguments need the same tests for falsity as closed ones. Unless you understand what the negotiator claims is true, and the reasons behind their claim, you will not know whether their argument has any merit at all.

You have to be careful here, because the instinctive reaction on hearing a statement with which you profoundly disagree, is to dismiss it outright. Statements like: 'I don't agree'; 'Rubbish'; 'Stuff and nonsense'; 'You must be joking', and so on, have a minimal impact on their willingness to reconsider their position, and, worse, identify your own behaviour as no different from what they could expect from a closed arguer. Nobody, I speculate, has ever heard someone respond, except sarcastically, to dismissive statements of their stated case with: 'Oh, I see. So you think I am talking nonsense. Well, I had better change my position immediately!' Normally, they dig deeper into their trenches.

The best response to somebody stating a case or making a claim with which you disagree is to ask them questions such as: 'Where did you get that data?' or 'What data supports your contention?' Sometimes it is sufficient to ask them why they believe or support their position.

Behind every case there is a reason, though not all reasons have as much merit in support of a claim as their sponsors assume:

O   'We should advertise in this publication.'
O   'Why?'
O   'It's in colour.'
O   'What is its audited circulation?'
O   'Not sure, but it's expensive looking.'
O   'How many of our customers read it?'
O   'Not sure, but we'll look prestigious.'

By inviting the negotiators to explain their reasons, rather than attack them, for supporting their assertions, they are more likely to expose the weaknesses, and often the irrelevancies, of their reasons, not just to you but, as often, though not so immediately obvious, to themselves.

Slowly realizing the weakness of their reasoning drains away their confidence. Conversely, your recognition that they have strong reasons backing their statements has the same draining effect on your confidence.

You are still better off in debate using questions to uncover their reasoning, because by questioning their reasons in a way that plants doubts in their minds about their own case, without humiliating them with public counter-arguments, you create the best possible context for them surreptitiously to alter their stance. The realization that their case is not as strong as they thought it was can be the prelude to their accepting that they will get less than they originally expected – in short, the closed arguer shifts to a more open negotiating stance by moderating their original position.

Once you identify the foundations of common argument ploys you can act appropriately if negotiators resort to them. This is not necessarily an excuse to become argumentative, nor an invitation for you to tackle every fallacious argument ploy that comes across the table. Recognizing an argument ploy neutralizes it as effectively as identifying a power ploy. Spotting argument ploys protects you against misperceptions of the merits of their case and, in conjunction with neutralizing their power ploys, makes a decisive difference in support of your own negotiating stance.

Years ago, a shop steward usually recited a little litany whenever he was representing anybody at a disciplinary hearing: 'Broken noses alter faces, circumstances alter cases.' His line of argument was clearly that whatever violation management has accused his member of, he was going to argue that the circumstances were different from other violations of the rules. The shop steward argued that though the cases were similar there were compelling reasons for treating them differently. Sometimes he was convincing, and sometimes he was not. Managers who questioned his reasoning – in detail – often did better than those who directly challenged the first plausible reason he gave them.

By 'better' I don't mean that the managers' disciplinary conviction rates were higher. I mean that by narrowing the grounds of an appeal to the specific, and not vague, variations in circumstances, they prevented a too easy slippage in standards of behaviour. If Jake got off for a relatively flippant reason, it would be more difficult to maintain discipline in a similar case with Quentin. It would also undermine support among employees and managers for discipline generally (let alone prevent additional unhappiness to those treated less leniently in the past).

The steward had an alternative and more difficult line of argument if an appeal to a dissimilarity in circumstances failed or looked too weak to press before he started. He would argue that they should delete the specific rule. He seldom did this because company rules were fairly robust, though those that had no merits at all were fair game to this type of challenge. To argue for a fundamental change in a rule, implies that there is a principle at stake. Asking him for a statement of the principle he thought was at stake in his proposal for a change in a rule was an appropriate response in debate.

People frequently argue this way. They either extract a statement of the principle from the proposer, or they provide their own version of the principle they allege is behind the proposed changes. For example, companies producing consumable goods insist on the right to random searches of employees' bags and cars leaving the premises. In government buildings this protects national security; in alcohol plants it ensures payment of excise duties. It can be a 'hot' potato in some plants. They search Justin from the stores department and find a sealed packet of company produced gas lighters. He is dismissed. They search Samantha, the senior manager in IT, and find 20 unused floppy diskettes. She escapes with a warning. The principle states that all theft from the company is a dismissable offence. In practice, the application of principles varies.

Likewise, when somebody argues for something to happen, one argument ploy is to convert it into an extreme principle and argue for or against the event happening (argument ploys can work both ways!). 'Nobody should be charged for health treatment', is a principle, therefore, 'private health care is immoral'. The latter assertion is an argument. Do the merits of the argument arise from the stated principle?

Suppose somebody needing urgent surgery is treated at a private hospital and the taxpayer pays the invoice. Is that a breach of the principle that nobody should be charged for health treatment? I don't think so, but I have had many a (lively!) argument with people who insist that it is. For some arguers, the principle that 'nobody should be charged for health treatment' is sacred and, by extending the principle to support the argument that 'private health care is immoral', they protect themselves from questions and examples showing that their argument did not (and could not) follow from their principle. Mind you, this does not necessarily invalidate their opinion of private health care; it merely separates their opinion from their principle.

Similarly, it has never followed that because that state of Israel has an inalienable right to exist (a principle) that, therefore, its governments are immune to criticism for specific actions or that, necessarily, any criticism of them is anti-semitism (an opinion).

In similar vein, can you see the argument ploys in the following?:

O   *'We must introduce minimum wage laws because we are the only country in the European Union not to have them'*   If this was a safe argument, how safe is its reverse in the early nineteenth century: 'Britain should not outlaw slavery because no other country in the world has done so?'

○   *'We cannot pay authors for loans of their books in public libraries because that is a tax on knowledge'*   If true, how do we justify paying wages to public librarians?

○   *'We must not allow women pilots to fly combat missions because, if captured, they might be raped'*   If true, why do we allow male pilots to risk homosexual rape?

○   *'Your opinion is wrong because the majority of people disagree with you'*   'Your opinion is wrong' is another opinion, and how many people agree or disagree is not a proof of rightness or wrongness – at best it is a fact; at worst it is another opinion.

○   *'We must spend whatever it takes to eradicate Aids because famous people are dying of it'*   TB affects millions of poor people and eradicating that disease is a more efficient use of scarce health resources.

○   *'You should buy this product because famous celebrities endorse it'*   Do they buy it and use it, or are they just paid to 'endorse' it?

○   *'You must make this change because other employers have done so'*   What are the merits of the change? How about: 'you must smoke because your friends do'?

○   *'You must vote for Bloggs because it is time for a change'*   It may be 'time for a change', but why Bloggs? He might be a change for the worse. Why not vote for Fred Nerk instead?

The statements come from arguments I have observed, some of them at surprisingly high-level conferences. I am sure you can quote others from your own experiences. To help you recognize phoney arguments in your negotiations, following Gilbert I shall identify ten common fallacies of argument, which, when used in a negotiation, are straight forward ploys (Figure 3.2).

I shall discuss briefly how these fallacious verbal ploys work by giving some examples:

PROMINENCE

Whatever is most prominent is more influential in the case for a decision. In annual appraisals, for example, the most recent failure sometimes counts more than a year's good, even excellent, performance. The extremist gets more attention than the moderate. The 'squeaky wheel, gets the grease' syndrome.

O   Prominence

O   Popularity

O   Expertise

O   Changing the subject

O   Defective personalities

O   Provenance

O   Straw man

O   Slippery slope

O   Selective evidence

O   Phoney dilemma

Figure 3.2 The ten most common fallacious argument ploys in negotiation

POPULARITY

The popularity of an idea often, and fallaciously, determines its merits. The fads and fashions of management gurus can cost millions before they run into the sand, and the latest 'popular' ideas are not necessarily good ideas. Beware of arguments involving statements like 'everybody knows', 'everybody agrees', 'nobody doubts' and such like. If you don't know or agree and you have doubts, then none of these arguments ploys has merit.

EXPERTISE

Because she is an expert in something, it is implied that this makes her an expert in everything. It is closely aligned to the authority ploy. Her views carry authority by dint of something she did elsewhere or long ago. Retired air marshals, admirals and generals, are not necessarily correct in their arguments for or against current military decisions solely because of their past and loosely related experience. Do they have relevant expertise or experience of the current decision?

CHANGING THE SUBJECT

When a proposer meets resistance on a specific proposal they change the subject to an 'unchallengeable' assertion or an appeal to a higher set of values. For example, 'we should buy Henderson's company to acquire his outlets' is a specific proposal. Detailed resistance to it may well produce a change in subject: 'Look, are you opposed to growth by acquisition? Do you want us to stand still and stagnate? Whose side are you really on?'

If the debate moves to the new issues he raises, you may end up endorsing the specific acquisition of which you are sceptical. By keeping focused on the original subject, you are more likely to prevail.

Recently, while negotiating a change in a pay and benefits system and meeting strong resistance from the employees' representatives, they attempted to change the subject by raising the issue that their members were 'comfortable with and used to the current system'. Very true, but this had nothing to do with the fact that the current system did not, and could not, deliver the pay and benefits packages that were necessary to accompany significant changes in the way the business operated.

DEFECTIVE PERSONALITIES

Here, the merits of the issues are not debated because the arguer shifts to the alleged (or real) defects of the people proposing them. This verbal ploy is much used by politicians and by their ilk in corporate life. By discrediting the proposer, they bury the proposal with opprobrium. It often works – that's why it is so common. It is highly dangerous as a deciding factor in a negotiation decision:

○ 'We can't possibly agree to talks with the Smythie's Group; their financial director was recently charged with indecent assault!'
○ 'How can we negotiate with terrorists?'
○ 'Your demand for us to share confidential information with you is what we would expect from a self-confessed right-winger.'
○ 'I am not surprised that you are demanding my resignation, given your weird sexual tastes.'
○ He would say that, wouldn't he?' (This is popularly known as the 'Mandy Rice Davies' ploy. She used it to deflect comment on statements made about her by a man implicated in a 1960s sex and politics 'scandal'.)

PROVENANCE

A ploy that attacks the origins of the idea and not its content or merits. In many ways, this is similar to the defective personality ploy, except that it broadens out the area for attack from the person to ideas, politics, religions, associations, even geographical locations.

- ◯ 'This is not acceptable, gentlemen, especially as it is another brainwave from the Brussels bureaucrats.'
- ◯ 'Trust the French to come up with that one!'
- ◯ 'I'm not interested in your plans to import commercialism from the market place into considerations of health care.'
- ◯ 'Your pension proposals smack of creeping socialism to me.'

STRAW MAN

To make a case against something, the straw man ploy alleges views that, in reality, are highly distorted from the truth or the merits of the issue.

A short extract from a debate on changing a company's policy to promotion regardless of sexual orientation illustrates a 'straw man' argument:

> 'Gays, they're all nuts. Do you know what their latest proposal is? Well, they are demanding separate cemeteries for gays, because – wait for it – lesbian grief is different!'
> 'My God. They *are* mad'.

It does not follow that the gays working for the company are as silly, nor do the straw man's alleged views have anything to do with the company's promotion policy. But the straw man ploy, though unfair because it is unrepresentative, can be devastating against a case, which is why it is used.

SLIPPERY SLOPE

This ploy is used to deflect attention from the merits of the initial proposal by looking at its alleged negative consequences. She wants to stop a company sick pay scheme being accepted by your managerial colleagues? Watch for her slippery slope ploy: 'Once they get paid for being off sick they will gradually increase their sick days until they are more off work than on.'

He wants your support for a 'no exceptions' debtor policy: 'If we don't chase every single debt, no matter how small or what it costs to collect it, the debtor's book will just keep growing and when word gets out that we're too soft to collect what we are owed, we'll be swamped with bad debts.'

She wants to sack a cleaner who ate an after-dinner mint left on the board room table she was clearing: 'Look, I know it sounds draconian but if we allow cleaners to eat left-over mints, before long they will be tucking into four-course dinners'.

All these reasons may or may not be true. Your response should be to ask for evidence that a real slippery slope exists and that appropriate counter-measures are impractical. Above all, keep a sense of proportion.

SELECTIVE EVIDENCE

By selecting evidence that supports a case and ignoring evidence that doesn't, the ploy misdirects the negotiation to a fallacious remedy. Sometimes this is easy to spot because the contrary evidence is known. At other times the evidence needs to be studied carefully to find out what is selective about it.

For example, managers of a research fund were debating whether to support a research project to study the effects of violence on television and the propensity to engage in violence by viewers. Supporters of the project drew attention to the researcher's excellent academic qualifications (an expertise ploy?) and to a recent case in which a serial killer had in his apartment a large collection of videos from particularly violent television programmes (a prominence ploy?). Opponents questioned the researcher's impartiality because of her known political affiliations (a provenance ploy?) and her lack of research in this area (a non-expertise ploy?).

The committee of 'experts' ran through more fallacious methods of debate per minute than a group of ordinary citizens debating religion, politics or football in a public bar. The professional experts didn't ask questions about the researcher's proposed methodology for interviews with prisoners convicted of violent crimes, though this was the only relevant criteria for their decision. If a significant number of her interviewees admitted to watching violent films on television this would still not show a link between TV violence and their own violent behaviour. Can you see why it is a selective evidence ploy?

Everybody who watches TV, including the small minority prone to violence, sees violent films. The researcher would have to demonstrate why violent films on television do not prompt most viewers into violent acts. Otherwise she has only selective evidence for the association she seeks to establish. This line of questioning might have saved the budget committee from hours of bad tempered debate on a hot and sticky afternoon.

PHONEY DILEMMA

One of the most widespread argument ploys in play. The speaker presents only two choices, and excludes everything else, to force you to choose the one she favours. The fanatic shouts: you are either for us or against us! If the fanatic is armed and dangerous, you might think it prudent to deny being against him. But you don't have to be a fanatic to use this ploy. Academics use it too.

Two Harvard academics, Roger Fisher and Bill Ury,[119] use a version of the phoney dilemma ploy to make the case for their negotiating method. They showed that the defects of 'soft' and 'hard' bargaining were so overwhelming that a third way just had to be found. Not surprisingly, the third way – principled negotiation – is their way. Anybody denying that their way was the only way, is thrown back on relying on one or other of the discredited soft or hard negotiation styles that they had combined as a phoney dilemma. Not much of a choice is it? Of course, the truth of their claim depends on their ability to exclude alternatives to their phoney dilemma. If there is no dilemma then their proposed negotiating methodology would have to stand on its own merits.

These ten common ploys are not the only verbal ploys used in the debate phases. Verbal ploys are as varied as they are numerous. Armed against these top ten, however, gives you a sufficient start to cope with others.

 DESTRUCTIVE ARGUMENT BEHAVIOUR

I called the opening of a face-to-face negotiation the argument phase because this is what I observed people doing, but before long it was clear that there were two divergent forms of argument, one broadly destructive and the other broadly constructive, so I divided the two types of behaviours to reflect this difference and renamed the phase as debate.

In the Negotek® TimeTrack™ (Figure 3.3) I show the two forms of behaviour as *destructive argument* and *constructive debate*. Time is measured in minutes down the left-hand column and the other columns are labelled accordingly, from destructive threats to constructive signalling.

TimeTrack™ enables observers to track the behaviours throughout a negotiating session.[120] The device allows the observer to tick a column when she observes a negotiator behaving in a specific manner at that precise minute in the discourse. The observer ticks the left-hand side of each column to denote the behaviours from the negotiating team on her left and the right-hand to denote the negotiators on her right.

TRAINING

Negotiating Behaviours

	Destructive Argument						Constructive Debate				Negotiation	
	Threat	Blame Attack	Block	Disagree	Irritate Interrupt	STATEMENTS	Assure	Question	Summarise	Signal	Propose	Bargain
T												
I												
M												
E												

Figure 3.3 The Negotek® TimeTrack™

I often use an OHP slide version of TimeTrack™ as an observation tool because it shows the participants what they and their colleagues were doing, according, at least, to the observer. You can use TimeTrack™ in conjunction with a video recording of the negotiation or on its own. You can also use it when consulting a client team about their behaviour in front of their customers or suppliers – though be careful: I demonstrated TimeTrack™ for a client once and inadvertently revealed the boss to his staff to be the most persistent user of destructive argument behaviours!

Irritate	Irritating remarks usually start off bouts of argumentative behaviour. Sexist, ageist, racial and such like remarks can be extremely provocative. Even ascribing to yourself high moral tones and a monopoly of 'fairness' and 'generosity' can start an argument.
Interrupt	Interruptive behaviour can also be intensely irritating, especially when it becomes competitive and you interrupt each other's interruptions.
Disagreeing	Telling people they are wrong or that you disagree with them is usually unhelpful. They switch off listening and compose their rebuttal. Before long neither of you is listening to the other.
Blocking	Blocking is like slamming a door when somebody is about to step through it. It is a rejection behaviour, shutting down possibilities of increasing your understanding of their wants and of their revealing themselves.
Blame Attack	If you blame somebody they justify themselves; if you attack them they defend themselves. There is no surer way to pick a fight. Most attacks and blaming behaviours are taken personally and your relationship and your ability to influence the other negotiator can be irretrievably damaged.
Threats	Making threats seldom achieves what is intended. You threaten, often out of frustration but it does not make them comply with your demands. They usually push the threatened into digging in and they prolong the dispute.

Figure 3.4 Destructive argument behaviours

Most negotiators, when made aware of their behaviours, see the positive and negative sides of argument and debate. Breaking old habits is not easy unless you constantly avoid destructive argument (Figure 3.4) and practise constructive debate.

Negotiators verbally transmit most information. Some of it is intentional, some of it unintentional. Rojot[121] suggests four categories of information exchange (after Gottchalk[122]):

○   information the negotiator wants to give;
○   information she can expect to get;
○   information she does not want to disclose;
○   information she would be surprised to receive.

These categories usefully remind you that while the delivery of statements should be neutral in tone, the information that we give in them is not neutral at all. What we disclose informs the other negotiator of our wants, intentions and commitment. Slips of the tongue can change a negotiator's perceptions of what is possible in a dramatic way. When one of my colleagues tried to close a management–union negotiation with the words: 'And that gentlemen, is the company's final offer ... [pause] ... for the moment!' he undid much of his earlier work convincing them that the company was at its exit point. It cost his company another 1 per cent over his authorized budget, and much ribald comment from his colleagues.

Opening statements are usually made of the strongest case for whatever the negotiator seeks. Queuing up to shoot them down is not the most effective response that you can make. All statements provide you with information. By listening carefully and checking that you understand what they want – and why they want it – you can shrink uncertainties and you can confirm or modify your assumptions. You need to be alert to take into account the surprises in the issues they include, or exclude, in their agenda, and to assess the strength of their determination, or lack of it, to achieve their entry positions.

Information can alter your perceptions quite dramatically.

○   You expect a large movement in their prices, but they limit price movements by disclosing the puny profit margins they make in that range of goods.
○   You expect a high price for the land for redevelopment. Their land engineering surveys, however, show the need for additional piped water supplies to the site, but the local council refuses to prioritize a water project on the site for at least ten years. Hence, you cannot maintain your aspirations on price.

What you disclose – when you disclose it – has a tactical role. This, of course, implies that their withholding of information could be as important for your perceptions as the information you reveal to them is important for their perceptions. There is nothing in negotiation that requires them to make a full disclosure of everything you regard as pertinent for your proper judgement of the pros and cons of a decision.

EFFECTIVE BEHAVIOUR

The 1970s were a particularly negative and bizarre period in labour relations history. The UK then had one of the worst strike records in the world, indicating that most UK management reacted to the credible threats of strikes by surrendering control of their labour costs to their employees. One researcher, Neil Rackham, expressed his mood at the time:

> Working in the industrial relations field ... had convinced me that nothing short of a major cultural change could significantly improve the negotiating climate in Britain.[123]

Rackham and his associates (The Huthwaite Research Group) sought new training methods to develop negotiating skills. They recoiled from the emotive storms of the opening sessions of negotiation, because 'people stopped behaving in a civilised way and try to cheat and deceive each other without scruple'.[124]

Rackham set out to develop new training methods that worked, because of the 'obnoxious practices' in industrial relations training, which were only moderated by the fact that many of the courses he studied were so ineffective and inept that they were 'comparatively harmless'. He asserted that:

> At the company level British industrial relations is based on the interactive practices of point scoring, overstating, emotionality, withholding information and so forth. Because these malpractices are perceived to be necessary managers demand training in them. Consequently many simulations, negotiating games, role-playing exercises and case studies centre around all those grass-roots malpractices which make industrial relations in Britain an international joke.[125]

Of the 45 negotiation role plays that Rackham observed, he concluded that 40 of them plunged 'participants into the mire of malpractice'. Only in selling skills courses did he find that 'the positive skills of persuasion were all important and the negative behaviours of invective and attack were avoided at all costs'.[126] It was no wonder, Rackham suggested, that most 'people confirm their suspicion that industrial relations is about the process by which an irresistible force plays poker with an immovable object'. Rackham wanted a new approach.

One trainer's simulation I read in the 1970s introduced 'Frank's' role as the production manager of a unionized shop thus:

> Frank is 46, a heavy drinker, and his marriage is in trouble, all of which problems were exacerbated by the killing of his 19 year old son by the IRA, while serving with the Army in Belfast. As Frank entered the plant he saw Seamus O'Rourke, the chief shop steward, smoking near a no-smoking sign ...

So what was already a difficult case to negotiate, became infinitely worse by bringing in the politics of Ireland. More's the pity, if the person role-playing 'Frank' was 22, a graduate, and female. In 1971 I dropped *role* playing and switched to *case* playing where the participants play the case without any reference to phoney personalities they did not have, or to moods they were not in. They study the briefs and negotiate them as professionals, playing themselves. A sample of Negotiate's simulations are in *The Negotiate Trainer's Manual*.[127]

Rackham's solution came from research into what negotiators did in practice. He used behaviour models from the social sciences to analyse what happened and produced 'controlled pace negotiation' or 'slow motion negotiation' as a training tool.[128] It is quite startling at first because the idea of negotiating over a cup of tea (or a room change) is different from what we normally conceive as a negotiable issue. But this difference is productive because it diverts training away from replicating the 'malpractices' of negotiation.

You may wish to try out a controlled pace negotiation with two small groups of your colleagues by following the simple rules outlined below. This should take in all about two to three hours. You divide 12 players into two groups and tell them that at tea time there will only be seven cups of tea available and that they have until then to negotiate to 'obtain an equitable volume of tea or compensation in lieu of tea'. They cannot meet face-to-face for their negotiations and must only communicate through yourself.

You start with one syndicate and invite them to assume that they are face-to-face with the other syndicate. First, they must decide individually what is the 'first thing you would say if you were now opening negotiations with them on behalf of this group'.[129] You write the six contributions on a flip chart. In the example Rackham reported these were:

○ 'I would like to hear your views about what a cup of tea is worth.'
○ What compensation would you consider adequate for a cup of tea?
○ We need to settle this question of compensation.
○ How much is tea worth to you?
○ I suggest we begin by establishing the value of a cup of tea and then negotiate from there.

○   What compensation would you give us for each cup of tea and what compensation would you expect from us?

The group then select one of the contributions for the tutor to convey to the other group. This group chose to send: 'What compensation would you consider adequate for a cup of tea?' Before leaving, you give them a list of definitions of behaviour categories and ask them to fit each person's contribution into one or more of the categories. The categories are shown in Figure 3.5.[130] The group assign their six statements to these categories. In Rackham's case these were: seeking information; seeking information; giving information; seeking information; proposing and seeking information. In sending their chosen message they decided they were 'seeking information'.

Behaviour category	Defined as
Proposing	Putting forward a new concept or course of action.
Building	Extending or developing a proposal which has been made by another person.
Supporting	Involving a conscious and direct declaration of support or agreement with another person or his concepts.
Disagreeing	Involving a conscious and direct declaration of difference of opinion, or criticism of another person's concepts.
Defending/ Attacking	Attacking another person or defensively strengthening an individual's own position, usually involving overt value judgements with emotional overtones.
Blocking	Placing a difficulty or block in the path of a proposal and without offering a reasonable statement of disagreement. These behaviours tend to be bald: 'it won't work', 'we couldn't possibly accept that'.
Open	Exposing the individual who makes it to risk ridicule or loss of status. It is the opposite of defending/attacking and includes admission of mistakes or inadequacies providing these are made in a non-defensive manner.
Testing under- standing	Seeking to establish whether an earlier contribution has been understood.
Summary	Summarizing, or otherwise restating in a compact form the content of previous discussions or considerations.

| **Seeking information** | Seeking facts, opinions, clarifications from another person or persons. |
| **Giving information** | Offering facts, opinions, clarifications to other people. |

Figure 3.5 Definitions of behaviour categories

Meanwhile, you inform the other syndicate of the first team's message and tell them that they are 'to assume that you were face-to-face with the other group' and 'without consulting each other' invite them to 'write down exactly what they would say in response' as if 'you were now opening negotiations with them.'

As before, each member of the group writes down their response, and then they discuss all six responses, selecting one as the collective response via you, for the other syndicate. Before leaving, you give out the list of the definitions of the behavioural categories and ask them to categorize all six statements and the opening statement they sent to the other team.

You continue this process until either they come to an agreement on the distribution of the seven cups of tea and the amount of compensation for those who do without tea, or until they exhaust the time allocated for the exercise.

In the three hours Rackham allocated for this exercise, he reported that he expected to process 15 to 20 exchanges of messages, with each participant analysing up to 133 behaviours from herself and her five team members, including the 10 or so exchanges that the other team sent for their consideration.[131] By any measure this constitutes extensive practice in identifying negotiating behaviours. Group discussions and private contemplation supports each person's identification of the behaviour categories.

From a training point of view, Rackham suggested that stand up lecturing for three hours on behaviour types would not accomplish anything like as effectively the learning benefits of participating in a controlled pace negotiation.

Rackham observed that teams seldom categorize the messages they receive in the same way as the team that sent the message. For example, one team sent the message: 'Despite your selfish claim to the tea, we would still like the answer to our question', which they categorized as 'seeking information', while the receiving team categorized it as 'defending/attacking'. They focused on the word 'selfish'.[132]

Practitioners sometimes forget that the message they send is not necessarily the message their partners receive, and rediscovering this truth in the exercise is an excellent way to remember it. Misunderstood messages and the confusion of language are a formidable barrier to progress in a negotiation, and Rackham's methods demonstrate vividly why negotiators should pay attention to this problem. I recommend you to try this exercise.

Neil Rackham and John Carlisle[133] did further research on 'effective' and 'average' negotiators. The absence of research into what happens when people negotiate struck them as challenging. One reason for this was lack of opportunity (my own research time at Shell-Haven was extremely unusual in this respect) and another, and more important, reason was the lack of a research methodology. Rackham solved the latter problem using behavioural analysis,[134] and direct observation of real negotiations, to produce an objective and quantified record of how skilled negotiators behave.

The proposition was simple: 'find some successful negotiators and watch them during actual negotiation to find out how they do it' (Rackham and Carlisle, 1978, p.161). Like the first line in the recipe for rabbit stew: 'first catch a rabbit', the challenge is to first find some successful negotiators and then observe how they perform in comparison to average negotiators. Rackham and Carlisle selected negotiators who met three criteria:

1.   They were rated as effective by both sides.
2.   They had a track record of significant success.
3.   They had a low incidence of implementation failures.

They identified a comparator group of negotiators who either failed to meet the success criteria or of whom they knew nothing. If the latter group contained unidentified successful negotiators, this would tend to narrow the observed differences between the two groups, adding credibility to conclusions asserting that the observed differences in behaviour were significant.

This was a different research methodology from that of Karass,[135] who recruited experienced negotiators and measured their performance in an insurance claim simulation. Karass used assessments of their negotiating traits to separate them into skilled and unskilled negotiators.

Rackham and Carlisle wanted to avoid what they described as 'the common trap of laboratory studies – looking only at the short-term consequences of a negotiator's behaviour and therefore favouring those using tricks or deceptions'.

Since 1978, evidence from replicating their methodology across many negotiation interactions has confirmed their broad finding[136] that skilled negotiators show marked differences in their use of the specified behaviour categories compared with average negotiators.

Though all negotiators draw upon all of the behaviour categories, skilled negotiators use certain types of behaviour more frequently and in those relative frequencies resides the key to effective negotiation behaviour (see Figure 3.6).

The 15 behaviour differences that appear critical to differences in performance produced a negotiation training programme that permits the participants to identify these differences, practise applying them and then transfer them into their negotiating role.

While they uncovered some interesting surprises, Rackham and Carlisle confirmed what others had asserted from unstructured observation and assumption. Their unique contribution was to establish the differences quantitatively for the first time and show that they were statistically significant. The hypothesis that follows from their research is that if you train negotiators to replicate the proven identified skills of successful negotiators, then they can replicate their relative successes. In particular, this also means training negotiators to avoid irritating behaviours, diluting their arguments, instantly counter-proposing, attacking and blaming, and labelling their disagreements, while training them to increase their seeking of information (questioning), to test understanding by summarizing, and to be prepared to state their feelings.

Behaviour	Comments	Measured differences	
		Average	Skilled
Irritators	Gratuitously favourable statements about one's own positions or offers ('generous', 'fair', 'reasonable', etc.).	Use per hour 10.8	2.3
Counter-proposals	Immediately counter-proposing, which is perceived as blocking, being unreceptive and disagreeing.	Frequency per hour 3.1	1.7
Defend/ attack spirals	'Can't blame us', 'It's not our fault', 'You screwed up, not us'.	Percentage of comments 6.3	1.9
Argument dilution	Using too many reasons to support a case – weak arguments diluting strong ones.	Average number of reasons given to back their case 3.0	1.8
Behaviour labelling	'Can I ask...?', 'If I may make a suggestion' – permits a formality that keeps debate unemotional.	Percentage of all behaviours preceded by a label 1.2	6.4

Labelling disagree- ment	'I disagree', 'You're wrong' followed by reasons, in contrast to explaining first then labelling.	Percentage of all behaviours preceded by a disagreement label
		1.5 0.4
Testing for under- standing and sum- marizing	Checking if previous statement has been understood and compact restatements of previous debate.	Percentage of all behaviours: 1. Testing under- standing
		4.1 9.7
		2. Summarizing 4.2 7.5
Seeking information	Skilled negotiators seek significantly more information than average negotiators. Information is needed for the debate and for bargaining.	Seeking information as percentage of all behaviours: 9.6 21.3
Stating feelings	'I feel some doubts', 'I'm very worried', 'I'm not sure how to react', rather than expressing opinions, remaining silent.	Giving internal information as percentage of all behaviours: 7.8 12.1

Figure 3.6 Variances in behaviours between skilled and average negotia-tors[137]

THE LANGUAGE OF NEGOTIATION

In negotiation 'language is everything'. What people say, how they say it, who they say it to, what they don't say, and how they react to what others say, affects the course of a negotiation. In 1991 Joan Mulholland, at the University of Queensland, published a major contri-bution to our understanding of language in negotiation.[138] All students of negotiation should absorb Mulholland's work, and most practition-ers would benefit likewise. It is one of those all too rare major contri-butions to negotiation behaviour, already, in my view, destined to become a classic of the genre.

There are, of course, two main activities in a negotiation interaction. One person performs by speaking and the other reacts by listening. Language is the medium through which they communicate. The speaker performs one of several acts and the hearer reacts in various ways.[139] These are detailed, with my own slight modifications, in Figure 3.7.

Speaking acts:

O   articulating a view on the matter under discussion;
O   bringing into discussion topics, opinions, needs, purposes, etc.;
O   adjusting, adapting, altering, qualifying and omitting from these those elements which are unacceptable to the listener;
O   prioritizing the matters represented, ranking them and choosing from among them what can be put together to form an acceptable whole;
O   formulating what will be the finished proposal;
O   formulating the final communicative act, whether it is a plan, contract, verbal agreement or whatever.

Hearing acts:

O   noting what others do as their main acts, for example, proposing, reporting, dismissing or arguing;
O   analysing what criteria are being used by the participants to establish major and minor acts;
O   noting what acts are not performed by others (which may be of significance);
O   learning about the ideas of others;
O   knowing when to provide support or refuse it.

Figure 3.7 Speaking and listening acts

This realistically assumes that negotiation is a sub-variety of conversation, with a narrower range of speech acts available to it because there is some 'degree of disagreement or opposition among its participants which is to be settled' and 'there is a need to produce some action or policy decision'.[140] Negotiation is not just a wandering discourse; it focuses on an outcome, but be clear that the method used to reach an outcome is linguistic and subject to misunderstandings and confusion and the distortions of frail memories.

By *speech acts*, Mulholland means definitive and individual behaviours formatted by speech. It is a linguist's concept but is accessible to non-linguists by taking it at its commonsense meaning. Saying 'good morning' is a speech act separate from a follow-on speech act, such as asking 'what are you doing today?'. One is a greeting, the other an enquiry. Linguists divide speech into separate acts to analyse the speech. You might note here, that Anne Douglas[141] used analysis of speech acts to develop her three phases model and that Morley and Stevenson[142] used comparative speech acts to test her model.

Negotiation imposes certain speech rules and conventions not found in non-focused conversation. Extreme breaches of these speech conventions interfere with the bonding effect of negotiation as a *joint* decision. Mulholland gives many examples of this assertion, far too many to include here in detail. A couple will give a flavour as they conform to common experience.

One obvious example is *interruption*, which offends the convention that allows a speaker to finish what they are saying. I have often asked negotiators to put their hand up if they like being interrupted, and to date, out of the thousands of people I have asked, not one hand has been raised. I have also asked them to indicate if they have never interrupted anybody else. The response is the same – nobody claims they never interrupt other people!

Mostly, we can get away with an element of acceptable interruption but where that tips over into unacceptable behaviour differs from person to person and conversation to conversation, not forgetting the negative impact of constant interruption on those who observe it happening.

Another, less obvious example, is where a person abruptly *terminates* an interaction, such as when they make a remark that demands, or is likely to provoke, a response and then they break off the interaction by leaving the room (perhaps slamming the door) or they cut the phone connection. Negotiation sessions terminated in this way are extremely difficult to handle. What do you do? Shout your response ever louder as they disappear through the door? Send a rude fax? Negotiators normally close meetings formally and safely by preliminary signals to each other: 'Anything else before we close?'; 'Any other competent business?'; 'When's the next meeting?'

Interestingly, Mulholland divides speech acts into *four phases* for negotiation: preparation and initial, central and closing phases (recent contributions to the approach that negotiation is a phased process have come from the most surprising of sources!).

Preparation concerns preparing for the speech acts of negotiation. Once articulated, these speech acts form the experience of the negotiators as to this person's thoughts on these or those events. This is an interesting slant on preparation, which is often thought of as the preparation of the data (issues, positions, etc.,) only. By addressing the preparation of the speech acts – in my terminology, the justifications, counters and responses – Mullolland reinforces the message that we negotiate using language and that this medium requires preparation as much as the data.

Speech acts affect those involved and, therefore, the negotiator should prepare for not just the consequences of the chosen speech acts and how to perform them well, but also prepare for the qualities that are important for the negotiation, such as the: 'equivalence of the participants, seriousness, clarity, viability of subject matter, specificity'. The negotiator, should 'note the kind of speech acts that are appropriate: inform, tell, ask, discuss, advise, accept, etc., and note also the modulations that will be needed: adapt, modify, qualify, reduce, recognise the contribution of, analyse, as well as ignore, dismiss, reject'.[143]

Mulholland points out that speech conventions impose constraints on speech acts in negotiation. She alludes to the convention that if one of the parties is 'speaking too slowly, or too formally, and offering only the polished product or thought' it is an inappropriate form of negotiating behaviour if the sharing of ideas or a bonding relationship is a main concern of the negotiators at that moment.

I have often observed negotiators failing completely to elicit positive responses when they open a negotiation on some fairly complex issue by presenting their own complete solution to the problem. Mulholland explains why this behaviour usually fails: 'because the fact that he is not offering to share the thought processes that created' his complete solution, means that his unilateral announcement is taken to be an attempt to exclude the other person from contributing to what is supposed to be a joint decision process'.[144]

Excluding the other negotiator, through your speech acts, is a real problem. This is seen most starkly in 'Boulwarism' — the tactic employed in the 1950s by Lemel Boulware of General Electric in the US. He made a single non-discussed, and non-discussable, offer to the unions, which created in its wake enormous resentment at the time because it deprived the unions (as was his intention) of a role in wage negotiations.[145] Michael Edwards, at British Leyland in the 1970s, faced similar resistance, and eventually provoked crippling strikes, when he announced repeated non-negotiable unilateral wage awards.

Simply announcing to one's family that you have decided where to go for the holidays, and that you have unilaterally selected the dates and made all the arrangements, would likely cause some resentment, even if the holiday destination you had chosen was a spectacular surprise. It would also cause resentment if your choice enabled you to do what you preferred (golf, football, fishing, quiet reading or drinking) and excluded the rest of the family's enjoyment of sea, sun, discos, shopping and noisily fooling around.

It is necessary when negotiating complex and sensitive issues to allow for the needs of the other negotiator to contribute and to feel that their contribution matters in some way, before announcing complete solutions. Unintentionally, your solution could provoke an avoidable breakdown. This suggests that rushing in with complete solutions before they have expressed their views and concerns, can be counterproductive. I suppose the advice of 'softlee, softlee, catchee monkey' might apply here.

Speaking only in clichés, and nothing else, is boring and is against the convention that you should provide some interest in what you are saying for your hearers. As a former chairman of the UK Social Science

Committee for UNESCO, I listened to many arid speeches punctuated with so many political clichés that it was tiring just to be in the same room.

In selling, there are cliché conventions ('we value your custom', etc.,), as there are in industrial relations ('the offer falls well short of the aspirations of my members'; 'we've taken full cognisance of the management's views and reject them,' etc.,), and in buying ('we are looking for value for money', etc.). Mulholland, however, sees a supporting role for clichés in that a total absence of them creates information overload to the hearer: 'Clichés interspersed with new or complex information make for a more comprehensible speech action',[146] which suggests that there is a positive role for some 'jargon', if it is familiar to both parties. And for well-known sayings too, perhaps?

In Mulholland's *initial phase* (the rapport-building part of our debate phase), speech act conventions are about re-establishing or establishing for the first time, the nature of the relationship between the parties, providing information about the mood, attitude or personalities of the speakers, and the making of 'decisions about the appropriate psychological tactics, speech acts and politeness strategies to be used from that time forward'. [147] She also points out that strangers 'will use the time to become used to other speakers' speech patterns, voice qualities, mindset and personality traits'[148] and characterizes this phase as 'an opportunity for interpretative work'.

The negotiators move from the initial to the *central phase* by signalling ('Let's start'; 'now then, what are we going to do about . . .', etc.) that it is time to begin the main activity of addressing the purpose of the meeting. Which of the parties takes on this role, or concludes it, by speech acts indicates which of them dominates the other, or which, perhaps, has the upper hand in the decision. In management meetings, the most senior person present usually undertakes this role and it would be unusual (a career decision, perhaps?) if the most junior member present usurped the boss's role and called the meeting to business.

Well-known conventions in speech interactions include:

O   turn taking
O   yielding a turn
O   holding a turn
O   claiming a turn.

Negotiating texts and courses do not normally cover this kind of material, yet it is important in Mulholland's view to do so, and I think she is right.

Years ago, I was surreptitiously making notes at an unofficial strikers' meeting in London, when, in the occasionally heated outbreaks of several people trying to talk at once, the chairman, and leader of the strike, used the microphone to call everybody to order, saying: 'Brothers, we can all sing together but we can't talk together'. This brought some order to the discussion, until the next outbreak of speakers failing to take their turn provoked the chairman to repeat his litany.

Holding the floor is a socially important act – one speaker, many listeners, in the context of a meeting; one speaking, the other listening (or more correctly, hearing!) in a meeting of two people. The convention is that all present may hold the floor on an equitable basis, though no one speaker holds the floor for too long, especially if this denies turns to others.

Speakers can use a variety of strategies to signal their willingness to yield a turn to the hearer. A completed sentence could signal a willingness to yield, and the hearer can come in at that point without risk of breaking the 'no interruptions' convention, whereas cutting in during a sentence would break the convention. Other signals include a slowing down in pace, an increase in drawling and a drop in voice pitch, as can certain phrases, such as 'and so on', or 'so, anyway', or other phrases, or bodily signals (e.g., sitting down or slumping back in your chair) peculiar to that speaker.

If the speaker does not wish to yield she can play several strategies, not the least of which is announcing from the start that she has a lot to say, perhaps by enumerating the number of points she intends to make, turning away a possible interjection ('Just a moment, I've not finished'), speaking at a fast rate, without pauses, almost without stopping for breath, or by pointedly ignoring somebody trying to get in with a turn (in the House of Commons, this is called 'trying to catch the Speaker's eye').

Conventions about claiming a turn include intervening at a natural termination point (at the end of a grammatical sentence), or less acceptable, whenever the speaker pauses. It is not uncommon to observe a convention when intervening to claim a turn, for the intervenor to start with a few words and pause to see if the speaker gives way and then continue if he does.

I recently watched a member of a management team try to claim a turn, using this stutter-pause technique six or seven times. Her colleague refused to give way because, when she paused after the stutter her colleague just re-commenced again. The union side, I noticed, thought the failed intervenor's grimacing reactions at being cut off each time amusing. They smiled to each other as her frustrations visibly mounted and they lost interest in what the speaker was saying. She should have used one of the 'strongest initiating moves' [149] to claim a turn by calling out 'Philip', her partner's name, to which he would likely respond with a question like: 'Yes, What?', or acknowledge with his head looking at her in a sloping stance. These are invitations, albeit involuntary ones, for her to intervene.

'Topic' is another of the speech subjects Mulholland discusses. Not all negotiations have agendas, i.e., topics or propositions, when they start. Negotiations fixed in the calendar by over-structured recognition agreements between employers and unions inevitably spend their initial phases agreeing on topics to negotiate.

'Once a proposition is settled on,' writes Mulholland,[150] 'the speech acts produced will affect it in various ways to suit the participants. They will reinforce it, explain its terms, repeat it, seek to vary some term in it, select parts of it for attention, argue that it needs amended, [sic] seek to weaken its force by adding qualifications, generalise to show its strength and validity, exemplify it (either to strengthen or weaken it by the selection of the particular example), narrow its applicability, distract others from its weakness.'

They repeat this process for every proposition introduced as a topic, and for each sub-proposition. This makes for those diversions, irrelevancies, and distractions so common in long negotiation sessions. It only takes a word or two to suggest possibilities as topics and it can take some time and effort to get the focus back onto the central issues.

There are standard signals that diminish the impacts of meetings. They include:[151]

- O   'That reminds me'
- O   'Oh, by the way'
- O   'Incidentally'
- O   'Oh, I forgot to tell you'
- O   'Talking of which'.

The extent to which dilution occurs depends on the relationship of the negotiators. A verbal struggle can ensue with one negotiator trying to push his preferred topic and the other trying to get back on track.

Speech acts used include: 'I know what you mean, but'; 'Or, in other words'; 'I agree with you that it is a problem for sales, but it is a problem for everybody, in particular my production people'. The last is a classic switch from the other negotiator's topic, about the impact on his sales people, to the speaker's preferred topic about its impact on her production people (no prizes for guessing which department she manages!).

This is only a flavour of the rich seam that Mulholland has mined in negotiation language and its use in dialogue. Follow-on research could produce many more insights into the use of forms of language peculiar to negotiators, especially in different uses of language between different cultures. In South Africa, a Zulu trade union leader told an Afrikaner General Manager, 'I laugh at your offer', causing him, the manager told me later, 'to realize that Apartheid was finally over'.

THE ART OF QUESTIONING

Questioning is one of those obvious skills everybody knows about and for which nobody requires training. Wrong. Questioning is one of the least accomplished of the skills of the majority of negotiators. Questioning is one of the main separators of skilled from average negotiators. According to Rackham,[152] average negotiators ask half as many questions as skilled negotiators. In some negotiations I have observed, 45 minutes or more go by without anybody asking a question, not even a rhetorical one. We tick poor questions in the TimeTrack™ question column, even like: 'Do you think I'm stupid?' Negotiations that suffer from question deprivation eventually run into the sand.

Advice abounds on questioning skills. Books on sales negotiation are usually full of questioning techniques, and some sales techniques consist solely of questions. Barristers train in advocacy skills, of which the art of questioning features as a major topic. For advocates their questioning skills are probably more important than their rhetorical skills.

Almost everybody in interpersonal skills training knows of the differences between 'closed' and 'open' questions. Yet, with all of this effort, why is it still common practice for negotiators:

O   not to ask enough questions?
O   to ask them badly?
O   not to listen to the answers?

This, for long enough puzzled me, both as a practitioner and as a trainer.

The TimeTrack™ technique exposes the lack of questioning demonstrated in a negotiation. Reviewing the TimeTrack™ record usually promotes an increase in questioning in the next negotiation. When it does, the impact on their negotiating performance is profound.

But what questions? Are some better than others? Does it matter? Given the paucity of your questioning I suggest that before you complicate your thinking with a thesis on questions, you should just start asking them without concerning yourself with the subtleties of form, purpose and content. I know it is dangerous to assert that any question is better than none at all, and you can pillory me for saying so, but for those who do not ask enough questions, and TimeTrack™ shows you ask fewer questions that you think you do, I will risk your scepticism in the cause of getting you to ask questions – any questions – rather than merely talk.

For those negotiators who do ask regular questions – and listen to the answers – some comments on the functions of questions and their language formats are appropriate. I shall summarize, therefore, some contributions from specialists in negotiation.

Gerard Nierenberg, an attorney, has been on the international negotiation seminar circuit for over thirty years. He founded a company called The Negotiation Institute in New York and has addressed thousands of negotiators on his questioning model.

Nierenberg's original questioning model was from a trial lawyer's point of view.[153] A shift in focus was necessary because if Nierenberg wanted to train negotiators he had to address negotiation practice.[154] Nierenberg's question functions are shown in Figure 3.8.

○   **Cause attention** ('How are you?')

○   **Get information** ('How much is this?')

○   **Give information** ('Do you know how you could?')

○   **Start thinking** ('What would your suggestion be?')

○   **Bring to a conclusion** ('Isn't it time to act?').

Figure 3.8 Nierenberg's five-question functions

He then offers 25 combinations of different types of questions, causing his readers, in my view, severe information overload. Incredibly, Nierenberg presses on with another 15 categories of questions,[155] relating them to the five functions in Figure 3.8, as shown in Figure 3.9 (with some variations of my own in the examples).

I have found Nierenberg's treatment of questioning too daunting for practical use (though you may feel differently). He includes far too many categories for you to remember, let alone for you to use under the pressure of a negotiating situation. But his concentration on questioning is beyond reproach and is worthy on that ground alone of the space allocated to it (also, I might have saved you a seminar fee!).

In contrast to Nierenberg's esoteric approach, the most common topic on questions in negotiation and sales courses is that of the simple differences between open and closed questions. Here there are only two categories to remember.

Question type	Example
Open-end	'Why did you do it?'
Open	'Did you do it?' (as in open-ended)
Leading	'You were very surprised then?'
Cool	'What is the square root of 4?'
Planned	'Having found the range, how do you correct for height?'
Treat	'Could you help with your excellent insight?'
Window	'Why do you feel that way about her?'
Directive	'How excessive do you think their profit is?'
Gauging	'How do you feel about my proposal?'
Close-out	'If you thought it dodgy you wouldn't invest, would you?'
Loaded	'Have you stopped beating your husband?'
Heated	'Having wasted today can we move on?'
Impulse	'By the way, how would your boss handle this one?'
Trick	'Are you going to end your marriage with a divorce?'
Reflective-mirror	'Do you think this plan won't work because it is too costly?'

Figure 3.9 Nierenberg's 15-question categories

1. *Closed* questions are those that, in principle, invite a 'yes' or 'no' answer. Such answers can be important if a 'yes' or 'no' answer fits the purpose of the question.

2. *Open* questions invite fuller responses than closed questions but not everybody takes up the invitation. In my experience, people sometimes answer closed questions with detailed elaborations of their 'yes' or 'no' answers without prompting. I have also heard open questions answered abruptly with a single word: 'What did he say to you?' – 'Nothing'.

It is not so clear cut, is it? But the difference between open and closed questions can be significant, as in the case of the question put to a sailor during an inquiry into a ferry collision. 'Did you take appropriate safety precautions?' produced the unhelpful answer 'Yes'. This told the inquiry nothing about how useful were the saftey precautions that he alleged he took. The question should have been: 'What safety precautions did you take?', which would have been more helpful for a judgement to be made on their usefulness.

Returning to the common problem of getting negotiators to ask more questions, I found the answer many years ago. We need something besides tutor talks that have limited impact on behaviour. The method I employ removes trainer's exhortations and substitutes a practical demonstration of the power of questioning. The results were, and continue to be, remarkable. Recently, for instance, while coaching some company directors who were about to begin merger negotiations with another company, I got them to rehearse their carefully prepared proposals on the merger package.

Those managers chosen to case play as the directors of the other company, complained to me, when I visited their syndicate room, that they were stumped for ideas about what to do in the opening session. Yet, beforehand they had contributed enthusiastically to their own company's negotiating agenda and now they did not know where to start in the rehearsal.

For a coach, this situation poses problems. If you intervene and tell them what to do, they no longer learn to the full extent of their capabilities; if you don't intervene at all, they effectively 'drop out' of a potential learning experience.

My 'solution' was to give them a clue, and then leave them to it. Therefore, I suggested that they simply asked questions. From their body language it was clear that this idea was like a life-line. So, I left them to it and went to the other syndicate room, where their colleagues were rehearsing their presentations of their company's proposed merger package. I did not mention, of course, what their colleagues were doing meanwhile.

Two hours later, the teams met. The target company's side listened to the merger proposals of what it could mean for their company (and themselves) and how both companies would benefit commercially. When they responded, they did so solely with questions, supplementary questions, and yet more questions, and they stuck to their plan of not making any comments on the answers they were given. They simply stuck to their questioning agenda.

The impact of their questioning on their colleagues' behaviour was almost too painful to watch. Everybody soon realized that the singular role of questioning behaviour they were witnessing was devastating to their company's proposals. This had serious implications for the real negotiations.

Their colleagues' persistent questioning exposed the weaknesses of much of what they had planned to present to the other company. They realized just how bereft of credibility were their merger proposals, once they were subjected to questioning and how demoralizing it was to see the product of several hundreds of man-hours of preparation crumble so easily. If the real company's directors were to behave likewise, and just ask questions, the merger was doomed. They had only hours to put it right.

Two learning points emerged, one for them as a company and the other for them as negotiators. Everybody realized that they had a lot more preparatory work to undertake to make their merger proposals more robust, and second, everybody – questioners and questioned alike

– realized the power of questioning through an experience that they would not forget quickly.

This coaching technique answers the problem of a lack of questioning behaviour among a company's negotiators – don't just tell them about what they should do about it, get them, instead, to practise asking questions in as close to a real situation as possible. The lesson, I can assure you, sticks!

Apart from the need for close questioning of an opinion, a stance, a story-line, an allegation, a complaint, the data, a proposal or a bargain, etc., as part of the information exchange in all negotiations, questioning has a pivotal role in the sales sequence, in influencing strategies and in the management of meetings.

In 1987, Rackham reported that his SPIN® questioning developed from observing 30,000 sales interviews, using an elaboration of the behavioural model he had earlier developed for analysing negotiation behaviour.[156] The methodology was similar: study what successful sales people do that is different from what the average seller does, and build sales training around the differences.

Huthwaite research also found that relying on the distinction between open and closed questions would not help the seller in the larger value sale, nor would relying on the traditional approaches to objection handling or revealing the distinction between features and benefits (both major topics in standard sales training).

In 1994, I sat through a presentation given by an English sales training company to a mutual client (I was waiting at the back of the room to deliver my negotiation course). They called their questioning model 'SPIPAC', which was SPIN® in disguise, with some sensible elaborations.

Sales trainers widely use SPIN® type questioning methods (mostly renamed). Given the vast appetite of the selling profession for new techniques, there is no shortage of people supplying them. New questioning techniques rapidly disseminate into the selling culture such that we take them for granted in double-quick time. What was startlingly revolutionary about SPIN® in 1987, is, alas, almost blasé ten years later.

All sales sequences use questions, but SPIN® identifies crucial additional questions to secure a higher hit rate in making the sale.

Sellers in front of a prospect ask *situation* questions:

○   'How many people are employed here?'
○   'How long have you used this process?'
○   'What is your annual turnover?'

These provide background information presumably useful to the seller.

The researchers found that situation questions do not correlate with success, that inexperienced sellers asked more of them, successful sellers asked fewer and that situation questions bored buyers if you asked too many of them.[157]

Too many situation questions raise questions in the buyer's mind like:

○   'Why am I telling her this?'
○   'Can't he get this information before he comes here?'
○   'How much longer before she gets to the point?'

None of this implies that you should not ask situation questions; it just suggests that you should ask them sparingly and move on (and that you should do sufficient preliminary research on the buyer's company before you meet him).

Experienced sellers deliberately move to *problem* questions (while some inexperienced sellers inadvertently discover problem questions in their desperation to make progress):

○   'Are you satisfied with your present equipment?'
○   'What disadvantages do you find from using external trainers?'
○   'Are there any reliability problems with the system you use?'

While problem questions correlate with success much more than situation questions, the researchers found that there was a difference between their success in the smaller compared to the larger sales. Success in the smaller sales correlates strongly with you asking problem questions, but the evidence does not support this correlation if you ask as many of them in the larger sales.[158]

It seems obvious that sellers who identify sales prospects who have problems should be in a good position to sell their product, if it addresses the prospect's problems. Not quite. It all depends on what you do next once you uncover the prospect's problem ('the unreliability of the current fire alarm system', say).

If you switch from asking problem questions to trying to sell your fire alarm product that allegedly solves the buyer's problem, you might make a small value sale (one battery for a fire alarm) but you are unlikely to make a large one (fitting out 20 plants with complete electronic fire and smoke sensitive alarm systems).

Lower-level customers make the decisions to buy smaller value products, usually on a one person-one-meeting-one-decision basis. More than one senior person, after several meetings, is involved in making a decision to buy value products, and the higher their value the greater the corporate and personal risk to the decision makers and, therefore, the greater the time taken over the decision to purchase. Jumping in with solutions as soon as you see a problem for your product to solve is foolhardy in the bigger sale.

Instead – and the better sellers do it – you should ask follow-on questions that take the implied buyer's need ('the unreliability of the current system', say), identified through your problem questions, and turn the implicit need into an explicit statement *by the buyers* of their need for reliability.

Remember, you have competing implicit needs jostling for your attention at any one moment and merely identifying an implicit need, such as 'I need a drink', does not mean that you will get up from your comfortable seat on the veranda and go to the refrigerator to satisfy your need. Other needs ('Will he score a six?', 'Is it worth leaving this lovely shade?') may be pressing much harder for your attention than a vague need you feel to quench your thirst.

The role of the *implication* question is to bring to a fore, in the mind of the sales prospect, your active desire to address their problems.[159] The seller, by building up the seriousness of the problem, asks implication questions to bring out the costs of not attending to the prospect's need:

○   'What is the unreliability costing you in emergency out-sourcing when that machine goes into downtime?'
○   'How much is absenteeism costing you in extra overtime working and in hiring temporary staff?'

Sellers who ask implication questions when they identify problems make more sales than those who solely describe their product or services. The main reason for avoiding a selling pitch immediately you identify a problem is that it usually invites the question: 'How much will it cost?'

Don't be wary of answering price questions (heaven forbid that your prices embarrass you!) but the buyer has not yet determined the full cost to him of the problem nor has he focused on the value to him of doing something about it. Implication questions bring out these costs, perhaps in forms that the buyer was not consciously aware of until now. If you jump this step in the sequence you lose an opportunity to allow the buyer to become aware of what this problem costs him.

The implications' step in questioning is so important that I prefer to follow another trainer's lead and call it 'wallowing'. Now, wallowing is a lovely word because it is a foghorn message. Negotiators latch on to the word wallow – sometimes provoking hearty renditions of a popular song about hippopotami wallowing in the African mud! – and by calling it wallowing you get the chief learning point across.

To make the prospect, or anybody you wish to influence, wallow in the implications of their problems is a sure-fire way of raising their consciousness of the need to address their problem and it also strengthens their bonding with you, the person sympathetic to their wallowing. If you practise getting people to wallow in any aspect of their lives you will improve your negotiating and influencing performances. People who share in wallowing behaviour cease to be strangers. If you consider your closer friends, I think you will find that mutual wallowing, albeit unconsciously and perhaps unnoticed, played a part in developing your friendships.

Before your wallowing with the buyer totally overwhelms her with depression at the size of the problem, you must switch her focus to the positive benefits of solving it. To switch from problem to solution, the researchers found that successful sellers used *need-payoff* questions:

O   'What benefit would there be in reducing absenteeism?'
O   'Would this only save on costs or would it also raise the morale of those who work their shifts by creating a sense of fairness?'
O   'How would you estimate the importance of improved morale to your operation?'

You ask about the value or benefit to the buyer of solving their problem so that in their answers they state these benefits in *their own* words and not yours. You do this before you mention your Absence Control service, your shift scheduling software or your morale-boosting incentive scheme, thus maximizing the chances of the buyer's receptivity to your solution.

The buyer's receptivity creates the most favourable conditions for downplaying what it costs because she has already stated the benefits she thinks she will obtain from buying a solution, which greatly exceeds the price for her to obtain it. Whenever the value of the benefits exceeds the costs of acquiring a product, price falls into its proper place. Thus, if the buyer values the benefits of training to eliminate hidden production costs from poor sourcing practice, estimated to be, say, £3000 a missile or £7 million a year, he is less likely to be unduly price resistant to ten training programmes that improve sourcing practice and cost only £5000 a workshop.

Need-payoff questions prevent, or reduce, the usual price objections of buyers as their knee-jerk reactions to the usual jerks trying to hard-sell them products they don't need, or, if they do, this is no thanks to those who neither ask about their needs nor attempt to satisfy them. Their more effective colleagues use wallowing techniques to induce the buyer to want to buy.

By imbedding questioning techniques into negotiation practice, participants will ask many more questions than they presently do and they will become familiar with, and exponents of, the different functions and formats of questions. For those who can reach Nierenberg's level of sophistication in questioning, fine; for the rest of us, reaching a higher rate of questioning, that's more than good enough.

But note, I regard wallowing as an important part of the negotiator's repertoire of skills. I advise you to practise your wallowing, along with your questioning.

 ## CONSTRUCTIVE DEBATE BEHAVIOURS

The main task of debate is to find out what each other wants. In disclosing what you want you do not reveal how far you may move on any of the negotiable issues. It is enough to state your entry positions. You do not have to move into your negotiating ranges until you are ready to formulate proposals.

Another useful word for debate is exploration. You decide what you want in preparation and explore what they want in debate. Until you know what the other negotiator wants you cannot safely make and exchange proposals.

Constructive debate involves:

○ Establishing some degree of rapport and building on it.
○ Offering an agenda for the meeting or a summary of what in your view the negotiation is about.
○ Asking for confirming or contrary views by inviting them to contribute to the agenda.
○ Searching for and disclosing wants to each other.
○ Asking questions and listening to the answers and answering questions and seeking understanding.
○ Summarizing regularly.
○ Signalling your willingness to consider movement if it is reciprocated.
○ Responding to their signals in a positive manner.

The key debating behaviours that the skilled negotiator must be adept at are as follows:

MAKING STATEMENTS

The most common behaviour in the debate phase, particularly in the early exchanges, is the making of statements.

You explain why you have this or that view, you answer questions, you state your views, your policies and your concerns, and you comment on what they say. Doing this without creating rancour is difficult, as is getting the debate back to neutral statement making after there has been an emotional outburst.

Making statements is the most common activity in the debate and proposing phases, according to our detailed observations. By the time the parties make specific offers to bargain they are in the decision, or the 'yes/no' crisis,[160] and, while continuing with questions and clarifications, they have the bulk of the information about their own and the other's views and positions.

Statements are the vehicle for information exchange. In defining the task of debate as finding out what the other party wants, remember that this is a two-way process – what's true for you is true for him. You both need information about each other's wants and the debate phase largely consists of this activity and that of trying to influence or persuade them that their wants, as originally conceived and articulated, need modification before a joint decision is possible. This is why it is so easy to slip from exchanging information into arguing about it.

Ideally, exchanging information should be neutral in tone. In practice, it can be turbulent. As Gulliver noticed, the opening exchanges can be fraught, with each party emphasizing their commitment to their positions, or the principles and interests behind their positions, by using language and tone to demonstrate their seriousness and commitment.

ASSURANCES

These include:

O   'Yes, it is a difficult problem, but we are in the solution business.'
O   'I can see why you are disappointed. Let's see what can be done.'

Assurance language oils the interchange. When people are anxious and concerned about their fears and assurance statements are more helpful than threats. I once dealt with a local government official who opened the negotiations – just after the personal introductions – on a right-of-way dispute, with the statement: 'If we don't get agreement from you to forgo your alleged right-of-way, we will CPO you this afternoon'. His threat to issue a Compulsory Purchase Order (CPO) went down like a lead balloon with my client, the opposite, presumably, of what was intended.[161]

ASKING QUESTIONS (AND LISTENING TO THE ANSWERS)

This includes questions such as:

○   'How did you calculate these figures?'
○   'With what aspects of my proposal are you unhappy?'
○   'Why is that important to you?'
○   'What if we could address that problem, what difference would it make?'

These are questions of the 'open' kind. Normally, a mixture of open and closed questions are required throughout debate because it is always possible to block an open question by saying 'I don't know', or to expand on a closed question with supplementary commentary, such as 'Yes, but'.

Questions are very powerful debate behaviours. They are more successful than 'I disagree' statements that you tend to utter whenever somebody says something with which you disagree or which you 'know' to be contrary to the 'facts'.

SUMMARIZING

Summarizing has important and simultaneous effects on the conduct of debate. Summarizing assures others that you are listening to their views and concerns, especially when you can summarize their views in words that satisfy them, whatever your own views on what they have said.

Summarizing gives you and your colleagues time to think because, in giving a concise summary of the differences between the parties, it helps to put your own thoughts into order too.

Summarizing clarifies what both sides are saying because, if your summary is inaccurate in any way, they have the opportunity to inform you of what they really meant and you too can clarify what you meant.

Summaries should be neutral, truthful and brief. Saying, in effect, that you have made a positive and helpful contribution while they have been obstructive, etc., is not a summary; it is an attack and is usually treated as such.

SIGNALLING

Negotiation is the management of movement from entry towards settlement positions. Negotiators start with at least two solutions to the same problem: yours and the other party's. The tactical question facing all negotiators is how to make movement towards a settlement without giving in? This is the root cause of the phenomenon of positional posturing. Taken to extremes, digging in behind ramparts is self-defeating, because it can initiate a breakdown or deadlock.

Stating the problem does not remove it, for if you do move unilaterally, will they reciprocate or will they remain firmly entrenched? And once you start moving unilaterally, where or when will you stop?

In my original eight steps, signalling was a (separate) third step and demoting signalling in the four phase's version was not a denial of the importance of signalling. Far from it, because signalling is one of the key behaviours in negotiating and the good news is that you do not have to learn how to signal. You already signal and respond to signals in your everyday interactions with other people. What training does for you is to make you aware and sensitive to their role in creating the possibilities for movement from the debate to the proposal phases. Signals when responded to are the bridge to proposals.

You learn to distinguish between absolute unconditional statements and their qualification into signals. Briefly, for example, a statement that 'we cannot accept those schedules' can become a signal if re-stated as: 'we cannot accept those schedules *in their current form*'. The words in the qualification 'in their current form' are the signal, implying that if the debate shifts from the absolute rejection of the schedules to the form they might take, then progress is possible.

Everything depends on how the negotiator, to whom you send the signal, responds, if they respond at all. If they ignore the signal, deliberately or from not recognizing it, they miss the moment for possible movement. If they dismiss the signal ('You will have to accept the schedules as they stand'), then the moment for movement may not recur and the dispute may go into rigid deadlock. If they respond positively in some way, the signal unlocks the gridlock: 'When you say, for instance, "in their current form" are you suggesting that if we discuss the format of the new schedules we might make progress?' Alternatively, they might simply ask: 'What do you mean by "in their current form"?'

To become aware of the signals that pass between you both it is essential to listen to what they say. It is the lack of awareness of the signals crossing the table that makes a debate difficult for untrained negotiators but it is an easy problem to put right. Just start listening and responding to them.

SUPPORTING

Finding something, no matter how tenuous, to express some measure of support in the other negotiator's suggestion or proposal, is far more productive than being wholly negative. Examples include:

O   'That is a most interesting suggestion and I can agree with some of it.'
O   'I can see some merit in your views.'
O   'While I have some reservations, I think your proposal is a basis for further exploration.'
O   'I would like to explore along the lines you have suggested.'

Supporting works wonders (not miracles!) for the tone of the negotiation. It is a behaviour that can be common enough in debate and in the response to proposals if you choose to practise it.

It is worth remembering that nobody ever achieved a worse deal by being well-mannered, though plenty of people have acquired worse deals and no deals by being ill-mannered. You will spend most of your face-to-face negotiating time in the debate phases, so it makes sense to do your very best to remain effective in these phases by following the advice set out above.

CHAPTER

4

PHASE THREE – PROPOSING AND BARGAINING FACE TO FACE

HOW IMPORTANT IS PERSONALITY IN NEGOTIATING?

What is the role of personality in negotiation? Clearly, if personality influences negotiation behaviour then practitioners, seeking to improve their performance, will want to know about it.

Psychologists, particularly those interested in the effects of personality on behaviour, moved into negotiation research in a big way in the 1970s.[162] What, however, may be interesting from a theoretical point of view, may also be impractical when you try to apply personality profiling under time pressure and with inadequate information. Thus, worthy insights from personality theories remain insights and not guides to practical negotiating behaviour. In practice, I believe, personality is a dead-end for working negotiators.

It is possible to adapt sound theories for practical purposes when time is scarce but not that scarce, in the preparation phase for instance, but it is less practical to adopt complex interpersonal analyses when eyeball-to-eyeball across a negotiating table during fast-moving interactions. By the time you identify the other negotiator's personality and consider what you need to do, it is too late to apply what you think you now know.

This drawback has not prevented the application of psychological profiling to negotiators. Apart from several books in this area, at least one computer program[163] allows you to input into your PC the details of the other negotiator's personality. Having previously inputted details of your own personality, within seconds your PC prints out the most opportune responses you should use to negotiate with that person.

I became convinced that personality was not a practical tool after reading several academic books and some trainers' manuals on it, and then talking to practising negotiators. For example, I presented a follow-on workshop 12 months behind a trainer who used negotiating styles extensively in his course, and none of the participants could remember the names of the four different personality styles the trainer introduced to them (some could not even remember their own style!). In consequence, they had not practised personality styling in their negotiations.

I readily accept that this sort of example is not a decisive objection to the validity of personality styles as a training topic. The most that some practical negotiators admitted to me was that with certain people that they knew well and with whom they had negotiated on a regular basis, they 'knew' how to adapt their own behaviour to 'get round' them and how not to phrase their remarks and proposals. This is the only slight evidence of some implicit influence from personality on behaviour that I have found.

Certainly most people like to answer personality tests that appear to tell them about themselves (an area not unnoticed by editors of popular weekly magazines). Harmless egotism is useful if it encourages interest in people's behaviours and the realization that other people see issues and themselves differently. Hence, personality typing is not entirely useless as a training topic. I am sceptical, however, about its practicality at the bargaining table. My preference, instead, is for a model of negotiating behaviour that can be applied under any and all time pressures, irrespective of the personalities of the people with whom you negotiate.

 ## THE PERSONALITY STYLES OF NEGOTIATORS

It is almost trite to acknowledge that personality is an inescapable aspect of human behaviour. We all have at least one personality! That said, is there much else to it? Psychologists answer 'yes, there is much much more', and many trainers wholly agree (for some trainers, I suspect personality fills up spare time on their thin programmes). Some psychologists also complain that not enough attention is 'given to how personality affects negotiation'.[164] The sales pitch for personality research and for its infusion into negotiating training is easy to state.

Personality, of course, affects everything people do. Patterns of behaviour re-occur in many different situations. You display certain traits which, when identified, mark your personality. Your traits are your 'predispositions to respond in characteristic ways' and different 'situations simply trigger what comes "naturally" to each individual'.[165]

If their personality is stable enough, then you could produce predictable responses to different negotiating situations and this may be sufficient for you to secure a better negotiated outcome. If you become aware of your personal traits, and learn how to control or manage them, perhaps you could improve your performance as a negotiator, parent, colleague, or team player?

Moreover, if you could develop the skills of identifying other people's personalities, especially those you deal with on a regular basis, this too might improve your negotiating performance. With practice, you could improve your ability to 'read' someone's personality from limited acquaintance, and do well even in negotiations with relative strangers. Convinced? Well, as you need to make up your mind about the role of personality in negotiation we will discuss this in more detail.

All of the popular versions of the role of personal traits or styles in negotiation originate from the work of Rubin and Brown,[166] who postulated that two variables determine the influence of personality on negotiation. First, there is *interpersonal orientation*, or the degree of social ability and social awareness:

○   If you are high on this variable then you are responsive to the interpersonal aspects of your relationship with the other negotiator.
○   If you are low on interpersonal orientation then you are non-responsive.

The highly interpersonally oriented negotiator reacts to changes in the other person's behaviour; her counterpart at the low end of the continuum does not.

The second variable is the negotiator's *motivational orientation* – are you one of nature's competitors or co-operators? Laying these variables across each other we can get the four-box matrix as in Figure 4.1:

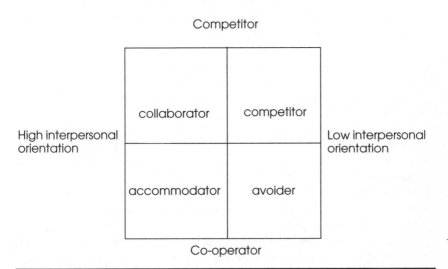

Figure 4.1 Rubin and Brown's personality styles

The four styles are: competitor, avoider, accommodator and collaborator. Their characteristics are as follows:

○ *Competitor style*   Achieving results through power, rather than relationships, matter to competitors. They are aggressive, domineering and seek to win at all costs. Openly manipulative, they use ploys and tricks, including threats, and they talk much more than they listen. They make demands – they are takers – and seldom make offers.

○ *Avoider style*   They prefer to avoid conflict, as implied in negotiating, and are happy to hide behind procedures, rule books and precedents. They avoid decisions, except those that maintain the status quo, and are suspicious of change, and are generally pessimistic (the bottle is half empty). They have few social skills and are not good at using them.

○ *Accommodator style*   They are relationship-oriented, and hence try to placate persons by making early (and unnecessary) concessions if conflict threatens. They involve people in the negotiation process, they seek friendly agreement and they work at ingratiating themselves with friendly responders, often by smoothing over difficulties with verbiage.

○ *Collaborator*   They are results-oriented through pragmatic problem solving and establishing good relationships. They are good team players and seek not to dominate the other negotiators but to involve everybody in solving the problem. For them, prolonged discourse to make the right decision is not a problem. They are good 'fixers' and even manipulative at a high enough level of intrigue, though a trifle Machiavellian. They are networkers who play the informal influence game.

Of these, which style makes for the best negotiators? A rather pointless question, in my opinion, because all personality types have to negotiate at some time or other. Some, surely, will shine in some negotiation circumstances and fail miserably in others?

It is not possible, in my view, to predict the comparative success rates of the four personality types because personality is neither the sole nor the dominant determinant of the outcome. However, certain behaviours, as distinct from specific personalities, work less well in certain circumstances than others. I offer the alternative hypothesis that it is possible that all personality types can change their behaviour for a negotiation without necessarily having to change their personalities. Indeed, if this was not true, what would be the point of training people in appropriate negotiation behaviour? If behaviour can override personality, why bother with personality?

Gilkey and Greenhaugh,[167] on the contrary, consider personality to be a dominant influence in determining the outcome. To illustrate their hypothesis that personality really matters in negotiation, they summarize how traits might manifest themselves in, for example, negotiations for a divorce settlement:

> If the husband tends to be highly *competitive*, he is likely to define the situation as one in which he must win as much as possible in the settlement. If the wife tends to be highly *accommodating*, she might submit to his exploitative demands and not preserve her own interests ... [if] both parties are *compromisers* ... they would be likely to seek outcomes that split the difference between his interests and her interests. The result might be a solution that is not optimal for either party. Suppose, for example, that the couple had a breeding pair of championship Siamese cats but, since the value of the cats is in there being a breeding pair, both husband and wife would lose some value in this settlement. If instead of being compromisers, the couple both tended to be collaborators, they would search for solutions to the problem that would benefit them both. Perhaps one party would keep the breeding pair and the other could keep all of the kittens in the next litter. Even worse ... is the situation in which parties are conflict *avoiders*. Here the couple may let the marriage drag on after it should be ended.

Their summary does not exhaust all the possibilities of the interplay between partners. For example, perhaps the problem in the marriage is sourced in the incompatibilities of living with someone who has the same personality traits? If, then, either similar or different traits produce incompatibilities, how does this approach help us to acquire insight?

Imagine two competitive people divorcing each other. They would both be out to win in a classic stand-off. But what of the others? Would an accommodator negotiating with an avoider exacerbate his tendency to make early concessions to placate the avoider's nervousness about negotiating, perhaps even making extra-generous concessions just to keep the avoider interested in making a decision?

How would a collaborator fare with an avoider? If the avoider can distinguish between competitive and collaborator pressure on her enough to become involved in a decision, which is contrary to her personality, there is a likelihood that the collaborator, mindful of the need for him to establish his relationship with the avoider (who does not want one), could get over involved himself and slide into concession making to create a motive for the avoider's involvement in the decision!

If almost anything is possible when personalities interact, what is unique about the influence of personality on the outcome? This is reason enough, in my view, to be sceptical of the validity of the personality approach, but because it features so strongly in some training programmes it requires further elucidation.

 ## PSYCHOLOGY AND NEGOTIATING PERSONALITIES

It occurred to me, when considering the interaction between personality types, that as a training tool it rests on the two weak assumptions that we:

○   are able to identify accurately our own and our counterpart's personality traits

and, having achieved that by no means assured feat quickly enough, it assumes that we

○   can remember how to deal with any of the 16 combinations of the four personality styles that are possible (which become much more complex when we negotiate in teams).

If you consider that Gilkey and Greenhaugh[168] used no fewer that nine psychological tests (Thematic Apperception, Roschach, Bem Sex-Role inventory, Empathy Measures, Interpersonal Orientation, Assertiveness, Leadership Opinion Questionnaire, Locus of Control, and the Conflict Resolution Mode) to assess the personalities of their co-operative subjects, the likelihood of anything remotely conducive to practical use in a live negotiation (unless the stakes were very high and the preparatory budgets were extraordinarily generous) must be severely limited.

If personality is the independent variable – the driver – of negotiating behaviour and it takes eight or nine scientific tests to uncover the other negotiator's personality, the arithmetic of the task becomes impractical, without considering the possibility that our assessment is wrong, or that our subject deliberately manipulates the tests. This is not to decry personality research, but insights remain insights, not guides to practice. The prospect of asking the other negotiator to complete several personality tests before we negotiate with them is somewhat daunting, unless of course you have the appropriate personality to ask and get what you want and they have the appropriate personality to give it to you!

Two other researchers, Herman and Kogan,[169] make the interesting point that personality affects initial behaviour but has a lesser or no impact on later behaviour. As negotiation is a process taking place through time, the demarcation between initial and later behaviour has some relevance. They suggest that your personality can influence initial behaviour because, in the earlier phase of the negotiation, you have little else to rely on, other than your predispositions and experiences in defining the people and the negotiating situation.

When you have little or no information you rely on your own personality to guide your behaviour – personality, remember, encompasses your 'predispositions to respond in characteristic ways' and certain situations 'simply trigger what comes "naturally" to each individual'.[170] However, once the interaction gets under way the behaviour of the other negotiator becomes a more important influence on your own behaviour. Each of you reacts, in turn, to the other's behaviours. The mesh of the predispositions of you both as negotiators helps to determine how each of you perceives the other's motives and intentions and how sensitive each will be to the other's behaviour. Through this process, the role of your own personality as the main determinant of your behaviour declines.

Herman and Kogan derive from various personality traits a tendency to be either behaviourally co-operative or competitive in a negotiation (though they confined their research to the outcomes of 'prisoners' dilemma' games).[171] Among their conclusions they report:

1. The more anxious a negotiator is, the more competitive is his negotiating behaviour ('They expect the worse and try to minimize their losses by adopting a competitive strategy').[172]

2. The less authoritarian a negotiator is, the more co-operative her negotiating behaviour ('high authoritarians ... have an egoistic orientation – self-interest is what the world is about – and thus are more competitive in dealing with others').

3. The more cognitively complex a negotiator is the more co-operative is his negotiating behaviour ('they persist in decision making tasks until they find an *acceptable* solution').[173]

4. The greater the negotiator's tendency is towards conciliation as opposed to belligerence, the more co-operative is her negotiating behaviour (she has 'a generally favourable view and reaction to people').

5. The more dogmatic a negotiator is, the more co-operative is his negotiation behaviour ('once such subjects have selected a co-operation strategy, they can be expected to pursue it tenaciously').[174]

6. The greater a negotiator's desire to avoid taking risks, the more co-operative her negotiating behaviour ('they are more co-operative in reaching bargaining agreements than in using a competitive strategy, and bargaining agreements are more likely to occur if co-operative goals prevail over competitive ones').

7.   The more self-esteem a negotiator has, the less co-operative his negotiating behaviour ('they think they probably deserve more on the average than do their opponents, and they intend to manipulate their opponents to guarantee themselves success').

8.   The more suspicious a negotiator is, the less co-operative her negotiating behaviour (they 'probably suspect the motives of any person in an interpersonal encounter and will expect the worst').[175]

Within these eight propositions there are variations when people with greater or lesser traits of a particular kind meet to negotiate. Two authoritarians, one highly and one less authoritarian, are likely to be least co-operative because the low authoritarian 'who may be easily exploited at the beginning of the relationship, may overreact and match or better the competitiveness of the high authoritarian'. Similarly, whereas negotiations between conciliatory persons will be the most co-operative, negotiations between a pair with one person more conciliatory than the other, are least co-operative, because the more conciliatory individual overreacts to the competitiveness of the less conciliatory person.

Now imagine, for a moment, trying to 'read' these complications as they work their way through a live negotiation? Can you now see why as a practitioner I remain sceptical? These complications add greatly to the existing problems of identifying personality traits, because an imbalance of the same trait can produce an entirely different orientation and thereby a different negotiating behaviour – as different as between co-operation and competitiveness – which could prove to be confusing to a negotiator, who, trying hard to identify another's personality traits, is handed the additional, and no less difficult, task of matching the degree to which a person has a particular trait compared to somebody who has, to a greater or lesser degree, the same trait.

I conclude that outside a psychology laboratory, instead of this complicating and possibly unresolvable puzzle, it might be simpler to rely on your direct observation of how the other negotiator actually behaves, rather than on an eight-factor analysis of his personality, which may not even manifest itself in the manner predicted.

 ## A TRAINER ON PERSONALITIES

Trainers, not wishing to cast aside a theoretical construct that could yield rich pickings for those gifted enough to be able to use it, have tried to simplify the identification of negotiators' personalities. While these simplifications are commendable they still do not address the question of how to grapple with 16 possible combinations of personality in a two-person negotiation, or the many more combinations once multi-person teams come into play.

The search for a practical link between personality and negotiating behaviour is like the search for the fabled north-west passage to India. If such a passage existed its finders would have become rich and famous, but as it didn't exist sailors died fruitlessly searching for it. In the case of negotiation trainers, their search for the link only wastes the resources of those clients who pay them to find it.

I shall reveal my own solution to this problem later but it suffices to note here that it involves switching from identifying numerous personality types to identifying the behaviour of the negotiators. After all it is easier — and ultimately more reliable — to identify their behaviour than it is to identify their personalities. However, we shall discuss an example of personality styling as taught in a well-established and highly credible training seminar.

Of the various contributions of practitioners and trainers to personality styling, I shall, because of its provenance, select the work of Gottchalk.[176] Gottchalk, a psychologist, taught for many years at the London Business School, and has run successful negotiation seminars for senior business leaders since the early 1970s. He is familiar with the experimental research normal in academic psychology and he has had an extensive association with high-level business negotiators. In short, he is highly credible.

He supports his four comprehensive psychological styles on two other behavioural concepts which he calls the 'habit zone' and the 'managed zone'. His work is a step towards what I consider to be the more relevant behavioural approach that I advocate, but he remains (1997) stubbornly linked to psychological typing.

Habits, Gottchalk observes, change slowly — after all it took a long time for your core beliefs to form into their current shape — but your *managed*, or adaptive, behaviour can change speedily to suit circumstance. And your attitudes to a specific event can override your beliefs about norms and values. Your habit zone is fixed in the short run but you can expand the managed zone by widening the repertoire of effective behaviour through training in new skills not commonly produced by your particular personality style.

This welcome conclusion weakens the case for personality typing because, if behavioural training can override personality (as, indeed, it can), what is the case for investing in difficult analysis to identify the four styles?

Managers are expected to be situationally flexible and not solely driven by their beliefs, such that they make every decision or implementation requirement a potential resignation issue. Those managers that are not flexible to some minimal degree tend to get weeded out, either by their resignation 'on principle', or by the company 'letting them go' for failing to 'fit in' with the need for flexibility in the organization.

In a negotiation, you display a mixture of your habit and managed behaviours. The more in control you are, the more you adapt to the requirements of the particular negotiating situation and to the specific behaviours of the other negotiators. Your personality style, which you relapse to in moments of loss of self-control, underpins your behaviour.

Gottchalk identifies four main styles (Figure 4.2) and specifies that each style has both positive and negative attributes that work for and against their impacts on the negotiation. Rojot[177] provides a summary of Gottchalk's analysis of personality (my direct quotations of Gottchalk's work are from his seminar materials).[178]

- O tough

- O warm

- O numbers

- O dealer

Figure 4.2 Gottchalk's four personality styles

Gottchalk defines style as 'the way we come across. It's the pattern of behaviour that other people see and hear when we negotiate. Each negotiating style is a recognisable "bundle" of behaviours.'[179] He asserts that your style comes from your genetic inheritance, upbringing, social background, education and training, national culture and job experiences.

He also acknowledges that you do not neatly fit into one style 'but most of us come pretty close to one or other of them' such that 'we have a 60–80% fit'. This presumably means that up to 40 per cent of your personality fits into another style mode or it is spread across several modes. This is another disconcerting problem for using styles to improve performance. A slight misreading of somebody's behaviour that supposedly links with their personality, can mislead you as to their personality type. Errors at this level of sophistication are potentially catastrophic if, in turn, they determine your own behaviour towards the person whose personality you have just misread.

Gottchalk also asserts that people can only change their styles by cathartic events and he mentions a mid-life crisis, a major career change or a bereavement, as examples of these events. But could you experience some event, slightly less than cathartic, just enough to switch a few percentage points from your previously dominant personality typing to your previously minority personality style, and thereby shift the balance of your personality? Someone who became temporarily depressed by some event could switch personality styles for a single negotiation only. Unless you are relatively intimate with them, your assessment of their personality type could be flawed.

Let's take a brief run through Gottchalk's four styles and then you can judge their practical value (bearing in mind that Gottchalk is probably the most credible original source for this approach).

The *tough* style is played by a dominant, aggressive and power-oriented person. Positively, the tough negotiator is clear in what she wants, likes to take control and exudes 'presence' to control agendas. She does not avoid conflict and is decisive in a crisis. She has stamina, can seize opportunities as they arise and is a risk taker, who is competitive and assertive.

On the negative side, she is off-hand ('take it or leave it') and is unconcerned with how others think or feel. Her assertiveness runs easily into aggressive traits — bullying, threatening and coercive, she argues too readily. Easily upset if she does not get her own way, she can criticize unfairly, make impulsive decisions and enjoys manipulating others. She is inflexible and obstinate.

In dealing with a tough stylist, Gottchalk advises[180] that you should avoid small talk, emphasize common goals and give them recognition (but something short of flattery). You should slow down the process in case you get 'bounced' into something. You do not have to give in and you can say 'no'.

A *warm* style negotiator is supportive, understanding, collaborative and is people-oriented. He is friendly, interested in other people, listens well and is good at asking questions. He understands the needs and values of other people and emphasizes common goals. He will support proposals from other people and bring them into the decision process, while being self-effacing about his own contribution. He is trusting of others and seeks and takes advice. He is patient and calm under pressure and is generally optimistic.

On the negative side, the warm stylist, being too concerned with relationships, seldom puts his own views, or states what he wants, in a negotiation. He can be soft on the issues, even personally submissive, and can jeopardize his own interests. He is not credible in the making of threats — even apologizes for appearing to make them — and is easily disillusioned. His trusting traits can slip into gullibility, and he is a dependent joiner and follower. He relies on time to solve most problems and prefers 'jaw, jaw to war, war', and he panics under pressure.

Gottchalk advises[181] that to deal with a warmer you should build trust but keep a friendly distance. You should trade information to get them on your side, but ask for more, only putting on pressure if it is necessary, and go slowly, continuing with caution. You should also check with him that his colleagues will agree to deliver whatever he offers to arrange.

The *numbers* stylist is analytical, conservative, reserved and issue-oriented. She has a good grasp of the facts, logic and detail. Mainly concerned with the practicality of the deal, she weights the options in a methodical and orderly manner. She always prepares properly and she is well organized with her files and notes. She is confident of her analytical skills and is a valuable technical resource in a negotiating team. She is strong on evidence and on practicality (will it work?) and is difficult to upset emotionally. She is good at side-stepping issues and blinding you with 'science'. When she says 'no' she hides behind official policies, procedures and briefs.

Negatively, she is emotionally cold to others and does not volunteer information and considers that a 'yes' or 'no' will suffice. She will not decide until she has number crunched the data and can find it difficult to 'see' the problem rather than focus on tiny details. She can suffer from 'analysis paralysis'. She is impatient with the sloppy arguments of others and will question their logic before offering her own reasons for or against their proposals. She can be obsessive and pessimistic.

Gottchalk[182] advises that you build and use the agenda to keep it moving and refrain from parking it to return to it later. You should take an interest in her 'facts' as they might reveal more than she thinks. If you do use numbers at all, make sure that they are accurate, as she cannot pass a set of numbers without checking the count. Emphasize mutual gain and show respect for her expertise.

The *dealer* is flexible, compromising, and oriented to the results. He sees opportunities and ways to make it work. With charm and almost cynical manners he deploys formidable persuasion skills and avoids giving offence. His adaptability and flexibility makes him open to new ideas and can be imaginative as well as pragmatic. He is above all articulate and a fast talker, who thinks on his feet and will use any available argument or fact to make progress.

As a dealer he can be too much of a compromiser, an 'all things to all men' debater, and can sacrifice his own interests, perhaps from insufficient consideration of the details. He shifts positions too fast, too often and can thereby seem to be too tricky, insincere, and even 'too clever by half'.

Gottchalk's[183] advice for dealing with a dealer is to be positive and focus on your target, even repeating your demands. You must prepare to trade information, to let them talk and to let them collect more information. You must avoid being side-tracked, so you must regularly summarize and take notes.

Recognize these personalities in the people with whom you deal? Can you see your own style in any one of them? Check them out with people who know you and ask them to select one that covers your personality. After that, study Gottchalk's recommendations and see if, in practice, you can apply them to people you negotiate with over the next month. It is, after all, a purely empirical question of whether it works for you or whether you can make it work for you with some degree of effort. (I invite you to send me your conclusions after a month's practice!)

Several other authors and trainers use slightly different, even whimsical, names for Rubin and Brown's four styles (product differentiation?). This makes their personality types verbally more accessible to practitioners but after twenty years the subject, in my view, has made scant, if any, progress.

Your personality consists of mixed degrees of one or all four of the personality traits (maybe you are a *warm dealer* with *tough* tendencies and a nagging weakness for *numbers*?). The unbalanced mixture or degree of adherence to the same trait could reverse your predicted behaviour into its very opposite – from hyper-cooperative to highly competitive, for example. Therefore, I have the same reservations about the effect of your personality traits as I have about feasibility of predicting your behaviour from whether you are culturally a Japanese or a Belgian.

If you can switch your behaviours as a result of the 'chemistry' (or lack of it) between personalities at the negotiating table, surely you can also switch between personality styles to suit circumstances? Might there not be a time to be 'warm', a time to be 'analytical', a time to be a 'dealer' and a time to be 'tough'? Why should you be the mere plaything of your so-called personality as if nature hard-wired your personality into you like a robot? Might you be capable of switching styles at will?

Of course, the more consciously you can switch personality traits, the more effective you might become, but if all of us, whatever our personalities, can also switch or shade – even hide – our personality traits too, in so far as this manifests itself in our negotiating behaviour, you will have to do much more than merely consider the 16 possible combinations of the four styles. You might have to consider umpteen combinations of varying shades of the four styles.

 ## PRISONER'S DILEMMA GAMES

Having raised some doubts, I hope, as to the practicality of the psychological styles approach, it is now time to 'put up or shut up', as my betting friends put it. If we are to abandon a 'scientific' contribution to negotiating practice we must put something better in its place. That is what I shall now do.

To do this most effectively, however, it is best to do it through interactive exercises, which is precisely what negotiators do in our workshops. They play the 'red-blue' game. This might seem a long way from the modestly simple game played at Rand in the 1950s, an institution dedicated to research for 'the public welfare and security of the United States', to the training of negotiators almost 50 years later. It so happens, without exaggeration, that it is the most important journey you can make towards your understanding of negotiation behaviour. Therefore, your effort will be well worth your while.

But it is not possible to play an interactive game on your own, so I shall have take you through an alternative route to achieve the same outcome. To assist your quest, I shall cut your journey time considerably by making a diversion. Initially you may find it perplexing but stick with it, because from this diversion you go right to the heart of negotiating behaviour.

The Rand researchers playing the dilemma game discovered something that has intrigued the social (and other) scientists ever since.[184] But, unlike the higher sciences of psychological profiling, you do not need a PhD to play dilemma games. Indeed, in over ten years' experience of thousands of participants playing our dilemma games, less than a handful have had trouble with it.

So let us try a mind game, beginning with the original game, known the world over as the 'prisoner's dilemma'. The original games were about two prisoners and a prosecutor who does not have enough evidence to convict them of the serious crime which he has reason to believe they have committed. The scripts for prisoner's dilemma games vary quantitatively but the essence of them all is the same.[185] The one I use is:

> Two prisoners are kept in separate cells with no means of communicating. The prosecutor offers the same deal to each prisoner: 'If you confess to the crime you will be released after testifying against your partner, who will receive a ten-year sentence; if you don't confess but your partner does, you will receive ten years and your partner will be released. However, if you both confess, you will both be sentenced to five years and if neither of you confesses you will get one year each on the lesser charge we are holding you on.'

Different authors allocate different prison terms for each option but this does not affect the outcome, provided they are roughly proportionate and they are in the same order. The question you must answer now is: what should a prisoner do if she is offered this deal?

Please ignore such irrelevancies (it is only a game!) as you feel that the prisoners should not have committed a crime, or that you do not know if they are guilty, or that you feel unable to comment on hypothetical cases, etc. This exercise is not about your morality, nor the prisoners' alleged lack of it, nor the prosecutor's misuse of 'due process'. The game concerns the dilemma of choice and it has real repercussions for the game of life.

Perhaps if the prisoners could communicate they might agree not to confess, which, because it gives them both a one-year sentence only, is also their best choice (though not perhaps the best choice for the judicial system). But like the game of life, choices in a dilemma game are not clear cut.

For example, even if, before their arrest, they jointly agreed never to confess under any circumstance, there is always the possibility of one of them (and, therefore, of both of them!) defecting on their sacred pre-arrest agreement. They could defect by privately meeting with the prosecutor and confessing, safe (?) in the knowledge that their partner would abide by their prior agreement not to confess. That way, the confessor walks free and the non-confessing erstwhile partner gets ten years.

But how safe is the assumption that while they can defect with impunity, their partner would not come to the same conclusion and defect for the same reason? What is true for one is true for the other, so a mutual defection is likely which would ensure that they both get five years, instead of the one year if neither confessed.

Does a prohibition on communication worsen their dilemma? Not really, and neither is it eliminated by allowing them to do so. Communicating makes no difference to the dilemma, once they part and return to their separate cells. With or without communication, jointly sticking to a determination not to confess, which means neither of them defecting, is their best option. But once out of sight, or in private contact with their lawyers, it is possible for one of them to defect to win a personal advantage. As neither of them can be sure that the other one won't defect, their next best choice is to defect to *protect* themselves. They risk five years against ten if they both defect and confess, or immediate release against ten if they defect before their partner comes to the same conclusion.

This is the meaning of the dilemma for the two prisoners. A dilemma is a forced choice where there is no one obvious best choice. The choice they make depends on what each prisoner, independently of the other, decides is in their own best interests. An independent observer can see that the optimum choice for them both is non-confession if, *and only if*, both make and stick to this choice. The prisoners, however, cannot be sure that their partner will make the best choice for both of them and not succumb to temptation and make the better choice for herself.

Well, what has this got to do with negotiation? A great deal more than it looks. Some of it we discussed in the section on the 'bargaining problem' (p.10) and the work of John Nash.[186] For the moment, I remind you that Nash stated that the bargaining problem – how two parties divide up a set of goods between them – is solved by them dividing the goods such that the agreed division maximizes their joint gains in utility. To do this the negotiators must *co-operate* to bring about the optimal solution for both of them.

Prisoner's dilemma games suggested that it was not evident that independent parties would jointly choose co-operation. Rationally, negotiators should co-operate because they are both made better off by co-operation, but this choice simultaneously requires them both to ignore the undoubted advantage that one of them could gain for herself by defecting. Because this personal advantage is obvious to both of them, it is as rational for one or both of them to defect as it is to jointly choose to co-operate, but in jointly defecting they risk becoming worse off. Something is not quite right here and this makes prisoner's dilemma games immensely interesting. Hence, the spending of US defence funds supporting Rand's esoteric research was a proper use of taxpayers' money.

I came across the red-blue game for the first time in the mid-1970s,[187] when I observed a version of it played on a training course for shop stewards. Later, my Australian collaborator, Colin Rose, introduced me to his version of the game and I know of no more effective a way to demonstrate the superiority of relying on the other negotiator's behaviour, rather than his personality, as the guide to one's own negotiating behaviour. Since then, I have observed thousands of managers playing this game in teams or in pairs.

You are still sceptical? Let us play, then, a mind game without content, without side references to prisoners and jail terms and the many other formulations of these games. Let us play at least two rounds of the red-blue dilemma game.

Briefly, you are told, without elaboration or further discussion, that your objective is 'maximize your positive scores'. Some players complain, after the game, that they should have been told whether the objective was to maximize their own or their joint scores with their partners, because 'this would have altered their behaviour'. Of course it would, which is why they were not told – it is the whole point of creating a dilemma that the players choose their own behaviour, uncontaminated by other people's advice!

How you interpret the red-blue game, or the game of life itself, depends on what you think are the 'rules' and 'what are the objectives' of your interaction with others, and these thoughts depend on your attitudes and beliefs about life and your relationships with others.

The red-blue game deliberately has minimal content and you get nothing other than an exposition of the rules in the briefing. Without hints or explicit guidance, you must interpret through your own personal filters the stated objective 'to maximize your positive score' and it is up to you to select the appropriate behaviours (i.e. to play red or blue) that you believe will deliver your perceived objective.

Each player has two pieces of paper, on one of which you write the letter *R* for red and on the other you write the letter *B* for blue. Each round of the game requires that you and your colleague independently choose to play either red or blue and, having made your choices, you then reveal them simultaneously to each other. According to the specific combinations of red and blue that are revealed you both receive scores, positive or negative.[188]

The scores for the three possible combinations of red and blue are set out in Figure 4.3.

○   blue – blue: 4 points each

○   red – red: minus 4 points each

○   red – blue   the player who played red wins 8 points
                 the player who played blue, loses 8 points

Figure 4.3 Scoring combinations for the red-blue game

The similarity with the choice in the prisoner's dilemma game is clear:

○   If you believe that the other player is an opponent, with whom you are necessarily in competition for points, you will play red in round one (equivalent to defecting by confessing in prisoner's dilemma) and hope to gain 8 points if your opponent plays blue.
○   If you consider that you will gain more by co-operation, you will play blue in round one (equivalent to not confessing) in the hope of gaining 4 points if your partner plays blue (but at the risk of losing 8 points if she plays red).

In a one-round game like the original prisoner's dilemma, you only get one chance to make a choice. In the red-blue dilemma game you play ten rounds and have ten choices (the players in the first recorded play of this game had 100 choices).[189] Obviously what happens in round one may alter or confirm your perceptions of the nature of the game – to compete or to co-operate with your partner? – and, therefore, you may alter your choices (behaviour) in the subsequent rounds.

In a ten-round red-blue game, the possible scores range from a maximum of plus 96 to a minimum of minus 96. These scores can only occur if one of you plays red in every round, and the other consistently plays blue. I have only seen this outcome once, when a magistrate said he considered his 'integrity' was more important to him than 'your silly game', a view not shared by his partner, who thought she had died and gone to heaven! No matter how many times she played red she kept getting blues back from the magistrate. Presumably, he does not behave so tolerantly with persistent offenders brought before his court, otherwise he would jeopardize law and order in his home town!

Most people in the game of life react to negative feedback (i.e., hurt or losses) by stopping their (blue) behaviour if all they get from the other player is persistent (red) harmful behaviour – which is why a child normally only touches a hot iron once. In red-blue games, after a couple of defections, you change from blue to red play to block your partner gaining points at your expense.

How do you see the game of life? Is it a Hobbesian 'all against all' nightmare, or are you constrained by fears of consequential retaliation, or is it that your moral code prevents you from defecting in your relationships? Is life just a game (of chance like cards or dice, or of skill like tennis, football, golf, etc.) where you behave as if your playing partner is an opponent? In poker bluffing is expected and in Scrabble attempting to disqualify unusual words is allowed. Normally no harm is done. Why should it be different in the red-blue game and in the game of life?

That is the beauty of a dilemma game without content. It allows for behaviour governed solely by the rules. Because the rules prohibit talking during the rounds, each player must 'read' their opponent's intentions only through what they do and not from what they say, or could say, they meant to do or why they do it.

Take round-one behaviour as an example. For both players the choice is red or blue. If the player reasons competitively and tries to maximize her positive score at the expense of her partner, she plays red and, if her partner plays blue, she wins 8 points and her partner loses 8 points. This opens a 16-point gap between them in her favour. If her partner plays red in round one too, they both lose 4 points. But this is a better outcome for her than playing blue in round one and losing 8 points if her partner plays red. But is it? The answer depends on how she reads the game. In the post-game analysis, players are asked to reveal their reasons for playing red in round one. Unambiguously, playing red in round one is 'rational', *provided it is a one-round game*, because plus 8 versus minus 4 gives red play a higher expected value than blue play. But this is pure 'short termism'.

For one thing, her partner notices what colour she plays because her behaviour immediately affects him. Consider the message he receives from her behaviour. Let us assume he played blue in round one, as approximately just under half the players do in my experience. Her red play is perceived as antagonistic to him because she gains 8 points at his expense. In the prisoner's dilemma game her partner would certainly notice her behaviour when he ends up serving ten years and she gets off.

What does this analysis tell us about the role of behaviour in negotiation? Let us reflect a little. The game is concerned with pure behaviour unsullied with your verbalizations about your intentions or reasoning. You make a simple choice, red or blue, and reveal it to your partner, who does exactly the same. But whichever colour you play, you send a message that may not be the one they receive. They judge your intentions on how your behaviour, not your intentions, affects them.

From the rules of the red-blue game, the maximum joint gain is 48 points each. I have found that about 8 per cent of players achieve 48 each (though Carlise and Parker report that 12 per cent of their players did so). This means 92 per cent of players do not maximize their joint scores, and this is disappointing contrary evidence if you passionately believe that co-operation necessarily triumphs over non-co-operation in human relationships.

Here we can clear up some confusion about so-called 'win-win' outcomes, made popular over the years. It has almost become what someone called a 'win-win religion' which, like motherhood and apple pie, makes the pursuit of the win-win outcome unchallengeable as an intention. The matrix diagram that usually supports the win-win cause is shown in Figure 4.4.

Player B

		Blue	Red
	Blue	Win – win (Both win)	Lose – win (A loses, B wins)
Player A			
	Red	Win – lose (A wins, B loses)	Lose – lose (Both lose)

Figure 4.4 The standard win-win matrix

Win-win is not by itself a strategy, or a style, it is an outcome, and though desirable, it is still a consequence of certain combinations of behaviour, that must occur simultaneously to achieve it.

Win-win behaviours contrast with win-lose behaviours, usually as a series of opposites, such as are summed up in being co-operative (keeping one's promises) as opposed to being non-co-operative (defecting on one's promises). Because it takes two to tango, the choice of co-operation versus non-co-operation is not an independent choice unique to one of the parties only. Circumstances can force the negotiator to behave non-co-operatively, irrespective of his desire for a win-win outcome. In practice, to behave co-operatively, irrespective of the other negotiator's behaviour, is profoundly silly because it does not lead to a desired win-win outcome. That is what the red-blue game illustrates directly in a fog horn manner to the practitioners who play it. However you can see that whether by playing the game or reading a book, you still must come to the same conclusion that was uncovered by the original experiments with the prisoner's dilemma:[190] while win-win is rational, in practice, negotiators defect.

When I first began to think seriously about this problem, I wondered why John Nash appeared to be wrong. If maximizing the joint gains of negotiation is not an outcome common to practical negotiators, why did negotiators, who knew of the benefits of win-win negotiation, still opt for behaviours that were likely to produce sub-optimal outcomes?

The dilemma game illustrates the discontinuity between intention and behaviour, and observation supports the belief that this discontinuity is dominant in the real world. Unless negotiators can rely on their partners refraining from defecting, they cannot rely on experiencing, nor safely can they practise, the behaviour necessary for the desired outcome of win-win. Hence, one or both have a rationale for defection: they defect (play red) not because they necessarily want to do so (though *some* clearly do), but because they must!

When asked what they think the red-blue game is about many players cite '*trust.*' This is only partly correct, because *risk* necessarily constrains trust and the dilemma game is about risk too. And it is the risk of defection of the other negotiator that tempts you to defect to protect yourself. Experts define security as 'the elimination of trust'. But trust and risk in the game of life are inescapable companions. You can't have one without the other. As trust is partnered by risk, the behaviour of the majority of negotiators who do not choose to behave in a manner that produces a Nash solution, of maximizing their joint gains, is fully explainable. The task, however, is to do something about it.

And with this conclusion, we end our diversion and go back to behaviour as the alternative to the dead-end of personality profiling.

THE PRIME COLOURS OF NEGOTIATION

A negotiator's behaviour is a more reliable guide to how you should react than what you might think of her personality. Behaviour is what counts. To transform this insight into a practical tool we first sketch a model of behaviour.

In Figure 4.5 there are three boxes, one behind the other, each slightly off set. Behaviour, the nearest box, is the most visible to other people, reflecting the fact that behaviours, and/or their consequences, do not pass unnoticed.

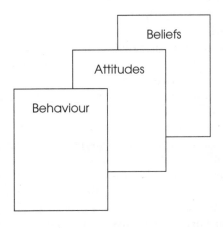

Figure 4.5 Behaviour, attitudes and beliefs

Behind your visible behaviour, but not perfectly correlated with it (hence its box is slightly offset in Figure 4.5) lie your partly visible attitudes. You make these partly visible by verbalizing them but as you can verbalize any attitudes of your private choice, they are not really so visible and, therefore, as reliable a guide to your intentions, as your behaviour. While you can mislead people about your attitudes, it is much more difficult to mislead them about your behaviour – you either did something or you did not. You put yourself at risk if you choose to ignore what they do but, perhaps, naively trust their explanations for doing it.

Behind your attitudes lie your private core beliefs, which are less flexible than your attitudes because you can choose different attitudes for every situation, while your beliefs tend to consist of a more rigid 'rule' for all situations. Again beliefs do not perfectly correlate with either your attitudes or your behaviour.

Beliefs are private and deeply held. They mature over many years and most people (but not fanatics and proselytizers) keep them to themselves. True, people may shamelessly, or fearfully, profess to believe in certain precepts from politics, religion or morality, when privately they neither believe in them at all, nor do they behave in accordance with them. Embarrassment or fear can prompt people to conceal their true beliefs, while manifesting in public whatever is conducive to their personal safety, or their enjoyment of a 'quiet life'. As true, many people honestly profess to believe in certain precepts, sometimes at great risk to their person.[191]

Whether your beliefs or values, that is the way you see the world and your place in it, dominate your behaviour is another matter, but for sure, experience suggests, when dealing with other people it is best to steer well clear of implied criticism or challenges to their beliefs, whether truthfully or hypocritically professed, or implied by whatever labels they give for them. For these reasons, the most reliable evidence for what they are about in negotiation, is not what they profess they are about but what they do. Again, behaviour is what counts!

Your attitudes and beliefs, indirectly to some extent, drive your behaviour because you do not behave in a vacuum. If we could reliably tap into your true attitudes and beliefs (which I don't believe we can), we could predict roughly how you would behave in given negotiating situations. Unfortunately, it is far more complex than that because you have a multitude of attitudes, some of which might guide you on one occasion to behave one way and others, on another occasion, might guide you to behave in a different way.

In the main, you are situationally flexible. When challenged on inconsistencies in your attitudes (and you are bound to have inconsistencies), with perfect justification you can reply that how you behave depends on the circumstances. Discussing this problem with negotiators over many years, I have found that they often 'explain' their contradictory attitudes to almost similar negotiating scenarios by saying: 'it all depends'.

We sometimes obtain believably candid evidence of the attitudes of negotiators when we debrief with them the results of the red-blue game in our workshops. The first question we ask[192] is: 'who played red in round one?' Usually, just over half the participants indicate that they did so. The next question is: 'why?' The answers are interesting. They fall into two categories:

O   'I played red because I wanted to get 8 points from the blue play of the other player (the majority of red players).'

O   'I played red because I expected red play from the other player.'

Playing red with the intention to gain 8 points from a partner whom you expect to play blue, unambiguously, is an intention to *exploit* your partner's blue play. Alternatively, playing red because you expect your partner to play red is unambiguously an intention to *protect* yourself (this way you only lose 4 points, not 8). These admissions are candid glimpses of their attitudes to the rules of the dilemma game and of their interpretation of the objective of maximizing their positive points.

In one workshop, a senior corporate banker asserted that her partner had not intended to exploit her because it was her unintentional mistake to play blue. I asked her how she knew what were her partner's intentions? You cannot see into the heads of the people with whom you negotiate. Their intentions are opaque, to say the least. All you should rely on is their behaviour: did they play red or blue? If they played red, the safest and the most reliable assessment of their intentions is to impute malign, not benign, motives to them and certainly you should not seek to justify their intentions in the reasons for your own behaviour.

From the red player's perspective, how do they regard blue or red play by the other player?

O   If you are out to exploit them, your partner's blue play confirms that you are dealing with a *naive* player who has not got enough sense to protect herself.
O   If the exploiter gets a red in round one from his partner, he has the choice of imputing a desire to exploit him on their behalf or a desire to protect themselves. Observation suggests that they impute the *exploitation* motive to their partner more often than they impute a protection motive. Malign motivations in one's self tend to promote malign interpretations of other people's motives!
O   If the protector gets a red in round one, this confirms their own motivation to protect themselves because they expected their partner to *exploit* them.

From this analysis, it is no wonder that red play provokes, in the main, a red response and that exploitative interpretations of the rules and objectives of the dilemma game predominate, if not quite in round one, certainly by rounds two or three: 'the best way to maximize my points is by taking them from the other player'.

What of those players (just under half) who played blue in round one? Why did they play blue? Answers vary. They fall into two main categories:

○   'I wanted to signal a willingness to co-operate.'
○   'I misunderstood the rules (e.g. played randomly).'

The more interesting point is what did they do next? This will depend on how you, the blue player, see your partner's play:

○   If you got a blue back, then there is every chance that you can develop a *co-operative* joint play to maximize your joint scores (remember this happens in only 8 per cent of our games).
○   If, however, your partner plays a red, you should take this as a gesture of *non-co-operation* and act accordingly – you should respond with a red in round two and see what your partner plays.
○   If you get another red, your partner is clearly out to *exploit* you and this suggests that you should play red yourself in round three.
○   If you get, instead, a blue from your partner, you should treat this as an 'apology'. Implicitly they are saying by their behaviour: 'I'm sorry I did not mean to take 8 points from you as I was *protecting* myself in case you played red'. Both can play blue in round three and expect a blue back.

The least helpful course for a blue player in round one, who gets back a red, is to 'give them another chance' by playing blue in round two. Sure, it is a co-operative play but it increases the risks of further red play by confusing the message signalled to the red player. If the round one red player plays red again in round two, a round two blue player is now 16 down and, worse, signals to the red player even greater naivety on his own part.

If, on the other hand, the round one red player plays blue in round two and receives a blue again from the round one blue player, he could conclude that he 'wasted an opportunity to play red and gain another 8 points'. Only the 'punishment', or more correctly the willingness to inflict punishment on the red player by retaliating with a red in round two, sends a clear and assertive signal: 'I want to co-operate with you, which is why I played blue in round one, but don't mess with me, if you want me to resume co-operation!'

That there is a connection between behaviour and attitudes in negotiation is unquestioned. To understand the implications of this relationship I shall introduce the prime 'colours of negotiation'. We move from dilemma games to the more complex interactions of negotiation by taking with us labels for the behaviours.

The prime colours of negotiation are *red* and *blue* (other versions of the dilemma game reverse the colours so that red is for co-operative plays and blue for 'selfishly competitive' plays).[193] Because the dilemma game clearly illustrates the consequences of choosing to play either red or blue, it is a convenient label for the negotiating behaviours and attitudes that lie behind your actions in a negotiating interaction. For make no mistake, in the pressure zone of interactive bargaining you do not have more than seconds – usually much less – to react to what they are doing. Using colours to identify their behaviour and to guide your own is an effective way to remember what to do. Think of red and blue as the colours at the extremes along a continuum, with red at one end and blue at the other.

Figure 4.6 summarizes some of the characteristics of extreme red and blue attitudes to a negotiator's behaviour. The most important summary expressions are:

○   'more for me means less for you' (non-co-operative);
○   'more for me means more for you' (co-operative).

A joint co-operative stance maximizes their joint gains. Individual non-co-operative stances can only improve one person's gains at the expense of the other. Experience shows that most people opt for, or end up, trying to maximize their own gains by exploiting their partners. As often, of course, sub-optimal play reduces, or if deadlocks are included, eliminates, the potential gains of both parties through negative feedback and the need to protect oneself.

RED	BLUE
'More for me means less for you'	'More for me means more for you'
Aggressively competitive	Assertively co-operative
Prefers to dominate	Prefers mutual respect
Seeks to win	Seeks to succeed
All deals are one-offs	All deals lead to others
Use ploys and gambits	Prefers to be non-manipulative
Favours bluffs and coercion	Doesn't bluff or coerce
Exploits the submissive	Yields to the aggressive

Figure 4.6 The prime colours of negotiating behaviour

Red behaviour derives from attitudes that see negotiation as a non-co-operative contest. Blue behaviour derives from attitudes that see negotiation as a chance for a co-operative sharing of the potential gains *but blue behaviour only works if reciprocated by the other party's blue behaviour.* In *ultimo extremis*, blue attitudes tip over into submissive behaviour, such is the intensity of an extreme blue commitment to co-operation.

Neither red nor blue behaviour is 'right' or 'wrong'. You must not naively trust others and in consequence you behave in a cautious, that is untrusting, manner. While your intention is to be more trusting, when you see how the other person behaves, often it is too late by then because your own caution provokes the other negotiator's suspicions of what you are up to and they play red to protect themselves: too suspicious and you provoke suspicion, too trusting and they assume your naivety.

Extreme red and blue behaviour manifests itself into one or other of the following:

○ Red players are *takers*: they seek to take something for nothing, and usually succeed against submissive extreme blue players.
○ Blue players are *givers*: they seek to give something for nothing and usually lose against extreme red players.

From observation certain attitudes are linked to certain behaviours and this can be illustrated by categorizing certain attitudinal statements about negotiation by whether they are red or blue, as in Figure 4.7. The extent to which you agree or disagree with the statements is a clue to your likely red or blue behaviour.

Red attitudes

1. My interests are far more important than preserving relationships.

2. I will not re-negotiate profitable deals just because the other negotiator claims he is in difficulties – a deal is a deal.

3. I look after my own interests and leave them to look after theirs.

4. Something for nothing always beats something for something.

5. You have to be cruel to be kind in business.

6. Power is more useful than a good case.

7. If they buckle under pressure I should push harder.

8. I do not reveal my true feelings in case the other negotiator takes advantage.

9.   If they give me an opportunity to take advantage of them, that's their problem.

10.   It is not my responsibility to consider the consequences to them of my ploys.

Blue attitudes

1.   It is not fair to take advantage of the other negotiator if she makes a mistake.

2.   Negotiators should not conceal their feelings and intentions.

3.   A marginal deal is better than no deal.

4.   If the relationship is important I should be more accommodating.

5.   Developing a good relationship is more important than taking advantage of their weaknesses.

6.   It is generally beneficial to be open about one's true intentions.

7.   Just because they are soft and cannot look after themselves does not mean they deserve to be manipulated.

8.   It is better to preserve goodwill than upset them by rejecting their marginal deals.

9.   I should give in to difficult people if it means I lose their business.

10.   I am worried about rejection when negotiating.

Figure 4.7   Typical red and blue attitudes to negotiation[194]

With how many of these, or similar attitudes, are you comfortable? This could indicate your proclivity for red or blue behaviours. Note that your proclivity for this or that set, or mixture, of attitudes is not ethically significant. It is most important that you do not assume that red players are 'bad' while blue players are 'good', since neither assessment is justified.

As shown in the dilemma game, blue players in round one, who receive a red, should themselves switch to red play in round two. If, in these circumstances, they cannot switch from blue to red plays they perform badly in the dilemma game and, if their incapacity to play red is replicated in analogous circumstances in negotiation, they will also do less well as negotiators.

Red play can be – must be! – instigated by negative feedback. If your ancestors had tried to have close relationships with dangerous predators, irrespective of the negative feedback from their observations of others vainly trying to do so, key people missing from the chain of the generations from them to you, might have meant that you would not have been around today to read this.

People who do not learn from negative feedback (e.g. water and electricity do not mix well; crossing roads without looking is deadly, and jay walking in mine fields is unhealthy, etc.) are destined to shorter lifespans, or to be incarcerated in protective care.

Where your attitudes come from – which experiences led you to adopt this or that attitude to negotiation – is interesting perhaps to you, but not really relevant to the people with whom you negotiate. They must cope with your behaviour. Your therapist copes with your rationalizations of it.

Behaviourally, your red or blue attitudes influence how you read a particular negotiation and what you do during it. Some people will tend to act and react the same way in that and every other negotiation. Where this forms a regular pattern, you are a slave to your attitudes.

 ## RESULTS VERSUS RELATIONSHIPS

Running through the categories of red and blue attitudes, sometimes explicitly, sometimes implicitly, is a thematic question of your negotiating objectives: which is the most important to you in this negotiation – the substantive results or the relationship between you and the other negotiator? Or, put another way, to what extent is your need for results constrained by your need for a relationship, or your need for a relationship constrained by your need for results?

Results orientations are associated overwhelmingly with pure red behaviour; relationships orientations are associated overwhelmingly with pure blue behaviour. Few people are so single minded as to be wholly red or blue and most of us are a mixture of both. Negotiators are pulled in different directions by the mixture of their orientations to results and relationships.

The substantive *result* of negotiating is its outcome ('who gets how much of what, where, when?') and, if this is the predominant determinant of your behaviour, you hold predominantly reddish attitudes. Your attitudes are justified through the results you believe you achieve and the results you achieve justify your red attitudes.

A one-off negotiation with a used car seller, or an estate agent, or a market trader in Casablanca, is seldom the beginning of a lifetime relationship. People who do well in these situations tend to be results oriented. The sellers in one-off deals, however, may relax you with behaviour that suggests that they are about to become your best friend. You would do well to eschew any thoughts of how 'nice' he is and simply concentrate on the deal and nothing but the deal, for you can be sure that is what he is doing. If you negotiate in a one-off deal and cannot switch to a results-oriented red approach, perhaps because you are too influenced by the seller's phoney relationship lines, you will do less well than those who switch because they are not taken in by the sales pitch.

Multiple negotiations with the same suppliers or customers usually create some kind of *relationship* with them, if only bred of constant contact and acquaintance. The extent of the relationship can vary from casual or contemptuous familiarity through to a deeply involved alignment of interests. This situation requires people flexible enough to constrain their redness and to deploy more blue-ish behaviours in search of ways to improve the relationship. In long-term business relationships, the parties co-operate to serve mutual goals. They become part of each other's added value chain. This outcome of a relationship orientation is at present relatively rarely achieved, though many are striving for it.

Some researchers have asserted that the quintessential negotiation dilemma is the tension between the results-relationships orientation.[195] Most negotiators aim to satisfy both orientations, with a few satisfying solely one or the other and a corresponding few satisfying both orientations to a high degree. In Figure 4.8, the boxes in the matrix illustrate the range of combined orientations.

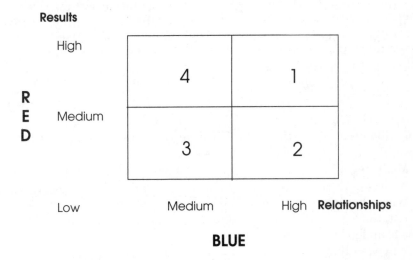

Figure 4.8 Results-relationships orientations matrix

The degree to which you are results or relationship oriented is marked on the vertical and the horizontal axes by the scale from low, through medium to high. The more you are oriented to results, the higher up the vertical axis you are placed; the more you are oriented to relationships the further along the horizontal axis you are placed. Co-ordinates from your places on the vertical and horizontal axes will intersect at some point in the matrix and you will be placed within one of the four boxes.

If you are highly results-oriented (extreme red) and only low, or even zero, relationship-oriented, your intersecting co-ordinates would place you close to the top left-hand corner of box 4, while if you are wholly relationship-oriented (extreme blue) and low, or zero, results-oriented, you would be placed by the co-ordinates close to the bottom right-hand corner of box 2.

If you are of a low orientation on the results and relationship dimensions you would be close to the bottom left-hand corner of box 3 and, if you are of medium orientation, you would be closer to the top right-hand corner of box 3. The stronger your orientations to one or other of the results or relationships dimensions, the closer your co-ordinates would be to the relevant axes in boxes 4 and 2.

Box 1 is that much sought for but difficult to attain combination of orientations, that is you are highly oriented to both results and relationships and ideally as close as possible to the top right-hand corner of box 1. This combination is not a trade-off between the orientations, it is a combination of the strengths of each orientation in that you are achieving both strong results and strong relationships with your customers and/or your suppliers. You are neither all red nor all blue – your negotiating colour is deep *purple!*

In Figure 4.9, the matrix is reproduced with positions marked on it that are representative of some common experiences of companies. Over the years I have tested negotiators for their awareness of their results-relationship orientations and while making no claims for the scientific accuracy of the tests, I believe they are at least indicative. Several points emerge from these tests.

Many negotiators, self-assessing their results-relationships orientations, locate themselves in box 1 (Figure 4.9) close to the point marked *x*. When, however, they answered a short questionnaire testing their orientations most of them moved to the left in the matrix, closer to the line bounded by *b* in box 4 and *a* in box 2.

Why was this so and what might it mean? For a start, it suggests that negotiators exaggerate the degree to which they satisfy their results-relationship's orientations. Box 1 is a worthy ideal goal and they think they are better at achieving some position in it than perhaps their underlying attitudes and their consequent behaviours, as drawn out from the questionnaire, suggest.

Second, those negotiators whose self-assessed positions in the matrix place them in either box 4 (predominantly results-oriented) or 2 (predominantly relationship-oriented) also move their positions after the questionnaire closer to the axes. This supports the view that negotiators believe they are better at optimizing their combined orientations than, probably, they are in practice.

The sloping line in Figure 4.9 crosses three boxes (4, 2, and 3) and it divides negotiators into one of three orientations: predominantly red results (4); predominantly blue relationships (2), or weak in both results and relationships (3) (a very pale purple). From assignments I undertake, I wonder if this explains the diverse goals that companies switch between in occasional triumphs of hope over practice, variously called 'culture change' programmes? For example, a bank, concerned about its results, looked at the way its managers dealt with their customers. It found that a typical bank manager's approach to business customers was, frankly, to coddle them. As a group they were firmly positioned around a in Figure 4.9.

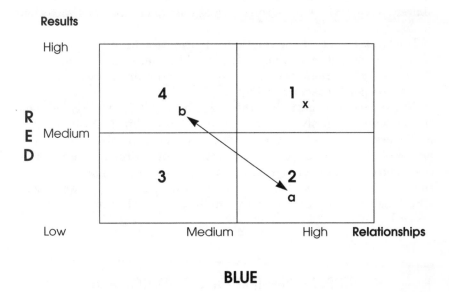

Figure 4.9 Representative results-relationships matrix

In the bank's culture the ultimate 'sin' of banking practice was 'to lose a customer', and hence losing customers was not a good career move. The consequence of this all-pervasive culture was to make it easier for managers, when negotiating fees and interest rates with unsettled customers, to give in, that is act extremely blue. This was good for their relationships with their connections but not so hot for their results as bankers.

The bank embarked on a programme of improving the results orientations of its managers, aiming in effect to move them from *a* towards, or further to the north-east of, *x* in Figure 4.9. However, this objective is not achieved by top-level fiat alone. Pushing for a redder results orientation in a deeply blue relationship climate usually damages relationships with at least some of the existing customers. Unless the losses are replaced with new customers it must have a downward impact on the bank's market share. The managers' orientations do not move the bank towards *x* in box 1, as intended, because they move instead towards *b* in box 4.

Presently, I have just started working on the reverse assignment with a different bank. This bank is concerned that its managers, using our terminology, are too oriented towards results at the expense of their relationships and, in consequence, the bank is losing market share to rivals who have stronger relationship orientations with their customers.

The bank feels that the relationship orientations of their managers need to be strengthened and, again, would prefer it if they could move their managers' orientations from somewhere around *b* towards, or further to the north-east of, *x* in Figure 4.9.

I have a feeling that unless this transformation is properly handled, the bank will certainly increase the blue relationship orientations of its managers but, by moving their orientations, not towards *x*, but towards and beyond *a* in a south-easterly direction. Is it, therefore, the case that some cultural change programmes merely move their managers along the line *ab* and not into box 1? Becoming aware of the results-relationship tension is the first step to handling these change programmes properly.

 THE PURPLE PRINCIPLE OF CONDITIONALITY

There are other behavioural dilemmas for negotiators besides that of whether to be driven by the results or the relationship. These other ways of looking at the dilemmas of negotiation behaviour are related because they stem from the basic choice of whether to be co-operative or

non-co-operative. As non-co-operative negotiation is the norm in practice, it is not surprising that trainers and practitioners have picked up
different ways of looking at basically the same phenomenon.

People have observed the contents of the red-blue continuum and
have given it different labels. Red and blue behaviours link and overlap
with what is popularly known as hard or soft ways of playing the negotiation game. They identify approaches to negotiation that are fundamentally different. Because they are set up as two extremes, the
dilemma they create is about which way to play. Some people play
either one or the other game more or less permanently, others switch
between them, gravitating to one or the other in an effort to match
their behaviour to whatever they make of the circumstances. As neither game is appropriate, this dilemma causes practitioners a lot of
grief. It has led some trainers to opt out of both ways of playing
the game by creating a new game altogether, called Principled
Negotiation.[196]

Our discussion of Principled Negotiation is postponed until Chapter
5. What I want to do for the moment is to develop the alternative to
the choice of 'hard' (red) or 'soft' (blue). Figure 4.10 (see page 190) is one
such useful categorization of the differences between 'hard' and 'soft'
behaviours.

The hard bargainer is the archetypal positional posturer – he determines his position, fortifies it, won't move, doesn't move and doesn't
blink while demanding that you move. He is a *taker* and like all red
players he wants something from you for nothing.

The soft bargainer is the archetypal namby-pamby – determines
the relationship, works to keep it alive, has no fixed ideas let alone
positions, won't stop moving, doesn't stop moving and doesn't flinch
when you demand he gives you more. He is a *giver* and like all blue
players at heart he wants you to have something from him for nothing.

The other approach in traditional negotiation practice is that of a
trader. This behaviour is neither hard nor soft, neither red nor blue. It
resolves the dilemma of choice by combining these separate behaviours
into a single consistent behaviour known as the *purple conditionality
principle*.

This principle owes its origins to the observed behaviours of effective
negotiators. A short analysis will demonstrate the credibility of that
assertion and, I trust, will indelibly imprint itself on your consciousness and in your practice.

Consider a hard player. What is their aim? Taking, of course. And
why do they take? Because they believe that making demands is how to
get what they want. They demand things from you and take scarce
notice of what you want. It is a one-way street, going their way not
yours. This is classic extreme red behaviour.

190 DIALOGUE

Hard	Soft
Participants are adversaries	Participants are friends
The goal is victory	The goal is agreement
Demand concessions as a condition of the relationship	Make concessions as a condition of the relationship
Be hard on the people and the problem	Be soft on the people and the problem
Distrust others	Trust others
Dig into your position	Change your position
Make threats	Make offers
Mislead as to your bottom line	Disclose your bottom line
Demand one-sided gains as the price of agreement	Accept one-sided losses as the price of agreement
Search for the single answer: the one *you* will accept	Search for the single answer: the one *they* will accept
Insist on your position	Insist on agreement
Win the contest of will	Avoid a contest of will
Apply pressure	Yield to pressure

Figure 4.10 Hard and soft negotiating behaviours[197]

Consider a soft player. What is their aim? Giving, of course. And why do they give? Because they believe that conceding is how to get what they want. They give things to you and take scarce notice of what it costs them, or whether they get anything back in return. It is a one-way street, going your way not theirs. This is classic extreme blue behaviour.

If neither of these behaviours is appropriate, what can we do? Well, it is like the separate elements of sodium and chlorine, both of which are hazardous to your health and neither of which you can do without for long periods. In order to ingest these life-saving elements without risk of harm, nature provides them for you in the form of common table salt.

Likewise, in negotiation. The elements of taking and giving are injurious of a proclivity to trade if taken separately. The red player runs out of people to do business with; the blue player runs out of resources to give away. In order to procure what we want without risks of deadlock or penury, negotiation provides the safe means for you to trade using the purple conditionality principle.

By combining your red demands with your blue offers you make a *purple* conditional proposal, which is the only assertive way to propose and to bargain (see Figure 4.11).

CONDITION	OFFER
'IF you give me . . .	THEN I will offer you . . .'
your red side	your blue side

Figure 4.11 The purple conditionality principle

Note that the conditional proposal uses an 'IF ... THEN' format. This has long been a theme of Negotiate's negotiating workshops – we call it the 'Big IF' to drum it home to those negotiators who flunked making their proposals in the conditional format. Of course, other similar meaning formats — 'provided that' or 'on condition that', and such like – are perfectly acceptable in practice, though over the years I have found the 'IF-THEN' version sticks in the memories of most negotiators and has the greatest impact on their degree of assertiveness when making proposals.

You don't have to choose between behaving in a red manner – 'gimme this, gimme that' – nor do you have to try to meld the behaviours in Figure 4.10. For a start there is no question of you having to 'accept one-sided losses', nor feel that you have to 'make concessions to cultivate the relationship', nor do you need to 'make threats', nor 'insist on your position', and so on. All of those choices are phoney ones. If you have got stuck into one or other set of behaviours, exemplified in Figure 4.10, you are in deep trouble as a negotiator, because neither of them is a viable strategy against a purple conditional proposer.

So-called hardness in negotiation carries with it a false image for personal 'toughness' and resolute 'strength of character'. So-called softness has the reputation it deserves. Up against a conditional bargainer, neither of these games can succeed. The conditional bargainer implicitly – and sometimes explicitly – makes the statement, by no means necessarily in a louder voice than it takes to talk intimately to one's loved one, that is the epitome of the only genuine toughness in negotiation that counts: 'You will get absolutely nothing from me unless and until I get something from you.' The determination to hold to that statement of the explicit trade and the constancy of applying it in practice at all times when negotiating is about as tough as you can ever get as a negotiator. It is also the most accommodating that you can get as well, because it is founded on the principle that a negotiated decision provides something for both parties – you get some of what you want and they get some of what they want. And if the parties volunteer to accept the traded bargain, what could be fairer?

My assertion, therefore, is that there are only three main behaviours, taking, giving or trading, that you have to identify and react to, often under time and other pressures. Identifying their behaviour is much more manageable than trying to read their personalities.

As the effective negotiator is always a trader, your response is always the same no matter what they are about. You are a conditional bargainer, nothing less, nothing more. At a stroke you can cope with any form of behaviour that comes across the table.

You read the game they are playing and you can respond using a conditional bargain as the most effective counter-measure available in negotiation. There is no need for special effects, complicated 16-box permutations, in-depth personality analysis or over theoretical strategies. More, you can learn and be trained to use conditional bargaining as the single most appropriate behavioural response in a negotiator's repertoire of skills and you can practise it immediately. In a short time, with some specific practice opportunities, it will become the single major contributor to your successful career as a negotiator.

To see why this is so, we shall explore the *conditional exchange principle*. Trading behaviour can be manifested by the questions that you ask ('What is in it for me?'), by the summaries that you make ('In return for your requirements, you are offering to meet some of ours'), by your signals ('On the basis of what you are offering to us at present, we would have difficulty making a recommendation to our board to make available to you the full range of our services'), and, of course, by the proposals and bargains that you make (always, always in the IF-THEN format). Almost everything you say to them in the face-to-face interaction implies, or, preferably, explicitly states, that the negotiated decision will be based on exchange, and not on them or you taking, or them or you giving. Your behaviour advertises your determination to trade.

What of them? That depends on their behaviour. If they appear not to be considering your requirements (they only talk about their own needs and do not refer to, or ask questions about, your needs, nor do they show any interest in them when they are raised by you) their behaviour suggests a taker's stance. Your determination not to subscribe to their taker's stance counterpoises the two behaviours, behind which are the two differing attitudes to what negotiation is about in general and what it is about in the circumstances you both face in this particular negotiation.

What happens next is as much up to you as to them. If you crumble, you will end up a giver not a negotiator; if they switch from trying to take to trying to bargain with you, they end up, like you, a trader. It can only get better for both of your from then on.

On the other hand, their behaviour can suggest that they are givers. They appear overly concerned, for instance, about your requirements, your interests, your needs, even to the exclusion of articulating their own needs at all. Though it might seem too good to be true that they want to give the store away, you may wish to consider the implications of taking advantage of their behaviour and the longer term disadvantages encouraging taking or giving as alternatives to trading.

Takers exist and prosper because their behaviour is rewarded by the behaviour of givers. If there were fewer givers around there would be fewer takers in the field. Behaviour is reinforced by the outcomes it produces and nothing reinforces takers' behaviour more than it being fed by the behaviour of givers. It is, therefore, in your interests as a trader to try to reduce the incidence of giver behaviour.

The behaviour of givers arises from their attitude towards their relationships with others. So besotted are they with the benefits of co-operation that they strive to enhance relationships by ensuring that their generosity is abundantly evident. They can go so far as to 'give the store away' by acceding to your requests in full, plus awarding you unasked for bonuses.

O   You ring them up for an emergency delivery and immediately they say 'yes' and offer you a discount on top, plus they agree to have the delivery made to you over a holiday weekend, for which they have to pay their employees premium rates in overtime and holiday pay, without attempting to recover these costs from you.

O   They eschew any sign of a conflict of interests, by denying that confrontation exists, or if its existence cannot be denied, that it has a role in their relationship with you, and to prove it, they give in at the slightest sign of you having a problem, no matter how costly solving your problem is to them.

What can you do about nature's givers? Surely it is their responsibility, and not yours, for them to look after their own interests? See how easy it is to wash your hands of them and to form the view that if they are stupid enough to give you what you want, and more, without asking for anything in return, that is their problem not yours? That is, of course, the attitude behind a taker's behaviour and is instanced in some of the red attitudes set out in Figure 4.10.

I have listened to many takers rationalizing their behaviours in numerous versions of what I call the takers' lament. Whatever way they express it, it is still a taker's attitude and it is still inimical to effective negotiation practice. The problem of the existence of givers is a problem for all negotiators. Temporary membership of the takers' club, when faced with a compliant giver, is no answer to the problem; it only compounds it.

We traders must educate those givers we come across, into doing something other than mere submission. This is not easy because the behaviour associated with trying to do this can have parallels with what a giver does! We try to elicit from them their needs, by questioning, clarifying and summarizing, what they tell us. Sometimes we are almost competing with them to find out what they need to the exclusion of what we need – a sure sign of a giver's behaviour. This is why we have to be very careful that we do not get carried away with our quest to uncover the giver's needs such that we forget to articulate our own.

Hence, we must always be sure to respond to any expression of their needs with references to the general needs we have and by implication, or explicit statement, we always link the two together into a conditional bargaining format: 'Yes, I see that you can deliver the stock in a hurry for me, and if you can do that before Saturday evening I would be prepared to consider paying something towards the additional costs you will incur on the holiday week-end'. An extremist giver would probably respond by offering to deliver without charging for premium costs, so we might have to offer to pay cash on delivery, or offer some form of early settlement of the account.

You might think this is silly, and consider that, if you have a 'live one' in play, you might as well exploit him, but then you would be forgetting what this attempted conditionality bargaining with the giver is about. We are trying to educate the giver into changing his behaviour, and not just with us, but with everybody else he meets, including nature's takers. For be sure, an extremist giver is not going to last too long in charge of any assets, including the possibility that those assets destined for your Saturday delivery will not be available for your benefit if his creditors move in just after your call to him. In this case, your, albeit 'temporary' or 'exceptional' taker's behaviour, means you lose too. Doing business on exceptional taker's terms can damage your interests as much as the interests of the givers.

Finally, a few additional points about the format of conditional proposals and bargains are appropriate before we move onto some typical red behaviours:

O   *Proposals are tentative, bargains are specific*   The most effective
      format is to always lead with your conditions (your red side) and

to follow with your offer (your blue side). But two other points
have to be noted and practised:

○   *Proposals are always stated as vague offers*

Condition	**Offer**
'If you consider my concerns	then I could *consider* your concerns.'
(vague)	(vague)

In proposing your condition may be vague or specific, but the offer
is always vague. For example:

Condition	**Offer**
'If you could improve your delivery schedule	then I could consider making minimum value orders'
(vague)	(vague)
'If you improve your delivery by three days	then I could consider making minimum value orders'
(specific)	(vague)

In both cases you are committed to considering – but not committed to
making – as yet unspecified minimum value orders. How much is a
minimum value has yet to be decided, as has whether the trade-off will
be in minimum value orders, or in some other tradable, if a minimum
value order agreement proves impracticable or too expensive.

Tentative proposals are more for exploration of what might be possible than for a genuine search for a 'yes' at this stage. In fact, it is not
easy to say 'yes' to a vague proposal because you do not yet know to
what you are saying 'yes'. People saying 'yes' to a vague proposal are
not listening to what they are being told.

Common avoidable errors when receiving proposals include:

○   interrupting because you disagree with all or part of it;
○   arguing against it because it appears to be unacceptable (remem-
     ber it is only their first offer!);
○   immediately dismissing it with a 'no', 'not bloody likely', or worse,
     'do you think I'm stupid?' (what answer do you expect?);
○   instantly counter-proposing, suggesting that you have no inten-
     tion of considering their proposals.

As always, the appropriate behaviour is drawn from constructive
debate. It is, of course, imperative that you listen to the proposal, and,
to make sure that you understand it, you should question either, or
both, the condition and the offer. This may produce supplementary
explanations, which reveal information of value to your current

negotiating position. Even your tone of voice, or your involuntary hesitations, or your body language can reveal something about your intentions and your strength of feelings.

If they merely state their own requirements in the manner of a red player, you can ask them for their views on why you should accept their suggestions – what is in it for me?; why should I accept that?, and so on. This lays the basis for your eventual response. If you want to stay in the proposal phase, you will need to formulate your own proposal. Its content would depend on the circumstances, but if you can incorporate into your proposal something they have included in theirs – building on what they propose – it will help to move the negotiations forward. If you cannot incorporate anything at all, you will have to settle for proposing something entirely different.

Many iterations may be necessary before the outline negotiated package takes shape. Each of you will be pushing for your own conditions, and mitigating theirs, pulling on what they are offering, and slowly modifying what you are offering, until the shape of the deal emerges. Here, you need to be careful. Keeping a large number of issues in the air at once is not easy; it can be downright difficult at times. It is tempting to curtail the complexity by separating out the issues and settling on them in turn.

Administrative or procedural convenience is a seductive influence with many negotiators in the proposing and bargaining phases. Settling on many of the issues early on can generate a false sense of progress. As you reduce the number of outstanding issues to be settled, you also tend to isolate the 'difficult' issues and, unintentionally, you reduce the flexibility you have for movement on them. In the extreme, you end up with one difficult issue to settle – usually the money! – and, bereft of an ability to trade across several issues, you are reduced to movement along the negotiating range of the difficult issue only. Your desire to make progress turns the negotiation into a zero-sum game, which may not be a game from which you can expect further progress.

Sometimes, re-negotiating the earlier clauses in a multi-clause contract does not cause problems but sometimes it does, if only for the party who feels required to settle, because of time or other pressures, despite the outstanding, usually, onerous issues. The thought of re-starting a multi-clause negotiation can be enough to put a negotiator's hackles up if they feel they are out of time, or if they are out of patience, or if they are more than satisfied with their 'gains' on earlier clauses, which may now be in jeopardy of a re-negotiation.

My advice remains: link everything together, beginning with phrases that your agreement to the wording of any clause is provisional on 'how the total deal stacks' and that you may wish to return to certain clauses if the negotiations stall on later clauses. Also, if you have to revisit earlier clauses, and to avert charges of 'bad faith', you can work into your debate behaviour phrases like: 'nothing is agreed finally until everything is agreed'.

The principal difference between a proposal and a bargain is that a bargain conveys the *specific* terms on which you are prepared to settle, while a proposal is only tentative.

If they say 'yes' to a specific bargain then you have a deal. It is as simple, and complex, as that. If they say 'no', you have to continue negotiating, if you think a deal is still possible.

To assist in the intense atmosphere of the bargaining phase, bargains are always conditional — there are no exceptions to this rule among effective negotiators. Hence, the bargain is always in the same format as the tentative proposal: IF-THEN. 'IF you agree to this, THEN I will agree to that': the condition and the offer are always specific. There is nothing tentative about a bargain. For example: 'If you agree to these joint and several guarantees, then we will agree to pay $100,000 immediately to your creditors.'

If they accept the specific bargain (joint and several guarantees in exchange for $100,000 debt relief, say) and comply with the condition (the guarantees), then you have made a legally binding contract to perform the offer.

When responding to a bargain, arguing is a weak response because it returns you to the debate. It is also unlikely to produce a revised bargain. People seldom say: 'Oh, I see, my offer is not acceptable because of clause 6. OK, I'll change clause 6 for you'. More often, rejected offers are argued about and arguments about offers often lead to more arguments.

Your best response to an unacceptable bargain is to propose a conditional counter-bargain containing your revision of their terms. If this happens at the start of the negotiation, then debate will follow on the gap between you; if towards the end of a negotiation, counter-bargains can lead quickly (sometimes too quickly) to an agreement.

This chapter ends with an exercise (Figure 4.12) for you to test whether you have grasped the importance of the language of proposing and bargaining. Figure 4.12 is an extract from one of our workshop exercises. Read the proposal or bargaining statements and identify what, if anything, you find wrong with they way they are formulated and then write your version of how you think they should have appeared.

1.   'If I accept a 10 per cent discount, will you give me a bigger order?'

2.   'How about a 7 per cent discount if you order 1 million units a month?'

3.   'OK. I'll accept liquidated damages but I expect something in return.'

4.   'If you give me a bigger order, then I will give you a 5 per cent discount.'

5.   'OK. I can live with a tighter warranty clause.'

6.   'Can you make it 40 instead of 50, if we give you exclusivity?'

Figure 4.12 Negotek® exercise on conditionality
       (For my comments on the exercise, see Appendix 2, p. 319.)

THE MYTHS OF CONCEDING BEHAVIOUR

There are several bargaining possibilities:

1.   They get what they want on your terms.
2.   You get what you want on their terms.
3.   You both get some of what you want on each other's terms.

These possibilities are likely to arise, by themselves or in combination, in a negotiated package when you trade issues, and changes in the issues, with each other, using conditional exchange language, preferably in an IF-THEN format.

However, there are two other (non-bargaining) possibilities:

1.   They get what they want on their terms.
2.   You get what you want on your terms.

These two possibilities arise when bargaining behaviour is replaced by conceding behaviour by one of you. By conceding behaviour, I mean your unreciprocated unilateral movement on an issue, a position, or on a quantum within a position. The possible motives of the conceding party are worth considering, if only to reveal the essential flaws in the conceder's expectations.

Conceding movement rather than trading for it, is as common a fallacious behaviour as can be found in negotiation. In another context, I referred to it as a curse and a disease[198] and reported on the fate of

Bjorn McKenzie, a travelling salesman, who almost introduced the practice in northern Canada in the 1890s, until the local folk sent him packing. What he had done in fact was to teach wolves that if they wanted to be fed they should chase sledges.

In *Everything is Negotiable* (1982) I advised negotiators to be 'more like Scrooge than St Francis of Assisi'[199] because, with negotiators, 'generosity is not contagious,' whatever the habits of Saints:

> Indeed, experience suggests that liberality in concession-making is the worst thing you can do if you want to get concessions from the other person. If you concede why should he do likewise? Surely, by remaining where he is, he might induce you to concede even more?[200]

I also reported that these remarks often provoked the stormiest of sessions at Negotiate's workshops (they still do!) particularly from people who rise to the bait to defend their practice of goodwill conceding.

Usually, two reasons are advanced for making unilateral concessions:

1. 'I concede a couple of little things early on, just to soften them up.'
2. 'Somebody has to push the boat out or we'd never get the negotiations going.'

Both of these defences are a triumph of delusion over experience and are born of utter confusion about the dynamics of successful negotiation.

What is the evidence that supports the first line of defence? Even the language used – their words not mine – indicate a breathtaking arrogance: 'little things' and 'soften them up'. What kind of people do they negotiate with, where a 'couple of little things' melts away their resolve? If the other negotiators are so easily 'softened up', may they always negotiate only with them and their ilk!

The fact is that almost all the evidence of research and experience suggests the very opposite result is induced by unilateral concessionary behaviour. Goodwill concessions by you do not 'soften up' the other side, they make them tougher. Unilateral conceding produces in the other negotiator either no reciprocal response at all – they simply take something for nothing – or timidly asymmetrical responses in favour of themselves.

Consider how the other party perceives your one-way concessionary behaviour. She can interpret it one of two ways. You are:

1. displaying goodwill by signalling a desire to co-operate (by playing one-sided risky blue);

2.   displaying your weakness.

Remember, a negotiation is not the same as a one-round dilemma game. A blue co-operative strategy is only sensible if the other player co-operatively reciprocates, otherwise it is naive, and could be treated as such by the other player.

There is no reason for her to reciprocate to your free gift concession and, because you made it unilaterally and not conditionally, she has to read, or more likely, guess, your intentions correctly if she is to respond in the way you want her to. Why should she necessarily do that? If your concessions truly amounts to a 'couple of little things' they are hardly going to impress her; if they are nothing at all, they will insult her, and, if they amount to major concessions because she values those specific 'couple of little things' highly, the chances are also as high that she will interpret your behaviour as proof of your weakness. Whatever you naively think she ought to do, experience shows that most negotiators respond to perceived weaknesses in the other party with toughness. Softness is not contagious.[201]

If you want her to reciprocate your offer of movement, it is surely more effective to tell her so and the best way to do that is to make your offer of movement explicitly conditional on her movement, using the purple principle of conditionality (IF-THEN) to do so. That way she does not have to try to interpret what you are about – and get it wrong – because the conditional proposal tells her that if she does such and such for you, you will do such and such for her. What could be clearer?

Interestingly, when academics have attempted to model negotiations they have developed their models around the theme of concession-convergence.[202] There are one or two points for practitioners that have come out of this research. The main issue for you is how bargainers might interpret your concessionary behaviour. In this context, a concession is defined as a change in the position of one party compared to some previous position they held. Thus, a new offer, different in some respects from a previous offer, is indicative of a concession. In those negotiations where the parties open with a statement of their positions – such as in a wages dispute or in international diplomacy, or in acquisition or merger negotiations – and where movement takes place by sequentially discussing the proposals from each side and adjourning and then repeating the proposing process, some concession-convergence models have had explanatory 'success'. Their success is extremely limited and highly specific to a very narrow interpretation of events.[203] A brief survey of some of their conclusions illustrates what I mean.

The formal analysis of concession-convergence bargaining asserts that two negotiators with different solutions to the same problem will accept the risk that they will incur costs (a strike, for example) from not agreeing, the greater is the difference between their solutions.[204]

So, if I am the company and you are the union, the higher your demands for a wage increase compared to my much lower offer, the higher the risk of a strike but the more willing I am to take that risk and suffer its costs. You are keener to strike for a large discrepancy in our positions and I am willing to take that risk because the difference in our positions makes it worthwhile to resist your stike action.

In another context, the logic behind this argument can be seen by considering a situation in which there is a life or death decision at stake. You will be more likely to fight harder for your life than you would be for a small change in your circumstances. You are prepared to risk the consequences of a dispute over something really important to you than you would over something relatively trivial. Thus, in concession-convergence models it is reasonable to assume that risk tolerance of a strike is higher when large issues are at stake than when smaller differences are in dispute.

Now, if you come back with a proposal that concedes some part of your claim for a higher wage, i.e. you reduce your demand by some amount, this will lower the difference in our respective positions (the greater your reduction, of course, the smaller the remaining difference). This in turn will lower the amount of risk I am prepared to take that a strike will occur. I am less willing to fight your strike over a much smaller difference in our positions. Note, that this also implies that concessions from the union *soften* my determination to adhere to my original offer.

If my risk tolerance of meeting the costs of a strike is now lower, then the only way I can bring the current risk of a strike into balance with my new lower risk tolerance is to make a concession by raising my wage offer. My higher wage offer reduces the risk tolerance of the union because it reduces the gap between the company's offer and the union's demand. Thus, the model suggests that concessions by each of us, by reducing our willingness to risk the costs of a strike if we adhere to our previous demands and offers, produces reciprocal movement and this leads to a process of concession convergence, which gradually reduces the gap between our different demands and offers until we finally agree on a new wage rate. This new wage rate will be higher than the company's first offer and lower than the union's first demand.

The problem with this neat analysis is that concessionary behaviour need not lead to reciprocation. When one of us concedes, the effect is to reduce our willingness to risk the costs of a strike for what is now a smaller gap between my new offer and your current demand. When the gap is smaller, why should you concede next? Surely, it depends on how you interpret my concession compared to your non-concession? It could be that the conceder attempts to lower the risk of suffering the costs of a strike, by making another unilateral concession to narrow the gap between his demand and my offer. In doing this, the same pressure to concede reasserts itself and the unilateral conceder ends up conceding right through to the other party's position.

The perceptions of the bargainers are what is missing from simple concession-convergence models. How do you perceive my concessionary behaviour? The conceder is certainly influenced by her risk tolerance of suffering the costs of a strike (or, in a wider negotiating context, suffering the costs of no agreement). She is also influenced by the value to her side of the company's current offer.

A wage offer well short of the union's aspirations, but which is still an improvement on the current wage rate, has some positive value. Even a zero offer that guarantees current employment levels has a positive value. The union negotiator will also consider the determination of the company to pursue its current position. The company's capability to take a strike and its willingness to do so are inputs into the union bargainer's incentive to stand firm or to concede something.

Similarly, the company is influenced by how it perceives the union's concession which, because it changes the current situation, can be interpreted in more than one way:

○   If the concessionary move, at that stage in the negotiation, is made earlier than expected and if the concession is larger than expected, the company may conclude that the union is weaker than it thought.
○   If it concludes that the union is weaker, it might re-assess the risks of suffering a strike have diminished and that it can safely take a tougher and not a softer stance.
○   If, contrarily, the union's concessionary move is later than expected and if the concession is much smaller than expected, the reverse analysis could induce a greater degree of softness in the company's determination.

Again we conclude that softness provokes toughness and toughness provokes softness.

Concessions have a limited scope as goodwill gestures. If there is a high degree of distrust between the parties, as there is with belligerents in wars and civil wars, there is a highly restricted role for such gestures.[205] If overdone they are treated as evidence of weakness and are punished, accordingly, by promoting greater intransigence by the receiver of the gesture.

They can have an effect if they are part of a carefully planned and nurtured trust-building process. But trust building is best, and can only be, conducted as a two-way process in which mutual trust grows through mutually conceded, and therefore mutually traded, trust-building actions and non-actions. Outside of this limited circumstance, goodwill gestures are fraught with unintended consequences for negotiators and I suggest that you avoid experimenting with them in your normal business negotiations.

After 60 years of development, concession-convergence models of negotiation behaviour have had a limited impact on practical negotiators. Those few researchers who have studied what negotiators actually do (which excludes those researchers who use students, and not practical negotiators, as their experimental subjects) have produced some useful conclusions about actual concessionary behaviour that have had a much wider impact on training and practice. This may also be because they have moved outside of those bargaining situations where coercive force, such as in strikes or warfare, and its consequent direct costs, have major visibility for the negotiators.

The common experience of commercial negotiations is that the costs of failing to settle focus on the missed opportunities of agreement, rather than the direct costs of the parties trying to influence the outcome in their favour by strike or military sanctions.

Dr Chester Karass for many years dominated the popular negotiating seminar market in the United States and elsewhere. His was a down-to-earth, no-nonsense approach (he is retired), based on his 20 years' extensive experience as a top-flight negotiator in the purchasing function, for such as Hughes Aircraft in southern California, and a well researched PhD in negotiating behaviour from the University of Southern California in 1968. His books[206] circulate widely and have long been source material for negotiators.

Karass[207] is an example of a practitioner turned negotiation researcher. He undertook an experiment with 120 professional negotiators from four aerospace companies. First, he had each negotiator assessed by two of his managers on scales of 45 separate bargaining traits and then he matched them into pairs to undertake the experiments.

The experimental negotiation consisted of a 30-minute case briefing on a lawsuit between a drug company and a plaintiff, whose eyes had been damaged after taking the drug. The plaintiff sued for a million dollars. At the end of sixty minutes the pairs had either negotiated a settlement or they 'went to trial'. Their settlements contained details of:

○   the amount they settled for;
○   the time it took to settle;
○   the concession history.

Each negotiator was also asked to record their assessments of their own and their rival's objectives before the negotiations commenced and then again at their mid-point.

Karass also introduced three power variations: first, when the power was equally balanced; second, when the power favoured the plaintiff's case, and third by introducing coaching to those whose low bargaining trait scores indicated that they were unskilled in negotiation. The power balance was altered by changing the number of precedents from other imaginary cases into the case briefing files, and by coaching a more aggressive stance in the unskilled negotiators' approach.

The Karass[208] results are instructive, and he summarized them for 'practical men of action'[209] to provide 'some new ways to look at age-old challenges' (Figure 4.13). (For details of the Karass experiments and the statistical merits of his conclusions, I refer you to his PhD thesis and to his book.[210])

○   'First, we discovered that skilled negotiators were very successful when they had high aspirations or were lucky enough to face unskilled opponents with equal power.

○   Second, we found that skilled negotiators were benevolent when they had power.

○   Third, we found that unskilled negotiators were losers except when they had power and *high* aspirations.

○   Fourth, we discovered that successful negotiators made high initial demands, avoided making first concessions, conceded slowly and avoided making as many large concessions as their opponents.

○   Fifth, our results indicate that successful negotiators used concessions in a dynamic way. They applied the above techniques to test the validity of their assumptions and the intent of the opponent. Losers did not test reality in the same way. Both were equally poor estimators.

○   Sixth, all negotiators, successful or not, expressed equal satisfaction with the final agreement.'

Figure 4.13 Conclusions from the Karass experiment

My own caveat can be summarized by reminding you that, while, in the experiment, power can be assigned by simply changing the partici-pant's briefing notes, in real life there is no objective assessment of the degree of relative power. Power is a subjective judgement. If somebody acts as if they have power and your perceptions coincide with that belief, then the influence of power on the outcome would be in line with the Karass conclusions. This suggests that behaving as if you have power, and playing the moves accordingly, improves your chances of a more favourable settlement.

Offers and demands that demonstrate that you have high aspirations, irrespective of beliefs about the relative power of each side, would also increase your chances of a more favourable settlement. Hence, at Karass seminars you are advised to 'aim high', irrespective of your skill level. If you express high initial demands, only moving grudgingly and with miserly concessions after the other negotiator has moved first, you can do better whatever your initial skills' level. This is a powerful line to follow.

Skilled negotiators with high aspiration levels were big winners, particularly when they were opposed by low aspirants. The fact that large initial demands improve the probability of success, suggests that initial wide differences between demands and offers did not necessarily jeopardize the possibility of a settlement.

The fact that Karass found that his 'losers' made the largest concessions in the experimental negotiations, and that people who made smaller concessions failed fewer times, has implications for training. Losers, he noted, tended to make the first compromise – perhaps they felt the tensions of disagreement more keenly than their partners, which caused them to 'blink' first.

The 60-minute deadline in the experiment was of significance. Karass found that skilled negotiators made smaller concessions as the deadline approached. This deliberate patterning of the concession rate has the affect of conditioning the other negotiator to expect less and, if a salient position on price is made obvious, it induces expectations of the likely settlement price. For example, a movement pattern from 150, through 130, 120, 115, 112, and 111, suggests a salient settlement price of 110, not 105 or 100, particularly if time pressure is mounting.

Time pressure mounts if there is an obvious deadline. Most settlements in the Karass experiment occurred shortly before the 60-minute deadline. If they followed the usual pattern that is observed in real-world negotiations, the rate at which there is movement increases the closer the parties are to the 'natural' or imposed deadline. A long period of apparent stalemate can suddenly be transformed into a concessionary rush, as if the negotiators are fed up stalling.

Karass concluded that a very high unexpected demand tends to lead to success rather than deadlock. Presumably this outcome was observed at the beginning of the negotiation rather than towards the end, because an initial high demand is likely to structure the other negotiator's expectations when negotiations have just begun, leaving them more time to negotiate the demand.

At the end of a negotiation, shock high demands can compel even a fairly compliant negotiator into stiff resistance, motivated by feelings of 'unfairness' and bullying. Outside of an experiment, negotiators who have commitment to their objectives are more sensitive to such tactics.

This is another caveat I have about concessionary behaviour being prompted by the high aspirations of the other negotiator. According to Karass, negotiators with extremely high aspirations fail less than those with low aspirations. They succeed or deadlock, he reports, more often than those who seek less. But they cannot do both simultaneously!

If the individual negotiator deadlocks she is out of the game. She gets zero. If across a number of negotiators, more high aspirants succeed than deadlock, a false conclusion might be prompted. Only if she conducts a large number of similar negotiations and pushes for her high aspirations each time, will she gain more from her successes than from her failures. It does not follow that aiming high succeeds, or is the appropriate behaviour, for each individual negotiation.

If the negotiation is a one-off, with terminal consequences for the player's client, her high aspiration strategy could mean her clients get nothing, when something less than everything was available. For their clients, there might not be a next negotiation to move on to.

There is also the case where two negotiators, each with high aspirations that are mutually incompatible – you want the lot, I want you to have nothing – are in dispute. The probability of deadlock is bound to be much higher than if there was some symmetry in our aspirations. This suggests that you choose your negotiating partners more carefully – only negotiate, as a high aspirer, with low aspirers!

I end my discussion of concessionary behaviour with a brief reference to what I believe is an erroneous conclusion by a member of the Harvard Negotiation Project, Gerald Williams, who is a Professor of Law at Brigham University, more as a warning to practitioners to avoid invitations to conduct similar experiments. There is a danger when training that the client wants an assessment made of the negotiating performances of her staff on the basis of the results of the simulation exercises. I have long resisted these requests and I think you should do likewise, either as trainer, a professional negotiator, or as a manager wanting feedback on your colleagues. Here is why.

Williams conducted an experiment with 40 experienced American attorneys, who were all given the same facts of a personal injury case. They were paired off and instructed to negotiate a settlement, after being designated as attorneys for the plaintiff or the defender. They all came back with different settlements (except three pairs who failed to agree and 'went to trial' and six other pairs who refused to reveal their results!). Williams reports that he was surprised at the range of results. More, he was embarrassed: 'it was one of those times when there is mass confusion and hysteria and you are afraid of the situation because you cannot learn from it'.[211] But what did Williams expect? That they would all come with the same award?

Williams went on: 'As I recorded these outcomes on the chalkboard, tension in the room began to mount. People were looking at each other, and they were wondering about their own competence.' The results showed that the lowest award negotiated for a plaintiff was $18,000 and the highest was $95,000. On seeing the results and hearing the explanations of the two lawyers concerned, Williams reports: 'We all chuckled sort of nervously, believing as a matter of etiquette we ought to let the two worst negotiators in the room defend themselves'. Note how Williams leaps from the two 'worst' results to the erroneous conclusion that these results make the defender's attorney in the $95,000 award, and the plaintiff's attorney in the $18,000 award, the 'two worst negotiators'.

A single outcome in this sort of 'experiment' is not a predictor of negotiating competence and it is doubtful if much about negotiating competence can be gleaned from the results, which will vary according to how the negotiators interact with each other, and a host of other variables. Some results will be 'high' simply because a negotiator gave in; some 'low' because another negotiator refused to budge. Others will vary according to how the negotiators interpret the facts and to the subjective views they hold on the available alternatives (including, in a legal case, the lottery of going to trial).

The least that would need to have been done in Williams' experiment is for each attorney to negotiate with several of the other 39 (changing roles from plaintiff to defendant) and for the results to be grouped for comparison, much as pairs playing in bridge competitions move round the tables until they have played the same cards as everybody else in the tournament. That would provide a better indicator of individual performance than a single negotiation exchange or a single hand at bridge (although it would still be flawed in other respects).

Better still, Williams should have established what were the necessary skills of a competent negotiator (as Karass attempted) and then sat in on each negotiation and witnessed whether those skills were demonstrated or otherwise, and then drawn some comparisons with what he observed across different pairs. Presumably time precluded that approach.

His prime and most flawed assumption was that because all the attorneys were 'experienced', they were 'skilled' negotiators. The only basis for their selection was that they replied to an invitation sent to an unstated number of 'experienced' attorneys living in Des Moines, Iowa, to participate in the experiment. Critically, no proper assessment was made of their competence as negotiators before the experiment began. In more than twenty-five years of watching negotiators at work, I remain unconvinced that experience and competence are necessarily strongly correlated.

Competence cannot be measured by the result of a single negotiation, either in real life or in a simulation, particularly a negotiation which has only one variable, the amount of compensation, in it. Competence is measured more accurately by a combination of observing how negotiators conduct themselves against a set of skills criteria, by testing for understanding of the concepts related to aspects of their activity, i.e., how they 'read the game', and by assessing the comparative results of a large number of their negotiations.

 ## PROPOSING AND BARGAINING PLOYS

It is time to return to manipulative ploys, particularly in relation to the proposing and bargaining phases, where the number of ploys are both numerous and, sometimes, deadly.

As suggested in the previous section, I have long admired Dr Karass as the leading entrepreneur in the global negotiation seminar business, so anything I say here about some other aspects of his work should be read with my admiration of him in mind.

My problem with the ploy's approach is that it is all too tactical and not sufficiently strategic for my liking. A tactical appreciation of a game is all very well – and some people have made good careers in sport and business on that skill alone – but it is well short of being sufficient for a longish negotiation on something important to the parties.

One-off selling interviews give scope for ploys because the buyer can say 'yes' or 'no' on the spot and the seller is relatively free to try the dozens of 'closes' ploys to get herself over her sales quota. For bigger deals, over many meetings, the scope for ploys is limited, if not frankly foolish, for a negotiator to put them into play. The stakes are higher and the players are more senior and experienced and they talk to each other. They can see ploys coming round the mountain waving large banners advertising the seller's intentions and they are likely to punish them for the insult. They also know how to use ploys in reverse against inexperienced sellers. Karass provides details of three well-known ploys, which are now classics in the genre.

THE BOGEY

The first of these is the *bogey*, which, writes Karass, 'is simple, effective and ethical'. [212] I have serious doubts about his claim that it is ethical. However, let us see how the bogey works. The buyer – for it is a buyer's ploy – lets the seller know that she 'loves his product', and even enthuses about its suitability for use in her operations. But, unfortunately, she has a limited budget and if the seller wants to sell his product to her company, he will have to come down in price to meet her budget limits.

Put like that it may not sound very convincing but anybody who has sold for a living will know just how persuasively she can play a bogey and how easy it is for a seller to slide into responding positively to it. It is difficult to become 'hostile with someone who likes you and your product' says Karass, and, before you know it, as a seller you are revealing your product's costings to convince her that your prices are sound. By doing so, you are also revealing data which she uses to trim your price.

'Before long it is discovered', writes Karass, 'that some things in the original price can be trimmed away, others can be changed and still others can be adjusted by the buyer himself to meet the budget'.[213] Karass claims that the bogey is ethical because 'each party has helped the other reach its overall goals'. Now just a minute. The ploy is based on convincing any seller, whose product you are seriously considering, that you do not have sufficient money in your budget to buy it at the price quoted by the seller, whether this assertion is true or otherwise. In short, you have to be 'economical with the truth'. You cannot ignore the ethics of this behaviour because it is almost certainly morally fraudulent to purvey a falsehood to induce a gain.

What are the overall goals of the parties? The seller wants to make a sale and achieve a price as close to his list (top) price as he can, and the buyer wants to make a purchase and at a price as much below her budget as she can. Their individual objectives of keeping their jobs depend on them achieving sales targets, in the case of the seller, and maximizing the variance between her budget and her actual spend, in the case of the buyer. What have they ended up with? True, he has achieved a sale but it is at a lower price than he expected; she has made a purchase and at a higher price than she wanted. Other than in the abstract, they both succeeded in making an exchange; she lied to achieve one of her tactical goals – buy cheap – and he fell for a falsehood to achieve his tactical goal of getting an order.

Their future relationship is now at risk of him wising up to the fraudulent bogey, and she whingeing, when, as a result of her forcing the seller to cut corners and trim costs, the supplier's people work less than wholeheartedly to supply orders with low or no profits. She could end up not getting what she thought she had bought and having to face some wrath, perhaps, from her colleagues who use the product as an input into their processes.

I once applied the 'bogey', or at least my version of it, which I named 'The Mother Hubbard' of the cupboard is bare fame,[214] but later rued my ploy play. My task was to buy a computer system with five terminals for the Business School, and I was challenged by the Dean to do better than the University's purchasing department – 'you being the hot shot negotiator', was how he put it. I rose to the challenge and pulled the seller's price down by 35 per cent using a bogey ploy. Brilliant?

Then it started. We had agreed, for example, that installation was included in the price; this was interpreted by the computer company's engineers as putting a three-foot cable into a wall plug but not running cables from the CPU to four different rooms along a 30-foot corridor. We also had a maintenance agreement with a four-hour service call out; this was interpreted by the maintenance department as a response to our calls whenever all other full price sites were serviced. I could go on, but you get my drift? Of course, we should have tightened down these clauses but my sights were on beating the budget to please the Dean, not getting it right to please the staff using the computers.

There is other damage to the relationship when a bogey is sprung. Buyers of a bogey disposition believe that all seller's prices are padded. The bogey ploy is justified by these buyers as a means of uncovering price padding. The seller pads to give room for a bogey in case one is used by the buyer; the buyer uses the bogey to test the credibility of the seller's price. If she succeeds in uncovering price padding, the seller reinforces her perception that all sellers' prices are padded. If the seller's price padding is not challenged, his company makes extra profits to pay for successful bogeys pulled on them elsewhere; if the buyer springs a bogey she saves costs but might do so against a seller's bottom line price – he did not pad it – with risky costs if the supplier falls into financial difficulties.

A bank I know of congratulated itself on springing an aggressive and successful bogey on the security printer which supplied its cheque books. The printer was compelled to take on the work at the low bogey price out of desperation, but they went bust before delivering the full order. The bank had to rescue the printer at enormous additional cost, just to have its cheques printed and despatched to its customers.

Ploys provoke ploys. Experienced sellers can counter-bogey by challenging the budget ceiling. They can seek flexibility in using virement facilities from one budget to another, on the assumption that all budgets are flexible upwards, and seek access to the financial controllers above the buyer's level of discretion. If she is genuine about her love of the product, it is difficult to block off too many of these moves without creating the germs of suspicion that she made it up about her budget ceiling.

Sellers can also switch sell from the product marque that the buyer is so enthusiastic about to an *El cheapo* version of it. This tests the buyer's alleged enthusiasm. If the *El cheapo* version is unacceptable, then she must either agree to internal company efforts to move the budget ceiling upwards, because her claim is genuine and not a ploy, or go through the charade of pretending to do so until it is safe for her to reveal her 'successful effort' to get new (higher) budgetary authority. Of course, as a consequence, a mutual bluffing culture in now brought into their relationship.

Sellers can use mini-ploys by referring to such bogey blockers as:

O   minimum order value ('no orders under £5,000');
O   minimum quantities ('it is in boxes of a gross only');
O   compulsory joint purchases ('we do not supply the mobile phones without a two-year contract to purchase our airtime');
O   fixed warranties ('warranties are 12 months parts only, labour is extra');
O   exclusive supply clauses ('franchisees must buy all consumables from us');
O   variations payments ('any variation from the standard spec is charged as an extra');
O   retrospective volume discounts ('you only earn discounts retrospectively in arrears for actual volumes you buy and pay for').

Like an arms race, bogey ploys, and counter-bogey ploys, escalate to neutralize each other. This might make life for negotiators more interesting but it adds little to efficiency. Tighter and tighter specifications, for example, lead to 29-page Ministry of Defence type specifications for simple one-gallon water cans to prevent sellers cutting corners; more detailed terms of business lead to pages of contract jargon excusing a supplier from every conceivable complaint, and the time taken up by one side trying to renegotiate contractual imperatives and the other side trying to defend them, adds to the transaction costs of bargaining.

Games begin that have nothing to do with the purchase or use of a product. Building companies open up teams of variation claimers to win 'extras' so that tightly tendered jobs can become profitable; teams of counter-variation claimers are set up to challenge everything that was done by the builder and to get re-work done without paying for it.

THE KRUNCH

Closely aligned to the thinking behind the bogey is the Karass ploy of the *krunch*. This is the most common stance of almost every buyer who is disposed to see his job as one of beating down the supplier. In the krunch the buyer tells the seller, 'you have got to do better than that on price'.

The krunch is a fishing expedition based on the buyer's belief that all seller's prices are padded and that there is always some slack in every price. It is better than the bogey because the buyer does not want to convey the impression that he is enthusiastic at all about the seller's product, which tends to suggest to the seller that she is in with a chance. He wants, instead, to put maximum pressure on the seller, such that unless her price is adjusted downwards, and fairly quickly, then the buyer will take his business to one of her rivals, whose sales literature is just visible among the pile of papers jumbled on the buyer's desk.

Karass, at least, is not so sure about the ethics of the krunch. He believes it is ethical but admits that 'there are many who do not'.[215] Contrarily, I think this is more ethical than the bogey because it does not tell a lie about a fictitious budget ceiling. It simply tells the seller that he will have to do better on price than he is at present, which merely expresses the desire of all buyers (readers included) to buy at lower prices than sellers want to sell.

There has never been a price so low that you would not be even happier as a buyer if you had paid still less for it; conversely, there has never been a price so high that you would not have been even happier as a seller to have got still more for it.

If you are in selling and have not yet come across the krunch, you have not been in selling more than a few hours! It is not used all of the time, of course, but the krunch is used so often by most buyers, it's like flies near a cow's tail – they go with the territory. Like the bogey, the krunch begets what it is aimed against – sellers pad prices to defend against the buyer's krunch, so buyers krunch to defend themselves against price padding!

To defend against a krunch, the seller tries the 'apples and pears' defence – 'my competitor's pear is not comparable with my apple'. They are both fruit but they are different fruits. No two offers are strictly comparable – if they were this might attract the attention of anti-cartel investigators – and it is often plausible to make the case for an apples and pears defence, providing the buyer lets you see the alternative quotes she has been hinting are in the folder on her desk. If it is a bluff on her part, pushing the issue to make her show her alternative lower price quotes may disqualify you on grounds that she does not like to be embarrassed by a called bluff showing her to be a liar. It is easier to get rid of you and give the business to somebody else (perhaps at a higher price).

THE NIBBLE

The Karass *nibble* is indisputably an unethical ploy. Karass reports: 'Nibbling pays. Somebody once said, "If you can't get a dinner, get a sandwich." The nibbler goes for the sandwich. It may not do much for his ego but it helps his pocket book.'[216] If it pays, it is a fairly disreputable way to get paid in my view.

What does the nibbler do? What it says – he nibbles away at the deal, cutting a cent here, a cent there, a promised service is amended unilaterally, or an extra charge appears for minor items (anything too big would provoke enquiries). It is take, take and take again.

'Buyers nibble on sellers and sellers nibble on buyers', reports Karass. Sellers nibble by 'making overshipments, by supplying slightly inferior merchandise, by not performing promised services, by delivering late, by adding special charges', while 'buyers nibble by paying invoices late, by taking discounts not earned, by requesting special delivery or warehouse services, by asking for slightly better quality than contracted for, by demanding extra reports, certifications or invoices, by getting free engineering charges, and by requesting extra consulting and training help for nothing.'[217]

If this does not create problems for vigilant negotiators, I don't know what does. All these nibbles are irritants to your customers or suppliers. Most may be too trivial to provoke a response but if you run enough of them together, you can discredit the deal that you struck.

Having been on the end of somebody's nibbling, I have hardly recovered three years later from my abhorrence of the practice. A course due to run from 9–5, began to extend into the evening before – 'you're on the premises that evening and I am sure we could begin the seminar for an hour or two before dinner' was how one client commenced a series of nibbles. They ended up expecting me to do a day and a half in contact hours for my daily fee. I was forced to say 'no' to the client, otherwise it would have raised questions as to why they were hiring me to improve their staff's negotiating skills, plus the fact that their nibbling had really begun to annoy me.

Accomplished nibblers abound. They do a great disservice to negotiation. They make the implementation of deals a nightmare and they give credence to critics of negotiation who decide to throw out the baby with the bath water in an effort to 'change the game'.

The problem lies in the overly tactical obsessions of the ploy players with the game as they think it is meant to be played. They seek to gain one-sided advantages and end up with increasingly complex barriers to straightforward dealing. They think they are cleverer than everybody else – the fastest ploy player in town – but like their movie forebears, the fastest gun in the West, they forget that there is always a faster gun or ploy player just round the corner.

THE SALAMI

The *salami* ploy is similar but different to the Karass nibble. Salami comes in slices. Unable to achieve agreement on a major change – such as a company pension scheme – the negotiator attempts to salami by trying for agreement a thin slice at a time. He suggests that only the longest serving employees qualify for company paid pension contributions, not everybody. Facing a couple of dozen people qualifying against a couple of thousand, the employer's representative feels able to justify committing to the smaller expense.

Of course, next time the contract is renegotiated, and every year thereafter, the union negotiator seeks new salami deals to widen eligibility among the employees until, in due course, the entire workforce is covered by a company pension scheme. The employer, meanwhile, saves pension contributions for the diminishing band of those not yet eligible. In like spirit, the employer could pave the way for agreement on a company pension scheme by rejecting the union's claim for everybody by disqualifying all but a few employees in a reverse salami, hoping to postpone the cost increases by dragging out the timing of changes in the eligibility criteria.

In contrast, the nibble is an unethical one-way slicing ploy because the player takes a nibble from you without your open agreement and relies on your administrative lethargy to let him get away with it.

As ever, you must deal with the nibble the instant it occurs, otherwise your passivity endorses it and the nibbler 'wins'. If the deal was 30 days, you must hit back hard at the first account unpaid on the 31st day, otherwise the credit taken will extend continuously; if it is for 'no-returns' after 60 days, you must not give them credit for any returns made at 65 days, otherwise this will become a norm instead of an exception; and if short deliveries are accepted, you must demand a firm requirement for a full despatch before you pay the account, otherwise short deliveries will continue, necessitating a messy and time-consuming reconciliation of despatch notes and invoices, with a high chance that you will pay for more than you received.

THE RUSSIAN FRONT

Slightly less common than salami is the *Russian front* ploy, the name for which I am responsible,[218] and, I am flattered to say, appears regularly in derivative literature. I am less pleased with an author[219] who ascribed it not to Lieutenant Wolfgang Mueller in Paris in 1943, in a dispute with his Colonel over his girlfriend, but to the Napoleonic invasion of Russia in 1812! Starkly, poor Wolfgang, told to go for a walk while his colonel entertained his girlfriend, protested, and was told by his Colonel, 'Either you do as I say, or I will have you sent to the Russian front *tonight*.' 'Mein Gott', said Wolfgang, 'the Russian front! Anything but the Russian front!' And he went for a (long) walk!' How Napoleon, and a non-existent nineteenth-century 'front' (a word unknown in the Napoleonic Wars) crept into twentienth-century negotiating texts, only the hapless author knows (and his explanation of his version of the ploy is simply silly).

You can be Russian fronted any time whenever the other negotiator gives you two choices, both unpalatable, but one more unpalatable than the other. If you believe that she has the power and the intention to impose one or other of the choices upon you, your likely course of action is to choose the least unpalatable one. If you do, you have been Russian fronted.

Versions of the ploy appear in discussions over alternative proposals – yours and theirs – in which they draw stark consequences for everybody, but particularly you, if your proposal were to be accepted. Here they are Russian fronting the consequences of the proposals rather than the proposals themselves. To avoid believable and unpalatable consequences, you choose to avoid the worst one and inevitably cast your lot in with their less onerous proposal.

SELL CHEAP, GET FAMOUS

The *sell cheap, get famous* ploy is legendary in the world of entertainment and in any circumstance where you are pitching for business for the first time. It is also controversial, or at least the appropriate response I recommend is controversial among some people at our seminars. So many people think unlike negotiators that I am not surprised that they get worse deals than they need to. The power of the ploy is founded on the sheer determination, nay desperation, of the target to put a foot in the door, that they will consider almost any pricing proposition put to them by a buyer with a plausible line in having some 'golden key' to their future.

The producer, for example, tells the young actor that as she is unknown, she cannot receive the top rates she wants – and probably deserves – but if she does this film on the 'cheap', she will become so famous that 'train loads of money' will be hers from then on. Its use is not confined to film producers. I have lost count of the corporations who have told me that just having them as clients will do 'untold good to my reputation'.

We are all familiar, I hope, with how advertisements refer not to 'low wages' but always to 'good prospects', and how buyers speak not of 'one-off low priced orders' but vaguely of 'the possibilities of high volume purchases'. The 'Chinese widget deal' is an extreme example of the sell cheap, get famous ploy. In this version the Chinese buyer places his demand for a low price in the context that there are a billion people in China. True, but the two facts of low price and large population are not necessarily connected. My advice is that if you sell yourself and your products cheap, you will get exactly what you demonstrate you think they are worth.

ADD-ON

Sellers use the *add-on* ploy in the often successful attempt to raise the final price paid by the buyer for the product. You negotiate what you think is the actual price for the product or service. Once this is agreed, the seller interprets your agreement as a signal to charge for extras. What you bought was the standard product or service and not the full one. This is sometimes called the *Brooklyn optician* ploy in which the price is built up using short pauses for you to stop the price getting any higher.[220] If you do not interrupt, the seller keeps adding on extras until she runs out of them.

It is essential, therefore, to know what it is you are buying by asking insistently: 'What do I get for my money?'; 'What does your offer include and exclude?'; 'Let me be clear, if I buy the all-inclusive package at the price you have quoted, give me examples of what is meant by "installation", "training", "access to helplines" and "upgrading".' Until you are satisfied that everything you want covered is included in the price, do not agree to anything. If you do agree too early to an unspecified package, you might regret it when the full bill comes in for payment.

LIMITED AUTHORITY

Limited authority gives the ploy maker a power he is not entitled to, though he is entitled to claim it if you are willing to acquiesce in his deception. If he tells you his authority to vary a deal is strictly limited, and you are already at that limit, you have a problem if you want the deal (he has a problem if you don't). He is not refusing to move, it is somebody else (echoes of 'tough guy/soft guy'?) who is the cause of the problem. How can you argue against that?

If company policy declares minimum order quantities, maximum volume discounts, large pre-order deposits, strict 'taken into use' provisions, and delivery charges, it is difficult to expect the seller to over-turn company policy on your behalf. If he does not have discretion he cannot use it. You either accept the deal, within the parameters of his limited authority, or you start again with somebody else.

HIGHER AUTHORITY

Akin to limited authority is *higher* or *escalating authority*, in which the deal has to be referred to the next most senior person in the organization, and the next, and perhaps the next above him. Union representatives explicitly require endorsement of what they agree with you from their members, and, to be frank, deals may not be worth much if the representatives are not allowed this facility. Of course, you are dependent on how they report on the deal – with enthusiasm or by them just going through the motions – and it can provide an excuse to come back for more because the members 'won't agree to what is on offer'.

Many deals are also agreed 'subject to Board approval', giving the negotiator a passable excuse for coming back with a couple of yes, buts, and at least one quivering quill. Karass[221] advises 'firm counter-measures' against the escalating authority ploy but warns that it 'takes an exceptional man to stand up to the tactic'. One useful tip he gives is: 'Do not repeat your arguments at each level. Sit back and let your opponent do it.' It is easier to critique, Karass correctly observes, somebody's (mis)interpretation of your position than defend somebody else's dissection of your recently spoken words.

 ## GO-BETWEENS AS RED BARGAINERS

The hard red bargainer is an extreme version of the ploy player. He also aims to influence your perceptions and to lower your expectations but as a hard bargainer he takes this aim to an extreme and is out to swing the outcome entirely in his favour. There is no other goal than an outright total victory and he will use everything in and around the negotiation process to achieve this end. Have no illusions about it because you are not paranoid – red bargainers aim to get you.

Red bargainers are prevalent wherever interests clash and they decide that their interests must prevail over yours. It's nothing personal – just business, or at least that is what they claim. They can be the 'hired gun' for one of the parties or the other party's principal. Too bad if you are unaware of the game they are playing. Plausibility is one of their strong suits, deniability is another.

A corporation with a red bargaining culture ensures that the people who succeed in it are the ones who adopt the red bargaining norms set by the successful top managers. Lawyers write their letters in numerous tones – the hard bargainer's letter, from the very first one they send, is uncompromising in its demands, brooks no argument, allows you no case to the contrary and assumes arrogantly that on receipt of it you will jump as high and as often as their peremptory demands require.

Part of your training for business negotiation should include a passing acquaintance with red bargaining behaviours. The selection that follows is representative but not exhaustive.

People who have been to the school of hard knocks, or as Ringer[222] puts it, to 'Screw U', play a strong hand in red bargaining. Ringer describes his 'undergraduate days at Screw U', in the real estate business, as learning 'through brutal experience, to face the realities of the business world', in which, he concluded, there were 'only three types of people':

O   *Type no. 1*: 'lets you know from the outset – either through his words or actions, or both – that he's out to get all of your chips. He then follows through by attempting to do just that.'

O   *Type no. 2*: 'assures you that he's not interested in getting your chips, and he usually infers that he wants to see you get everything "that's coming to you". He then follows through ... and attempts to grab all of your chips anyway.'

O   *Type no. 3*: 'also assures you that he is not interested in getting any of your chips ... and sincerely means it [and] ... due to any one of a number of reasons – ranging from his own bungling to his personal standards for rationalising what's right and wrong – he ... still ends up trying to grab your chips.'[223]

Not much naivety here! From his perceptions of what business was about, Ringer went on to develop a dealing philosophy, candidly expressed by the titles of his best sellers: *Winning through Intimidation* (1973) and *Looking Out for Number One* (1977). He climbed a steep learning curve. Ringer describes his direct experience of a number 1 type of negotiator:

> He was as hard as nails and could be as mean as cat dirt when the
> going got tough. He looked at the real estate business as one big
> game, and, almost naively, seemed to assume that everyone else
> was also playing the game just for the thrill of winning ... (Just so
> there's no misunderstanding, however, 'winning' *means* getting as
> many chips as possible. The nature of the chips, of course, is deter-
> mined by individual objectives and can take many forms – such as
> money, trophies, or the love of another person – in fact, an infinite
> number of forms) ... He was a stern teacher who often tongue-
> lashed me for being too careless or too trusting. Whenever my incli-
> nation was to give the other person the benefit of the doubt, his
> position was that there was no such thing as the 'benefit of the
> doubt' in business dealings. His approach was to tie the other guy's
> hands behind his back, bind his feet, close off all exits of escape, and
> then 'negotiate'.[224]

His example of the hard bargainer setting about his business, exempli-
fies the red style of bargaining. Ringer found a 'desperate builder' in
need of a $150,000 second mortgage, who had nine small apartment
properties to offer as collateral, which were already subjects of a first
mortgage. The number one type lender whom Ringer introduced to the
builder 'shook his head and indicated that he would need more collateral in order to make the loan. The prospective borrower protested,
insisting that the nine properties he was willing to give as security con-
stituted excessive collateral to begin with'. The lender 'thanked him for
his trouble and indicated that he was going to fly back to New York; the
prospective borrower – desperate for cash – quickly backed off and
agreed to give him, as additional collateral, a first mortgage on a ten
acre parcel of land that he said was going to be rezoned to an industrial
classification soon'.

The lender not only took the land as collateral, 'but, as he got nearer
to closing, insisted on inserting a clause in the loan agreement which
stated that if the land was not in fact rezoned "industrial" by the end of
one year ... that borrower [would] pay off an additional $20,000 on the
principal of the loan'. The lender 'after reviewing the figures very carefully', told the borrower 'there was no way he could make a $150,000
loan based on a collateral they had been discussing; he said that
$100,000 was the top figure he was willing to go. The borrower then
became downright hostile. He emphatically refused to agree to the
change, someone again [the lender] thanked him for his time and indicated he had better things to work on ... and once again the borrower
limped back to the "negotiating table". They finally compromised at
$105,000 dollars.'

The lender was not through with his red bargaining. He 'required
that the borrower "deposit" with him (the lender) each month, one
twelfth of the annual real estate taxes on the various properties', which

meant the lender would have the use of the borrower's tax money until the taxes were due. The lender also noted that one of the newest properties still had a considerable number of vacancies. So he 'insisted that $20,000 out of the $105,000 loan be retained by him until that property reached an occupancy rate of approximately 80 per cent. The same objections, the same gestures, the same result. Intimidation was the deciding factor: the borrower ended up agreeing to all of the ... conditions'.[225]

Ringer describes similar deals that he observed or did himself. The problem Ringer faced is known as 'back-dooring' or 'circumventing', and is common to all deal making go-betweens who are not directly one of the parties. Two parties who want to do a deal but do not know of each other's existence, can find each other through a go-between. This is good news for the parties but risky for the go-between, who only gets paid if the parties cannot avoid doing so. Having been introduced and having decided that they can do business, why should they pay anything to the go-between? Hence, some don't and many others try not to. Ringer offered some memorable advice to all intermediaries when dealing with potential red players:[226]

> With a written agreement
> You have a prayer;
> With a verbal agreement
> You have nothing but air.

Back-dooring as a problem is universal. Americans call it the 'hooker's principle': 'services are valued far more before they are rendered than afterwards'. Hence, like hookers, you should get paid up front.

A friend of mine is a licensed FIFA players' agent. A football club looking for an experienced 'mid-fielder', say, might let him know of their interest in finding such a player from another club. If he finds someone who fits the bill, how does he ensure he is paid? Once the two clubs talk to each other directly, they can negotiate the player's transfer, with each plausibly arguing that they had agreed that the other club would 'take care of the agent's fee'. To prevent temptations to back-door him, he gets agreement to his fee in writing, preferably in the form of a separate agreement one from each club before he puts them in touch with each other. He has learned, the hard way, not to take on such quests without written confirmation of the clubs' 'understanding' of the deal. He agrees with Ringer that: 'Closing deals is so much trash, if you, my friend, don't get no cash.'[227] (Ignore Ringer's double negative – he's American!) Ringer writes, partly in confession, partly in exhortation:[228]

Regardless of the 'product' or 'service', selling is not an end in itself; selling is only a means to an end: receiving income. Contrary to the emphasis in many 'success' and 'how to' books, closing deals is not the name of the game: it is only a means to the end of walking away with chips in your hand. Reality dictates that the mere closing of deals will not pay your grocery bills; only getting paid will do that. In business, love, and life in general, 'getting paid' is what it's all about ... like most people I've known, [I] often hid my eyes from the realities of the jungle because they seemed too 'brutal' to accept. But whether or not I accepted them did not change the fact that they were realities. It wasn't until I finally forced myself to stop being an ostrich that I was able to start making some headway in the jungle. 'Brutal' is another of those freely used relative words. Relative to the candy land rules of goody-two-shoesism taught in many 'success' books, the realities of the jungle may seem 'brutal'; but relative to the fantasies which actually support those rules, the realities of the jungle are comforting ...

Reality is such that it simply isn't true that if you do a good job, you'll get what you deserve ... And remember: looking out for your best interest does not conflict with your doing a good job at whatever it is that you're supposed to get paid for; it simply means that you make sure you *do* get paid for the good service you render. You have the right to be remunerated for a good performance, and don't allow *anyone* to intimidate you into thinking otherwise.

Coming from the experience of a red bargainer that is very good advice indeed. Red bargainers are not confined to the streetwise graduates of 'Screw U'. The professions are also exponents of red bargaining, and most of them went to academic universities not 'Screw U'.

 ## RED BARGAINERS IN INSURANCE

One obvious place to look for red bargainers at work is within the legal profession, in particular within the personal injury sector, though corporate litigation is a rich source too for evidence of red behaviour. Businesses have to insure their employees during working hours – and must display their Employer's Liability Certificates at their place of business – and they are liable for the products or services that they sell. Litigation arising from claims are common enough for you to benefit from some knowledge about how these claims are handled and what can happen to you if you leave your fate in the hands of insurance lawyers.

While personal injury is widely, if thinly, spread throughout the population – no particular group being more prone than others – the defendants tend to be a finite number of insurance companies that took on the risk of your being injured in exchange for regular premiums. If you suffer injury they sometimes deliberately contest their liability for your injuries.

Plaintiffs (the injured party), according to one expert in the field, come from 'varying backgrounds and histories, no experience of personal injury litigation, and ill-formed expectations of the outcome of their actions'. Defendants (the insurers) in contrast 'have common characteristics, endless experience of personal injury litigation, and clear expectations of the outcome of claims'.[229] In short, plaintiffs are at a disadvantage – like when you buy a used car from a professional who sells them every day.

Litigation plays a major role in personal injury negotiations. The 'coercive menacing character of the court process ... is the anvil, against which the hammer of negotiation strikes'.[230] That most cases settle out of court has been remarked upon for years.[231] Litigation is necessary to concentrate the insurer's interest in a private compromise – it being better to achieve a limited gain 'than to pursue complete success and in so doing take the risk of no gain, or worse, palpable loss'.[232] Recently, some lawyers boasted that it is the sheer costs of litigation that drive people to settle before the case gets to court, as if this was a justification for the cost of the legal process.

Comparing the number of personal injury incidents to the number of cases pursued by those injured, you find that only a small proportion of the persons affected 'initiate claims for damages' and, of these, 'only 80 per cent of those claims initiated achieve any kind of settlement' and that 'the settlements reached are generally for relatively small amounts'.[233] This alone ought to get you worried before you embark on a disputed insurance claim.

Of interest to negotiators is the unsurprising evidence that in 'two thirds of the cases the settlement is concluded on the basis of the *first* offer made by the defendant's insurers'.[234] This suggests that a Karass inspired negotiator would have plenty of scope for a successful and remunerative legal career ('act tough, aim high, move niggardly', etc.) in personal injury claims whether working for the plaintiff or the defendant. This is precisely the profile that typifies much of the negotiators in personal injury claims.

Raiffa[235] provides an analytical insight into negotiations over personal injury.[236] Raiffa's case facts are that Anderson, a 19 year-old woman, picked up her car from a repair garage not realizing that the off-side front light was not working, perhaps due to negligence by the garage. It was a misty, rainy evening with poor visibility. Driving alone in a 'no overtaking' zone, she 'peeked out' from behind a truck and had a head-on collision with an oncoming vehicle. She was permanently disfigured, disabled and blind. It was alleged that she was doing 70 in a 50 mile-per-hour zone.

Her solicitor sued the garage, for $1.63 million. The defendant's insurance company had issued a policy to Anderson that covered her for up to $500,000 for bodily injury caused by faulty repairs. The insurers, following their usual procedures, notified the regulatory authorities that they had entered $10,000 as their reserve for settling the case. As is also usual in these cases time passed and Anderson's lawyer wrote to the insurers two years later (and four years after the accident) offering to settle for the $500,000 for which the defendant was insured. He intimated that he believed a jury would award $1 million to $1.2 million.

The garage urged its insurer to settle in case the jury award was not covered by the insurer's limit of $500,000, in which event the defendant would be left to cover the difference between that amount and any higher award. They also offered to pay the insurers $25,000 of any amount less than an award of $500,000 from an out-of-court settlement and threatened to sue their insurers themselves in a 'bargaining-in-bad-faith' case, if the insurers did not settle out-of-court. The insurer said 'no' to both Anderson's lawyer and to their own client, the garage.

From the insurer's point of view they had to decide upon the reservation price that they should lodge to cover a settlement. This depended on how they assessed the chance of a successful claim in court; if the plaintiff did win, the likely probability distribution of the award, and, if the award exceeded $500,000, the uncertainties of their secondary negotiations with the, by then, aggrieved garage (who were liable for the difference).

Suppose the insurer assessed the probability that a jury would find in favour of the plaintiff as being 0.8 (giving only 0.2 probability that the court would find in favour of the garage). The next question is how much is the court likely to award? Using a cumulative probability distribution, the insurer could conclude that the jury would award $400,000 with a 0.5 probability, and an amount in excess of this, say, $500,000, with a 0.3 probability. This gives a mean expected value of the insurer's judgmental distribution of about $360,000, suggesting that the insurer should settle out of court for any claim of less than $360,000.

From Anderson's point of view, she follows a similar analysis, except she has to take account that part of her award – assumed to be 30 per cent – is paid to her lawyer on a contingency fee basis. If she uses similar probabilities to the insurer, she has a 0.8 probability of winning and applying this to the likely awards (of which she gets 70 per cent) ranging from $200,000 to $850,000, she would have an expected reservation price of $350,000. This compares to the insurer's calculated likely court award of $360,000. This is a small zone of agreement based on (unrealistic) assumptions about the plaintiff's risk neutrality, the sharing of probability assessments, the insurer's transaction costs and the plaintiff's anxiety costs.

Raiffa reports that negotiators, who were given the case information in experiments and who were asked to assess the probabilities that the plaintiff would win, produced a 0.75 probability when the players took the role of plaintiff and 0.55 probability when they took the role of the garage. Each party in negotiation tends to view its own chances of winning as much better than the other side which must mean that their expectations are incompatible, because the above probabilities of success (75 per cent and 55 per cent) do not sum to 1. Other research supports the view that negotiators make over-optimistic assessments about the strengths of their own case. Only when the negotiators make assessments without being given a role – akin to being neutral outside observers – do their assessments fall into the middle (50–50).

Plaintiffs, dealing with their own case only, tend to be more risk averse than lawyers who deal with numerous personal injuries cases regularly. If the lawyer gets it wrong, she loses her commission; if the plaintiff gets it wrong she loses the lot. This probably explains why plaintiffs settle for first offers and press for settlements for relatively large amounts that are certain, than try for often justifiably much larger amounts that have only a probability of success (and, therefore, of failure too!).

When it is personal (it's your compensation) you are bound to be more risk averse and personally more anxious than when it is an every-day item of your professional business (it's one among several cases you have on the go at any one time that might pay you commissions). For the big players in the insurance business, they know from the high per-centage of cases (90–95 per cent) that do not reach a court, that they can risk playing 'chicken' with risk-averse plaintiffs by letting time work against the plaintiff's patience.

The more risk averse the plaintiff, the greater the pressure on them of living without a settlement and the more anxious they are to 'get it over with'. Yet, if your case is one of the 5 per cent that gets to the court house steps, the chances of a jury taking your side as a victim and inflicting huge damages on the insurer – assuming you have case – increase sufficiently in your favour for the insurer to expect to be 'pun-ished' for letting the case into the court, or, once in court, of letting it go to a jury decision. How does this work out in practice?

There is no doubt that insurers, acting on behalf of their clients, and more pertinently, in the interests of their shareholders, can provide rich pickings for people in the legal profession who are prepared to be red bargainers. To the extent that these red bargainers deal with 'soft' blue solicitors, acting for uninformed plaintiffs, the red bargainers can win hands down. Even if a solicitor, acting for a plaintiff, is naturally pugnacious and inclined to act 'in an uncompromising way',[237] the chances are not good of them achieving what Karass would describe as a highly successful settlement.

Many general legal practices – where an injured person is likely to go for advice, if they go at all – do not undertake enough personal injury work to be more than 'one-shotters' and they are nowhere near as good as the 'repeat players' who enjoy regular work from the insurance companies. Hence, the insurer's lawyer 'will almost always come out "ahead" in litigation', or more accurately, in the long process leading up to it.[238] For a similar reason none of us is as good as a professional used car seller – we buy a car once in three years, they buy and sell cars every day.

Some insurers have made abrasive red bargaining into an art form, in that they have a reputation for never making an offer on a claim and for taking the 'most hard and uncompromising' stance on all occasions.[239] To get regular work as a defendant's solicitor, you have to establish a reputation for successfully contesting any and all claims on behalf of the insurers, which means consistently achieving low or zero settlements.

Some solicitors represent their clients by trying to be 'palsy-walsy' with the insurers' solicitors. By being 'reasonable' they hope to develop 'trust' and avoid having to 'outflank' them, and in this way they aim to 'sort out and settle things' on a co-operative basis.[240] They are the archetypal 'co-operative negotiator' who, in fact, are always vulnerable to exploitation.

Not surprisingly, other solicitors consider blue behaviour delusory. 'Insurance companies get away with murder', they claim, 'with hundreds of thousands of solicitors. They're ripping them off right, left and centre. There are under settlements. There are cases not pursued. That's why they [the insurers] don't want to talk to you. They don't want everybody to wake up'.[241] Again, not surprisingly, solicitors who hold to this view have a different behavioural perspective from those who want to 'talk it over' and get a settlement without litigation. Genn reports one senior partner as proclaiming:

> The difference between us and many so-called litigation solicitors is that we love litigation. We do litigation. We try to litigate. Most litigation solicitors seem to spend half their time avoiding litigation in personal injury cases for plaintiffs because they think they shouldn't unless you have to. Our philosophy is that you do it as a matter of course, because its the only way to pressurise insurance companies to get the maximum money in the quickest possible time.[242]

Some other players compromise in that they combine both litigation and negotiation – they issue proceedings first and 'don't mind negotiating in the meantime'.[243] They believe that litigation causes 'insurers to settle higher than the figure they've got marked in pencil in their files'.[244]

Interestingly, co-operative blue negotiators appear to be in the majority, at least in their self-stated explanations of what they are about, and claim that they are concerned with 'ethical conduct, meeting their clients' needs without the necessity of litigation, and maintaining a good personal relationship with the opposing "attorney"'.[245] Meanwhile, red negotiators 'were characterised as dominating, competitive, forceful, tough, arrogant, and unco-operative'.[246]

Professional negotiators may have an interest in a longer term game they play with solicitors, claims adjusters, and claims managers. An overly blue co-operative stance in one instance with an insurer, may conflict with the long-term interests of their client – who only gets one shot for the pot – while an image-building aggressive stance that establishes a 'tough' reputation, could also undermine their client's best interests, if the deal goes sour and the insurers 'win'.

Here, being either 'too close to' or 'too far from' the other party, in pursuit of the solicitor's own ends can be in conflict with the needs of their clients. The defendants' solicitors, likewise, are only concerned with a professional evaluation of liability and an estimate of the likely quantum to settle and are guided by the sole objective of saving the insurers money. Any 'sympathy for the injured plaintiff has no legitimate role in this decision-making process'.[247]

A minority of claims are based on frivolous – even dishonest – grounds. An even larger number of claims with merit are not pursued. The insurer deals with claims in the knowledge that some of them may be contaminated by fraudulent intent. The insurer needs to check the details first before deciding whether to contest or pay up, and if the latter, how much to pay. It is seldom the case that a claim is clear cut, with unambiguous liability set squarely at an insurer's door. And it is probably inevitable that those claims that are unambiguous are challenged as a matter of course, on the grounds that delays will reduce some claims because they are settled on low first offers, and that scrutiny might uncover some holes in the unambiguous claim not foreseen by an early reading of the 'facts'. In the meantime, the insurer hangs onto the disputed money.

Insurance is essentially a bet: the insurer bets that the event against which you insure will not happen; you bet that it will. The stake is your premium, and if the insurer gets it right more than they get it wrong, by the events they insure happening on fewer occasions to fewer people than the total number of insured people who pay premiums, they make profits. But whatever the event, it makes good business sense for the insurer, before they pay a penny, to ensure that the claimed event did take place, and that it happened to the person they insured, and that the person they insured did suffer what they claimed to have suffered, and that they did not contribute to the event happening in any way or to any degree.

The thin line between prudently checking for error and fraud and that of seeking excuses not to pay, is easy to cross. Many people believe that insurers deliberately avoid paying out on claims if they can get away with it. They hire red bargainers to limit their payouts and the claimant's interests are at the mercy of how well or otherwise their solicitor bargains back.

Where claims are unambiguous, the insurer asserts they wish to settle as quickly and efficiently as possible (one UK insurer currently has a marketing slogan about 'not turning a drama into a crisis'). It is the ambiguous claims, including those not properly documented, or that are in some way unsupported by witnesses and evidence, that create most of the work and which induce an adversarial contest between them and the plaintiff. Those that become embroiled in one of these contests have varying attitudes to the delivery of an outcome. A legal counsel, who acts for plaintiffs and defendants, put it thus:

> I take the view usually that there is no certainty in litigation, there-fore it is best to take the money offered rather than to fight on for something more. But I don't take the view that a bird in the hand is so desirable that I'm prepared to have that rather than the possibil-ity of getting four birds or five birds if I can get my net over the bush. But one never knows what is going to happen. One may get an ungenerous judge. One may find that counsel on the other side can pull some hole in the case that one didn't know was there. One usually has not seen the witnesses. One doesn't know how inarticu-late and stupid one's own client is going to be. You know, he's going to do something which makes it look, whether it be true or false, as if he's trying to milk the injury.[248]

There are pressures on the parties which are unquantifiable, except as classroom exercises, about how things will go in a court, what award will be made on the basis of the evidence (not the deserts) of the plain-tiff, how long the delays might be before a judgement is made, and what it all will cost. The plaintiff feels these pressures more than the defen-dant's insurers. This leads to insurers deliberately delaying proceed-ings, or gleefully taking advantage of the tardiness of busy solicitors responding to their correspondence.

Genn reports that one-sixth of the cases going to court are aban-doned by plaintiffs without achieving any settlement.[249] How much this is due to the weariness of plaintiffs or to neglect by their solicitors is not known but we can surmise that if one-sixth give up, another size-able proportion will press their cases with diminishing conviction and will probably settle for whatever the insurer deigns eventually to offer.

We can also assume that professionals in the insurance business are well aware of this factor and that it is exploited in miserly offers to settle well below what they privately believe the claim is worth. If the plaintiff's solicitor is herself under pressure to realize some income from the multitude of unsettled cases that she has in her files, it could be that she will encourage depressed plaintiffs to settle for what is on the table, rather than pursue their cases further, thus delaying her practice receiving income out of whatever they settle for eventually.

This coincides with the need for insurers to settle what they call 'nuisance' claims which have no real merit other than that the cost of fighting them is not worth the cost of settling. This particularly applies where the plaintiff is on legal aid, which does not pay the defendant's cost should the plaintiff lose their claim. A counsel who works for both plaintiffs and defendants provides an insight into the nuisance claim from both sides of the fence:

> There's always a nuisance value in a claim. Now, in a way, as a plaintiff one can play on that, particularly as, I think, and it's probably naughty to do it, but if one is legally aided, as of course so many plaintiffs are, then even if the defendant wins, they are not going to be able to recover their costs, which means that there is a nuisance value to the extent of their costs, and in a small claim that's quite a large proportion of what the claim is, so it shouldn't be too hard to get something out of the defendant. As a defendant, particularly as an insurance company on a claim like that, well, one says one can't be taken to the cleaners all the time and every so often one has to crucify somebody just to show it cannot be done.[250]

Sorting the wheat from the chaff is always a tedious business, more so when the defendant has a clear monetary incentive to find more chaff than wheat. The claims inspector – the person who decides on whether to contest a claim, or if to pay, how much to aim to settle for – studies the paperwork and, from experience of the large number of insurance claims that have crossed her desk over the years, divides them into two piles:

1.   those for which the insurer has no liability, or she can make a case in court that they are not liable (not necessarily the same thing!);
2.   those for which they are liable, or a court could be convinced that they are (again, not necessarily the same thing!).

The claims in the first pile are resisted, maybe right up to the corridors of the court on principle. The claims in the second pile might be settled for nuisance value at a very low, even nominal, amount in 'full and final settlement'. She will try to settle these as low as possible, and all the factors, quantitative and qualitative, raised by Raiffa's example of the

Chevrolet case, will be implicit in whatever method of analysis that she uses.

If 60 per cent take the first offer, she might as well make it a low one, but how low? If time wearies the claimant, or circumstances prejudice their abilities to hang on for the full claim, how long can she delay the process before she must talk serious money? She need not do this abstractly in an office. She can glean information to help her to decide what course to follow, by arranging for face-to-face meetings between her representative and the plaintiff's solicitor, with a view to uncovering any weaknesses in the case, judging the standard of representation of the plaintiff's solicitor, or any weakness of personal circumstances or aspirations in the plaintiff. She is looking for anything at all relevant to the case that might tip the settlement amount downwards. In these situations, the plaintiff's negotiators had better be careful. It is difficult to bluff your lack of preparation and your tenuous grasp of detail when exchanging views with a two-legged barracuda. Those negotiators of an extreme blue disposition are easy meat.

Will the insurer's negotiator take advantage of any usable weaknesses in the plaintiff's case? You can bet the settlement amount, and then some, that they will. Genn[251] found that every company claims inspector and defendant barrister that she interviewed admitted that they would certainly take advantage of anything the plaintiff's solicitor offered, intentionally or otherwise, and they justified their behaviour as an integral part of the adversarial system of personal injury litigation and negotiation. If blue style co-operation is present, it is only one-way: the plaintiff's negotiator co-operates but the defendant's negotiator doesn't hold fire in return.

I suspect that desires to co-operate generally stem from weaknesses of poor preparation, inadequate investigation, lack of grasp of the detail, the time and trouble demands of their other cases, and a proclivity for bluffs and threats in the plaintiff's negotiator. Astute defendants can spot a bluffer at a distance, and just in case they're not too sure if it is a bluff, they call it anyway. Periods of long silence between plaintive letters and demands, with neither an acknowledgement of receipt of a letter or a reply, test the mettle of the negotiator and his client. Doubts about a case or its chances of success soon unravel a bluff into an embarrassed silence. The case dies, unless a ludicrously low offer appears (don't bank on it) enabling them to take a very small amount in 'a full and final settlement'.

The three experiments I have mentioned[252] all took a claim for personal injury as their topic for a negotiation exercise. I put this down to the prevalence of claims negotiations in the United States. Injury claims are about a single variable: *money*. You either get more of it or less of it. There isn't anything else to trade (except, perhaps time, but even that expresses itself in the amount of money you get or forgo). These insurance cases have the characteristics of pure haggles.

The negotiators have a range of monetary values they will settle for, ranging from what the claim is really worth through to a 'favourable' settlement, i.e. the least/most they can get away with. Distributive bargaining is the game, slicing up the negotiator's surplus is the means. And in these conditions it is no time for the plaintiff's negotiator to go 'wobbly'. It should not be forgotten that while the negotiators do their business, the plaintiff's future is in the balance. They have to live with whatever their negotiator agrees to, or more likely, without whatever she fails to press for.

 ## RED BARGAINERS IN BUYING

Commercial buying, a common enough business activity, is rife with red bargainers. So it is not surprising that there is a controversy underway among commercial buyers about the appropriate behaviour to successfully negotiate with suppliers.[253]

It is fashionable, for instance, in certain large corporations for them to embark on developing long-term partnerships with their suppliers. They have reasoned that adversarial bash-ups with cowering sales people endanger their own products, if their suppliers mess up with whatever they send over for whatever pittance they have accepted merely to get a signature on a purchase order.

It is also fashionable to take a different point of view and to practise red bargaining with suppliers. David Sheridan,[254] is one of the exponents of red bargaining in buying and he bases his assertions on his extensive buying experience, latterly at Whitbread, the beer company, and in his role as a trainer of buyers for the Chartered Institute of Purchasing and Supply and, from the other side of the table, his earlier career as a seller.

Sheridan is not one of nature's 'hard men' simply because it is an affliction of his personality. He bases his advice on what is practical and on what he appreciates about the virtues of competition. Capitalism is about competition, and competition is its primary driver, he asserts. Without competition, or with competition heavily modified by custom, laws and regulations, capitalist economies would atrophy and decline, living standards would not grow as well, if at all, and millions of people would merely subsist rather than approach their full earning potential. To avert tough consequences, he believes, it requires tough remedies. Red bargaining with suppliers is good for us all, irrespective of some of the discomforts it causes to those sellers who seek protection from the power of the market. Markets are there to protect consumers, not producers.

Sheridan urges the use of the competitive forces of the market to maximum effect. The buyer's role, in the quietness and privacy of his office, is to act as the market's conduit into the seller's prices. Feeling that he is serving our interests, the buyer works on the assumption that all sellers pad their prices and that his stripping out the padding makes for a more efficient economy.

'Should a supplier,' Sheridan asks, 'be permitted to make a reasonable profit?' Answer 'yes' and you are not thinking through the implications of what you mean. 'Reasonable' is subjective and a matter of personal interpretation, and enables sellers, in those firms affirming it as their supplier philosophy, to 'breathe easily' in their dealings with buyers. Sheridan neatly turns the question on its head, and asks 'Why should suppliers ever sell at a *loss*?'[255] and, more to the point, if they do sell at a loss, whose business is that but the seller's?

The motivation of sellers to sell at any price is revealing (remember, Sheridan has been there as an industrial seller). Prices are different for the same products for different buyers. If the seller can sell higher to one buyer than another, she can sell lower to other buyers. This results in subsidizing sales to one buyer at the expense of another. Losses in selling to you are compensated by selling profitably to your less determined rival, which, according to Sheridan, is good for competitive pressures in your sector.

The convention that volume earns its appropriate discount might provoke a seller to set her price at its 'marginal cost', because it suits her company to keep a production line running even when it is not fully recovering its costs in volume sales. Why should a buyer not exploit the opportunity offered to him if this is the case? The seller may be doing this, coincidentally, to 'buy in' to a customer's future potential (in response to a buyer's sell cheap, get famous ploy?), or because of cash-flow problems and creditor pressure.

Therefore, there are many reasons why a seller agrees to sell below list price and even below cost. But why should the buyer worry about that? A bankrupt supplier is an expensive over-cost problem for a buyer caught midway between a low priced deal and his stocks in a receiver's warehouse. Sheridan asserts that the 'seller's profit margin is of no direct concern to the successful buying negotiator'.[256] You can rely on most sellers to avoid loss-making contracts – they are as aware of the consequences of bankruptcy as you are and they are in a better position than you to spot one coming – and they can always walk away from your offered deal and the methods by which you set about securing one. For Sheridan, 'the moral is clear':

the buying negotiator inherently concerned with establishing a win/win position in every transaction will be likely to be consistently outperformed by the negotiator determined to find the best outcome, without, it is stressed, any deleterious effect on quality, contract performance or continuity.[257]

Sellers are expected – and 'there is nothing wrong with that' – to submit prices in excess of what they are prepared to accept. Their entry price is higher than their exit price, as it should be. What can be done about this? 'If a consistent, aggressive, competitively based negotiating attack is not mounted in *every* case, no buying negotiator can be reasonably confident that the best deal overall has been achieved.'[258] This applies just as much to a one-off deal as it does to repetitive deals with the same supplier. Of course, the one-off deal can stand a much higher degree of aggression because repetitive orders signal to the seller that their bargaining position is stronger than otherwise. This means that long-term deals tend to even out the power balance and soften the buyer's price challenges.

Sheridan urges critics of aggressive stances by buyers to remember that he is advocating '*consistent* pressure to the maximum that the circumstances will allow' and that he accepts that 'the conditions will vary between the high favourable and the extremely difficult'.[259] Sheridan acknowledges the possibility of an arms race developing from sellers padding prices and slackening specifications to create negotiating room, and from buyers stripping out prices and tightening specifications to remove what the sellers create. It is still not a waste of time to be aggressive because the buyer can introduce competitive pressure on the seller, even 'if competition is scarce or non-existent', despite 'holding inferior cards'. Note the metaphor, a sure sign of a ploy player at work.

The aggressive buyer practises one of four modes of buying:

1.   sealed tenders to find the lowest price;
2.   pressure on the lowest price to find an even lower price;
3.   the Karass krunch ('you'll have to do better than that');
4.   conning the sellers to compete among themselves.

Sheridan recommends the fourth mode. It works like this. The buyer accepts none of the bids he has invited for a contract to supply something and sits quietly waiting for the keen sellers to enquire about their bids. Any that do not enquire he calls after a decent wait. The message is the same to all of them: 'your price is too expensive'. It has an added twist. The buyer does not disclose how far any seller is away from the lowest bid – for this would start a negotiation between the buyer and the seller, with the latter trying to compromise between his and the buyer's lowest price. Neither does the buyer reveal which firms are in the competition for his business. He only repeats to each enquirer that the gap in their bid is considerable and, 'sorry, the names of competitors are commercially confidential'.

Some suppliers (correctly) drop out quickly, and the prices of those still contending drops, sometimes considerably. The suppliers compete with each other, without knowing who is in contention. To stay in the game they have to sharpen their pencils.

The buyer, it is assumed, is buying a standardized package with clearly defined specifications and performance standards. The sellers know this and bid for his business. Sheridan claims that he has rarely seen even one seller drop out of the first round, 'for there is an irresistible desire to uncover the likely eventual selling price, competitors' proposals and sources',[260] showing that sellers in price negotiations are often their own worst enemies.

Most, perhaps all, sellers tend to re-bid at lower prices. The buyer again intimates that 'the price is still too high' and again adamantly refuses to comment on how high it is, or against whom they are bidding. The seller is no wiser, having reduced her prices perhaps through more than one round of this 'relatively rare negotiating technique' (though what is negotiable about it is not clear), and some of them will come back again and again with new lower bids, only to be told truthfully, though with tongue in cheek, that she 'is not as far out as previously'.

Meanwhile the buyer is in a strong position. He has used the competitive pressure of the market (or, more likely, the seller's imagination about it) to find 'the lowest price at which someone is *prepared to sell*' the product he requires. If the buyer indicates a willingness to accept a price quotation, the game is not over, for he can now turn to the other parts of the contract (terms, conditions, performance standards, etc.) and apply his techniques on them.

Sheridan derides those who consider such red bargaining tactics as unfair and resembling entrapment of the seller into a game of 'blind poker'. He considers traditional bargaining behaviours as much more 'lamentable and ineffective'. Open competitive bargaining, he points out, results in competitors' prices and terms and conditions being bandied about the sector, with confidential information treated derisively and individual elements of a contract treated as public knowledge. Sheridan denounces 'other ploys' that exaggerate the volume of potential business (sell cheap get famous), promised payment terms which are never adhered to (the nibble) and the defection of a buyer or seller to another more profitable contract if one comes along. He considers his red bargaining methods as ethical in comparison with what happens under other modes of buying. It is a 'fundamental principle of trading' that while every seller has a right to obtain the maximum possible price, every buyer has a right to try to obtain the lowest.[261]

The seller, Sheridan insists, can always walk away and seek better profit margins elsewhere, for, in a freely competitive market, nothing compels him to sell, any more than anything compels the buyer to buy. Whether the competition is real or imaginary is not relevant as long as the selected supplier *thinks* it is real and acts accordingly, with the buyer doing everything he can to 'keep the supplier in that frame of mind'.[262] This leads to Sheridan's seven 'Golden Rules' for buyers (Figure 4.14).

1. Never reveal the price at which she is prepared to buy until it reaches an acceptable level.

2. Never reveal the names of competitive sources – whether they exist or not should be left to the seller's imagination.

3. Never reveal the terms or conditions of another supplier's quotation.

4. Never promise volumes of business known to be false.

5. Never give payment guarantees that are unlikely to be kept.

6. Never enter negotiations with 'targets' in mind relating to financial elements of a deal, as they are success inhibitors.

7. Never castigate a supplier for reducing the price as the supplier needs as much encouragement as possible.[263]

Figure 4.14 Sheridan's Golden Rules for buyers

Applying Sheridan's rules in a recession could be plausible but in a boom it might be much more difficult. In a major dairy business that I consulted for, the suppliers eventually revolted against a Sheridan-type buyer and demanded that he be sacked. The problem for the 'successful' buyer was that the market turned from excess supply to excess demand and the 'price' they extracted for their continuing to supply their product to the multi-billion pound business was the removal of their tormentor. This was a great personal shock for the individual but his company duly complied and the sellers restored the company's supply of bulk milk. It's alright exercising power when you can get away with it, but tides turn and if you have trampled all over others for years you may well reap what you have sown.

Interestingly, Whitbread, a few years ago, also switched from a classic Sheridan red-buying style, which he had perfected while working for them, to a more partnership-oriented style in which his seven buying precepts were alien. If the wheel of fate turns again, perhaps his precepts will be restored?

RED BARGAINERS IN BUSINESS

Philip Sperber appears to be an ethically confused author on negotiation and a few extracts from his work might underline my point that the sort of behaviour he advocates does very little for trust building and constructive negotiation practice. Sperber offers suggestions to implement the ploy of *fait accompli* (Figure 4.15) in which there are echoes of the Karass nibbling ploy.

O   If there is a dispute over a bill, give the seller a 'paid-in-full' check for an amount less than what is being asked.

O   Let the seller begin preliminary work or at least conduct extensive research and evaluation on the basis of an anticipated order. Then back off.

O   Serve the seller with a summons and complaint. Then talk. Have a machine installed or at least delivered. Then reject it and bargain for better terms if the other party wants to avoid taking it back.

O   Tell the seller that the material delivered is already assembled or cut up. It can't be returned, and you can't pay.

O   Tell the seller that you are insolvent or bankrupt. Ask if he or she will settle for 20 cents on the dollar.

O   Pick up and repair the equipment you are servicing prior to an agreement on price. Keep it if the buyer does not go along with the price you give.

O   Make a change in quality, price, delivery or some other key term when it is too late for the buyer to go elsewhere for his or her needs. Then negotiate.

O   Stop work. Then negotiate on a new price based on unforeseen circumstances.

O   If the buyer phones to cancel the order, say it is already on the freight car or it was already modified to meet the buyer's specifications.

O   Tell the buyer that you need a little more money to finish the job. Say that if there is no money there is no completion.[264]

Figure 4.15 Sperber's fait accompli *ploy*

At what point the patience of the other party will evaporate and Sperber's red ploy player will end up in court is an open question. At the very least, the other party will consider whether to do future business with so obvious a manipulator and in time the Sperber player will run out of customers.

Sperber's other gems include his:

- ○ 'strategy and tactics of asking for less and getting more';
- ○ 'when and how you achieve goals through threats';
- ○ 'omission and face-saving negotiating techniques';
- ○ win 'more profitable deals' than could be 'obtained by putting all of your cards on the table regarding your demands';
- ○ 'critical terms before whetting the other's appetite for what you are offering'.[265]

He calls one of these techniques 'low balling'. The seller makes a convincing sales pitch to the buyer about the benefits that a new machine, say, could have on his costs and quotes a 'low ball' price, extremely favourable to the buyer. Once the buyer is hooked he delivers his red bargaining ploy. He tells the buyer that a price increase has just been imposed 'beyond his control' (shades of tough guy/soft guy?). In theory, the buyer continues with the sale but on higher, though still reasonable, terms.

Sperber advocates using similar red techniques in other circumstances too. Here is a selection of them:

- ○ You let a prospective buyer wait in your reception room with other competitors. This justifies your claims for a better offer.
- ○ You notify the seller that management has decided to drop the product line you have been buying components for because of heavy losses, and then you proceed to negotiate a more favourable purchase price.
- ○ You tell the seller that management has decided to make the components in-house, which panics him into selling them to you at a lower price.
- ○ You tell the buyer that the purchase order will have to be rejected because it looks like there will be a strike and existing inventory is being delivered to long-term customers. After you tell the buyer that these preferred customers are paying a premium, the buyer equals or betters the increased purchase price, and you reluctantly give in due to the buyer's pleas for equal treatment.[266]

Now if Sperber's ethics do not make your toes curl, I suspect that nothing will. He provides clear evidence of the red bargainer's approach to deal making.

I am not encouraged by the prospect of Sperber-style negotiators at work on the innocent and I certainly would be more than cautious if one of them wanted to do business with me.

THE LAW AND RED BARGAINERS

Without getting too legal, you should note what the law says about the activities of certain types of red bargainers, which you might need to consider before you attempt your own red bargain, or after you have dealt with a red bargainer. In the UK, the law, under freedom of contract, mostly – and properly – leaves the contents of business contracts to the parties who negotiate and sign them. However, the law intervenes in certain circumstances and declares some contracts to be invalid.

The fact that a contract was made between parties with unequal bargaining power is not of itself a cause for vitiation of the contract terms. It is necessary to show that the relative bargaining positions were abused (Cartwright, 1991, from whom I have drawn on for my remarks and quotations, unless otherwise noted).[267]

Originally, the law was minded to step in between contracting parties if the plaintiff could prove, or it could be proved on his behalf, that 'he was poor and ignorant, had had no independent advice and that the sale was at considerable undervalue'. The law does not intervene on behalf of those suffering from seller's (or buyer's) 'regret' and those claiming redress in law have to prove an 'unconscionable bargain' has occurred, always bearing in mind that the other party had to be aware of the state of mind or relative inhibiting position of the plaintiff.

For example, Richard Branson's well publicized regret at selling his Virgin Music business is no cause for legal intervention. That it is now worth ten times what he sold it for is a consequence of his well-informed business decision made at the time he signed the contract to sell being overtaken by subsequent events.

Evidence of 'duress or undue influence' would count against the buyer who took advantage of a seller, but the making of a poor deal, all other things being equal, would not. Presumably, the famous line from *The Godfather*, that 'he made him an offer he could not refuse' could be examined closely by the plaintiff and his lawyers, should he live long enough to seek the protection of the courts!

In the exceptional circumstances that you have a problem with a trustee of some funds of which you may be a beneficiary, you have the security that the law is 'astute to prevent a trustee from abusing his power or profiting from his trust: the shepherd must not become the wolf',[268] which edict should join the well-known warning to professional consultants who charge for their advice that 'you can't eat your cake and have it'. So beware of charging fees for your advice and hoping to disclaim any responsibility for how your client uses it.

An unfair contract is not sufficient grounds to have it vitiated. Lord Brightman expressed it thus:

> If a contract is stigmatised as 'unfair', it may be unfair in one of two ways. It may be unfair by reason of the unfair manner in which it was brought into existence; a contract induced by undue influence is unfair in this sense ... call this 'procedural unfairness'. It may also, in some contexts, be described (accurately or inaccurately) as 'unfair' by reason of the fact that the terms of the contract are more favourable to one party than the other ... call this 'contractual imbalance'. The two concepts may overlap. Contractual imbalance may be so extreme as to raise a presumption of procedural imbalance, such as undue influence or some other form of victimisation. Equity will not relieve a party of a contract on the ground only that there is contractual imbalance not amounting to unconscionable dealing.[269]

In other words, the terms of a contract are not inequitable unless the bargaining behaviours themselves are conducted unfairly.

It is not right, said Lord Denning, that the 'strong should be allowed to push the weak to the wall'. He went on to distinguish five categories of pushing the weak to the wall:

1. *Duress* – where the 'urgent need of goods' forced the weaker to submit to unconscionable demands.
2. *Unconscionable transactions* – where the stronger party 'imposed terms on the weaker'.
3. *Undue influence* – covering both actual and presumed influence.
4. *Undue pressure* – a creditor under pressure from a debtor to accept less than the full amount due under threat of obtaining nothing at all (putting a bar on Sperber's advice of offering 20 cents in the dollar or nothing).
5. *Salvage agreements* – attempts by salvage tug captains to force payment for assistance beyond 'fair and just' terms.[270]

The law, stated Lord Denning, gave relief when the party, without independent advice, entered into a contract upon terms which were unfair, or where she transferred a property for a sum grossly inadequate to cover its real value, or when her bargaining power was grievously impaired by reason of her 'own needs and desires, or by

ignorance and infirmity, coupled with undue influences or pressures'
brought to bear on her for the benefit of the stronger party.

Lord Scarman in 1980 qualified the unfair use of bargaining power
as a reason for vitiating a contract:

> It is unnecessary because justice requires that men, who have
> negotiated at arm's length, be held to their bargains unless it can
> be shown that their contract was vitiated by fraud, mistake or
> duress ... Such a public rule ... would be unhelpful because it
> would render the law uncertain. It would become a question of fact
> and degree to determine in each case whether there had been, short
> of duress, an unfair use of bargaining position.[271]

If you are misled by a negotiator's representations, the mere fact of
having been misled by false statements disturbs the balance of the bargaining positions, and, for the person who was misled, gives them
access to legal remedies. This is why commercial negotiators, taking
over a business, support their efforts at 'due diligence' with, if they can
get them, written warranties from the seller, backing the affirmations
and statements that the seller makes in the course of their discussions.
You should resist having to rely solely on the findings of your efforts at
'due diligence'. It is only prudent that the buyer incorporates representations as to the rate of profit, the expectations of future sales performance, the non-existence of undeclared liabilities, the extent of the
debtors book, etc., into the contract of sale.

An unwillingness to give warranties or to agree to their representations being included in the contract, should produce caution in the
buyer; though a seller rightly may be cautious to agree because of the
possibility that the buyer is attempting to entrap him into warranties,
which the buyer may have discovered are of doubtful or controversial
value from his due diligence procedures. The buyer may merely suspect
that they have not been given verbal cast iron representations by the
seller and wants those that were given to be incorporated into the contract, in order to claim later that she has been misled, enabling her to
seek remedies, which, if the 'misrepresentations' are serious enough,
would enable her to acquire the business at a much reduced cost.

Far-fetched as this red ploy might seem to be, I know of a seller
where this is almost certainly the case, and that his agreement to
specific warranties, given in good faith, but now subject to controversy,
is being used as an excuse not to pay him anything like the agreed full
price for his business. A case of red bargaining in reverse, using the law
against red bargaining to strike a surreptitious red bargain!

Parties should be free to bargain, writes Cartwright, 'well or badly',
but if 'one party, by his words or conduct, or by abusing a position of
strength ... disturbs the balance of negotiations, the disadvantaged

party should have appropriate remedies'.[272] It might be more sensible, when negotiating for things that are important to you, to consult others well versed in these matters before committing yourself to the consequences of what you sign. Unwilling as I am to direct business to expensive lawyers (there are no cheap ones!), and in the absence of a negotiation consultant in your vicinity, I suggest that you consult your local Yellow Pages under 'legal services'.

 DIFFICULT NEGOTIATORS

Extremist red takers usually exhibit behaviours which are problematic to deal with. Being difficult includes somebody demanding movement from you while offering none from themselves. They can be just plain intransigent. They can express their intransigence quietly but firmly or noisily but firmly. They can be domineering, bullying, threatening and outright abusive. They can also be calm, dispassionate, even charming, and only implicitly abusive.

In whichever form their behaviour is manifested, the objective is the same: to use their behaviour to get you to loosen your determination to protect your interests.

This problem was raised at so many seminars that I decided to address it in the programme directly. Not surprisingly I noticed that the problem was always raised as one of dealing with somebody else who was difficult, never any of the questioners! Their question about the remedies for dealing with these sorts of difficult behaviours was usually stated as whether to choose to *match* or *contrast* the difficult person's behaviour?

Matching a difficult person's behaviour is unsatisfactory as a response because a red response to red behaviour is likely to exacerbate the difficult person's red behaviour. It becomes a trial of strength. The red player reacts to a red response by raising the stakes. Quiet intransigence is stiffened with greater intransigence, albeit perhaps still expressed quietly, but, with enough provocation, it can switch into louder intransigence.

Louder forms of intransigence – the archetypal domineering red player – beget still louder intransigence, until the gloves come off – 'no more Mr Nice Guy' – and it's a clash of the titans until one of you gives way and quits. If you react to the increase in intensity of their troublesome behaviour – realizing that your matching play is not working – and you switch from matching to contrasting behaviour, you only encourage the red player to increase her pressure because your switch in behaviour signals that her red behaviour is working.

Starting by contrasting difficult red behaviour with your softer blue behaviour is no bed of roses either. The problem is that the red player's interpretation of soft behaviour is not as intended by the blue player. Red players see blue play as a sign of weakness and naivety. They believe that their own red behaviour is working and that you are about to give way. One more push, they believe, and you will roll over and play patsy. Hence, they intensify their red behaviour rather than abate it. If this does not work, because you are provoked into switching from contrasting to matching their behaviour, they blame themselves for not being tough enough and they increase the pressure even more.

It seems that whatever you do, match or contrast, or any combination of them, does not work. The difficult player plays red anyway, and, on the evidence of their perceptions of their effect on you, it is logical for them so to do. What then is it to be: match or contrast? My answer is neither, which is often treated sceptically by those who ask the question. Surely, they say, you are behaving in one or other manner? I prefer to step back a little way and approach the problem from another perspective altogether.

Behaviour is the major determinant of our perceptions of the intentions of the other negotiator. It is, after all, what we witness plainly before our eyes. Guided by our perceptions, and by our feelings that arise from those perceptions, we react, as we must, one way or another towards the difficult negotiator. We either stand up and fight back to deadlock, or give in after a nominal fight back. We can rationalize our reactions by some half-convincing thought processes, which often include some version of 'it is more important to get on with my life than engage in "macho" games for trivial ends' – some things, we conclude are just not worth fighting over.

This is an inadequate response but it goes to the heart of the problem. Other peoples' behaviour influences the outcome we accept. But are we as impotent to deal with difficult behaviour as our eventual climb-down suggests? Must we quit and forgo what we want? Not necessarily. We must simply disconnect their behaviour from the outcome they intend we must accept. This involves a determination on our part that whatever their behaviour – difficult, accommodating, or otherwise – *it will not affect the outcome.* Repeat that mantra until it is 'hardwired' into you and then you can tackle the discomforts of difficult behaviour. Convince yourself of this mantra and you will be immune to the intended effect of their difficult behaviour.

You can choose, circumstances considered, to inform them that their behaviour will not affect the outcome. Whether they believe you does not matter – you should expect that your mere assertion of the principle is unlikely to have quick results. After all, their behaviour works with other people and your assertions to the contrary in respect of yourself may not sound so convincing to them – at first. So stick at it.

It is important that you understand the full implications of what you are trying to assert. If their behaviour truly is going to have no effect on the outcome as far as you are concerned, it must follow that their behaviour is not, nor must it become, an issue between you and them. They may behave however they like, but as long as it does not affect the outcome, how they behave cannot be an issue. Not every negotiator sees it this way, and they pay a price as a result.

For example, employees go on strike or they 'work to rule'. To add to the issues that caused them to behave this way – which may be fanciful or vindictive – managements often make an issue out of their employees' actions. They utter the immortal lines: 'no negotiation under duress', or 'no negotiation until you return to normal working', or even adding 'no negotiation until you give a written undertaking not to strike, etc., again'. The result? The strikes and work to rules continue. Why is this so? Because if the management make an issue out of the strike, the strikers perceive that it must be hurting them. If it was not hurting, they conclude then that the management would not bother making an issue out of it!

Right or wrong, people act on their perceptions of your reactions to what they do. They strike to hurt the employer, sufficiently, they hope, to make the employer more compliant to their demands. That intention lies behind a child's tantrum, a lover's walk-out, a worker's strike, an act of war, or terrorism. If their behaviour has no effect on its target would they contemplate it so often?

Observing industrial disputes over the years, I have been unimpressed by the tactical stupidity of some managements (and governments) when a dispute is accompanied by a stoppage, or some other salient form of sanction behaviour. Dutifully, they tell the media 'how damaging' the stoppage is to those affected by its consequences – loss of business, loss of customers, loss of money, loss of jobs, loss of public sympathy, and so on. The intention of such pronouncements is to send a message to the strikers that their actions are having detrimental effects on others and that unless they stop what they are doing and return to work, they will cause 'severe damage' to their company at some time in the future.

The message received is totally different and actually entirely counter to the intended effect of the message the management sent. The reason why people behave in the way they do – strikes, overtime bans, work to rule, etc. – is precisely to inflict enough damage on the other side to affect their willingness to support another outcome rather than the one they chose initially. If the management is not giving in to their demands, or is persisting with some line of action against which the strikers feel strongly, the news reports, and direct sound bites from people detrimentally affected by the strike, actually strengthens, not weakens, the resolve of the strikers to continue with their behaviour.

Consider the mood of the strikers — it waxes and wanes over the course of a dispute: if their actions have no apparent effects on either their employers or their employers' customers, it takes some considerable effort — believe me, I have been there — to get employees to consider the prospect of continuing, what in the UK is euphemistically called, 'industrial action'.

In any group of people, opinions for or against any particular action vary right across the spectrum from relatively keenly in favour, through various shades of warm to luke-warm and neutral and out through luke-warm to various shades of warm to relatively keenly against.

In Figure 4.16 the positive vertical axis represents the degree to which there are feelings for a proposition and the negative vertical axis represents the degree to which there are feelings against a proposition. The central horizontal axis represents distribution of a population supporting or opposing the proposition. Those above the line to some degree are in favour of the proposition; those below the line to some degree are against the proposition.

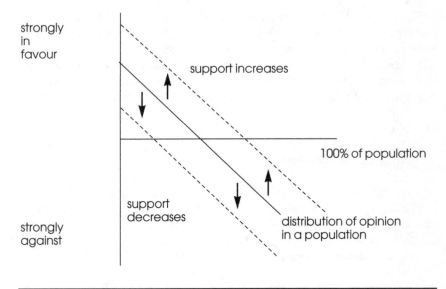

Figure 4.16 Distribution of positive and negative views on controversy

To shift opinion for or against a proposition in a population it is not necessary to win over every one of the people holding views on the opposite side to your own. You should not address your campaign to the extremists who are most in favour or most hostile. It is much more effective to address the larger number of the others less strongly opposed to you. In fact, concentrating your responses on those most passionately opposed to you at the expense of the usually larger group of less passionate opponents could be a tactical error, and a common one at that.

In short, we seldom deal with a monolithic opposition. In any striking group of employees there are various degrees of commitment to their action in support of whatever stance the union has taken on issues that are in dispute. Whenever you make the error of showing them that their actions are having an effect, you reinforce their current behaviour and you strengthen their determination and resolve. The greater the evident effect of their strike actions the greater it solidifies their determination to continue with it.

In Figure 4.16, the opinion line shifts upwards, because the inevitable waverers, thinking of quitting, are encouraged to hang on and the number in favour of the action grows rather than crumbles. There are many examples of this phenomenon. They happen every day, as a watching brief on the world's newspapers and television news confirms.

Having established this point, we must return to the second part of the strategy for dealing with difficult red negotiators: what do we do if we neither match nor contrast their red behaviour? How do we enforce the stance that the behaviour of the difficult negotiator will not affect the outcome? The only criteria by which the outcome will be decided, in the absence of allowing their behaviour to have the impact they intend, are twofold:

1.   the *merits* of the case
2.   the principle of *trading*

or some combination thereof.

We do not accede to any other criteria, though the content of the chosen or combined criteria is an open book, as variable as the parties want to make it. I have no prescriptions on the content of negotiated deals. These are the private business of the people who make them.

The selection of merit and trading as the sole criteria for a negotiated decision is a practical consequence of dealing with the difficult negotiator, though everything said here applies with equal force in any negotiation with anybody, difficult or not.

Consider the difficult negotiator you are dealing with (remember that it is always somebody else who is difficult!). Why are people 'difficult'? Some people habitually use red behaviour and are difficult to deal with because they believe that red behaviour gets them what they want. They are takers, through and through, and they use red behaviour to take from you whatever you are intimidated into giving them. Put this group to one side for a moment. What other reason could cause them to be difficult? Surely, it is possible – please do not discount it as a possibility at least – that they are being difficult because of what you have done, or more accurately what they believe you have done, to them.

OK, it is unlikely that you could have done anything to annoy anybody, of course, but it is possible at least that they could, albeit, mistakenly perhaps, perceive you have done something to cause them to act so uncharacteristically and badly towards you. We need to separate the habitual red behaviourist from the uncharacteristically difficult person who behaves this way because she believes she is your victim.

Assessing the merits of their cases is an essential step to separating these two types from each other. To do so, you have to refrain from imputing motives to them because motive imputation is the antechamber of even greater strife between you. It is more important that you listen than that you stoke the fire.

Years ago, Hamish, a hotel manager, explained to me his method of dealing with irate customers. His hotel was close by a major television studio and he often had high-minded prima donnas as guests, plus the usual number of hotel incidents that enflame the rest of us. When a guest blew their top at the front desk he would invite them into his office and say three things to them, without pausing:

> *First*, I unreservedly apologize for the stress we have caused you, *second* I am going to listen to what you say, and *third* I am going to put it right.

He said this before he knew what the problem was and before he had assessed whether it was an outburst of prima donna-*ism* or a genuine error on his staff's part. He reported that in almost every case, the guest calmed down and the problem was sorted out quickly to both sides' satisfaction. I recommend his approach to you.

To decide on the basis of merit there must be a discussion with you listening to them. If you decide that you have made a mistake, put it right. There is little point in defending the indefensible. Of course, they could have contributed to your mistake and, if you have created the right conditions, you can discuss the implications of this for the eventual outcome.

If a customer, who is meant to supply data to you for a job evaluation exercise you are conducting for them, supplies incorrect data, and your computer operators fail to notice this, the mistake is a shared problem and so are the costs and consequences of having to do the exercise again. Insisting on a one-way burden of costs, when there was a two-way contribution to the mistake, is a purely red ploy. Pressed to a direct answer to their direct question as to why your operators did not spot the mistake, you would be forced to prevaricate, and, perhaps, lie. You could get away with it but you are forever vulnerable to an upset employee spilling the beans to them (and, perhaps, to their lawyers) if he subsequently falls out with you. If asked, you may prefer to answer truthfully and take the consequences because shared blame means shared costs.[273]

Problem solving on merit is well covered in the literature[274] and you should consult it for practical recommendations. For a traditional negotiator, decision on merit is part of the debate phases of negotiation. The search for a solution is by way of listening to statements reporting their version of events and defining their criteria for their solution. Scoring points, sarcasm and direct rebuttal, and so on are not useful behaviours for this purpose.

It is seldom the case that the entire problem is susceptible to a decision by merit only. Bank managers report that some customers preface a meeting to discuss bank charges and fees with a list of alleged errors and omissions committed by the bank's staff in administering their accounts over the previous months. While a sensible opening move by the customers, it does not follow that the errors and omissions that are agreed to be the bank's fault are of sufficient weight to warrant the bank drastically reducing its legitimate revenue requirements that still need to be negotiated. The merits of their complaints may feature in the negotiations on the issues and they can influence the tone of the subsequent agreement.

Discussion on grounds of merit inevitably plays a role whenever the parties attempt to influence and persuade each other. Decisions arising from the purple conditionality principle are formed in the proposal and bargaining phases and they are quite distinct from decision by merit alone. I can relate a distinct example of them both at work in a case I worked upon as a consultant.[275]

John Fryer was an irascible union official. By all accounts he was a difficult person with whom to negotiate. His behaviour was aggressive, physically dominating, loud and very abusive. His manners were not much to write home about and his language was unsuitable for polite company. After playing the red-blue game and covering 'take, give or trade' behaviour, an action plan for all 24 of the region's managers who dealt with him was agreed.

In retrospect, not enough emphasis was placed by me on not allowing

Fryer's behaviour to influence the outcome, for only 11 of the 24 managers managed to keep the plan working after three months (with another six claiming to do so 'intermittently'). Seven of the managers had reverted altogether to their old style of matching the union official's behaviour. I shall give two examples of how managers coped with Fryer as a difficult negotiator, one an example of the application of decision by merit and the other an example of decision by trading.

Fryer was always complaining and he felt he had much to complain about on behalf of 'his long suffering members' (his regular 'catchphrase'). On this occasion he arrived at one of the company's depots and demanded that the toilets be cleaned up immediately as one of them was 'flooded' with urine and excrement (not the words he used) and 'his long suffering members were forced like animals to wade through [filth] to use the toilet'. Normally this would have provoked a row, with the manager insisting that the complaint be put through the official grievance procedure. As this procedure took two or three days to produce a decision, an insistence on using it would cause Fryer to erupt into an even louder rage.

On this occasion the manager immediately accompanied Fryer to the toilets to see for himself the extent of the problem. Not surprisingly, it was nowhere near as bad as Fryer had described it – more a thin smear of leaking effluent that only an ant would need to 'wade through'. However, the toilet was leaking and it was unacceptable that this disamenity should wait three days before a decision was made to fix it. The manager judged that immediate action was merited and he ordered the supervisor to have maintenance re-plumb the toilet bowl and clean up the mess.

When Fryer left the depot he appeared to be satisfied. The manager was also satisfied with the merits of the case and he thanked Fryer for bringing the problem to his attention (he said nothing about the manner in which Fryer had raised the subject nor his threats about what would happen if something was not done 'pretty damn quick'). He did chastise the supervisor for not dealing with the leakage as soon as it was brought to his attention by one of his drivers several hours earlier.

The trading incident, dealt with by another manager in another depot, was slightly more tricky because the merits of the case made by Fryer were suspect. The manager, in short, did not think Fryer had any merits in his case at all. Briefly, Fryer arrived at the depot with a demand from 'my long suffering members' that they be given Saturday off with pay so they could go to a local football club's cup tie. The work they should do on Saturday he suggested could be done on Sunday at premium overtime rates.

Now, while cup ties are important local events they are seldom that important that everybody wants to go. Moreover, it is unlikely that in a depot of 120 men and women that all of them would be interested in football. In this case, the town had two football teams, United and Rovers, and the chances of them all being Rovers supporters was so remote as to be risible. Fryer, as usual stood his ground: it was 'Saturday off, Sunday on'. Anything else would be 'typical management tyranny' which prevented his members enjoying a 'unique local event such as a cup tie'.

The manager did not argue with him, even though he knew he had strong grounds to reject Fryer's claim as spurious. Instead, he offered Fryer a deal: 'If all the deliveries are completed by 12 noon then everybody can take the afternoon off with a full day's pay. Those who want to can go to the cup tie. Nobody is coming in on Sunday.' Fryer protested at this 'miserable' offer and went off to report to his members that the management's offer was 'totally inadequate'.

The members, however, voted to accept the management's offer. Fryer returned to the manager's office and alluded to non-specific allegations of managerial 'intimidation' and stated that he had warned them that the offer was a trap 'to get them to do a day's work in half a day and create a precedent for redundancies' (itself, you may note, a fine example of his own intimidatory style).

The manager avoided being drawn into the ridiculous charge of intimidation – he had not left his office nor had he spoken to anybody about the problem. He had concentrated on planning the delivery schedules and other details necessary to implement the deal. He also stated that he had not even thought about reporting the deal to the regional office so there was no precedent to be set.

The manager had resolved a problem by trading. He had not been influenced by the usual bullying, abusive and accusative behaviour of Fryer. If customers received their parcels on Saturday morning and the drivers had the afternoon off to do with it what they wanted, it was 'no skin off my nose', he reported. That, after all, is what management is about and he had no interest in the agendas Fryer was pushing when he made the demand in the first place.

The manager retained control of the remedy through a traded solution rather than make concessions merely to seek peace with an obstreperous union official. As far as he was concerned, whether the offer was accepted or rejected it did not cause major problems for him. Predictably, if normal working ensued those (few) keen football supporters rostered to work on that Saturday would have made the usual private swapping arrangements with colleagues rostered for a rest day and, failing that, they would probably 'go sick'. In all, he reckoned this would involve six or so drivers at the most, with two or three of the 'sick' drivers risking disciplinary action if they were found out. He was not surprised that the union meeting voted overwhelmingly for the offer he had made. 'Folk around here', he asserted, 'do not look gift horses in the mouth'.

POWER IN PROPOSING AND BARGAINING

It is time to return to practical applications of dependency theory for the proposing and bargaining phases.[276] Power issues and their effects are not confined to preparation and debate. They are felt throughout the negotiation and beyond during the relationship as a whole. For complex, higher value negotiations, power is omnipresent and it is appropriate that you consider some aspects of what we have discussed about power in the context of the proposing and bargaining phases, though, as before, what we discuss has relevance to the other, earlier, phases too.

For example, a debate I often have with practitioners is whether there is in some sense a fixed amount of power in negotiation such that an increase in your power automatically reduces my power. We must distinguish here between what a negotiator might believe is happening and what in fact is happening. No negotiator can see inside the other's head and you are therefore blind to the other's perceptions.

If total power is a fixed quantity, the dependency relationship is a zero-sum game – what one gains in her power the other loses in his power because the fixed total amount of power is divided between both of them. If power, on the other hand, is a variable sum game then an increase in your power over me need not be accompanied by a decrease in my power over you – we have, in fact, a non-zero sum dependency relationship. Sounds horrifically verbose, I agree, but these ideas lie behind some very practical debates that negotiators have when discussing appropriate tactical moves in an adjourned negotiation.

Because power is a perception not a tangible – it is subjective not objective – how can two perceptions be joined together to form a total amount of it? If power is about what you believe, often in practice on the scantiest of data, and your beliefs are intangible, then they cannot be aggregated in any meaningful way with somebody else's. More so, if I keep my perception of your power private to myself, and if, whatever influences your judgement of my power over you, you keep private to yourself, it is not practical to act as if either of us know how 'the power' is divided between us. It is not all that uncommon for negotiators to believe that each of them is stronger than the other, which by definition, cannot be true.

In practice, there can be shifts in my perceptions of your power of which you are unaware and vice versa. As you are unaware of my power perceptions, the only way you can notice changes in them is if they affect my behaviour. This leaves wide scope for a misreading of each other's intentions and for me to engage in behaviours to manipulate your power perceptions.

Negotiators do not aggregate their perceptions of the mutual power balance. That they act on their perceptions is not the same thing as explicitly, or even implicitly, combining or netting their perceptions together. Total power, like total love, is a mental construct and not a guide to action.

Power is a variable not a zero-sum game. By this, I do not claim that you necessarily see changes in your perceptions of power having no effect on me. You may very well believe that if you reduce your commitment or increase your alternatives (using a BATNA[277] technique) you can shift 'more' power to yourself *at the expense* of 'less' power to me. Remember, it is changes in your dependency that change my perception of my power over you. Lowering your dependency does not necessarily increase your power just because you believe that it reduces mine.

Your dependency might increase because circumstances force an increase in your commitment and a fall away in your alternatives. In a zero-sum model a consequent increase in my power would lower yours. But this is incorrect for non-zero sum models. Increasing your dependency increases my power – should I become aware of these changes – but your power over me depends on my dependency on you not on your dependency on me.

Concealing your increasing dependency on me, even deliberately misleading me about its true state, either on the alternative or the commitment dimensions, corresponds to your best interests and I surmise that this is roughly what happens in practice. If I read correctly your dependency status or changes in it, and conclude that my power is high or increasing, it is likely to alter my negotiating behaviour. Observation suggests that I will increase my demands and lower my offers. Hence, obfuscating clues to your current dependency is an appropriate behaviour for you. And what is true for you is also true for me.

Negotiators not only have an incentive to conceal their changing dependencies but also are incentivized to deliberately mislead the other party as to their current dependency. In summary, my perceptions of your power depend entirely on the transparency or otherwise of your true dependency and, as important, the transparency depends on what you reveal to me about them.

Moreover, you are able by tactical play to manipulate what I perceive as my dependency in respect of my alternatives (you will attempt to limit them) and my commitment to the outcome (you will attempt to increase it). Whether this behaviour works in practice is an empirical question, conditioned by context and circumstance and the credibility or otherwise of your tactical plays.

Another relevant contribution from Bacharach and Lawler was to put into an appropriate context Hirschman's work[278] on 'exit, voice and loyalty', the broad themes of which were circulating among economists in the 1970s. Hirschman illustrated possible consumer reactions to indifferent quality and poor services in competitive markets. Bacharach and Lawler realized the rich implications of Hisrchman's work for understanding bargaining relationships.

Hirschman's three rather strangely named themes (exit, voice and loyalty) are quite revealing and much mileage can be got from them by negotiators. 'Voice' describes situations where you attempt to influence the party that has done, or is doing, something that you consider to be 'bad' for you. For instance, if a restaurant supplies an appalling service you have the choice of 'voicing' your complaints and thereby giving them an opportunity to correct their errors, or of paying the bill and silently 'exiting' and leaving them ignorant of their bad service in the hope that their professional failings will eventually drive them out of business. Why do them a favour by giving them a chance to do better?

The 'exit' choice is common in conflict situations where you go to some lengths to avoid open conflict and prefer to submit, or quit, rather than face the tensions of a dispute. You might rationalize this behaviour along the lines of statements like: 'I didn't want to create a fuss' or 'The last thing I wanted was a public scene'.

In the 'loyalty' choice you accept the negative conditions of the relationship and neither 'voice' nor 'exit'. This occurs, for example, in family 'Christmas truces' in family 'wars'. Similar 'truces' occur in families celebrating religious festivals such as Yom Kippur and secular festivals like Scotland's Burns' Night, America's Thanksgiving, France's Bastille Day and Australia's Anzac Day. People continue to live in difficult relationships, too, for the 'sake of the children' or the simple poverty of their alternatives.

Bacharach and Lawler[279] give five examples of the practical application to collective bargaining of exit-voice-loyalty behaviours. In exit, some of the employees voluntarily leave the enterprise with which they are in conflict and seek employment elsewhere. For example, in the preliminary build-up to what became a prolonged strike of 2000 workers in an engineering company, the Convenor of Shop Stewards quit and went to work in a flower shop as a delivery man (he was a highly skilled tool-maker). His exit was as surprising to the employers (and close observers like myself) as it had dramatic consequences for his former members (they lost the strike). In most cases, while some people can exit, most have no option but to stay.

In a strike we have a limited form of exit. The employees refuse their labour but remain in a relationship with the employer. In fact, their withdrawal of their labour is aimed at enhancing the relationship of the union with the company and not at reducing it. They suspend their individual relationship by a temporary exit in order to enhance their collective voice and to secure a better offer from their employer.

Explicit bargaining is a very clear example of voice – you tell them what you want, why you want it and you debate proposals and bargains with them to reach an agreement. In contrast, Bacharach and Lawler suggest that tacit bargaining is a mild form of loyalty, through which you seek only to influence the outcome, perhaps through the consultative rather than the open negotiating process. In an act of complete soft blue submission you exhibit total loyalty. Submissive blues prefer to keep their collective head down rather than risk the consequences of an open challenge to those in control, who can't or won't listen. This was a major theme in the film *High Noon,* except that Gary Cooper did not exit, nor choose loyalty – he went for a particular violent form of voice!

Linking Hirschman's themes to bargaining, Bacharach and Lawler point to the connection between judging whether to choose exit, voice or loyalty, and your assessment of the probability of the potential bargaining outcomes that you might expect from exercising one of the three options.

They express it thus:

> An increase in the perceived dependence of B on A increases the perceived probability that an influence attempt by A will secure a given magnitude of outcomes and thus increases the subjective expected utility of A's voice option.[280]

In other words, if you perceive that the other negotiator, B, is increasing her dependence upon you (perhaps she has lost the services of a key rival supplier – it went bust, say) then the probability of success if you take a stronger stand on your prices for your services, increases the number of outcomes you can expect – what you might gain – if you persist with forcing the issue to a negotiation (the voice option). A corresponding result comes from a decrease in your own dependence on the other negotiator.

Bacharach and Lawler's experiments to reveal the consequences of their theories can be summarized neatly, though I am not entirely convinced that they take practitioners much further than would result from introspection about their experiences and I have reservations about the zero-sum implication of their first five experimental propositions because they imply a somewhat mechanistic cause and consequence role for changes in the basis of bargaining power. I have adjusted Bacharach's and Lawler's language only to make it less formal:[281]

○   An increase in your bargaining power increases your toughness while decreasing the other negotiator's toughness.
○   An increase in your dependence on the other negotiator increases her toughness and decreases yours.
○   An increase in her dependence on you decreases her toughness and increases yours.
○   An increase in your alternatives decreases your concessions and increases her concessions.
○   An increase in her alternatives decreases her concessions and increases yours.

These assertions are a zero-sum version of the balance of power, and for non-zero sum, or variable sum, situations the outcomes are slightly different in that your concessions, upwards or downwards, do not produce a corresponding effect on the other party's concessions. It depends on what happens in the sequential interaction. Your bargaining power might increase but you might fail to exploit this effectively or I may block this effectively with counter-behaviour.

Both negotiators act on their perceptions and not on an objective assessment of their mutual bargaining power. You may act as if you have bargaining power and this may influence my perceptions that you have the power that your behaviour suggests. On the other hand, it might not. The point is that one cause can produce more than one consequence when consequences are mediated through the perceptions of two or more people.

Tidy cause-consequence conclusions, particularly if they are translated into negotiation behaviour that is bereft of reference to the principle of assertive conditionality, rely too much on concession-convergence processes. The conditional proposal format precludes unilateral concession movement. In the concession-convergence format, the parties move to a greater or lesser extent towards each other sequentially. Using conditionality proposal formats, they move simultaneously or not at all. True concession-convergence behaviour is more like a haggle than an IF-THEN type of negotiation. For completeness, however, I will briefly summarize Bacharach's and Lawler's more interesting propositions:

○   An increase in your commitment increases your concessions.
○   An increase in her commitment increases her concessions.

This leads to, at first glance,[282] to two surprising contrary conclusions:

○   An increase in your commitment decreases your concessions.
○   An increase in her commitment decreases her concessions.

These conclusions assume that the party with greatest commitment to an outcome pushes more strongly in the negotiations on certain issues and thereby provokes deeper concessions from the less committed party. I am not entirely convinced that this is an outcome likely to be experienced in practice, though I can see the rationale that a party which is uncommitted to a particular outcome, and that recognizes the importance of the outcome to the other party, might – only might – be willing to concede more to that party, perhaps in some expectation that this will strengthen their longer-term relationship. This is speculative in my view.

 ## APPLYING ATKINSON'S POWER ASSESSMENT METHOD

An example will illustrate the application of Atkinson's method in the proposal and bargaining phases and how it helped produce agreement. First a summary (Figure 4.17) of Atkinson's method from Chapter 2 p. 87.[283]

○　State the proposal you wish to test as accurately and with as much of the detail as you would be required to specify in the negotiations.

○　List the disadvantages to the other party as they will assess them both above (disadvantages of rejecting) and below (disadvantages of accepting) the line.

○　Rate each disadvantage on a scale of 1–10, where 1 is a minor and 10 is a major, disadvantage (i.e., 10 is a worst cost or most harmful hurt) of them rejecting or accepting the proposal.

○　Weight each disadvantage in the other party's eyes for the probability that this disadvantage would have to be borne on the usual scale of 0.0 to 1.0:

　　　0.0　 –　impossible
　　　0.25　–　possible
　　　0.5　 –　even chance
　　　0.75　–　likely
　　　1.00　–　certain.

○　Now multiply each disadvantage by the likelihood of it occurring to give a weighted total for each disadvantage and add them to give a grand total for the elements above the line and then for the elements below the line.

○　If the disadvantages of rejection exceed by more than 3 :1 the disadvantages of acceptance you have negotiating power; if the disadvantages of acceptance exceed the disadvantages of rejection by less than 3:1, you don't. These results are assessed *before* you prepare a negotiating behaviour strategy to enhance or mitigate them.

Figure 4.17 Atkinson's method for assessing power

Recently, I negotiated on behalf of a client the purchase of a small restaurant chain. The restaurants were on the market at £500,000 for their average 18-year leases and their all important licences to serve alcohol with meals. The stock was of no value to the purchaser, as they intended to change the format from steak houses to a bistro chain. The kitchen equipment and restaurant furniture, cutlery and crockery of the chain were included. The market value of the 'goodwill' of the current clientele was not a consideration to the purchaser.

The power assessment is set out in Figure 4.18 and shows a ratio of 38.7:37.9, which is as good as parity (1:1) and therefore the power balance was neither in favour or otherwise for either party. The proposal was negotiable.

My offer on behalf of the buyer was based on a break-even analysis of the revenue that was required to pay for the cost of borrowing, or the cost of money for that portion of the purchase price and initial running costs which were to be invested out of the purchaser's capital, the cost of sales and the costs of materials (food and wine) and the usual overheads. This produced a purchase price of £350,000 to be safe from contingencies, and a top price of £370,500, where the risk was unacceptable against likely first-year earnings.

The initial offer price was set at £320,500 to provide a negotiating range up to £370,500. This was well below the restaurant owner's stated entry price of £500,000 (this itself was a reduction against £700,000 which had been mentioned to the 'scout' who had found the seller some weeks earlier).

As events unfolded, I suspected that £500,000 was a ranging shot to see what they could get as it was well above their reservation price of what they probably needed to clear their debts (the restaurants were not trading too well). Any price above our exit price of £370,500 was not to be considered and when negotiations stuck with the owners at £450,000 my client turned to the market to see what else was available.

The factors which are identified in Figure 4.18 as being the disadvantages to them of rejecting our proposal could only get worse for them as the weeks ticked by, because at the price they were at (£450,000) nobody could seriously make the restaurants pay (unless they had 'silly money' – always a possibility from new entrants to the restaurant trade!) and this exacerbated the pressures from creditors and the bank on 'Steaks R Us'.

There were also some obvious pressures on my client. She wanted to settle the purchase before the Christmas season began, otherwise she faced buying some other restaurant chain too late to achieve a seasonal lift in custom followed by two or three months of slow trade between January and March. Also, the alternative restaurant chains on the market all had one problem or another – no licences in some of them (careless management or police objections) or they were in need of substantial internal renovations or major investments in kitchen equipment.

The parity of the ratio, 38.7:37.9, indicated that a price was negotiable, provided nobody else came into play to make an offer for the chain or for individual restaurants within it. This assisted my client in accepting a need for some patience to bring matters to a head. In a final negotiation, we upped our price to £340,500 for immediate entry, assignment of the leases and licences and all of the fittings and furniture, and so on.

To purchase the restaurants' leases, licences, kitchen equipment, furniture and utensils, for a price of £320,500. Our negotiating power:

		Weight ×	Likelihood =	Total
	A. Bank presses for cash	9	0.7	6.3
	B. Only buyer interested	7	0.6	4.2
	C. Offer may not be increased	8	0.2	1.6
	D. Creditors take action	7	0.5	3.5
	E. Go bust	10	0.3	3.0
Disadvantage	F. Interest burden increases	7	0.9	6.3
to 'Steaks R Us'	G. Securities called in	10	0.4	4.0
of rejecting	H. Face closure	8	0.4	3.2
my proposal	I. Cannot sell as going concern	4	0.4	1.6
	J. Lose more money	5	1.0	5.0
				38.7
Disadvantages	1. Offer substantially less than they required	10	1.0	10.0
to 'Steaks R Us'	2. Might get better offer	10	0.4	4.0
of accepting	3. Some creditors not paid	10	1.0	10.0
my proposal	4. Loss of face	7	0.7	4.9
	5. Uncovered losses	9	1.0	9.0
				37.9

Figure 4.18 Example of a power assessment

The owners were willing to come down from £450,000 on the condition that my client paid them the rent for the early entry because they had already paid this to some of their landlords. The early entry could commence that weekend enabling the client, at her own risk, to redecorate the restaurants before the lease was signed.

In our tactical plays we emphasized two items (B: we were the only buyer interested; and J: they cannot sell as a going concern, in Figure 4.18) in the list of the disadvantages to them of rejecting our improved offer, with a view to raising these costs in the minds of the owners of 'Steaks R Us'.

I selected item C: our offer might not be raised, for special treatment by continually stating that any hope they had of this happening was of limited value to them because any movement by me on price was strictly limited by our financial analysis of the break-even point. We needed to plant the idea that the probability was much higher that no further movement was likely, and, if it was, it would only be marginal. This was meant to have the effect of raising the weighted value of item 'C' as a disadvantage to them and that somewhere below £350,000 was a major price barrier for ourselves.

We pushed Item T ('cannot sell as a going concern'), by emphasizing that the other restaurant chains we were looking were no longer going concerns and, in consequence, would attract a discounted price from us on that ground alone. As to their other concerns, such as the pressure from the bank, their creditors and other uncertainties, it was not considered politic to articulate these too much, on the grounds that the owners of 'Steaks R Us' would be well aware of them without our intrusion into what, for them, would be private concerns. Again our intention was to increase the spectre of the disadvantages to them of rejecting our offer by concentrating on those items we could influence, and allowing those we could not – the creditors and the consequences of going bust, with their personal securities being called in – to work on their resolve in the background of our discussions.

Of the disadvantages of accepting our offer, I thought we could overtly only influence two of them, namely, the prospect that they might get a better offer from somebody else and the presumed loss of face they might feel by them coming down from £500,000 to £340,500. Specifically, items 1: 'offer was substantially less than required', 3: 'some creditors not paid', and 5: 'uncovered losses' (Figure 4.18), were not factors that I wanted to remind them about.

As it was they disclosed to me their inhibition of accepting our offer because it left them with a £22,500 unpaid debt to a refrigerator company, which was threatening to repossess them. If they did repossess the refrigerators (necessary under the hygiene Acts for a restaurant's licence), my client would have to purchase new ones (at £30,000 plus).

Alternatively, we could do a deal with the creditor, which we did privately, and we settled on a price of £20,000 to be paid over two years. This removed their disadvantage of accepting our offer and it made our offer price even firmer.

The likelihood of my client making a better offer was also knocked by the same statements I made in respect of their disadvantages of rejection, illustrating that statements can work on the disadvantages on both sides of the line simultaneously.

Concerns about a loss of face are much more difficult to address, except indirectly. For one thing, I never mentioned at all their opening demand of £500,000, (let alone the scout's reported price of £700,000) nor any movements they had made in between to £450,000.

It is senseless – though I see it too often – for a negotiator to taunt, by implication, the movement of a person's positions, or to attack them for their earlier 'unrealism'. This only creates or adds to a 'face' problem. I felt able, however, to make statements to the effect that we were offering to pay 'over the odds' compared to other restaurant chains on the market only because of the excellent trading and internal conditions and its status of the 'Steaks R Us' chain with its full liquor licences. I also made remarks to the effect that this was a testimony to the hard work they had obviously put in to make their restaurants such a sellable proposition.

This is a simplified illustration of a low value transaction, but it gives you a flavour of what is involved when preparing for a negotiation. Of course it is crude and of course it is subjective. It cannot be accurate by its nature. But it is far, far better than leaving power assessments to the proverbial 'black boxes'. An 'opaque' box, such as provided by Atkinson, is much more useful.

The discussions that this method promotes are most productive, not just in identifying where the power lies *before* a negotiation but how it might change *during* a negotiation as a result of tactical action by yourself. I have found that once the table, like Figure 4.18, is completed, negotiators can successfully resist any temptation to 're-calculate' or re-assess the numbers to produce the results that they want.

There is no question of 'adjusting' numbers to produce a different result from the first ones entered in Figure 4.18. The ratio that is produced first is the one with which you must work. 'Errors' in any item's weighting are best dealt with by your tactical actions and not by massaging the numbers. You can adjust the numbers *after* you take action – assuming your actions have been productive in increasing the weightings of the disadvantages to them of rejection and of reducing the weightings to them of acceptance. Anything else could be kidology of the worst kind – you would only be kidding yourself!

CLOSING THE BARGAINING PHASE

Closing ploys tend to be pressure ploys. Momentum is building up towards agreement and the final shape of the deal is looming. Careful pressure here by a manipulative negotiator can pay him dividends at your expense. It is often observed that the most dangerous time in a negotiation is when the euphoria of agreement is building up, the more so when the negotiations have been difficult and time consuming and you are ready to go home.

QUIVERING QUILL

Extra concessions can be extracted by the *quivering quill* (named thus because 'quivering fountain pen' does not sound quite right!). This relies on your enthusiasm for a settlement overcoming your judgement so that you do not see what they are doing. The deal is close, they have their writing instrument in their hand, hovering above the page, and then they spring it: 'I'm still not happy with clause XI', he says, laying down his pen, 'for reasons I have already stated. It leaves me vulnerable to price swings. If you could agree to cover them, then I could sign now and we could get on with the deal.' If you are desperate to sign and the concession is palatable (too high a demand and they would interrupt your drift into euphoria) the chances are you will move enough to get their pen over the page again. And if you do, it is not unthinkable that they might try another quivering quill ploy to keep you moving.

A more blatant quivering quill is the *yes, but* version of the ploy. Here she tells you directly, euphoria looming or not, that there is this or that minor difficulty in the way of a deal. It can be infuriating to deal with a 'yes, but' player. No sooner do you resolve one 'yes, but' and another one pops up. But you only have yourself to blame.

If you only moved conditionally and kept the deal as a package – 'nothing is agreed until everything is agreed' – you could insist that all of the remaining 'little difficulties' were identified before you responded to any one of them. You could also insist that these new items could be discussed only if they were taken care of within the present package limits, otherwise you would have to re-open the package to make adjustments across the other items which you had put forward as a basis for your solution. This places the 'yes, but' person in the uncomfortable (for her) position of having to move to get concessions from you, instead of getting them for nothing. Therefore, check for all the 'yes, buts' she has and never take them one at a time, because she will likely think up as many as she can get away with as long as you appear willing to accommodate her.

NOW OR NEVER

The *now or never* closing ploy is usually foreshadowed by hints of a pending deadline. The hints become more explicit as you near deadlock over some of the issues. If the deadlock is right across every issue, now or never becomes an ultimatum and it is less effective. It is the gentle hint of a 'natural' termination of the negotiations that works most effectively, particularly if the deadline has some credibility, albeit spurious.

The pressure intentions of now or never are obvious. It works when you accept that you are under time pressure to accept what is on offer and, though you are dissatisfied with aspects of the offer as it stands, you are more concerned that prolonging your search for better terms might jeopardize the deal if it runs into a credible deadline imposed by the other party. Deadlines are always questionable. Some are serious, many are dubious. This is hard to determine in advance. If the deadline bluff is called and it is a bluff all well and good. If it isn't a bluff, you end up without a deal.

Koch[284] suggests that you test a deadline by running right up to it to see what happens when it looks like it will not be met. You can also turn the deadline against the person who has introduced it by asserting that 'this is the best I can do ... in view of the deadline'. Deadlines are like threats and in my experience are best ignored. Responding to them, or looking as if you accept them, only legitimizes them.

TAKE IT OR LEAVE IT

In similar vein, *take it or leave it* is an ultimatum close. It is the antithesis of negotiation, hence the earlier it is tried in the negotiation the less credible it must be, but the later it is tried the more credible it becomes, in the sense that they probably mean it. Your choice is to do exactly what they demand: take it, if you believe this is the best you can do or leave it, if you can do without whatever they are offering. It is not just your problem, of course. They, too, have to cope with the consequences of you leaving it.

Presumably they prefer you to take it, though the ultimatum suggests they are indifferent and that is the significant deciding factor for your reaction if you are at the receiving end of one. Only context can inform you of the likelihood of it being a bluff, though you always have the choice of rejecting a deal which is less than satisfactory to you. This is a large part of the case for developing what Fisher and Ury call your BATNA (best alternative to a negotiated agreement).[285] If your BATNA is better than taking the deal, you can opt to leave it.

SPLIT THE DIFFERENCE

A seductive closing ploy, masquerading as a fair and sensible compromise, is the old stager, *split the difference*. It seems so reasonable and equitable. A difference is proving difficult to bridge, so she suggests that you split the difference with her. This is tempting, sometimes too tempting, and so you agree. In doing so, you have moved 50 per cent across the remaining gap between you and her. Fine, if you can afford to do so. But you have also missed the point that by making this suggestion she has revealed her own willingness to move at least 50 per cent of the way towards you. This leaves her vulnerable to you insisting that while she obviously can afford to move, you cannot. You can now acknowledge that the gap has been halved by her unilateral offer. Splitting the difference, while attractive, is deficient as a bargaining move because it is unilateral, unconditional and vulnerable to rejection. What next? Split the split difference?

Most closing ploys are obvious though they consistently work if you bring to the table a state of mind susceptible to them. Long distance negotiations away from home for long periods, or the influence of pressing social engagements on timetables for your departure, can work against your resolve. With modern air travel you now have an alternative to waiting for days or weeks for further meetings, though you must be careful that you do not leave merely because your patience is driven by the pace at which business negotiations are conducted in your own culture. Expecting strict timetables to be adhered to in cultures less driven by clocks is going to end in tears unless you adjust your pace to theirs. While waiting for an answer, why not go home and return when they are ready? You'll probably save more than the airfare by doing so.

 ## BARGAINING CLOSES

Rackham's books[286] demolished several well-established certainties in sales practice and sales management. Closing techniques, staple certainties for sales trainers, were discovered to actually lose you the larger ticket sales, whatever they might do for the smaller sale. There is a vast literature on sales closes which continues to grow. Some trainers made their reputation presenting 'unique sales closes that really work', and many more make lucrative livings at expounding them across the globe.

One of the top performers in this genre is Zig Ziglar, whose book[287] appropriately, perhaps, closes my select bibliography. In it, Ziglar describes how 100 specific sales closes are supposed to work. To give you what I hope is an off-putting flavour, read some of the names of 20 of the 100 closes in his book:

> The Gloomy Gus, The Snooker, The Bride, The 1902, The Columbus, The Get 'em Smiling, The Puppy Dog, The Impossible Child, The Abraham Lincoln, The Rainy Weather, The 20/20, The Cokes and Smokes, The Oooh and Aaah, The Mother, The Hat in Hand, The Neiman-Marcus, The Kreepy Krawly, The I Can't Get 'Em, The Hep Em Git It, and the Greatest Salesman.

Other sales trainers, in pursuit of product differentiation, re-name these and other closes with exotic imaginations. For you, the issue is whether to waste time and resources on buying into books and seminars on 'closes' that purvey what is to negotiating what astrology is to astronomy.

When should you close and stop bargaining? When the gaps are almost closed, or when you have no more room to move, you can use different forms of closes to attempt to conclude the deal. The bargain proposal itself is an attempted close because if they say 'yes' to a specific condition and specific offer in return, you have an agreement and the negotiation is concluded. If they say 'no', or 'maybe', the negotiations must continue or close without agreement.

So the language of the conditional bargain and its timing can influence the close of the negotiation. In ascending order of difficulty we can identify five main forms of bargaining closes:

1. *Summary close*   Summarize what has been agreed, how far you have (both?) moved from your original positions and call for an agreement on the terms you have offered. Avoid assertions of 'final offers', 'take it or leave it', etc., as these threats are usually ineffective and, if you are bluffing, they might call your bluff to produce 'final offer no. 2'. The summary close does not require elaboration, for like all negotiating summaries, it should be brief, neutral and truthful.

2. *Traded movement close*   Summarize as above but you propose a (small) *traded* movement on an issue which they regard as important to clinch the deal. It is essential that the issue or position which you amend is of small significance to them, that it is not a significant change in policy, nor a major issue of principle, and

certainly that it is not presented as a unilateral concession on your part. The movement must be specifically and clearly presented as a conditional trade: 'if, and only if, you agree now, then we will make the following (little) move on item x'.

3. *Adjournment close*   Summarize what has been agreed and suggest an adjournment for both parties to re-consider the merits of agreement on the current terms. You take a risk in adjourning because they can seek other counsel or become influenced by other people or events, or somebody else can get to them in your absence, hence combine the adjournment with a definite duration (hours, day, weeks) before meeting again and present the consequences of not agreeing as a disappointment only.

In labour relations negotiations it is usual for bargainers to consult their constituencies before formally agreeing to the proposed settlement. There is no point fighting this common practice because an agreement not endorsed by the workforce is unlikely to be workable. Forced agreements are unpopular and ultimately founder in implementation. There is no point in a union forcing a wage increase that the management cannot fund nor the management enforcing changes in working conditions that the union cannot deliver.

The management should try to influence their employees by proper communication strategies and should try to commit the union in the closing moves to positively recommend the deal to their members. Signing deals with unrepresentative union officials is an avoidable form of self-delusion, usually rudely shattered by disaffected employees. Our experience is that when union officials commit themselves to a positive recommendation they usually carry their commitments out in good faith.

Similar considerations apply in business to business negotiations. 'Subject to board approval' is a familiar condition on the closing of a bargain. True the condition can be abused by a board trying to squeeze some extra conditions from you in a quivering quill ploy.[288] Such behaviour informs you of your future partners' (?) red intentions and you must make a policy judgement on how best to react.

In some negotiations you would wish to terminate the relationship on grounds of suspected bad faith. In other negotiations, this is too drastic a response if you consider the merits of their case. Remember, you always have the option of re-opening some other issues yourself for reconsideration and trading to match their board's proposed changes in the deal. You too have a board!

4. *Either/or close*   Summarize what has been agreed and where appropriate offer them two alternatives for an agreement: 'We can

do it this way or that way. It's up to you.' By leaving them the choice they are encouraged to choose one or the other. But, clearly, the message is that you are closing the negotiation. They might decide to adjourn to consider the matter. The considerations relevant to the adjournment close apply in this case too.

5. *Ultimatum close*   This is a high-risk manoeuvre because people usually react negatively to threats, implied or explicit, and sometimes do so when they have no hope at all of hurting you more than they hurt themselves. In this most difficult of the closes you summarize the deal and present the consequences of non-agreement with whatever degree of bluntness is suggested by the circumstances: 'de-list your products'; 'cancel all purchases'; 'hire a new workforce'; 'activate your pre-signed letter of resignation'; 'introduce commercial sanctions'; 'appoint liquidators', and so on.

 ## AGREEMENT

If the bargain is accepted the negotiations are concluded. Always summarize what has been agreed and, if practicable, record the agreement in an acceptable form before the meeting is closed. It is most essential that you do not lapse into euphoria at this moment and neglect the necessary staff work of formally completing the negotiation properly because what happens here can have high costs for you if you neglect to do it properly.

Euphoria is understandable. If it went well, you are pleased and excited; if it did not go too well, you are at least glad it is over. If you are under time pressure, you can create a tendency not to jeopardize what you think has been gained by your intense attention to detail. A need to catch a plane can mean loose ends, and you may risk it costing you more than an extra night in Djakarta if misunderstandings arise on what was agreed. Better, far better, to tie down the details, if necessary line by line, while the negotiators are present.

Misunderstandings, like incorrect hotel bills, are seldom in your favour and if they are, they cause the same mistrust and suspicion in the other party as they would in yours. Certainly, watching negotiators close the relatively simple simulations we use on workshops, and asking them separately to write on a flip chart what they think they agreed to, is instructive. In almost every case, where they did not summarize the deal there is a discrepancy of some sort between the parties. Those negotiators who not only summarized the deal but wrote it down and read it out as their summary for final agreement never experience these misunderstandings.

Negotiation, it must always be remembered, is a means for making a decision. Management is not just about making decisions, it is also about implementing them. You negotiate to manage and most of your time will be spent in implementing decisions, not just making them. You must, therefore, arrange to implement the agreement and to closely monitor its implementation. But this moves beyond our subject of the negotiation process to that of effective management.

5

RATIONAL NEGOTIATION?

 THE LURE OF RATIONALITY

With practical negotiation so messy and humans so unreliable, a preference for rationality in negotiation is understandable. By assuming that people are rational it is possible to develop models of negotiation that produce normative principles of behaviour. You can contrast these rational behaviours with the kind found in everyday negotiations and you can use insights from the rational models to signpost improved behaviours.

Economics, for example, uses assumptions of rationality, in the sense that people are assumed to maximize their utility, which produces elegant mathematical models of concession-convergence negotiation, more appropriately labelled haggling.[289] These models are largely of limited practical value. There is also a growing academic literature in philosophy that uses rational bargaining models and prisoner's dilemma games to explore justifications for morals and ethics.[290] Again, these models have limited practical value outside the fascinating world of philosophical discourse.

The main problem with assuming rationality is that it is at variance with how people behave. While the derivation of rational behaviour from the assumptions produces insights into what would happen *if* people behaved according to the assumptions, it is more than a trifle academic to rely on rationality if people do not behave that way. And practitioners are at risk of compounding their errors if they follow plausible right-sounding but deductive prescriptions derived from preferences for rationality in circumstances that are contrary to the assumptions.

That negotiation research has travelled down the rational road is evident from published work over the past forty years. Whether we consider the work of games theorists[291] or economists[292] or philosophers,[293] the predominance of rational modelling is immediately evident. In earlier chapters I questioned the gaps in the Nash solution by observing how people play dilemma games and how they negotiate. People do not instinctively behave rationally and only a small minority opt for joint maximization. That proportion can be increased by prompting and training but it is still difficult to achieve – even approach – the much lauded 'win-win' outcome without considerable investment in long-term relationship building. Companies that have tried to change to win-win relationships have found it difficult and many have been disappointed.[294]

Maybe negotiators ought to behave rationally but they do not (an ought is never an is) and while analysis of the defects of non-rational negotiating is insightful[295] it is not yet apparent that these insights influence practice. Starting from observing how negotiators behave in practice, you can improve your performance. To do this effectively you must go from description to prescription and not from assumption to prediction, though this does not disallow considerations of both approaches. The very fact that you attend training courses to improve your negotiating behaviour is clear evidence that you do not naturally act as a rational bargainer and nor do you find such behaviour commonly exhibited by those with whom you negotiate. If it was natural to behave rationally, why would you need training?

In the following sections you will explore the contributions that rational decision-making theorists can make to your understanding of negotiation behaviour and you will explore their prescriptive advice to negotiators. Some of their prescriptions are useful insights and worthy of consideration by practitioners, while others remain insights.

 ## COMMON NEGOTIATING ERRORS

The case for rationality in negotiating behaviour stems largely from observation of the common errors of non-rational negotiators.[296] On the grounds that recognition of these common errors prompts a desire for alternative behaviour, researchers have concentrated on identifying the cognitive sources of these errors and on creating learning exercises to demonstrate how to avoid them. This alone causes negotiators to behave more rationally without having to take on board the formalistic models and analyses of pure rational behaviour. Bazerman and Neale[297] have been extremely proactive and successful in this work.

'Negotiating rationally means making the best decisions to maximise your interests' say Bazerman and Neale.[298] They aim to help you 'decide when it's smart to reach an agreement and when it is not' and to help 'you avoid decisions that leave both you and those you negotiate with worse off'.[299] To realize their aims they identify the six common errors that require changes in behaviour if they are to be overcome.

In their work with executives in US business they observed that they appeared to have 'decision-making biases that blind them to opportunities and prevent them from getting as much as they can out of a negotiation'.[300] These biases included the following.

IRRATIONAL ESCALATION

Escalation is best illustrated by Bazerman's and Neale's lively and amusing auction game. You show participants a $20 note and offer it for auction in bids of $1. Whoever bids the highest amount gets the $20 for whatever price they bid. Thus, if they bid $5, and nobody bids more, they get $20 for $5 ($15 net profit).

They have a rule that the second placed bidder must pay the auctioneer whatever they bid, hence, somebody, in the above example, bidding $4 pays the auctioneer $4. In this case the auctioneer has paid out $20 and received $9 in return which suggests she has lost $11.

Rationally the auctioneer is at risk but how likely is it that she will lose? According to Bazerman and Neale (and supported by my own experiences of running their auctions) the likelihood is much higher that the participants will escalate irrationally and produce a net profit for the auctioneer.

Somebody joining the auction is soon trapped into continuing to bid long after it is rational to do so. You continue bidding to avoid losing whatever you have bid so far, but what is true for you is true for the other bidder. To win, you lose!

Your most rational course is not to join in the bidding at all but the temptation to do so rests on the (greedy?) desire to bid $1 and win $20. So you enter the bidding. Samantha sees you about to make a $19 certain profit for your $1 bid and so she joins in with a bid of $2 giving her a certain profit of $18, *but only if you stop bidding*. But if you fail to bid $3 you lose your $1. And by bidding $3 you have a certain win of $17, *but only if Samantha stops bidding*. And so it goes on. You bid to avoid losing your previous bid and so does Samantha and every time you escalate your bid you reduce the certain winnings of the highest bidder and increase the certain losses of the second highest bidder.

Obviously a bid of $19 still gives you a net win of $1 *if Samantha stops bidding*, but as not bidding imposes a loss of $18 on Samantha, she bids $20. The auctioneer wins a certain $1 when the bids reach $10 and $11 respectively because the bidders pay her $21 in exchange for her paying a prize to one of you of $20. At bids of $19 and $18 she wins a net $17 profit. Once you bid over $20 she is well ahead.

In practice bidders irrationally escalate well beyond $20 and Bazerman and Neale report an auctioneer's profit as high as $407 in one of their workshops and they claim to have made $10,000 running their auctions over four years.[301]

Escalation behaviour is common in auctions, strikes, marketing campaigns, price wars and competitive acquisitions. You commence a course of action fully determined to succeed but you forget, or irrationally discount, the likely reaction of others who can influence the outcome.

You cut a price by a small amount to gain market share but your competitors follow suit and wipe out any gains you might have made if they had behaved differently. You know from experience that price wars are irrational but you irrationally believe that the other guys will quit price cutting first – 'we'll see who has the deepest pockets' – but if it is 'rational' for you to believe that they will quit and leave you with a price advantage, so it is for them to believe the same of you.

FIXED PIES

We have already discussed at length the fixed pie assumptions of zero-sum bargaining, which lead people to believe that they can only gain at the expense of the other party.

Bazermman and Neale report Congressman Floyd Spence's fixed pie philosophy in the Cold War:

> I have had a philosophy for some time in regard to Salt, and it goes something like this: the Russians will not accept a Salt treaty that is not in their best interest, and it seems to me that if it is in their best interest, it can't be in our best interest.[302]

Of particular additional interest in Bazerman's and Neale's account is their poignant identification of the advice to negotiate the 'easy issues first' as a form of fixed pie philosophy. Asserting that it is best to negotiate the 'easy' issues before the 'difficult' ones ignores the potential for trade-offs between the preferences of the negotiators, and this views negotiation as the division of a fixed pie.

ANCHORING

Your initial entry position acts as an anchor against which the changing pressures in the negotiation pull you towards a settlement or deadlock. The anchor influences perceptions of the other negotiator about what is possible. Karass advocates that you open 'high' which is another way of saying that you should strongly anchor your entry point.

The problem arises when you decide on where to open. Upon what information is your decision based? The irrationality of anchoring on non-relevant information leads to entry points that deter the negotiation commencing if they appear to be too unrealistic for the other party. Certainly, outcomes are influenced by opening positions because your entry point can structure or influence their expectations but they can also influence the outcome negatively – they walk away because you are too extreme.

If you remember that an entry offer is only a first offer and that you should always challenge the first offer, you have an antidote to over-reacting to initial stances. If anchoring is unrealistic, so is walking away when they first reveal their aspirations to you. You can counter-anchor too. This might set a large gap between you but what works on your expectations also works on theirs. You both have, perhaps, a long way to go before a definitive judgement that the anchors are too entrenched, so too early a reaction is irrational, collapsing towards the other's extreme position is irrational and so is taking too personally what they are doing.

REFERENT BEHAVIOUR

The way you frame an option can determine your willingness to accept an agreement. While fairly subtle this idea is widely applicable in negotiation. For example, bank customers are more willing to pay increases in charges and fees than they are increases in interest rates, even when the total amounts paid out in a year are exactly the same. The referent frame for interest rates is easily quantified and has a public standard reference point – what are current interest charges today? Bank charges and fees are less visible and hardly comparable. For a start you do not know what other customers are paying, but you do know what the bank rate is set at because it is published daily in the press and is constantly updated online.

Buyers value the same items at lower prices than sellers. The sellers' referent point is regarded as a loss of a possession and they tend to over-value the item to compensate for the loss they feel. Buyers under-value acquiring the item because they have no sense yet of possession of it. Experiments have shown this to be the case and it corresponds to observations of buyer–seller behaviours, not the least the common experience that the seller's entry price almost invariably is higher than the buyer's offer price.

Where this is not so, usually it is because the seller has little or no attachment to the item. For example, distant relatives often have the deceased relative's house contents cleared at a knock-down price because they have no attachment to the house contents. It is different if they are familiar with the house and its contents, as shown in those ghastly bereavement squabbles between family members in disputes over 'treasured' items – 'promised to me by Aunty Rebecca' – that can exhaust the money value of their inheritance in legal fees.

Reframing referent points is a more rational response to unintended deadlock over them and can dramatically change your choice of alternative outcomes. Consider a management-union dispute over the size of a wage rise. If you see the management's offer relative to your initial higher demand, you will perceive the offer as a loss from what you would have gained if they had paid your entry demand in full. If you see the management's offer as an increase over your current lower wage, you will perceive their offer as a gain. In this context, I have seen a union leader denounce a management's offer of a £1 a week increase as 'stingy', 'insignificant' and 'wholly unacceptable' and, in his other role as the leader of a tenants' rent strike, denounce the local council's rent increase of £1 a fortnight as 'draconian', 'wildly excessive' and 'outrageous'.

Reframing is psychological. Is the glass half empty or half full? The former are usually described as pessimists by nature and the latter as optimists. Which is more rational: to relate your salary increase to the amount of the increase you obtain or to relate it to what others are paid in your department? It used to be the case that employees were more concerned with their differentials over less regarded work groups, particularly unskilled people, than they were with the amount of increase they obtained. The 'rate for the job' is a strong referent for many employees.

FALLACIES OF PROMINENCE

Whatever is prominent attracts most attention. This is true in the use of information. Negotiators are influenced more by whatever information is easily available than they are by its relevance to the current decision.

Bazerman and Neale note[303] that functional managers see their company's problems almost total from within their own specialism. Attend any company's 'away-day' on its current problems and you will see functions lining up behind that which they know most about: the company's problems through their function's eyes. Finance sees the main problem in the efficient use of resources and the excess of work in progress and unsold products stored in its warehouses; accountants see it in the failings of accountability and costings; production in the lack of equipment and the scheduling of small batches rather than long runs and sales in the lack of innumerable quantities of everything that any customer might require at short notice.

Unions see headline inflation rates as the main case for higher wages; managements are more cost conscious about wage increases. In public debate, led by the varying intensity of media coverage, whatever is prominent in the news is disproportionately the driver of awareness of the need to do something. For instance, while the rate of child abduction and murder has been steady for ten years, the recent prominence given to some individual cases has prompted widespread fears that this particularly odious crime is on the increase and that our children must be more intensively warned to stay away from strangers. The facts are different. It is not on the increase and the majority of abductions and murders (83 per cent) are committed by people known to the children.

The rational remedy for negotiators is a more thorough search for relevant data and proper analysis of what is available. It is not that a little knowledge is dangerous as much as it may not be relevant.

OVERCONFIDENCE

Overconfidence in the likely success of your preferred position is one of the more common errors of negotiators. When you prepare your negotiating stance you often overestimate the likelihood of your prevailing. You do not take the other party's role sufficiently into account. The implication of your overconfidence is that the other negotiator is irrational and that he will accept from you settlements that are contrary to his aspirations. This results in behaviour that is less likely to be flexible than it needs to be if an agreement is the ultimate aim.

Deciding what you want is the main task of preparation but remember that finding out what they want is the main task of debate. You cannot get what you want without considering what they want and the extent to which your wants are incompatible as entry positions, either one or both of you must move to a more accommodating position.

I have observed negotiators confidently adopt positions that imply that the other negotiator will give in. The more certain they are of the viability of their own position the less viability they impute to the other party's position. Rationally this is odd. If you are 75 per cent certain that your position will prevail, the arithmetic of probability ascribes only a 25 per cent probability to their chances of success ($0.75 + 0.25 = 1$). Now, why would somebody adopt a position that only has a 25 per cent probability of success? Are they not as rational as you? Apart from

considering your risk-aversion sensibilities it must occur to a rational person that perhaps your 75 per cent confidence is misplaced? If they also are 75 per cent certain of success, something will have to give to get a result because the sum of the probabilities of an event occurring and not occurring must always be unity $[p + (1–p) = 1]$.

Overconfidence produces inflexibility, lack of movement, lack of trading, impasse and deadlock. If these are the main errors of irrational negotiating behaviour, what is the remedy?

 ## SIMON'S SIMPLE MODEL

Phased models[304] map what people do in social interactions. They have an inductive bias. Nobel prize-winner, Herbert Simon,[305] deduced a behavioural model for individual rational choice. The original three steps in Simon's 1955 deductive model are shown in Figure 5.1.

Simon assumed rational choice on the part of the decision maker. He also acknowledged that there was a possibility for feedback between each step, so that his model is not a linear one-way process. If, for instance, subsequent information reveals inadequacies in the previous step, you may return to that step and re-do your work there.

O   Identify the problem

O   Search for alternate solutions and their consequences

O   Preference order solutions and select a course of action

Figure 5.1 Simon's rational decision model

Walton and McKersie,[306] authors of the landmark study of American labour negotiations, endorsed Simon's individual choice model because they believed that his three rational steps were demonstrated in the three stage bargaining sequence observed by Douglas.[307] This is a significant shift in application of rational choice from the individual to bargaining pairs and, in its extensions in the model of principled negotiation, may explain the source of important flaws in its applicability.

Walton and McKersie, in identifying bargaining processes with Simon's rational individual choice, asserted that the early phases of negotiation, possibly even the pre-negotiation phase, involve the uncovering, identifying, and understanding of problems. As negotiations progress, the negotiators' attention turns to the search for possible solutions to the problems they have identified. Finally, Walton and

McKersie noted, under the pressure of a deadline (a decision crisis?) how decisions are reached. Briefly, they argued for parallel steps as follows.

How you *define the problem* (step 1) is crucial to how you approach it. If you conceive that the problem is the other player's problem only and not a problem shared by you both, this will provoke what Walton and McKersie famously called a 'distributive' or zero sum bargaining situation – what you gain the other loses. If the problem, however, is defined as a shared one, then there are prospects for what they called an 'integrative' solution, or joint gain sharing from solving the problem.

Information exchange dominates step 2, and not just about the potential solutions but of the consequences of each of them. 'Invention and creativity', more commonly called brainstorming nowadays, are essential here. The search can cause feedback to produce a clearer and more accurate definition of the problem, perhaps widening it to include other problems not at first glance obviously connected with the original one. This opens up new possibilities for finding a solution.

Step 3 is heavily influenced by modern utility analysis and seeks to integrate *utility maximizing* into the choices and behaviours of the negotiators.[308] Crudely, you each make successive comparisons of the utility you derive from alternative solutions and you each have some tentative idea of a utility maximizing solution acceptable to you (though not necessarily to the other party). The tension of choice focuses on whether you should accept the current solution on offer (the one you are guaranteed if you say 'yes') or whether you should continue the search among the other possible solutions you have not yet uncovered (there is more than one needle in the haystack!). This makes the outcome of Simon's rational decision process uncertain but more realistic in the sense that there is no unique solution, such as found in the Nash solution.

The search for solutions involves testing potential solutions against some form of criteria, which can be changed if the solutions it suggests prove to be unsatisfactory to one or other of you. By iteration, you eliminate unsatisfactory solutions and use amended criteria to judge the replacement solutions. You do this until a mutually satisfactory solution emerges.

This is an interesting variation on recent[309] insistence on establishing objective criteria *before* you judge the various options that are thrown up by your brainstorming activities. Simon's approach of iterating between potential criteria – rejecting them until agreement is found – is more flexible and realistic. It is also less mechanistic.

Though Walton and McKersie suggest that bargaining parallels Simon's three steps, I have reservations about their assertion. Of course, bargaining processes can be fitted into Simon's rational decision model provided we are not expecting anything near a perfect fit. But we also have to accept that bargaining models are not suitable as subjects for rational individual decision-making theories. It is the very untidiness of the negotiation process that breaches the boundaries required for rational choice modelling.

Simon was not as extreme a rational decision theorist as the Nobel prize-winning economist, Milton Friedman[310] whose rational decision model imposed much stricter assumptions than Simon's.

Simon asserted that decision makers are not fully rational for they are necessarily bounded by crucial deficits in the information necessary to act like perfect decision makers. In practice, Simon's decision makers do not have the time, nor the access, nor the ability to process all the information required to make the perfect decision.

Therefore, they do the next best thing and make decisions that satisfy at least some limited or acceptable criteria rather than continue in the perfectionist search for the highest value solution. Simon's ideas of *satisficing* and bounded rationality won him the Nobel Prize. The differences between maximizing and satisficing behaviour are significant and not just because maximizing is more susceptible to mathematical analysis than satisficing. Behaviourally they are quite different because the maximizer's choice is determined by restrictive assumptions and the satisficing choice is determined by the negotiator's perceptions. Simon's model is closer to how we expect individuals to behave though it is still too formal as a description.

For many years on courses run for sales or purchasing staff I have set the participants a short exercise. They work in pairs and have 15 minutes in which to produce a minimal three- or four-step summary of how a person makes a decision. That is about all the briefing they get before they are sent off to do it. Almost every pair comes back with a model of decision-making which is as close as you can make it to Simon's 1955 model, even though few if any of the pairs have ever heard of Simon or any other author of formalized decision-making models.

Broadly, the pairs return with something like the edited version in Figure 5.2, though the language they use is often different, even vaguer. The argument for this sequence is easily justified by participants and is usually persuasive. Not everybody gets it totally right but sufficient do and I have interpolated below what happens in each step from several versions presented at the seminars.

You become aware of a need for something – say, to quench your thirst. Whether you do something about this need depends on what else is pressing for attention. If you are busy with some other more pressing need (will your team score in the TV game?) you postpone doing something about the need to quench your thirst.

O   awareness of need

O   search for options to satisfy the need

O   selection of one of the options

O   satisfy the need.

Figure 5.2 How participants describe a rational decision process

If the need successfully competes for your attention you consider what ways are open to you to satisfy the need. In the thirst example, you could consider what drinks were available in the fridge, how long it would take to make a cup of coffee, whether a glass of water would be sufficient, and so on. If the effort to acquire one or all of the options is too much (your house is bereft of drinks and the water is contaminated) compared to your desire to quench your thirst, you might postpone doing anything about your need for the moment.

Having searched for options you select one of them – make a cup of coffee – and having done this you satisfy your need by drinking the coffee to quench your thirst. How you select among the options is potentially an interesting question. You might use some relevant criteria, such as the option that minimizes your absence from the TV. This is a 'higher' order of consideration in the model that few participants identify unless prompted in the debrief.

Remarkably, almost everybody reports the steps in the same (correct) order, though step 4, 'satisfy the need', is identified by a minority with most people reporting steps 1 to 3 only. On questioning why they chose only three steps, the most common retort is that if you select an option to satisfy the need that implies that it is satisfied.

Now, if people in only 15 minutes' introspection can move so close to deriving a Simon's type rational decision model without prompting it must indicate that his model corresponds to perceptions of reality to a sufficient degree for us to have some confidence in it. Participants are usually fairly pleased with themselves when I show them how close they are to Simon's model (prompting some *sotto voce* remarks about how 'easy' it is to win a Nobel Prize, until I point out that the prize was for much more than this version of his model or that what made Newton a genius is now accomplished by fourth form school children with little or no sweat!).

Where a deductive process is so closely aligned with people's own perceptions of what happens, we can see why such models are so attractive when offered as the appropriate way to negotiate. Deviations from the rational process are easily side-lined as sub-optimal departures from what is in their best interests. Applying the model must be an improvement – even a changed game – on what happens when people are trapped into irrationality in their negotiating behaviour. The prescriptive bias in such thinking is irresistible and most people swiftly succumb to it.

As you will see, I am sceptical that rational decision models are sufficient as guides to action and they can obscure important elements in a process that does not fit neatly into the model. Moreover, they make a strong case for prescriptions that might not travel well when transferred from the logic of individual decision making to multi-party decision making commonly found in a negotiation process.

 PRINCIPLED NEGOTIATION

Fisher and Ury's seminal work, *Getting to Yes: Negotiating Agreement Without Giving In*,[311] has significantly influenced the theory and practice of joint problem solving. Its prescriptive model is widely accepted among many practitioners in dispute resolution and mediation, though less so by practitioners of commercial negotiation.

Principled negotiation's prescriptive sequence is firmly rooted in Herbert Simon's rational individual's decision model. This is its significant problem. Simon's rational decision model is for a rational individual not a negotiating pair. A model that plausibly describes what works for the rational individual may be inadequate for the negotiating pair, if only because the pair are subject to their conflicting prejudices and the impact of their interactions, whereas the individual can mediate between herself and her differing views on the options in private and she can override her private views by finding subjective reasons, personal only to herself, to justify whatever she decides to choose. In negotiation most of this rationalizing necessarily is in the semi-public domain. Your justification for one option is subject to critical examination by the other negotiator, for instance. Now, Fisher and Ury do not discuss this possibility, though it is unlikely that they are ignorant of Simon's work.

Principled negotiation 'or negotiation on the merits',[312] asserts the debatable premise that traditional negotiation inevitably means positional bargaining, which, in turn, because of its alleged in-built defects, inevitably opens stressful fault lines between negotiators. Principled negotiation as a method, it is claimed, is the only alternative to the errors of positional bargaining. From Fisher and Ury's examples of these errors, however, they appear to confuse positional bargaining with *positional posturing* (where bargaining is certainly not manifest).

Nevertheless, they enjoin practitioners to abandon traditional negotiation.

One example from their text supports my contention that positional posturing is not the same as positional bargaining. Fisher and Ury write: 'Each side tries through sheer will power to force the other to change its position. "I'm not going to give in. If you want to go to the movies with me, it's *The Maltese Falcon* or nothing".'[313] Their example is not evidence of positional *bargaining* at all. It illustrates in fact the antithesis of bargaining and perfectly describes positional posturing in the form of an ultimatum. If the listener loses the contest of wills, the outcome has none of the characteristics of a voluntary bargain and their decision process has none of the characteristics of negotiation. Contests of will are what happens when the parties fail to negotiate, not what happens because they do.

Compare the above quotation with one re-written to articulate one of the main prescriptions of principled negotiation, namely that agreement on the use of principled negotiation methods by both parties is a *pre-condition* for participating in a negotiation: 'I'm not going to give in (*"never* submit to pressure!"). If you want to negotiate with me, its principled negotiation or nothing.' Sounds pretty arrogant? Advocates of principled negotiation often exhibit behaviours that are regarded by them as disreputable when used by traditional negotiators.

Fisher and Ury use a fallacious argument ploy (pp. 116 et seq.) by setting up two extremes, 'hard' and 'soft' positional bargainers to show that neither extreme can be 'efficient', nor 'wise' nor good for relationships ('bitter feelings generated by one such encounter can last a lifetime').[314] They also exclude the possibility of 'a strategy somewhere in between' the extremes, and they conclude that negotiators must change the 'game' of negotiation to the principled negotiation method.[315]

Practitioners can learn much from the method of principled negotiation, but there is no need to throw the baby out with the bath water. It is possible to reject the errors of positional posturing without rejecting the methods of traditional negotiation. By setting up two extremes and denying a third possibility, readers are driven to a forced conclusion, as if our options as negotiators were governed by an algorithm. This debating trick has no scientific merit, though it has a long pedigree.

As negotiators we could decide, in certain circumstances, to accept Fisher & Ury's advice to change the game from traditional to principled negotiation but only if it is to our benefit to do so (see Figure 5.3)

PROBLEM Positional bargaining: which game should you play?		SOLUTION Change the game – negotiate on the merits
Soft	**Hard**	**Principled**
Participants are friends. The goal is agreement.	Participants are adversaries.	Participants are problem solvers. The goal is a wise out- come reached efficiently and amicably.
Make concessions to cultivate the relationship.	Demand concessions as a condition of the relationship.	**Separate the people from the problem.**
Be soft on the people and the problem. Trust others.	Be hard on the people and the problem. Distrust others.	Be soft on the people and hard on the problem. Proceed independent of trust.
Change your position easily.	Dig into your position.	**Focus on interests not positions.**
Make offers. Disclose your bottom line.	Make threats. Mislead as to your bottom line.	Explore interests. Avoid having a bottom line.
Accept one-sided losses to reach agreement.	Demand one-sided gains as the price of agreement.	**Invent options for mutual gain.**
Search for the single answer: the one *they* will accept.	Search for the single answer: the one *you* will accept.	Develop multiple options to choose from; decide later.
Insist on agreement. Try to avoid a contest of will.	Insist on your position. Try to win a contest of will.	**Insist on using objective criteria.** Try to reach a result based on standards independent of will.
Yield to pressure.	Apply pressure.	Reason and be open to reasons; yield to principle not pressure.

Figure 5.3 Two extremes and a principled solution[316]

For the moment, I advise practitioners that they would be less than wise to abandon traditional negotiation just because of the avoidable (and objectionable) practices of positional posturing.

THE PRESCRIPTIONS OF PRINCIPLED NEGOTIATION

Principled negotiation is a prescriptive method of negotiation 'that can be used under almost any circumstance'.[317] The four prescriptions are set out in Figure 5.4.

O   separate the people from the problem

O   focus on interests, not positions

O   generate a variety of possibilities before deciding what to do

O   insist that the result be based on some objective standard.

Figure 5.4 The four prescriptions of principled negotiation[318]

Its popularity is founded on these sensible strictures – they appeal to the good sense of people who want to resolve problems rationally and in good faith. Examining the prescriptions of principled negotiation we can make some supportive as well as critical comments.

SEPARATE THE PEOPLE FROM THE PROBLEM[319]

At once, the appeal of principled negotiation is fully explained. This goes to the heart of the challenge to confrontational or adversarial approaches. People are often part of the problem (sometimes they are the problem!). Everything they say is conditioned by who they are and the state of their relationship with you. They bring a large emotional baggage with them too. When they throw this around during an inter-action of any kind it is more difficult for you to find a joint solution. Emotional baggage distorts perspective. Layers of abusive hostility make for poor problem solving and any advice to shift attention from the people to the problem is good advice, though like much good advice, it is difficult to apply if at least one of the parties is determined to keep it personal.

Outraged spouses, hunting for revenge, or worse, can make domestic disputes intractable and personally self-destructive when it comes to the disposal of the ex-family's assets – including the ability of the parents to generate future income streams – let alone to agree on access rights to the children.

One friend of mine who sought divorce from her husband, simul-taneously declared that her main goal was to 'ruin the bastard'. No amount of rational argument could divert her from this goal, even though if she was successful it would mean his ability to finance any worthwhile income support for herself and her children would be severely compromised (particularly if his goal was to make sure 'the bitch did not get a penny'). Both of them could ruin themselves financially in the process of ruining each other.

Emotional hurt from the collapse of relationships filters out good sense. In the heat of a conflict you lose perspective. Normally decent people lose their self-control and behave beyond accepted frontiers of personal conduct. If you follow competitive sports at all you will know how common it is for fired-up players to descend into unacceptable, even appalling, behaviour.

This is the bottom line, of course. Removing the people from the problem is a fine goal – and a necessary one, no doubt – but it is not so simple to enforce. The best you can do is make sure that on your side of the table you rise above personalities whatever the other side decides to do.

If the prescription to separate the people from the problem requires that the parties co-operate in making it effective, this suggests that people problems are not standing in the way of solutions! The prescription is only required when people are in the way of a deal.

FOCUS ON INTERESTS NOT POSITIONS[320]

Positions are *what* we want, interests are *why* we want them. The two are inseparable. Fisher and Ury emphasize the interests of the negotiators as the one way of resolving disputes and of exploring the acceptability of terms when positional stances alone might be unproductive. They are wrong if they assume that considering the interests of the parties removes the need for deciding on positions. As we shall see, interests and positions are *not* mutually exclusive; they are intertwined. It cannot be an Orwellian case that interests are good and positions are bad. This is a profoundly silly error.

Issues are the agenda of the negotiation, expressed (normally) in positions. It is not possible to negotiate without reference to issues and positions, except at the most general level of 'yes' or 'no', but even that 'yes or no' must be in reference to some position, otherwise to *what* are you saying 'yes or no'?

Let us take the vexed question of a proposal to build a new runway at an airport, an event usually accompanied by intense controversy from the residents who are most immediately affected by the proposal. Some residents may decide for or against a proposed new runway by how the new flight path affects their interest in the quiet enjoyment of their property. It is their interest that drives them to want or not want the runway and the more their interest in quiet enjoyment is affected – the closer, that is, their property is to the noise envelope of in-coming and out-going aircraft – the more likely that they will be against the proposal. Uncovering a party's interests helps you to understand what they are about; identifying your own interests likewise helps you to decide on your positions on the negotiable issues.

The issues are commonly addressed by some form of stance (build/not build; buy/not buy; yes/no, etc.). Less commonly they are explored by reference to your interests. If the stances on the issues, and the consequent alternative positions that are possible on any one issue are in conflict, this creates the need for processes of dispute resolution. If nobody took a stance on an issue there would be no dispute to resolve. What is non-controversial is not negotiated. Peace is the acceptance by all of the status quo and disputes (from differences of view through to violence) arise when at least one person wants to change the status quo and at least one other person does not.

The positional gap between 'no you don't' and 'yes we do' is bridgeable without recourse to positional posturing. Conflicts over positions are a fact of life, as are violations of the laws of football (which require, albeit fallible, referees to adjudicate).

Negotiation concerns the management of movement from conflicting positions towards an agreement, which often means getting beyond the positional posturing of some of the people with whom we must negotiate. To be sure, it helps when resolving disputes to focus on the interests of the parties concerned, but it is not essential that we abandon traditional negotiation or positional bargaining to achieve a workable agreement.

Parties adopt particular positions on an issue for many reasons. Some have a strategy of compelling the other party to surrender. Others do so because they believe that they need 'negotiating room' in the expectation that the other party will require movement to cut a deal. It is not always convenient (or wise, or efficient) to negotiate with no idea of what you want or why you want it. Aimless discontent is not negotiable. You can be sure that at some point into the dialogue, they will want to know what you want. Answering that you are not sure until there is a mutual exploration of each side's interests reads well in theory but may not help you in practice. It postpones the inevitable – a statement of what you specifically want – which itself could colour their attitudes to a discussion on interests because of fears about where this is leading them.

Following the identification of interests, Fisher and Ury recommend that you move from 'your interest to concrete options'.[32] Now, what are 'concrete options' but just another name for positions? Traditional negotiations accommodate such a progression from interests to positions, as shown in the Negotek® PREP planner, without obfuscating the meaning of words.

They also advise you to think in terms of 'illustrative specificity'.[322] Again, what does 'illustrative specificity' mean if it is not another word for a position? They assert that: 'Much of what positional bargainers hope to achieve with an opening position can be accomplished equally well with an illustrative suggestion that generously takes care of your interest'.[323] This is excellent advice, albeit that it uses weasel words like 'concrete options' and 'illustrative specificity' to avoid admitting that the principled negotiator, sooner or later, must move from considering interests to that of considering positions.

To cap it all, they advise the principled negotiator to be 'generous' to his own interests.[324] This sounds very like the prescriptive advice that your interests are best served by giving yourself generous (i.e. large) negotiating room by asking for much more than you expect. This again sounds remarkably like the positional posturing against which *Getting to Yes* heaps unrestrained opprobrium.

They also insist that the principled negotiator must 'be concrete but flexible'[325] that is, in the terminology of traditional bargaining, it means be specific in your opening position but flexible enough to move along a range of positions in search of agreement. Principled negotiation, on these weasel worded admissions, is only a special case of positional bargaining, complete with negotiation ranges and entry and exit points.

I have long found it remarkable that the negotiating literature appears to ignore Fisher and Ury's somewhat tortuous bobbing and weaving to avoid recognizing their affinities with positional bargaining.

INVENT OPTIONS FOR MUTUAL GAIN[326]

Like the previous prescriptions, inventing options for mutual gain is widely accepted by practitioners, though less widely applied, largely because of the constraints imposed by higher policy makers who often direct negotiation activities and overly restrict their negotiator's scope for movement. The rational theorist argues in favour of surveying all of the options in any management decision process; the practitioner would likely retort that this is just not practical most of the time. But, to be fair, this is not what Fisher and Ury are prescribing. They are advising negotiators to do more than just accept what appears to be the only two competing solutions on the table, particularly as these may be narrowly framed and also, as they stand, mutually exclusive.

Once the interests of the parties are illuminated other possibilities for solving the problem are highlighted. There is usually more than one possible solution to a problem, other than the first ones generated by the parties with the problem, particularly as your first reaction to a problem is usually to fight your own corner with your least accommodating position. Recasting the problem by reference to interests enables other options for a solution at least to be considered. Behaviourally, this requires a suspension of judgement while the possible options – some of them off-the-wall, perhaps – are identified and listed.

Brainstorming sessions are recommended for you to identify the options. Initially, you can conduct this with your own colleagues but, if confidence levels are high, a joint brainstorming session with the other negotiator is suggested. The rules are the same for a single or a joint session: no idea is too whacky; nor rejected because of who suggested it and all judgement is suspended until the well of ideas dries up. This atmosphere is reckoned to create the right conditions for looking at problems from new perspectives. Deadlocks can be broken by relatively risk-free consideration of other people's ideas.

How rich the well of ideas and options are that emerge from brainstorming sessions depends on the size of the problem, the extent to which 'big picture' macro-level solutions dominate over 'little picture' micro-level solutions. Switching from the 'yes versus no' decision to the conditions under which a 'yes' or 'no' decision could operate, opens up lots of possibilities, some of which could induce the parties to some mutual accommodation between their mutually exclusive initial positions.

In the dispute over whether the new airport runway can be built, it is impossible to reconcile a blanket 'yes' with blanket 'no' at the local level. Higher level policy makers – the government, for instance – may legislate over the heads of the local community in the 'national interest', and if they get away with this politically (not assured in a democracy), that could end the dispute. On the way to the government securing the necessary legislative authority to implement their decision, the local residents can impose a price upon the nation for their acquiescence in an outcome conceived by them as contrary to their personal interests. In the extreme, as at Japan's airport battles in the 1980s, violent protests can escalate and turn the environmental interests at stake into a test of the final authority of the state.

A brainstorming session on the micro problems raised by the local residents could produce various options palatable to them and the authorities. For instance, if the interests of the residents have been identified – remember, interests are the reasons, motives, concerns, or fears that motivate the residents in this case to say 'no' – micro policy responses can be addressed if the parties are willing to try them. This can be done by the authorities (if they have any sensitivity or political nous) or by the residents (if positions have not hardened to the point where to contemplate searching for other options is treated as a treachery by one's neighbours). In either case, it is a way forward, which is what motivates the principled negotiator.

Those in favour of the runway should consider meeting as many of the objections of those whose interests lead them to oppose the runway proposal as it presently stands. Among these objections will be:

O   *The residents living within the noise footprint of the aircraft* They can be generously compensated with double or triple glazing and other sound-proofing measures, or their properties bought at fair market value.

O   *The impact of airborne pollution*   This can be treated by specifying and enforcing re-fuelling non-spillage standards and lean engine burn.

O   *The effect on sleeping patterns*   This can be addressed by restricting flying hours and engine noise levels (e.g., 'whisper jets').

O   *The effect of increased airport-related traffic*   This can be ameliorated by road re-design and landscaping investments.

None of these options alone may be sufficient to break a mass consensus against an airport proposal, but together, with the micro-details fully aired, they might be sufficient to reduce hostility to the proposals to manageable levels, even reducing opposition to the futile condemnations of a small isolated minority. It is seldom possible to please everybody, but then you don't need to as Figure 4.16 shows (p. 243).

Again, the method of principled negotiation finds its best expression in assisting in the sorting out of public disputes. Just how far it is applicable for the myriad of small one-on-one negotiations that dominate private decision making and commercial business is debatable.

INSIST ON OBJECTIVE CRITERIA[327]

In the prescription on objective criteria lies the fatal flaw of principled negotiation as a distinct alternative to positional bargaining. What it sets out to remedy ends up with it playing the same role it criticizes in positional bargaining and it risks creating the same frustrations that lead to positional posturing.

The prescription to agree objective criteria is evidence of the influence of a judicial mind and it is not coincidental that Fisher and Ury are qualified attorneys-at-law. Justice depends on the existence of objective criteria for consistently judging appropriate remedies after the facts have been established to the satisfaction of a jury. In some countries the law is codified into specific criteria about what constitutes a criminal act and by default what does not. In other countries, the law depends upon the precedents set by earlier courts when they judged the remedies applicable to the same or similar facts.

Nobody is above the law and, therefore, the law has to be clear for everybody. If a jury decides on the facts and the judge decides on punishments for transgressing somebody else's rights, the system is freer of injustice than when these things are decided by the whims of individuals. For most people this is self-evident and is unchallengeable in any society I suspect most readers would want to live in.

When the authors of principled negotiation include the necessity for deciding disputed issues on objective criteria they are introducing a formal judicial method into informal negotiation. What could be surer of rational support than insisting that decisions made by negotiation should conform to a basic principle of natural justice, namely, that the criteria for a decision should be objective for those who submit to its governance and should not be the result of pressure?

I think the problem arises because Fisher and Ury were trained in these basic legal principles and they have introduced them into spheres of human activity for which they were not designed and for which they may not be applicable in practice. Lawyers think in terms of guilty or not guilty (and, in Scotland, the third verdict of 'not proven'). This is how lawyers are trained to think and there is not much point debating it.

But what might work for the justice system may not work for the process of negotiation as it operates around the world, including in those societies where the rule of law is more of a lottery than a reality. Agreeing on objective criteria to settle a dispute has great rational appeal but does it have practical substance?

When this method is applied to negotiation, insisting on objective criteria is open to question. Note first that negotiation is usually a private process between at least two parties who are not publicly accountable. Neither the state, nor its servants, normally get involved in the myriad of negotiations between private parties. Attempts to do so on occasion – such as in labour law – usually fail.

The law can enforce contracts but it rarely decides on the contents of a contract. If negotiators do appeal subsequently to law it is an appeal that takes place outside of the negotiation process. They cease to be negotiators and become litigants and the issues are decided by a third party. Whatever they do in their negotiations they must agree to do themselves. This sharply delineates judicial from private negotiation processes.

Now, here is the rub. It does not require the intelligence of an Einstein to make the connection between agreeing to use objective criteria and the likely determination of the outcome based on that criteria. Indeed, Bob, who cannot spell his name backwards, would have no trouble realizing the implication of accepting a prior commitment to using objective criteria. He would either resist the notion altogether or he would endeavour to import whatever selective criteria best suited the solution he wanted, with, no doubt, his opposite number doing exactly the same in support of his case.

Fisher and Ury fail to tackle the persistent problem that negotiators tend to select criteria that support their own preferred outcomes, and thereby produce a clash of solution criteria every bit as intractable as a clash over positions. In this manner they dodge the consequences of deep disagreement between the negotiators over opposed criteria by using a literary device in their book to make their case more plausible. Unfortunately, most readers – and exponents of their method – whom I have interviewed on this issue appear to have missed the significance of the device until I bring it to their attention.

Fisher and Ury always slip into their illustrative disputes a convenient third party who just happens to be available to show the near deadlocked parties how to use objective criteria to avert a positional crisis and, thereby, resolve their disputes:

O   In the case of the partners designing their future home,[328] there is a helpful architect who takes away their ideas – some of which appear to be mutually conflicting – and re-designs the house to meet their expressed criteria.
O   In the union-management dispute a 'facilitator' appears.[329]
O   'Someone' discovered an MIT brilliant solution in the deep-sea mining problem for the Law of the Sea negotiations.[330]
O   In the long example they provide[331] of a landlord and tenant in dispute over the rent, there is the fortuitous guidance provided by the Rent Control Board.

Principled negotiation apparently is no longer one between two parties because it requires an additional third party to get them to an agreement based on objective criteria. In legal disputes, that third party is always present too in the form of the pre-written or precedent law set down by the legislative process. In Fisher and Ury's exposition of principled negotiation the third party is conveniently brought into the scene by the authors with, in my view, diminishing credibility. I find their examples unconvincing as a guide to the daily negotiations entered into by the rest of us, for whom there is no convenient facilitator to hand.

Consider two individuals in dispute over something. Assuming that they have accepted the use of objective criteria, how do they set about finding, let alone agreeing, on which objective criteria to choose? It is not as easy as it appears. They do not have legally enforceable statutes enforced upon them (and if they had, it is hardly a negotiation). They must, in fact, create their own solution as they go along.

The prescription, however, ignores the obvious: criteria will be selected solely because they predetermine my preferred outcome not yours, and in consequence are likely to be rejected by you on those very grounds alone.

In 1982, the University of Strathclyde Business School, of which faculty I was a senior member, opened preliminary discussions on an emergency redundancy programme to bring the School's expenditure in line with its income. The Principal of the University asked the School to select potential candidates for possible redundancy. Two groups emerged within the faculty, each offering their 'objective criteria' to select people for redundancy (there was actually a third group who preferred to bury their heads in their hands and hope it would all go away).

One group was convinced that redundancy should apply to those members of staff who had high enough outside consultancy earnings for them to suffer least from losing their tenured low paid posts. Jokes circulated about the collective noun for professors being 'an absence of'.

Another group argued in favour of an altogether different set of 'objective criteria'. They argued that faculty who were unable to generate outside consultancy earnings from selling their business expertise in the market, clearly were unsuitable to be employed to educate managers of businesses in a reputable business school.

Which set of criteria would you adopt? Presumably, you would align yourself to whichever criteria applied to you and served your self-interest: in short, were you a consulting or non-consulting faculty member? And so it came to pass in the 1982 debate. I quit and took a Chair in another business school where professors were valued for their credibility as consultants in business rather than their ability to secure protection from the financial realities of market forces.

In negotiation, the choice of objective criteria is seldom left to third parties to decide, unless your negotiation process allows for the intervention of Fisher and Ury's conveniently placed third parties, who seem to pop up whenever their fourth prescription would otherwise run into the sand. Most private negotiating parties do not allow for third party interventions because neither time nor resources permit a role for them. Left to the parties, predictable differences in objective criteria take them back to positional bargaining and a reluctance to agree to objective criteria that predetermines the outcome in their favour, unless they are tricked into agreeing otherwise.

In asserting that this is the fatal flaw in principled negotiation I am not relying on a rhetorical trick. Negotiations I have participated in provide much evidence that each side, not surprisingly, selects criteria for settlement that are heavily loaded to support their own interests. Competing objective criteria often are immovable and can lead to the fallacious rhetoric of positional posturing. Battles over criteria need not improve the rationality of negotiators at all. They are just another part of the problem of the bargaining process.

To list all the examples of a failure of the fourth prescription to select objective criteria as a solution of a dispute would try your patience, but a short list of some examples might drive home the point:

○ The republican nationalists in Northern Ireland demand a referendum of all of the people living on the island of Ireland to decide the fate of Ulster because Ireland is a single country; the Ulster Unionists demand a referendum of the people of Ulster only, on the grounds that the rest of Ireland is a foreign country.

○ Argentina demands sovereignty over the Malvinas because the islands are on its continental shelf, though they were never settled by its people; the Falkland islanders demand that they remain British because they are part of a southern Atlantic island group that includes islands (Georgia) that are not on the Argentinean continental shelf and the fact that they have been settled by British Falklanders for nearly two centuries.

○ The Palestinians claim sovereignty over the lands of Israel because they occupied them for nearly 2000 years; the Israelis claim sovereignty over the same lands because they occupied them for over 2000 years, until they were forcibly evicted by the Romans in AD 79.

○ The Greeks demand the return of the Pantheon marbles on the grounds that they belong to the Pantheon monument and they were 'stolen' by Lord Elgin; the British Museum rejects the claim on the grounds that they were legally acquired from Lord Elgin, who bought them from their legal owner in the nineteenth century, and were legally transferred to the British Museum.

○ Citizens of Germany demand the return of their family's art treasures on the grounds that these were stolen by Russian troops at the end of the Second World War; the Russian authorities refuse to return the treasures because they were acquired as compensatory reparations for the enormous losses suffered by the Russians, when they were invaded by an army, led by German war criminals, in 1941.

What is noticeable about these statements (their historical veracity is not important for our discussion) is how closely the criteria by which each party wants the issue to be decided are related to their justifications for the positions they adopt on these same issues in dispute.

That should not surprise you, as people contesting disputed issues usually incorporate some form of justification for their stances and, therefore, the close affinity between a stance and the criteria for that stance should be unremarkable. The most common question in negotiation is always along the lines of: 'how do you justify your position?', which usually provokes some appeal to some form of selective 'objective' criteria.

Principled negotiators, who *insist* on joint agreement on the objective criteria by which an outcome is to be determined, simply ignore the fact that much of the debate phases of negotiation are precisely a conflict between the competing criteria selected by each party. To expect them to search for objective criteria to resolve the dispute is unrealistic because differences in positions usually reflect differences in the criteria each adopts to justify their positions.

An individual making a rational decision can develop objective criteria and use some form of surrogate for the utility maximizing mathematics found in rational decision theory because they only have themselves to convince. But negotiation is about joint decisions between more than one party which raises the complexity of the task by several magnitudes. The way through the dilemma is for the negotiators to trade themselves out of the impasse.

The principled negotiator in debate with a non-principled negotiator has the double task of proposing objective criteria for a joint solution, presumably similar to what he started with and of persuading the other negotiator to abandon her own criteria in favour of his (which as far as she is concerned is the criteria with which he started). Given that the criteria for deciding on the solution determines the outcome, why should she do this (remember she is not a principled negotiator)? Ah, replies the principled negotiator, but if she would only agree to this process, how much more efficient, effective and wise would be the negotiating process. Of course it would, just as it would be if the conduct of any negotiation conformed perfectly to the Nash assumptions and was not prey to the negative behaviours of positional posturing repeatedly alluded to in *Getting to Yes*.

But all that the search for agreed objective criteria achieves is to shift the focus of the negotiators' debate from their positions on the issues to their positions on their criteria for settlement. In an ideal world that may be a step forward, but in reality it achieves little for practical negotiators, particularly when the solution criteria are as controversial as their positions.

Whether the criteria they adopt are appropriate becomes a matter of dispute – which itself underlines that in most cases there are no unique objective criteria for the private negotiators to settle upon, especially as they are face-to-face and alone in their negotiating interaction and not subject to outside influence from conveniently placed third party mediators or the judgements of arbitrators. A dispute over which criteria to select could be just as unrewarding as a dispute over which position to adopt. Principled negotiation once again slides into a special case of positional bargaining.

Principled negotiation is largely about the conduct of mediation, conciliation, counselling, or joint problem solving and it provides several useful insights into the avoidance of negative outcomes by applying its four main prescriptions. Closely allied with its rational problem-solving methods, principled negotiation is mainly about uncovering the layers of distrust and other inhibitions on the parties in dispute by using these methods, rather than by using the purple conditional exchange principle. In this one sense it is an alternative to traditional negotiation but it cannot replace it.

It is preferable to see principled negotiation as another decision-making technique, appropriate in some circumstances but not in others, neither superior nor inferior to traditional negotiation, and, as such, one of several ways of making a decision. It is not a panacea for the failings of other decision-making processes nor it is guaranteed to resolve all of the world's intractable problems. Where principled negotiation is able to make a contribution to solving certain problems, we must welcome it but we must also recognize its limitations for use to resolve many other problems.

 ## RISING ABOVE PRINCIPLE?

Fisher and Ury's prescriptions for negotiators apply in special cases and are not, therefore, a totally new paradigm for all negotiations. There are numerous categories of dispute resolution, where the consequences of focusing on interests not positions and insistence on the use of principled negotiation methods only would be counterproductive.

Interests, issues and positions are inextricably linked, and denying a role for positions in favour of a wholly exclusive role for the party's interests is an avoidable error. If negotiators are stuck in a conflict of interests it makes sense to shift their attention to the positions taken by both sides on some of the issues. If people are stuck in a positional stand-off, it makes sense to switch to consideration of their interests.

It cannot be a case of always and only considering interests to the exclusion of positions.

In the Negotek® PREP planner you are required to consider your interests but you are not enjoined to elevate your interests to an all-exclusive concern. The negotiable issues form the agenda and in negotiating these issues you deliver your interests. As ever, what is true for you is true for them. Whether you focus on interests or issues at particular stages in the negotiation is a tactical question not a principle.

The long-running dispute between religious and secular communities in Israel is an example of where it might be better to switch from considering the overall interests of each side to negotiating on specific and immediate issues where ideology conflicts with the law.

How do you reconcile secular and religious differences that affect every aspect of the life styles and culture of their respective communities? We cannot hold our breath until a longer term accommodation is found when two adjacent communities are so driven with conflicts of interest that they slip into violent confrontations. In these circumstances, negotiation on issues is about the here and now. Negotiation on interests might take a while longer.

You cannot avoid the immediate issues and positions in these conflicts because the disputed issues are driven by the interests behind them. As neither side will forgo their principles or amend them, your attention must switch to what can be done about the disputed issues.

You might be able to negotiate, for instance, an arrangement that determines for how many hours a public road can be free of cars on the Sabbath on roads close to communities that hold the Sabbath sacred. Cars can absent themselves from a road for a short while without it becoming an issue of civil liberty (think of our resigned acceptance of traffic jams and diversions). If some people feel that strongly about it they can seek redress through the courts, in full knowledge of the consequences for the losers' civil liberties. The dispute can develop into severe civil unrest. What starts with verbal abuse, leads to stone throwing, road blocking and eventually to petrol bombs. Demanding that one side or the other forgoes their interests and beliefs is a ruinous route to disorder.

You cannot negotiate principles (if we could they would not be principles!) but we can negotiate their *application*. To do this successfully you must be prepared to negotiate details, which implies negotiating ranges on your positions on the issues. For the immediate negotiation, appealing to interests may be less productive than concentrating on the details of a compromise.

This has long been a part of British diplomatic practice. In circumstances where it is near impossible to discuss the substantive differences between two hostile parties because of their bitterly opposed beliefs and histories, it can help to move things forward by focusing on the 'Heads of a Potential Agenda' for the discussions. If the 'bigger' picture is fraught with pain, let us try looking at the 'smaller' picture to ease the pain, while making progress on the details.

In some bloody battles, such as during the Peninsular War, fighting was suspended for each side to remove its wounded, with stretcher parties from the combatant armies undertaking the same grisly tasks alongside and in the midst of each other, often nominally cut off from their respective lines.

The reverse applies if you are stuck on an issue: can you make progress by turning to the 'bigger picture' and to the interests of the parties? Traditional negotiators are not frozen into a belief that it is interests at the expense of the issues. A dose of pragmatism is the appropriate antidote to restrictive negotiating practice. The negotiator should adapt her negotiating method to suit the circumstances and not try to suit the circumstances to her preferred negotiating method.

That principled negotiators are urged, after examining interests, to develop 'concrete options', what in other words we know as positions, indicates a loophole in the purity of their prescriptions. For this reason, I recommend that you can integrate their prescriptions into traditional negotiation practice where such integration would be beneficial to finding a solution. Moreover, you can cease your sole dependence on the prescriptions of principled negotiation by switching between the prescriptions of principled negotiation and traditional negotiating practice to suit your circumstances.

Unfortunately, advocates of the stricture 'it's principled negotiation or nothing' find themselves in a dreadful tangle if they insist on the acceptance by the other party of the principle of principled negotiation before they will agree to negotiate. This is, admittedly an extremist version of the principled negotiation method but arriving at this position has a compelling logic, though Fisher and Ury do not go this far. The possibility of such procedural extremism is not just a flight of my fancy. It is the inevitable consequence of elevating tactical prescriptions ('insist on the four basic points of principled negotiation as the sole negotiating method') first into a principle ('never yield to pressure') and from a principle into a compulsion ('it's principled negotiation or nothing').

Disavowing bargaining over positions, if applied rigorously and in all circumstances, apart from causing perplexity in the minds of the people against whom it is directed and of whom is demanded their strict compliance, becomes a contest of will to secure an unshared preference for principled negotiation. A failure to convince, or to compel, the other person to use principled negotiation methods must mean that you are prepared to deprive both yourself and the other person of the benefits of the negotiated outcome that you could both enjoy through traditional negotiation. You prefer to do without an outcome – and enforce this deprivation on your luckless negotiating partner – in pursuit of an unshared principle. My recommendation is that you use whichever method is most likely to work in the circumstances. To do otherwise is almost 'otherworldly', safer, perhaps on an American campus than elsewhere.

Extremism may not matter too much when the principled negotiator and a shopkeeper are attempting to decide the price of an antique dish, but it might matter to wounded prisoners of war, waiting for exchange and relief from their sufferings, while, you, the principled negotiator, and their captors tussle over which method of negotiation you must use to secure their release or exchange.

Your attempts to force your preference ('it's principled negotiation or nothing!') onto their already irascible captors puts the prisoners in serious jeopardy of further deprivation, or worse. The knowledge that you 'won' a point of principle and went home 'victorious' – you did not give in to pressure and the integrity of principled negotiation remains safe and unsullied – might be the last thought the prisoners have as their captors take the view that as their negotiator cares more about the principle of principled negotiation than what happens to the prisoners, they might as well starve or shoot them instead.

How applicable is principled negotiation in these circumstances? Would a principled negotiator really jeopardize his colleagues' lives in pursuit of his principles or would he adapt his method of negotiation to suit the circumstances? Is it not clear that where you value the outcome, you would need to be adaptable and would have to be so if there was to be a favourable outcome at all?

Analogously, when negotiating, for instance across a cultural divide, to what extent should you insist that the other negotiator adopts your cultural norms and values or would you accept that it is you that might have to do the adjusting? This is particularly evident when cultural differences are expressed in the different pace at which, say, a Saudi might conduct a negotiation compared with, say, a Chicago futures trader. Forcing the pace to suit yourself and insisting on what might be perceived as a weird and unfathomable method, could cost you the deal.

It might be argued that positional posturing is more likely to lead to prolonged deadlock anyway and that there is a better chance of a settlement if both sides adopted principled negotiation. This I would have thought would depend on the circumstances and the time frame.

A plausible and abstract argument is not a proof, especially if we must first risk a deadlock and its consequences over the method we intend to use before we can access its alleged benefits. Similarly, the insistence on using objective criteria to determine the agreement, in practice requires stances not much different from that of positional or traditional bargaining and when this insistence is examined in closer detail it takes on many of the characteristics of the justifications articulated by some positional negotiators.

Principled negotiation is an insightful process but it is not the alternative to traditional negotiation that its proponents celebrate. As a sub-set of traditional negotiation, principled negotiation has a valuable contribution to negotiating practice and more especially to dispute resolution and problem solving. Abandoning traditional negotiation methods, however, in favour of the exclusive use of the four prescriptions of principled negotiation could be a serious error. As Dr Mates, a Yugoslav diplomat, expressed it to me in 1967: 'sometimes we must rise above principle'!

THE NEGOTIATOR AS MEDIATOR

Principled negotiation has spawned a large literature, which mainly has been uncritical (for an exception see Jandt, 1985[332]). It is no surprise to note that the bulk of this literature has been concerned with developing principled negotiation as a dispute resolution method, because its potential for these disputes is most obvious.

In the absence of a third party mediator, which for the overwhelming bulk of negotiations we must accept as datum, is there anything we can do if the parties are stuck on the issues (positional bargaining) or on the interests (principled negotiation) or on both (traditional negotiation)? I think there is and, in a spirit of being constructive about Fisher and Ury's contributions, I shall explain briefly what you could do by drawing on some of what they propose, while adding some interpretations of my own.

The absence of a third party mediator in a deadlocked negotiation imposes on those who want to make progress that one of you effectively considers taking over the mediator role, at least attitudinally. Now I do not pretend that this is easy nor that it will work, not least because the idea incorporates a number of serious contradictions.

Figure 5.5 defines mediation and it does not take much experience to know that neither negotiator meets, nor can comply with, the terms of the definition. For a start, as a negotiator, you are neither 'impartial' nor 'neutral'. If anything, both of you are exactly opposite in your orientations – which is why you have deadlocked! You both certainly have 'authoritative decision-making power' constrained by the requirement that whatever you decide is jointly decided and not unilaterally decided by one of you alone.

> Intervention by an acceptable, impartial and neutral third party, who has no authoritative decision-making power, to assist the disputing parties in voluntarily reaching their own mutually acceptable settlement of issues in dispute.

Figure 5.5 Mediation defined

The notion that one of you would knowingly permit the other to 'intervene', in the manner prescribed for mediation, is most unrealistic if your joint efforts so far have proved incapable of finding a 'mutually acceptable settlement of the issues in dispute'.

In summary, when there is no third party available, one of you acts as a surrogate third party without the knowledge or awareness of the other. But can you perform in some helpful way the role of a mediator while remaining one of the negotiators? On the surface, I would doubt it, unless you can switch your mind-set for a moment or two.

Bill Ury[333] makes a thought-provoking point that when in a deadlock you should 'go to the balcony' (Figure 5.6). This is the age-old advice of 'putting yourself in their shoes' but with an added twist. From your mental balcony you are looking down at both of you and not just across a table from the same level. You can relate to your own behaviour as well as theirs and mentally you can put some distance between yourself and them.

Behind the idea is the common observation that people who are in the thick of a dispute see the issues differently from those who are looking at it from the outside. When involved you are more emotionally committed to what is going on and what you believe is likely to happen than when you are not emotionally involved. The act of 'going to the balcony' may weaken that emotional commitment just enough for you to glimpse what is blocking progress on your side and theirs.

Don't react	GO TO THE BALCONY
Disarm them	GO TO THEIR SIDE
Change the game	DON'T REJECT – REFRAME
Make it easy to say 'yes'	BUILD THEM A GOLDEN BRIDGE
Make it hard to say 'no'	BRING THEM TO THEIR SENSES NOT THEIR KNEES

Figure 5.6 Ury's advice for negotiators as mediators[334]

Attitudinally, presumably you accept that other people have interests that are as important and valid for them as your interests are important and valid for you. This does not mean that you have to agree that their interests necessarily override your own – this is not about becoming a blue submissive! But the act of reminding yourself of the parity of interests could be enough for you to want to explore ways of meeting as many of their interests in the course of meeting your own.

The deadlock is caused by the currently proposed solutions of the problem not meeting enough (or any) of the interests of each party and the act of reviewing the shortfall should itself produce some new thoughts on how to do something to make a difference.

The fact that interests may be traded implies they can be prioritized like issues. To grasp the subtleties of prioritizing interests, it is necessary to review them and a good place to do that is from your mental balcony. You can invite them to share their perceptions of their interests from 'their side' of the table. A mediator would do something akin to this in private caucuses with each party[335] but you do not access them in that role. The more convincing you are in the role of trying to see their world through their eyes – the more you 'disarm' them – the more you will learn about the game they think they are playing with you and you with them.

One advantage you have in the negotiator as mediator role over the third-party mediator is your access to the real world of your private thoughts. This, combined with what you can glean about their world, must put you in a better position than you were as a negotiator in deadlock with them. You have access to a candour, albeit one-sided, normally denied to even a talented third party.

Understanding the other party's deeper interests and their perspectives of the world should enable you to make changes to your proposals by reframing them to accord more with their aspirations and, in this manner, you can lower their threat perceptions of what you are about. They are more likely to say 'yes' to movement if you address their interests than if you irritate their inhibitions. The latter deserves what it usually gets – a resounding 'no'.

In the role of a negotiator as mediator you try to 'rise above the fray' to search productively for agreement without compromising your role as one of the participating negotiators. Nothing outlined above should suggest that this is going to be easy or that it will necessarily work. It is only indicative of a novel line of approach when you are faced with the alternative of persisting in deadlock.

EPILOGUE

EPILOGUE

 A PRACTITIONER'S RESEARCH AGENDA?

The Dialogue's survey of the works that may be useful for negotiating practitioners is incomplete. It was never meant to be a comprehensive nor exhaustive survey. It reflects my selection of the works that I have found to be useful – and some of the works that I found to be wanting – from over twenty-five years as a researcher, tutor and practitioner in negotiation.

The many quoted authors of the original works have done a great service to negotiation practice. You should note in this context that even research that leads to a dead-end, or is found to be fallacious, is a necessary part of the process of improving understanding and performance.

Similarly, the works of those authors whom I have not mentioned may have important contributions to make to the subject. Their omission may be because, though aware of their work, I considered that they strayed from my agenda. It is also possible that I am unaware of their work, for which my apologies. I do my best to keep up with what is published, albeit only in English (more apologies all round, but as a Scot, English is the only foreign language I know!). Readers are invited to draw my attention to their own writings, or the works of others, that they consider make important contributions to the debate called for in my preface. I am grateful in advance for those who accept the invitation and I promise to follow up any references they cite.

However, there are some areas where negotiation studies are beginning to appear which I have not addressed in *Kennedy on Negotiation*. Much of my interest in these areas will depend on the direction my consultancy work takes over the next few years, as the demands of the market are always a sure indication of the direction in which trainers and practitioners want a subject to develop.

At the moment I believe that negotiation studies are in good shape. The structure of negotiation is well understood in the *phased process* models. I do not expect there to be much controversy in the near future about the common phases of negotiation, though whether there are three, four, six, eight or 12 phases is open to the welcome competition of presentational refiners and the illustrative examples of live cases from practitioners, particularly from those negotiating in different cultures.

The individual *skills of negotiation*, be they in planning, debate and interactive behaviour and in bargaining also appear to be well understood (though maybe not so universally practised!) and researched prescriptions of the type undertaken by Huthwaite are liable to sharpen the focus for those who have career, commercial or diplomatic consequences at stake. Behaviour can be changed by training, workplace practice and sensitive coaching, and this agenda is likely to be in a steady state for the immediate future.

Some future work is required on the use of language in negotiation (for example, in extending the work of Mulholland) and in developing assertive language tools for promoting agreement.

The dissemination of the ideas behind *principled negotiation* is already well under way, though it appears to be gravitating more to dispute handling (community conflicts, intra-organization conflicts, such as promotion, discipline, turf wars, etc.) than to the commercial arenas where *traditional negotiation* has long been dominant. In time, perhaps, some of the methods developed from principled negotiation, such as in the role of the *negotiator as mediator*, might prove to be fertile and practitioners would be well advised to keep in touch with this area.

In the meantime, applications of the prescriptions of principled negotiation to live cases, if possible in the commercial sphere, are needed so that evaluation of its precepts can be made from a practical rather than a deductive perspective. At present, much of the material on principled negotiation is about how it *could* make a difference to negotiations if only the principles would follow the prescriptions but solid evidence in the commercial field is lacking (as a perusal of the contents of the *Negotiation Journal* from Harvard shows). The Dialogue discusses these limitations in respect of its reliance on objective criteria but this is not to suggest a lack of potential for the method when it is exposed to wider commercial practice.

The more certain limitations of the streetwise credo of ploys and tricks are well documented and properly understood even by those most associated with it in the recent past. In evaluating a Karass Effective Negotiation programme a few years ago, we noticed that the emphasis had softened on the use of ploys to proposing more of a relationship orientation. In the more recent separation of the international Karass organization from its British counterpart, we noticed a further softening from a ploys approach. Now, the Karass organization is far from being totally results-oriented in their programme contents, nor would it be correct to identify them as purveyors of an extreme ploy philosophy (my personal admiration of its founder, Chester Karass, is well attested) but the trend from ploys to longer term effectiveness and the need to build relationships, is indicative in the weakening market among negotiators for the material espoused by Sperber.

This assessment of the streetwise school in no way suggests that I am recommending that you relapse into naivety about the way negotiations are conducted in the real world. The manipulative school of negotiation was more a product of the origins of the interest of practitioners into how to negotiate in the world they then worked in the 1960s, than a product of focused research into negotiation as a normative phenomenon. Once numerous observers moved into the subject, the first impressions that negotiation was a detail in a Machiavellian march to 'winning' or a Machiavellian necessity to avoid 'losing', were bound to be challenged and, thankfully, they were, as reported on in the Dialogue.

What I have called the *colours of negotiation* is a more fundamental assessment of the appropriate behaviour for your dealings with red players whom you suspect might prefer to *take* than to *trade*. The surface dialogue about ploys versus relationships is only understandable if the dilemma of negotiation is realistically confronted.

Nobel prize winner John Nash was right mathematically: the *Nash solution* is robust. But practitioners, without prompting, do not optimize in the way Nash showed that they should (an ought is not an is) either in the red-blue dilemma game or in the game of life. You defect not because you want to but because you must. From that assessment, negotiating behaviour – some of it of the ploy variety and some of it of the taking variety – is explainable.

Dealing with others on a consistent basis *as a minimum* requires that you assert the *purple conditionality principle* by neither taking (red) nor giving (blue) but combining your red demands with your blue offers in *IF-THEN* proposal formats.

Of course, much more work needs to be done on applying purple conditionality to live cases. Our evidence, so far, is that purple conditionality is more likely to move negotiators *towards* a Nash solution (the maximization of their joint net gains) than so-called 'hard' or 'soft' behaviours and, because purple conditionality is appropriate for the bulk of negotiations most people carry out, it is more likely to succeed than the, as yet, unproven precepts of principled negotiation.

This assertion is controversial, I am sure, with the authors of principled negotiation, many of whom are certainly confident that they

have found the solution to the frustrations of decision making by negotiation. In the Dialogue I characterized their prescriptions as a special
case of positional bargaining and questioned whether a dispute over
objective criteria is anything really different from disputes over the
justifications for positions. They can reply in due course, after applying
their own precepts to consider the merits of the criticism before attacking the messenger!

Turning then to a subject area not explored in the Dialogue that may
have importance for practitioners, I would select the main one to be
cross-cultural negotiation. That the growing global market is making
cross-cultural influences on doing business across borders a highly
visible activity is beyond question. The global market is penetrating
right down to the High Street, with consumer products in abundance
from cultures only barely known by the final customers.

Books that are appearing wrestle with this problem at two levels.
First, there are books on differences in the manners and courtesies
between related and unrelated cultures. One of several on my shelf is
compiled from the experience of the Parker Pen Company[336] and is
among the best in the genre. These types of books provide a useful
'safety' course for business people (and tourists) travelling abroad but
they are not sufficient for a more in-depth analysis of the potential
problems of cross-cultural negotiation.

The second level of approach is much more scientific but it still has a
long way to go before being a trainable product. Among my reasons for
not discussing culture in negotiation in the present Dialogue is the
simple one that while dissatisfied with what is available on the subject,
I am not yet in a position to make worthwhile corrective comments. It is
no good merely criticizing without offering something in its place. My
lack of advice at present may change in the near future as my negotiation consultancy and the setting up of overseas subsidiaries and
licencees of Negotiate Limited, means that I am negotiating increasingly with people from other cultures (plus my time for reflection is
increasing on long-haul flights!).

The two most prominent authors in this field are Geert Hofstede [337]
and Frans Trompenaars.[338] They have both looked beyond the surface
and taboos of different cultures to explore the basis of differences in
culture and how they might be manifested in differences in values.
Their work is also characterized by examining data rather than reflecting on impressions or codes of conduct gleaned from experience.

My reservations about the state of knowledge about cultural
influences in negotiation is similar to my approach to the influence
of personality in negotiation (though I express the definite view in
the Dialogue that personality is not a determinant of negotiation
behaviour). With culture I am not yet sure that its influence on negoti-

ating behaviour can be determined. Like personality, culture must have some influence but what it is and how it can be tackled behaviourally is by no means settled just yet.

At present, my views are impressionistic. Experience of negotiating with people from different cultures suggests that some level of awareness of the differences is important.[339] For instance, it's no good pushing the pace with people whose perception of time is different from your own. But be careful here. Just because they are from a different culture does not mean that they are imprisoned within their own culture's values and that they are incapable of translating them in a similar manner to which they translate your language into theirs. Indeed, this must be so if the study of another culture is a prelude to your adapting your pace, values and behaviour into forms acceptable to people from another culture. Surely, what you can do so can they?

Moreover, the method by which cultural norms are researched is necessarily arithmetically proportional – what proportion of people in culture A respond to a certain value, such as individuality versus collectivist – compared to people in culture B? If culture A has 80 per cent of the respondents registering different responses to 80 per cent of people in culture B, is this a significant difference and, if it is, what does this tell the negotiator from culture A to do if he is about to meet with a negotiator from culture B?

That a value difference may be significant does not assure a negotiator that it is behaviourally significant, and, if it is behaviourally significant, it does not mean it is safe for the negotiator to assume that the person from the different culture subscribes to the values shown by questionnaires to be significant in her culture. For example, the person from culture A may be a member of the minority 20 per cent who subscribes to values shared by the 80 per cent of the people from culture B. Therefore, how do you know to which segment of the population that negotiator belongs? As with personalities, you don't know and without detailed analysis, you have no means of finding out. Hence, I concluded for the moment, that while culture is an important agenda subject for further negotiation research and analysis it is not in a sufficiently settled state for me to include it in the Dialogue in much more detail than I have outlined above.

One last reflection on changes in client preferences. I claimed that negotiation studies are in good shape (what a hostage to fortune that could prove to be!) and, perhaps, we have taken them as far as we can for the moment. However, I am finding increasing interest among negotiating practitioners for materials on influencing and persuasion skills (which, naturally, I am responding to energetically) and it may be here that the next wave will arise.

Just as the autocratic management styles of the 1950s and 1960s gave way to more 'consensual' management and produced the demand for negotiation studies, perhaps it is time we looked a little deeper and see that while negotiation skills are necessary in modern management structures, they too are no longer sufficient, and the baton is passing to those who can help practitioners use influence and persuasion skills to help them to get what they want. Just a passing thought (though remember, you read it here first!).

 ## A PERFECT NEGOTIATION?

Some years ago I helped my brother-in-law at his hotel in Argyll by working a shift in the public bar. Hamish, a regular client, was celebrating by (uncharacteristically) buying drams of whisky for anybody who wanted one. He told his story with relish to all who drank his whisky. He owned an old waterlogged fishing boat in the nearby loch and that very week the county had issued a condemnation order on the wreck and had also ordered him to remove it within 21 days. That afternoon, however, he had sold his boat to a woman from Glasgow, who had paid him the amazing sum of £6000 for it. 'She could have had it for £600' he said and 'I'd have even paid her to remove it!' Clearly, Hamish was what Fisher and Ury would call a positional bargainer.

After my shift, I went to the dining room and on the way to my table I was surprised to meet Fiona, a former student of mine. She was drinking champagne and, yes, she too was celebrating, in her case because she had managed to acquire a boat for *only* £6000 from a local 'glaikit teuchter' – which is a Scot's Lowlander's mocking term for a Highlander.

Fiona was overjoyed because she was the props manager of a TV production company and she needed a boat – any boat – which her carpenters and painters could fit up to look like a luxury cabin cruiser. The script required the hero to escape by diving off a burning boat into the loch just before her pyrotechnical people blew it up. Her budget for the boat, she proudly told me, was £20,000, which would make her popular with her irascible producer.

Hence, two traditional negotiators, each delighted with their deal, celebrated separately the outcome of their negotiation within 50 feet of each other. To be sure, they could have insisted on settling the price by objective criteria, but would that have made either of them any happier with their private deal? I doubt it. Mutual satisfaction with a deal is the truest measure of the success of a negotiation.

In short, if it works, don't fix it.

Negotiate Limited presents workshops and training sessions based upon the concepts and methods developed in this publication. For details of these services, send your business card, or call:

> Dr Gavin Kennedy
> Negotiate Limited
> Consultant Negotiators
> 22 Braid Avenue
> Edinburgh
> EH10 6EE
> United Kingdom

> Tel: [44] (0)131 452 8404   Fax: [44] (0)131 452 8388

APPENDICES

SELECT BIBLIOGRAPHY OF WORKS REFERRED TO IN THE TEXT

Atkinson, G. G. M. (1975), *The Effective Negotiator*, Newbury, Negotiating Systems.

Atkinson, G. [G. M.] (1990), *Negotiate the Best Deal: Techniques that Really Work*, London, Institute of Directors.

Axtell, R. E. (1990), *Do's and Taboos around the World*, New York, John Wiley.

Bacharach, S. B. and Lawler, E. J. (1981), *Bargaining: Power, Tactics and Outcomes,* San Francisco, Jossey-Bass.

Bazerman, M. H. and Neale, M. A. (1992), *Negotiating Rationally*, New York, Free Press.

Bierman, H. S. and Fernandez, L. (1993), *Game Theory With Economic Applications*, Reading, Mass. Addison-Wesley.

Blau, P. M. (1964), *Exchange and Power in Social Life*, New York, John Wiley.

Bles, M. and Low, R. (1987), *The Kidnap Business*, London, Pelham Books.

Braudel, F. (1979, trans. 1985), *Civilisation and Captialism, 15th–18th Century,* Vol. 11: *The Wheels of Commerce*, London, Collins, Harper-Row.

Carlisle, J. (1980), 'Successful training for effective negotiators', *Journal of European Industrial Training*, Vol. 4, No. 1, pp. 99–102.

Carlisle, J. and Parker, J. C. (1989), *Beyond Negotiation: Redeeming Customer-supplier Relationships*, Chichester, John Wiley.

Cartwright, J. (1991), *Unequal Bargaining: A Study in Vitiating Factors in the Formation of Contracts*, Oxford, Oxford University Press.

Chamberlain, N. W. (1951), *Collective Bargaining*, New York, McGraw-Hill.

Coddington, A. (1968), *Theories of the Bargaining Process*, Allen & Unwin, London.

Coker, E. and Stuttard, G. (1976), *Industrial Studies 2: The Bargaining Context*, London, Arrow Books.

Connor, A. (1995), *Dirty Negotiating Tactics and Their Solutions*, Ely, Cambs, UK, Wyvern Crest.

Cross, J. G. (1965), 'A theory of the bargaining process', *American Economic Review*, Vol. 55, pp. 67–94.

Dahl, R. A. (1957), 'The concept of power', *Behavioural Science*, Vol. 2, pp. 201–18.

Douglas, A. (1957), 'The peaceful settlement of industrial and inter-group disputes', *Journal of Conflict Resolution*, Vol. 1, pp. 69–81.

Douglas, A. (1962), *Industrial Peacemaking*, New York, Columbia University Press.

Druckman, D. (ed.) (1977), *Negotiations: Social-psychological Perspectives*, Beverly Hills, Sage.

Emerson, R. E. (1962), 'Power-dependence Relations', *American Sociological Review*, Vol. 27, pp. 31–42.

Fisher, R. (1969), *International Conflict for Beginners*, Harper & Row, New York.

Fisher, R. and Ury, W. L. (1981), *Getting to Yes: Negotiating Agreement Without Giving In*, Boston, Houghton Mifflin.

Fisher, R., Ury, W. L. and Patton, B. (1991), *Getting to Yes: Negotiating an Agreement Without Giving in*, (revised edn) London, Century Business.

French, J. R. P. and Raven, B. (1959), 'The bases of social power', in D. Cartwright (ed.), *Studies in Social Power*, Ann Arbor, MI, Institute of Social Research, pp. 183–205.

Friedman, M. (1957), *A Theory of the Consumption of Function*, Princeton, New Jersey, Princeton University Press.

Fuller, G. (1991), *The Negotiator's Handbook*, Englewood Cliffs, NJ, Prentice-Hall.

Galanter, M. (1984), 'Words of deals: using negotiation to teach about legal proceedings', *Journal of Legal Education*, Vol. 34, pp. 268–76.

Gauthier, D. (1979), 'Bargaining our way into morality: a do-it-yourself primer', *Philosophical Exchange*, Vol. 2, pp. 15–27.

Gauthier, D. (1985), 'Bargaining and justice', *Social Philosophy and Policy*, Vol. 2, pp. 20–47.

Gauthier, D. (1986), *Morals by Agreement*, Oxford, Oxford University Press.

Genn, H. (1987), *Hard Bargaining: Out of Court Settlement in Personal Injury Actions*, Oxford, Oxford University Press.

Gilbert, M. A. (1980; 1996), *How to Win an Argument*, New York, John Wiley.

Gilkey, R. W. and Greenhaugh, L. (1986), 'The role of personality in successful negotiating', *Negotiation Journal: On the Process of Dispute Settlement*, Vol. 2, No. 3, pp. 245–56.

Glaser, R. and Glaser, C. (1991), *Negotiating Style Profile: facilitator guide*, King of Prussia, Pennsylvania, Organisation Design and Development Inc.

Gottchalk, A. W. G. (1974, 1990), *Teaching Notes, London Business School: Negotiation Course Manual*, unpublished.

Gottchalk, A. [W.G.] (1993), *The Negotiating Guide*, London, Group A. G.

Gottlieb, M. and Healy, W. J. (1990), *Making Deals: The Business of Negotiating*, New York, New York Institute of Finance.

Gulliver, P. H. (1979), *Disputes and Negotiations: A Cross-cultural Perspective*, New York, Academic Press.

Hall, L. (ed.) (1993), *Negotiation: Strategies for Mutual Gain*, London, Sage.

Hampden, C. and Trompenaars, F. (1993), *The Seven Cultures of Capitalism: Value Systems for Creating Wealth in the United States, Britain, Japan, Germany, France, Sweden and the Netherlands*, New York, Doubleday.

Hatsock, N. (1985), 'Exchange theory: critique from a feminist standpoint', *Current Perspectives in Social Theory*, Vol. 6.

Herman, M. G. and Kogan, N. (1977), 'Effects of negotiator's personalities on negotiating behaviour', in Druckman, D. (ed.), (1977), op. cit.

Hirschman, A. O. (1970), *Exit Voice and Loyalty*, Cambridge, Mass., Harvard University Press.

Hodgson, J. (1994), *Thinking on Your Feet in Negotiations*, London, Pitman.

Hoffman, E. (1951), *The True Believer: Thoughts on the Nature of Mass Movements*, New York, Harper and Row.

Hofstede, G. (1980a), *Culture's Consequences*, Beverly Hills, Sage.

Hofstede, G. (1980b), *Cultures and Organisations: Software of the Mind*, New York, McGraw-Hill.

Holmes, G. and Glaser, S. (1991), *Business-to-Business Negotiation*, Oxford, Butterworth-Heineman.

Jandt, F. E. (1985), *Win-win Negotiating: Turning Conflict into Agreement*, New York, John Wiley.

Johnson, R. A. (1993), *Negotiation Basics: Concepts, Skills, and Exercises*, Newbury Park, Ca., Sage.

Karass, C. L. (1968), *A Study of the Relationship of Negotiator Skill and Power as Determinants of Negotiation Outcomes*, PhD Thesis, University of Southern California, Los Angeles (unpublished).

Karass, C. L. (1970), *The Negotiating Game*, New York, Thomas Y. Crowell.

Karass, C. L. (1974), *Give and Take: The Complete Guide to Negotiating Strategies and Tactics*, New York, Thomas Y. Crowell.

Kennedy, G. (1972), *Productivity Bargaining: A Case Study in the Petroleum Industry, 1964–71*, Glasgow, University of Strathclyde, MSc Thesis (unpublished).

Kennedy, G. (1982; 1989; 1997), *Everything is Negotiable*, London, Century Hutchinson.

Kennedy, G. (1985), *Negotiate Anywhere*, London, Century.

Kennedy, G. (1990; 1996), *The Negotiate Trainer's Manual*, Edinburgh, Negotiate.

Kennedy, G. (1991), *Negotiation: a Distance Learning Text*, London, Pitman Publishing.

Kennedy, G. (1992), *The Perfect Negotiation*, New York, Wings Books.

Kennedy, G. (1993, 1997), *Pocket Negotiator: The Essentials of Negotiation from A to Z*, London, The Economist and Profile Books.

Kennedy, G. (1993; 1996), *Kennedy's Simulations for Negotiation Training*, Aldershot, Gower.

Kennedy, G., Benson, J. and McMillan, J. (1980, 1982, 1984, 1987), *Managing Negotiations*, London, Business Books.

Kennedy, G. and Webb, R. J. (1996), 'The game of strife', *Supply Management*, 23 April.

Kniveton, B. (H.) (1989), *The Psychology of Bargaining*, Aldershot, Avebury.

Koch, Jr. H. W. (1988), *Negotiator's Factomatic™*, Englewood Cliffs, NJ, Prentice-Hall.

Kolb, D. M. (1995), 'The love for three oranges or: what did we miss about Ms. Follett in the library?', *Negotiation Journal*, Vol. 11, No. 4, pp. 339–48.

Kreps, D. M. (1990), *Game Theory and Economic Modelling*, Oxford, Oxford University Press.

Kuhn, R. L. (1988), *Deal Maker: All the Negotiating Skills and Secrets You Need*, New York, John Wiley.

Lax, A. D. and Sebenius, J. K. (1986), *The Negotiator as Manager: Bargaining for Cooperation and Competitive Gain*, New York, Free Press Macmillan.

Lee, R. and Lawrence, P. (1991), *Politics at Work*, Cheltenham, Stanley Thorne.

Levin, E. (1980), *Negotiating Tactics: Bargaining Your Way to Winning*, New York, Fawcett Columbine.

Levinson, H. M. (1966), *Determining Forces in Collective Wage Bargaining*, New York, John Wiley.

Lewis, D. V. (1981), *Power Negotiating Tactics and Techniques*, Englewood Cliffs, NJ, Prentice-Hall.

Lewis, R. D. (1996), *When Cultures Collide: Managing Successfully Across Cultures*, London, Nicholas Brealey.

McMillan, J. (1992), *Games Strategies and Managers,* New York, Oxford University Press.

MacWillson, A. C. (1992), *Hostage Taking Terrorism: Incident-response Strategy*, Basingstoke, Macmillan.

Malin, S. (1984), *The Negotiation Edge*, Palo Alto, Calif., Human Edge Software Corporation.

Marsh, P. D. V. (1974, 1984), *Contract Negotiation Handbook*, Epping, Gower Press.

Mastenbroek, W. (1989), *Negotiate*, Oxford, Basil Blackwell.

Mauss, M. (1954; 1996), *The Gift: Forms and Functions of Exchange in Archaic Societies*, London, Routledge & Kegan Paul.

Morley, I. E. and Stephenson, G. M. (1977), *The Social Psychology of Bargaining*, London, George Allen & Unwin.

Morrison, W. F. (1985), *The Prenegotiation Planning Book*, New York, John Wiley.

Mulholland, J. (1991), *The Language of Negotiation: a handbook of practical strategies for improving communication*, London, Routledge.

Murninghan, J. K. (1992), *Bargaining Games: A New Approach to Strategic Thinking in Negotiations*, New York, William Morrow.

Nash, J. F. (1950), 'The bargaining problem', *Econometrica*, Vol. 18, pp. 155–62.

Neale, M. A. and Bazerman, M. H. (1991), *Cognition and Rationality in Negotiation*, New York, Free Press.

von Neuman, J. and Morgenstern, O. (1944), *Theory of Games and Economic Behaviour*, Princeton, NJ, Princeton University Press.

Nierenberg, G. I. (1968), *The Art of Negotiating: Psychological Strategies for Gaining Advantageous Bargains*, New York, Cornerstone Library.

Nierenberg, G. I. (1973), *The Fundamentals of Negotiating*, New York, Hawthorn Books.

Nierenberg, G. I. (1985, 1986), *The Art of Negotiating®: User's Manual for IBM PC's and Compatibles*, Berkeley, CA., Experience in Software.

Pigou, A. C. (1920), *The Economics of Welfare*, London, Macmillan, p. 11.

Pillar, P. R. (1983), *Negotiating Peace: War Termination as a Bargaining Process*, Princeton, NJ, Princeton University Press.

Polanyi, K. (1957), *The Great Transformation*, Boston, Beacon Press.

Poundstone, W. (1993), *Prisoner's Dilemma*, Oxford, Oxford University Press.

Rackham, N. (1972), 'Controlled pace negotiation: as a new technique for developing negotiating skills', *Industrial and Commercial Training*, pp. 266–75.

Rackham, N. (1987), *Making Major Sales*, Aldershot, Gower.

Rackham, N. (1988), *Account Strategy for Major Sales*, Aldershot, Gower.

Rackham, N. and Carlisle, J. (1978), 'The effective negotiator Part 1: the behaviour of successful negotiators', *Journal of European Industrial Training*, Vol. 2, No. 6, pp. 161–5.

Rackham, N. and Carlisle, J. (1979), 'The effective negotiator Part 2: the behaviour of successful negotiators', *Journal of European Industrial Training*, Vol. 2, No. 7, pp. 129–36

Rackham, N. and Morgan, T. (1977), *Behaviour Analysis in Training*, London, McGraw-Hill.

Rackham, N. and Ruff, R. (1991), *Managing Major Sales: Practical Strategies for Improving Sales Effectiveness*, New York, Harper Collins.

Raiffa, H. (1982), *The Art and Science of Negotiation*, Cambridge, Mass., Harvard University Press.

Rapoport, A. (1966), *Two-Person Game Theory: The Essential Ideas*, Ann Arbor, University of Michigan Press.

Rapoport, A. (1974), *Fights, Games and Debates*, Ann Arbor, University of Michigan Press.

Rawls, J. (1972), *A Theory of Justice*, Oxford, Oxford University Press.

Ringer, R. J. (1973), *Winning Through Intimidation*, New York, Fawcett Crest.

Ringer, R. J. (1977), *Looking Out for Number 1*, New York, Fawcett Crest.

Robinson, C. (1990), *Winning at Business Negotiations: A Guide to Profitable Deal Making*, London, Kogan Page.

Rojot, J. (1991), *Negotiation: From Theory to Practice*, London, Macmillan.

Rose, C. (1987), *Negotiate and Win: The Proven Methods of the Negotiation Workshop*, Melbourne, Lothian Publishing.

Ross, H.L. (1970), *Settled Out of Court: The Social Process of Insurance Claims Adjustment*, Chicago, Aldine.

Royal Bank of Scotland (1992), *Negotiation in Practice*, Edinburgh, Royal Bank of Scotland.

Rubin, J. Z. and Brown, B. R. (1975), *The Social Psychology of Bargaining and Negotiation*, London, Academic Press.

Sahlins, M. (1972), *Stone Age Economics*, Chicago, Aldine Atherton.

Schelling, T. C. (1960), *The Strategy of Conflict*, Cambridge, Mass., Harvard University Press.

Schelling, T. C. (1966), *Arms and Influence*, New Haven, Yale University Press.

Schoenfield, M. K. and Schoenfield, R. M. (1991), *The McGraw-Hill 36-Hour Negotiating Course*, New York, McGraw-Hill.

Shackle, G. L. S. (1957), 'The nature of the bargaining process', in Dunlop, J. T. (ed.), *The Theory of Wage Determination: proceedings of a conference held by the International Economic Association*, London, Macmillan.

Sheppard, P. and Lapeyre, B. (1993), *Negotiate in French and English: Negocier en Anglais comme en Francais*, London, Nicholas Brealey.

Sheridan, D. L. (1991), *Negotiating Commercial Contracts*, London, McGraw-Hill.

Sigmund, K. (1993), *Games for Life: Explorations in Ecology, Evolution and Behaviour*, London, Penguin.

Simon, H. A. (1955), 'A behavioral model of rational choice', *The Quarterly Journal of Economics*, Vol. 69, February, pp. 99–118.

Slaikeu, K. A. (1996), *When Push Comes to Shove: A Practical Guide to Mediating Disputes*, San Francisco, Jossey-Bass.

Smith, A. (1776), *An Inquiry in to the Nature and Causes of the Wealth of Nations*, London.

Smith, H. B. (1988), *Selling Through Negotiation: The Handbook of Sales Negotiation*, New York, Amacom.

Snyder, G. H. and Diesing, P. (1977), *Conflict Among Nations: bargaining, decision-making and system structure in international crises*, Princeton, NJ, Princeton University Press.

Sperber, P. (1983), *Fail-Safe Business Negotiating: Strategies and Tactics for Success*, Englewood Cliffs, NJ, Prentice-Hall.

Stevens, C. M. (1958), 'On the theory of negotiation', *Quarterly Journal of Economics*, Vol. 73, pp. 77–93.

Ury, B. (1991), *Getting Past No*, London, Century Business.

Ury, W. L., Brett, J. M. and Goldberg, S. B. (1988), *Getting Disputes Resolved: designing systems to cut the costs of conflict*, San Francisco, Jossey-Bass.

Valentyne, P. (1991), *Contractarianism and Rational Choice: essays on David Gauthier's 'Morals by Agreement'*, New York, NY, Cambridge University Press.

Walton, R. E. and McKersie, R. B. (1965), *A Behavioural Theory of Labour Negotiation: an analysis of a social interaction system*, New York, McGraw-Hill.

Weintraub, E. R. (1975), *Conflict and Co-operation in Economics*, Basingstoke, Macmillan.

Wildavsky, A. (1964), *The Politics of the Budgetary Process*, New York, Little, Brown.

Williams, G. R. (1983), *Legal Negotiation and Settlements*, St. Paul, Minn., West Publishing.

Young, O.R. (ed.) (1975), *Bargaining: Formal Theories of Negotiation*, Urbana, Chicago, University of Illinois Press.

Zartman, I. W. and Berman, M. R. (1982), *The Practical Negotiator*, New Haven, Yale University Press.

Zartman, W. (1975), 'Negotiations: theory and reality', *Journal of International Affairs*, Vol. 9, pp. 68–77.

Zeuthen, F. (1930), *Problems of Monopoly and Economic Warfare*, London, Routledge & Kegan Paul.

Ziglar, Z. (1984), *Zig Ziglar's Secrets of the Closing of the Sale*, Old Tappan, NJ, Fleming H. Revell.

2

EXERCISE ON CONDITIONALITY

You were asked to read each example of a proposal or bargain (Chapter 4, p. 198), and to note what is wrong with it. My suggestions follow below.

1. **'If I accept a 10 per cent discount, will you give me a bigger order?' (proposal)**
    It is a question proposal and not a statement proposal. Question proposals are unassertive.
    It is the wrong way round with the offer preceding the condition.
    It is specific in the offer (10 per cent) and vague in the condition ('a bigger order').

    'If you give me a bigger order, then I will consider a discount.'

2. **'How about a 7 per cent discount if you order 1 million units a month?' (bargain)**
    It is a question proposal and not a statement proposal. Question proposals are unassertive.
    It is the wrong way round with the offer preceding the condition.

    'If you order 1 million units a month, then I will offer you a 7 per cent discount.'

3. **'OK. I'll accept liquidated damages but I expect something in return.' (proposal)**
    It is the wrong way round with the offer preceding the condition.
    It is specific in the offer (liquidated damages) and vague in the condition.

'If you gave me (xxx), then I would consider some amount of liqui-dated damages.'

4.   **'If you give me a bigger order, then I will give you a 5 per cent discount.' (proposal)**
It is vague in the condition and specific in the offer.

'If you give me a bigger order I will consider a discount.'

5.   **'OK. I can live with a tighter warranty clause.' (proposal)**
It is a give-away. Nothing can save it as it is unconditional.

'If I got (xxx) then I could live with a warranty clause.'

6.   **'Can you make it 40 instead of 50, if we give you exclusiv-ity?' (bargain)**
It is a question proposal and not a statement proposal. Question proposals are unassertive.

'If you make it 40, we will give you exclusivity.'

APPENDIX

3

PRACTICE EXAMINATION

This practice examination should take you about two to three hours to complete. When you have completed your answers to the questions in the case study and the essay questions, please follow the instructions if you would like your answers to be assessed and if you wish to receive my comments on your answers.

PART 1: CASE STUDY

Read the case and then answer the questions by applying your knowledge and experience of negotiation. Each question is worth five marks (maximum 20 marks).

INWARD INVESTMENT

A government department has been processing tenders for the first $95 million phase of an estimated $315 million modernization programme for its national telecommunications network. Of the original four bidders, two, Totec (Europe) and CTT (USA), qualified for the final round of negotiations. One of the two non-qualifiers was disqualified for proposing to use vintage digital technology while optical cabling was offered by the two qualifiers, and the other was disqualified because of doubts about its financial viability.

Two requirements were stressed in the original Request for Proposals (RFP) as being crucial to the award of the first phase of the contract. First, there had to be a high proportion of local manufacturing incorporated into the bidder's proposals and the degree of technology transfer had to be specified and second, the bidder had to guarantee the system's performance.

The government is keen to use the modernization of the telecom systems to create inward investment and technological transfer, both to gain domestic added value (wages and local dividends) from the cost of the modernization and to develop a capacity for future exports of this product.

While no commitments were offered, the RFP stated that a bidder establishing local manufacturing capacity with a high content of technology transfer would be in a strong position when RFPs were issued for the follow-on phases of the modernization programme, commencing in two years' time.

The department officials prefer Totec's proposal over CTT's. The technical content of each bid was similar and so was their best and final prices (Totec: $95.5 million; CTT £94.2 million). As usual, the department would need good reasons to advise the Minister to accept a bid that was more than 10 per cent above their consultant's estimated price.

Totec's proposals on local manufacturing of its Optica 1 system are more attractive than CTT's, who proposed little more than local assembling of imported components, while Totec proposes a fully equipped capacity with a schedule for developing local sourcing.

Both bidders offered the industry norm of two-year warranties, but the department is keen to extend that warranty to four or five years, similar to that achieved by a neighbouring country with a supplier, even though that particular manufacturer was disqualified by the department for this contract on the grounds that it produces outdated digital and not optical fibre systems, and therefore its products would be less efficient than either Totec's or CTT's.

The normal life-span of a telecom cabling system is 25 years and a telecoms agency can recover its investment costs in four or five years, depending on its pricing policies, making the investment very attractive to a growing and modernizing economy.

A breakdown in a telecom system, even for a short while, would be damaging to a country's international prestige. The RFP required a warranty against breakdowns lasting above 20 seconds (an international norm) and it required a consequential loss penalty, at least during the warranty period.

Current government policy normally requires a maximum of 50:50 foreign and local shareholdings, though this sometimes is varied, but only slightly, when the investment is a key strategic project. The government's main concern is to prevent a variation in the shareholding ratio in favour of the foreign investor that could work against its strategic plans for technological transfer and the capacity for future exports of high-tech products.

The country's public procurement laws prevent the department from confirming contracts for phases 2 and 3 but they do not prevent the department from designating the successful bidder for phase 1 as the 'preferred bidder' for phase 2. Only if the supplier failed in phase 1 would it be likely that they would not get phase 2, but that 'understanding' must remain an unenforceable opinion and not a guarantee.

From Totec's point of view, investing in a local manufacturing capacity will cost $60 million, which realistically requires five years to depreciate against the output of the plant and therefore it is not possible to recoup this level of investment from the revenue of a single two-year contract. Totec requires some degree of certainty that it would win phases 2 and 3 of the modernization programme to justify this level of inward investment.

If Totec did not receive the follow-on contracts for phases 2 and 3, it could recoup some of its investment by selling it to the successful bidder at a time when it would be in a weak bargaining position. Otherwise, it would have to write off the investment. But to sell its manufacturing plant to a rival bidder for phases 2 and 3 would be detrimental to its commercial interests, particularly if the sale led to rivals gaining access to its advanced technology.

The shareholding ratio is also important to Totec because unless it was the majority shareholder of the local company plant it would be unable to contemplate serious technological transfer, as this would expose it to competition worldwide if the local owners were to export the plant's output. Totec envisages the local plant eventually as a production facility for its own worldwide exports to other contracts, but it has no intention of allowing a partly owned subsidiary company to join the bid lists as a competitor for worldwide telecoms contracts.

Totec cannot allow its intellectual property rights (IPRs), worldwide patents and the fruits of its research and development to slip into the public domain if it was a minority shareholder of a local company. Totec requires a majority shareholding with no blocking or golden shares held by the government or its agencies. It is happy for local partners to contribute equity in cash or its equivalent in land and construction costs to finance their minority shareholding, but management of the plant and the control of its technology must remain exclusively with Totec in all events. It must be free to repatriate its profits.

Totec has indicated that it cannot accept exposure to consequential loss from technical failure even during the warranty period of two years. If the system failed for any reason (defined in the RFP as a downtime exceeding 20 seconds) the consequential losses could exceed the entire resources of Totec. Effectively, the risk of consequential losses on this scale are uninsurable.

Totec has offered to consider retention by the department of 5 per cent of the contract price for two years as a performance bond, but the definition of performance must exclude downtime from all climatic, geological and environmental events, plus causes outside its control, such as power failures from the country's public utility, damage to cabling by public works contractors, and attempts by users to connect unauthorized telecoms equipment to the lines (all three of which are well-known features of the country's current telecom service).

Totec has developed a new system, Optica II, which has a built-in redundant capacity that dramatically reduces the risk of system failure and it could, therefore, safely give a downtime warranty of no more than 10 seconds. Optica II, for which Totec has a worldwide technological lead of about two years over CTT, was not bid for this contract because the RFP's specified standards are met by Totec's Optica I system. For another $12 million for phase 1, Totec could manufacture Optica II in the local plant and extend the warranty period to four years.

A meeting between the department and Totec is to commence soon and from this the department officials hope to advise the Minister on which telecoms company should be awarded the contract. The department officials can only make recommendations and any variations to the RFP they make are subject to the Minister's approval.

Assume that you are an adviser on negotiation to the department and have been asked for your opinions.

Please answer the following four questions:

1.   What are the prime interests of the department in this project and how might they shape its response to Totec's suggested variations to the RFP?

2.   Use a Negotek® PREP Planner to identify the entry and exit ranges of the department and Totec on the various issues.

3.   If Totec cannot persuade the department to commit to phases 2 and 3, how might it reduce its exposure on the capital costs of the local plant?

4.   How might a principled negotiator, compared to a traditional negotiator, approach the outstanding issues?

PART 2: ESSAY QUESTIONS

Write short essays (500 words approximately) on four of the following ten questions. Each essay is worth 20 marks. Four essays must be attempted to pass the examination (maximum 80 marks).

1. What are the uses and limitations of the Nash solution to the bargaining problem?

2. Why do some negotiators resort to 'streetwise' ploys?

3. Why might the method of principled negotiation be regarded as a special case of positional bargaining?

4. How would you prepare for a negotiation? (Please use a recent live case of your own for illustration.)

5. What is the appropriate behaviour for dealing with difficult negotiators?

6. To what extent does power influence negotiation behaviour?

7. How might a knowledge of the four phases of negotiation assist in improving negotiation behaviour?

8. What is the principle of conditionality and why is it so important for effective negotiation?

9. How can negotiators move without giving in?

10. How crucial a role does debate behaviour play in a negotiation?

For assessment and comment on your answers, please post them with a self-addressed enveloped to:

Dr Gavin Kennedy
Negotiate Limited
22 Braid Avenue
Edinburgh
EH10 6EE
United Kingdom
www.negotiate.co.uk

Note:

O   For readers in the UK, please send British postage stamps on your self-addressed envelope for the same amount it cost you to post your examination answers to me.

O   For readers resident outside of the UK, please include with your answers international postage coupons for the same amount that it cost you to post your answers to me.

O   Please allow 30 days for the return of my comments.

NOTES

1   Fisher and Ury, 1981, p. xi
2   Ibid., pp. 3 and 85
3   Mauss, 1954
4   Thomas Hobbes, *Leviathan* 1651, pt. I, ch. 14
5   Friedrich Nietzsche, 1857, second essay, sec. 1, p. 57
6   Ibid., sec. 6, p. 65
7   Hatsock, for example (1985, quoted in Kolb, 1995)
8   Smith, *An Inquiry into the Nature and Causes of the Wealth of Nations*, 1776, Book 1
9   Ibid.
10   Ibid.
11   Ibid.
12   Nash, 1950, p. 128
13   von Neuman and Morgenstern, 1944
14   Nash, 1950
15   Ibid.
16   Poundstone, 1993
17   Carlisle and Parker, 1989, p. 49
18   Walton and McKersie, 1965
19   Lax and Sebenius, 1986
20   Ibid., p. 89
21   Ibid.
22   Pigoun, 1920
23   Lax and Sebenius, op. cit., p. 90
24   Gulliver, 1979
25   Kennedy, 1972
26   Douglas, 1962
27   Gulliver, op. cit.
28   Simon, 1955
29   Fisher and Ury, op. cit.
30   Douglas, 1957, p. 53
31   Fisher and Ury, op. cit.
32   Douglas, op. cit., p. 77

33 Morley and Stephenson, 1977
34 Gulliver, 1979, p. 121
35 Ibid., p. 143
36 Fisher and Ury, op. cit.
37 Gulliver, op. cit., p. 147
38 Ibid.
39 Ibid., p. 153
40 Zartman and Berman, 1982
41 Gulliver, op. cit., pp. 162–3
42 Kennedy et al., 1980
43 Walton and McKersie, op. cit.
44 Kennedy et al., 1980, pp. 28–31
45 Kennedy, 2nd edition, 1984, pp. 30–7
46 Ibid., p. 40
47 *The Art of Negotiation*, video, Longman, 1982
48 *Do We Have a Deal?*, video, Gower, 1992
49 Royal Bank of Scotland, 1993
50 Rackham and Carlise, 1978, 1979
51 Kennedy et al, 1982, p. 44
52 Ibid., p. 48
53 Morley and Stephenson, op. cit., p. 40
54 Ibid.
55 Kennedy et al., op. cit., pp. 49–50
56 Ibid., p. 53
57 Ibid., p. 93
58 Ibid., p. 90
59 Ibid., p. 91
60 *The Art of Negotiation,* video, op. cit.
61 Rose, 1987
62 *Do We Have a Deal?*, video, op. cit.
63 Carlisle and Parker, 1989
64 Nash, op. cit.
65 Morrison,1985, pp. 35–9
66 Walton and McKersie, op. cit., pp. 13–45
67 Fisher and Ury, op. cit.
68 Ibid., p. 41
69 Ibid., pp. 41–2
70 Gottchalk, 1992, pp. 41–2
71 Raiffa, 1982, pp. 58–65
72 Walton and McKersie, op. cit.
73 Raiffa, op cit., pp. 45–6
74 Kennedy, 1993; 1996, pp. 61–5
75 Listings of potential negotiable tradables in a variety of sectors are in Morrison, 1985, and in Holmes and Glaser, 1991
76 Kennedy, 1982; 1989; 1997
77 Dahl, 1957
78 Emerson, 1962
79 French and Raven, 1959

80   Bacharach and Lawler, 1981
81   Blau, 1964
82   Emerson, op. cit.
83   Bacharach and Lawler, op. cit., p. 59
84   Ibid.
85   Fisher and Ury, op. cit.
86   Bacharach and Lawler, op. cit., p. 63
87   Atkinson, 1975
88   Kennedy et al., 1980, p. 21
89   Atkinson, 1990
90   Ibid., pp. 137–67
91   French and Raven, op. cit.
92   Atkinson, op. cit., p. 139
93   Stevens, 1958
94   Chamberlain, 1951
95   Levinson, 1966
96   Chamberlain, op. cit., p. 220
97   Levinson, op. cit. p. 8
98   Ibid., p. 141
99   Kennedy et al., 1982, p. 21
100 Kennedy, 1982; 1989; 1997
101 Karass, 1974; Connor, 1995
102 Ringer, 1973
103 Levin, 1980, p. 96
104 Ibid., pp. 156–73
105 Ibid., p. 10
106 Ibid., ch. 9
107 Sperber, 1983
108 Karass, 1974
109 Schoenfield and Schoenfield, 1991
110 Fuller, 1991
111 Gottchalk, 1993
112 Kennedy, 1982; 1989; 1997, ch. 15
113 Karass, 1974, pp. 90–92
114 Kennedy, 1982; 1989; 1997, pp. 72–6
115 Gilbert, 1980; 1996
116 Ibid., p. 12
117 Ibid.
118 Ibid., pp. 12–13
119 Fisher and Ury, op. cit., pp. 8–14
120 See *The Negotiate Trainer's Manual*, Kennedy, 1990; 1996
121 Rojot, 1991
122 Gottchalk, 1993
123 Rackham, 1972, p. 266
124 Ibid., p. 267
125 Ibid.
126 Ibid.
127 Kennedy, 1990; 1996

128   Rackham and Carlisle, 1978, 1979
129   Rackham, 1972, op. cit., p. 269
130   Ibid., p. 270
131   Ibid., p. 273
132   Ibid., p. 275
133   Rackham and Carlisle, 1978
134   Rackham and Morgan, 1977
135   Karass, 1968; 1974
136   Rackham and Carlise, op. cit., p. 162
137   Rackham and Carlisle, 1978, pp. 162–5
138   Mulholland, 1991
139   Ibid., pp. 41–2
140   Ibid., pp. 40–1
141   Douglas, 1962
142   Stevens, op. cit.
143   Mulholland, 1991, p. 42
144   Ibid., p. 44
145   Lax and Sebenius, 1986, p. 235
146   Mulholland, op. cit., p. 44
147   Op. cit., p. 45
148   Ibid.
149   Ibid., p. 57
150   Ibid., p. 61
151   Ibid., p. 64
152   Rackham and Carlisle, op. cit.
153   Nierenberg, 1968, pp. 92–6
154   Nierenberg, 1973, pp. 109–38
155   Ibid., pp. 125–6
156   Rackham, 1987; 1988
157   Rackham, 1987, p. 46
158   Ibid., p. 47
159   Ibid., p. 52
160   Douglas, op. cit.
161   Kennedy, 1996 'Right of Way'
162   Rubin and Brown, 1975; Herman and Kogan, 1977
163   Malin, 1984
164   Gilkey and Greenhaugh, 1986, p. 245
165   Ibid., p. 146
166   Rubin and Brown, op. cit.
167   Ibid., p. 246
168   Ibid., pp. 254–6
169   Herman and Kogan, 1977, p. 267
170   Ibid., p. 146
171   Poundstone, 1993
172   Herman and Kogan, 1977, p. 253
173   Ibid., p. 254
174   Ibid., p. 255
175   Ibid., p. 256

176 Gottchalk, 1993
177 Rojot, 1991, pp. 154–65
178 Ibid.
179 Gottchalk, 1993, p. two. 6
180 Ibid., p. 6
181 Ibid., p. 5
182 Ibid., p. 8
183 Ibid., p. 7
184 Sigmund, 1993
185 Poundstone, op. cit.
186 Nash, op. cit.
187 Coker and Stuttard, 1976, pp. 128–9
188 Kennedy, 1990; 1996
189 Poundstone, op. cit.
190 Poundstone, op. cit., pp. 115–8
191 Hoffman, 1951
192 Kennedy, 1990; 1996
193 Carlisle and Parker, op. cit., p. 46
194 The Negotek® Attitudes and Behaviour Questionnaire, 1995
195 Glaser and Glaser, 1991, pp. 10–11
196 Fisher and Ury, op. cit.
197 Adapted from Fisher and Ury, op. cit., p. 13
198 Kennedy, 1982, pp. 66–73
199 Ibid., p. 66
200 Ibid.
201 Ibid.
202 Young, 1975
203 Pillar, 1983
204 Zeuthen, 1930
205 Pillar, op. cit., p. 98
206 Karass, 1970, 1974
207 Karass, 1968, 1970
208 Ibid., 1970, pp. 14–24
209 Ibid., p. 25
210 Karass, 1968, 1970
211 Hall, 1993
212 Karass, 1974, p. 18
213 Ibid, p. 19
214 Kennedy, 1982; 1989; 1997
215 Karass, 1974, p. 91
216 Ibid., p. 121
217 Ibid.
218 Kennedy, 1980, p.160
219 Robinson, 1990
220 Kennedy, 1980, p. 169
221 Karass, 1974, pp. 58–9
222 Ringer, 1973
223 Ibid., p. 61

224 Ringer, 1973, p. 84
225 Ibid., pp. 83–7
226 Ibid., p. 152
227 Ibid., p. 212
228 Ibid., pp. 298–300
229 Genn, 1987, p. 8
230 Galanter, 1984
231 Ors, 1970
232 Genn, 1987, p. 11
233 Ibid., p. 13
234 Ibid.
235 Raiffa, op. cit., pp. 66–77
236 'The Sorensen-Chevrolet File', no. 9-175-258, The Graduate School of Business Administration, Harvard University, Cambridge, Mass., USA
237 Genn, 1987, p. 17
238 Ibid., p. 26
239 Ibid., p. 34
240 Ibid., p. 40
241 Ibid.
242 Ibid., p. 41
243 Ibid., p. 42
244 Ibid., p. 43
245 Ibid., p. 46
246 Ibid., and Williams, 1983, pp. 18f.
247 Genn, 1987, p. 52
248 Ibid., p. 98
249 Ibid., p. 104
250 Ibid., p. 115
251 Ibid., p. 132
252 Karass, 1968, Raiffa, 1982, Williams, 1993
253 Kennedy and Webb, 1996
254 Sheridan, 1991
255 Ibid., p. 90
256 Ibid., p. 91
257 Ibid.
258 Ibid., p. 92
259 Ibid.
260 Ibid., p. 96
261 Ibid., p. 97
262 Ibid., p. 98
263 Ibid., pp. 98–9
264 Sperber, op. cit., pp. 35–6
265 Ibid., p. 47
266 Ibid., pp. 47–8
267 Cartwright, 1991, ch. 9
268 Tito *v.* Waddell, 1977, quoted in Cartwright, op. cit., p. 208
269 Ibid., pp. 215–6
270 Ibid., pp. 217–18

271   Ibid., p. 220
272   Ibid., p. 231
273   Kennedy, 1990; 1996, see Hospital data
274   Fisher and Ury, 1981; Ury, 1991
275   Kennedy, 1991, pp. 153–5
276   Bacharach and Lawler, 1981
277   Fisher and Ury, op. cit.
278   Hirschman,1970
279   Bacharach and Lawler, op. cit., pp. 73–75
280   Ibid., p.76
281   Ibid., p. 91; p. 94
282   Ibid., p. 97
283   Atkinson, 1990, pp. 143–6
284   Koch, 1988, pp. 3–5
285   Fisher and Ury, op. cit., pp. 101–11
286   Rackham, 1987; Rackham and Ruff, 1991
287   Ziglar, 1984
288   Kennedy, 1982; 1989; 1997 p. 311
289   Young, 1975
290   Gauthier, 1979; 1985; 1986
291   Raiffa, 1982
292   Nash, op. cit.
293   Gauthier 1979; 1985; 1986; Rawls, 1972
294   Kennedy and Webb, op. cit.
295   Bazerman and Neale, 1992
296   Neale and Bazerman, 1991; Bazerman and Neale, op. cit.
297   Ibid.
298   Bazerman and Neale, 1992, p. 1
299   Ibid.
300   Ibid., p. 2
301   Ibid., p. 12
302   Ibid., p. 19
303   Ibid., p. 45
304   Douglas, 1962, Gulliver, 1979, Kennedy, 1982; 1989
305   Simon, op. cit.
306   Walton and McKersie, op. cit., p. 137
307   Douglas, 1962
308   von Neuman and Morgenstern, op. cit.
309   Fisher and Ury, op. cit.
310   Friedman, 1957
311   Fisher and Ury, op. cit.
312   Ibid., p.11
313   Fisher and Ury, op. cit., pp. 6–7
314   Ibid., p. 7
315   Ibid., pp. 11–14
316   Fisher et al., 1991, p. 13
317   Fisher and Ury, op. cit., p. 11
318   Ibid.

319   Ibid., pp. 17–40
320   Ibid., pp. 41–57
321   Ibid., p. 55
322   Ibid.
323   Ibid.
324   Ibid.
325   Ibid.
326   Ibid., pp. 58–83
327   Ibid., pp. 84–98
328   Ibid., pp. 118–20
329   Fisher et al., pp. 66–7
330   Ibid., pp. 87–8
331   Ibid., pp. 122–33
332   Jandt, 1985
333   Ury, 1991
334   Ibid.
335   Slaikeu, 1996
336   Axtell, 1990
337   Hofstede, 1980a and 1980b
338   Hampden and Trompenaars, 1993
339   Kennedy, 1985

INDEX